South Pass

SOUTH PASS NATIONAL HISTORIC LANDMARK
MONUMENT, CIRCA 1965

The crest of South Pass is located on the Continental Divide in Fremont County, Wyoming, about ten miles southwest of South Pass City, at 42.34.4° north latitude, 108.88.6° west longitude. After President Dwight D. Eisenhower selected South Pass as one of America's first National Historic Landmarks in 1960, this monument stood on Highway 28. Its fate is a mystery. *BLM file photo.*

South Pass

GATEWAY *to a* CONTINENT

WILL BAGLEY

University of Oklahoma Press ❧ Norman

Also by Will Bagley

A Road from El Dorado: The 1848 Trail Journal of Ephraim Green
Frontiersman: Abner Blackburn's Narrative
West from Fort Bridger: The Pioneering of Immigrant Trails across Utah, 1846–1850 (with Harold Schindler)
This Is the Place: A Crossroads of Utah's Past (with Pat Bagley)
The Pioneer Camp of the Saints: The 1846 and 1847 Mormon Trail Journals of Thomas Bullock
Scoundrel's Tale: The Samuel Brannan Papers
Army of Israel: Mormon Battalion Narratives (with David L. Bigler)
Blood of the Prophets: Brigham Young and the Massacre at Mountain Meadows
Always a Cowboy: Judge Wilson McCarthy and the Rescue of the Denver & Rio Grande Western Railroad
Innocent Blood: Essential Narratives of the Mountain Meadows Massacre (with David L. Bigler)
So Rugged and Mountainous: Blazing the Trails to Oregon and California, 1812–1848
The Mormon Rebellion: America's First Civil War (with David L. Bigler)
With Golden Visions Bright Before Them: Trails to the Mining West, 1849–1852

Library of Congress Cataloging-in-Publication Data
Bagley, Will, 1950–
 South Pass : gateway to a continent / Will Bagley.
  pages cm
 Includes bibliographical references and index.
 ISBN 978-0-8061-4442-9 (cloth)
 ISBN 978-0-8061-4842-7 (paper)
 1. South Pass (Wyo.)—History—19th century. 2. Pioneers—Wyoming—South Pass—History—19th century. 3. Immigrants—Wyoming—South Pass—History—19th century. 4. Frontier and pioneer life—Wyoming—South Pass. 5. West (U.S.)—Emigration and immigration—History—19th century. 6. West (U.S.)—History—19th century. I. Title.
 F767.F8B34 2014
 978.7'6301—dc23
                2013042693

The paper in this book meets the guidelines for permanence and durability of the Committee on Production Guidelines for Book Longevity of the Council on Library Resources, Inc. ∞

Copyright © 2014 by Will Bagley. Published by the University of Oklahoma Press, Norman, Publishing Division of the University. Manufactured in the U.S.A.

All rights reserved. No part of this publication may be reproduced, stored in a retrieval system, or transmitted, in any form or by any means, electronic, mechanical, photocopying, recording, or otherwise—except as permitted under Section 107 or 108 of the United States Copyright Act—without the prior written permission of the University of Oklahoma Press. To request permission to reproduce selections from this book, write to Permissions, University of Oklahoma Press, 2800 Venture Drive, Norman, OK 73069, or email rights.oupress@ou.edu.

For Terry Del Bene
Mentor, friend, and defender of South Pass

South Pass is par excellence *the continental pass. . . . Where the summit-crest of our continent is found; the focal source of its rivers and its sierras; where the cloud-compelling Cordillera culminates over the "Gateway of empires"; let these commemorate this name immortally, while the grass shall grow and the waters run, as firm and enduring as the loftiest mountain. Let the children of the world be taught to say: Behold the Pass and the Pillars of* WASHINGTON!

WILLIAM GILPIN
MISSION OF THE NORTH AMERICAN PEOPLE, 1873

South Pass was the only feasible crossing of the Rocky Mountains for the entire width of the United States. Mother Nature dictated those terms.

MERRILL J. MATTES

South Pass is one of the most deceptive and impressive places in the West.

WALLACE STEGNER

Contents

List of Illustrations	11
List of Maps	13
PREFACE	15
Acknowledgments — Editorial Procedures	
INTRODUCTION: THE GREAT GATE	21
The Way West — The True Northwest Passage: The Geography of South Pass	

1. "DARING AND INTREPID ACTIONS":
   DISCOVERING SOUTH PASS, 1812 — 33
   A Handsome Low Gap: The Astorians Find South Pass — Muddy Waters of the Missouri: South Pass Revealed

2. "MARSHALLING THE WAY":
   REDISCOVERING SOUTH PASS, 1824 — 51
   Enterprising Young Men: Reviving the American Fur Trade — We Could Go to Green River: The Quest for the Seeds-ke-dee — We Had Crossed the Main Ridge

3. "TWO FORTUNES APIECE":
   THE ROCKY MOUNTAIN FUR TRADE — 67
   Frolic: The Rendezvous — Through a Level and Open Country: The News — The Unusual Sight of a Train: First Wagons across South Pass — Business Is Closed: The Demise of the Rocky Mountain Fur Trade

4. "Unheard-of Journey":
   Missionary Couples Cross South Pass, 1834–1840   87
   A Hard and Most Toilsome March: Jason Lee — White for the Harvest: Parker and Whitman Go West — Wonder and Astonishment: Women Cross South Pass — An Immense Fund of Determination — In a Dangerous Country: The 1838 Missionary Band — Hardships and Perplexities: Women and South Pass — The First Train of Emigrants to Oregon: The Walker Family

5. "Treading Unknown Paths":
   Emigrants and Explorers, 1841–1848   111
   Fifty Roads: Evolving Trails over South Pass — A Thorough Fare for Nations: John C. Frémont — A Stern Reality to Fulfill: The Oregon Trail — We'll Find the Place: The Mormon Trail — Altogether Most Impressive: Travelers Admire the Scenery

6. "The Other Side of the World":
   The Gold Rush, 1849–1855   137
   South Pass Trails, 1849–1855 — To Cross the Devil's Backbone: Seminoe's Fort and Cutoff — Hail Columbia: Celebrating South Pass — Surpassing Grandeur: Gold Rush Views of South Pass — The Loneliest Land for a Grave: South Pass Memorials

7. Conflict and Catastrophe at
   South Pass, 1856–1860   163
   The Most Dangerous War Grounds in the Rocky Mountains — Disaster at South Pass: The First Handcart Trains — We Are Bound to Be Caught in the Snow: The Willie Company — Starved Forms, Haggard Countenances: The Martin Company — Fooled, Everybody: The Utah Expedition — Jaded and Worn Out: The Last Handcart Trains — Better Than the South Pass: The Cherokee Trail and the Overland Stage

8. "Emphatically an Emigrant Road":
   The Lander Cutoff   201
   Better Leave the Old Road: The Lander Cutoff, 1858 — A Full Corps of Artists: The Lander Cutoff, 1859 — Built at the Expense of the Govt.: The Lander Cutoff — These Dern Pilgrims: F. W. Lander's Legacy

9. THE U.S. MAIL AND THE WAR FOR
   SOUTH PASS, 1860–1869   227
   Cold & Disagreeable: The U.S. Mail at South Pass — Pony Express
   Stations at South Pass — The Paper City of South Pass — The Talking
   Wire: The Telegraph Crosses South Pass, 1861 — An Indian War
   Is Inevitable — To Rob the Trains and Destroy the Wires — The
   Road to the Wild and Romantic

10. "Gold, Slathers of It": The Rush to South Pass, 1867   271
    Rich Gold Discovery! The Rush — The Last Covered Wagons: South
    Pass after 1869

AFTERWORD: THE LEGACY OF SOUTH PASS   283
    Commemorating South Pass — Preservation and Protection —
    South Pass National Historical Park: A 1969 Vision — South Pass
    Today

Selected Bibliography   295
Index   315

Illustrations

South Pass National Historic Landmark Monument, circa 1965	*frontispiece*
South Pass Trail Today	32
Robert Stuart	37
Devils Gate	47
Jedediah S. Smith Crossing the Mohave Desert	61
James Clyman	62
B. L. E. Bonneville	79
Nathaniel J. Wyeth	83
Joseph Lafayette Meek	108
Father Pierre-Jean De Smet, S.J.	117
Col. John C. Frémont	120
Mysterious Marker at South Pass	123
The View at South Pass	136
Charlotte Dansie's Grave	161
Chief Washakie and His Men	166
Mormons Crossing the Plains	174–75
Gen. Frederick W. Lander, 1861	204
"Crossing the Platte"	215
Gravesite Overlooking Burnt Ranch	226
"Bull Trains" Crossing the Plains	237
Rhoba Sullivan	242
Wagons Nearing Mesa	246

ILLUSTRATIONS

South Pass Station, Idaho Territory, 1863	261
Treaty of Fort Bridger, July 2, 1862	262
Wagon Train, 1882	281
Wagons, Riders, and the Oregon Buttes	290

Maps

Route from the Missouri River to the Pacific	22–23
The Treks of Hunt and Stuart, 1810–1813	38
Stuart's Likely Route, 1812	44
Detail from Preliminary Map of Lander's Central Division, 1859	200
Roads through Greater South Pass	268–69

Preface

THIS STORY IS ABOUT A PLACE, SOUTH PASS. MOST OF THIS historic spot resembles a thousand other High Plains landscapes, caught between the land of little water and the land of virtually no water at all. Practically treeless, South Pass is the invisible divide between watercourses bound for the Pacific and the Atlantic or the Gulf of Mexico, and it marks the eastern border of some of the continent's most barren scablands. In many ways unremarkable—its scenery is far from breathtaking, and the American West encompasses ten thousand more impressive views—South Pass's classically western appearance disappointed the expectations of at least a hundred thousand travelers. Silence may be its most striking feature. The wind usually howls or whispers, but this spot is always quiet, very quiet. Some, like this native son, find its beauty singular.

Geography made South Pass the gateway to a continent and one of the most significant historic landmarks in the United States. Between Marias Pass near the Canadian border and Guadalupe Pass not far from Mexico, South Pass is the only corridor that anything on wheels could use to cross the massive cordillera of the Rocky Mountains without great physical or engineering challenges. Without this natural road, wagons could not have left the Missouri River and reached the Pacific in a single season, and the European conquest and settlement of the American West might have taken several more generations. A more daunting barrier might even have granted the first Americans the time they needed to establish their right to their homelands. Instead, between 1840 and 1870 South Pass made it possible for more than a half-million ordinary Americans seeking a better life for themselves and their children to cross the Great Divide at South Pass on the Oregon, California, and Mormon Pioneer National Historic Trails. This number is

PREFACE

a mere fraction of the six million African Americans who joined the Great Migration from south to north in the twentieth century, but it is still one of the largest peaceful—or relatively peaceful—migrations in human history.

Even better, with the American West seemingly doomed to have its public resources privatized, encouraging a swift and brutal transformation of our natural landscape into industrialized "sacrifice zones," South Pass belongs to you and me. As the twenty-first century begins, international corporations increasingly desire and demand unfettered access to the gold, oil, gas, coal, and the rare earths hidden in our nation's last, best places; they even strive to monetize—a horrific word—the wind and sun. Yet virtually all of South Pass is unchanged, and its classic open emptiness still belongs to the American people.

Acknowledgments

Like many books, this one owes its existence to the preservation and interpretation efforts of the National Park Service (NPS), the Bureau of Land Management (BLM), and the Wyoming State Historic Preservation Office (WSHPO). As a public historian, in the scope of work for the project, I agreed in 2004 "to conduct a South Pass historic context study and to prepare National Register nominations" for these agencies. The purpose was "to provide guidance in the management, protection, treatment, and interpretation of trails-related historic properties and landscapes in the South Pass area of Wyoming." I delivered the final study and four National Register nominations totalling more than sixty thousand words in 2007. Since this was a work for hire and your tax dollars paid for much it, the study is part also of the public domain and cannot be copyrighted. Some of the study material, including much of this book, is now available on the Internet. A version of chapter 1 appeared in *Wild West* magazine in 2013.

For two reasons, this book differs from the 2007 study. The report was a public document, so I sought to deliver a factual report for the general public that avoided political commentary or religious controversy, since many Americans see our entire nation's history as a chronicle of the works and special blessings of God. I tried to keep my opinions on this question to myself, since it involves a debate as old as philosophy and is better left to polemicists than to historians. I follow Alexander Pope's advice, "Know then thyself, presume not God to scan; The proper study of Mankind is Man," and stick with Carl Becker's definition: "History is the memory of things said and done." Therein lies the second reason the resource study and this book differ: history—what the historic records tells us about "things said and done" is constantly evolving and expanding, especially in the age of the Internet. Part of this is personal: history is either the world's most humbling or humiliating profession, since new evidence requires continually reinterpreting the past. In other words, I have learned a lot in the last seven years and have had to rethink what I thought I knew about South Pass and its past.

The research and fieldwork backing up this book would not have been possible without help from dedicated public servants, volunteers, archivists, librarians, and friends. My job required research, writing, and two field trips conducted July 12–14, 2005, and June 19–29, 2006. The 2005 trip with Craig Bromley and Terry Del Bene of the BLM and Lee Kreutzer and Kay Threlkeld of the National Trails System Office was a survey of the landscape on the Oregon, California, Mormon Pioneer, and Pony Express National Historic Trails between the Three Crossings of the Sweetwater, nine miles west of Jeffrey City, Wyoming, to the Little Sandy crossing, about six miles northeast of Farson, Wyoming. The 2006 field trip was more intense. With guidance from NPS and BLM archeologists, about a dozen volunteers from the Oregon-California Trails Association (OCTA) evaluated in detail 108 miles of the old wagon road and its cutoffs from dawn till dark for eleven straight days. We measured swales and ruts, identified known and likely campsites, and counted trail-related markers and landmarks. The surveyors established 193 panoramic photo points and took more than 4,800 photographs, located 20 surface artifacts, 40 possible graves, 5 inscriptions, 2 wells, 4 rock features, 3 springs, 3 campsites, 13 stream crossings, and more than a dozen archeological sites. The project collected a few artifacts such as a needle or awl and ox shoes, but left most relics of the trail in place.

Among those who participated in the fieldwork were OCTA volunteers Bill and Gail Robinson, Tom McCutcheon, Don Bailey, Dave and Wendy Welch, along with Lesley Wischmann, Barbara Dobos, Andy Blair, Todd Guenther, Dave Vlcek, and journalist Tom Rea, who offered excellent suggestions and corrections to this manuscript. Public servants and archeologists Terry Del Bene, Craig Bromley, Lee Kreutzer, Karina Bryan, and Colleen Sievers supervised the survey. Robert Hellyer of the Burnt Ranch Grazing

Company allowed us to cross his historic ranch at the Last Crossing of the Sweetwater. Joan Pennington graciously granted permission to use her map of the Hunt and Stuart treks, while Andy Blair, Kay Threlkeld, Lee Kreutzer, and former Wyoming state historian Russ Tanner contributed photographs to the project.

Editorial Procedures

Citations and the bibliography use the name of the original writer of a source, not the editor. Sources are cited at the end of sections using them, not by paragraph. Place names follow the official designations of the U.S. Board on Geographic Names, which do not use possessives for names such as Devils Gate. Newspaper citations contain the information needed to locate them and, when available, include the page/column: 2/3. Footnotes cite published sources by author, title, and page number. Full citations for other items are found in the bibliography. The selected bibliography lists all the books, articles, journals, and manuscripts referenced in the footnotes. The bibliography does use periods before colons. Book titles are in italics, while article, thesis, and dissertation titles are in plain text with quotation marks. Manuscript citations appear without quotation marks. Original sources preserve the grammar, spelling, and diction of the originals but capitalize the first letters of sentences and personal names, with periods at the ends of sentences. Underlined text is italicized. Otherwise they reflect the original's spelling and punctuation (or its absence). [Sic] is used sparingly. Brackets enclose added letters, missing words, and conjectural readings.

South Pass

Looking west from the heights above the Last Crossing of the Sweetwater River, the Wind River Mountains and their foothills rise to the northwest to break the long western horizon. This range forms the northern boundary of the passage through the Rocky Mountains known as South Pass. The bluffs rising above Rock Creek block the view to the east, but up close the drying grass and ever-present sage color a seared-yellow and brown landscape mixed with sagebrush green. Continental Peak, the Jack Morrow Hills, and both Oregon Buttes loom above the horizon to the south and southwest, while the long broad face of Pacific Butte forms the southern border of the wide tan-and-sagebrush blue-gray prairie that is South Pass proper. Directly to the west, the trail winds its way until it drops into the canyon of Willow Creek, but the vast, rolling western horizon is the twenty-mile-wide plain reaching from the foot of Pacific Butte to the foothills of the Wind River Mountains. A little farther west the trail divides, and one fork veers off to the northwest and South Pass City and disappears from sight. Now the two-track road and scenery before you is little changed from the landscape that would have greeted Narcissa Whitman in 1836, John C. Frémont in 1842, and Brigham Young in 1847.

South Pass National Historic Landscape Report
July 12–14, 2005

INTRODUCTION

The Great Gate

FUR TRADERS, MISSIONARIES, OVERLAND EMIGRANTS, MILITARY explorers, and historians have described South Pass as a twenty-mile-wide, sagebrush-covered plain in central Wyoming lying immediately south of the Wind River Mountains. Where the pass begins in the east and ends in the west has long been an open question. Some thought South Pass extended all the way from Independence Rock to the Green River, while others identified it specifically with the spot where they crossed the Continental Divide. "Modern scholars often debate the boundaries of South Pass," historian Todd Guenther observed. Based on the nature of the modern landscape and its historic significance, South Pass extends west from Independence Rock to the Little Sandy Crossing, 122 miles over the old Oregon Trail or about a hundred-mile flight for a crow.

South Pass will be forever remembered for its critical role in the lives of the half-million Americans who crossed it between 1840 and 1869 on their way to new homes in the West.[1] The initial wave of overland emigration brought missionaries and settlers over "the broad smooth highway" called the Oregon Trail, and they helped establish American control of the Pacific Northwest.[2] A second wave began in 1847, when thousands of religious refugees trod the Mormon Trail to their new Zion in the Great Basin. The end of the War with Mexico and the discovery of gold in the Sacramento Valley in 1848 transformed the road into the California Trail, which over the next four years witnessed an astonishing migration. Both the Pony Express and the first transcontinental telegraph crossed South Pass. Ironically, as its glory days drew to a close, the region became the center of its own gold rush.

---
[1] Mattes, *Platte River Road Narratives*, 5.
[2] Spence and Jackson, *The Expeditions of John Charles Frémont*, 1:445.

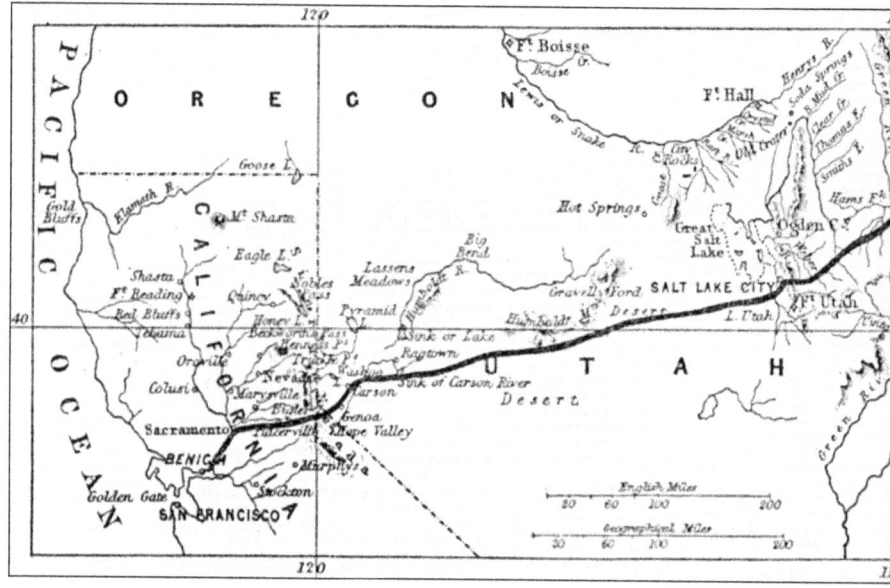

ROUTE FROM THE MISSOURI RIVER TO THE PACIFIC
The dark line shows the route of the overland stage across South Pass in 1860. *From Richard F. Burton,* The City of the Saints and across the Rocky Mountains, *1861.*

THE WAY WEST

Americans have long respected the historic importance of this gateway to the West: President Dwight Eisenhower selected South Pass as one of the first of ninety-two National Historic Landmarks proposed in 1960. "The only easy passage through the Rocky Mountains, South Pass has been aptly termed the 'Gateway to the West' and the 'Panama Canal of the Central Route,'" wrote Robert M. Utley, chief historian of the National Park Service. "The effective discovery of South Pass changed the character and direction of the fur trade and brought American trappers in large numbers to the central Rockies and the Great Basin. In the process they extended the territorial claims of the United States to the west and northwest and headed off the advance of British trappers to the southeast."

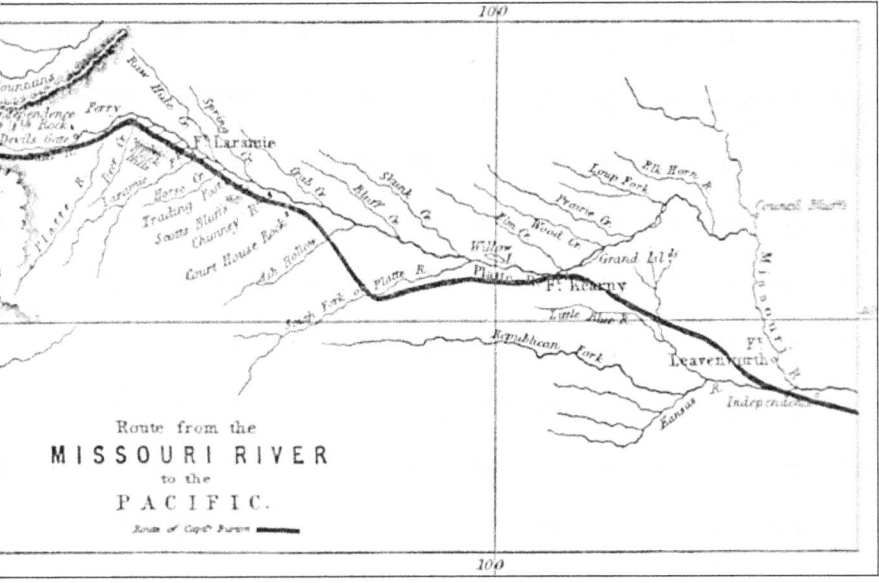

Route from the
MISSOURI RIVER
to the
PACIFIC.

The discovery of South Pass made the opening of a practical wagon road to the Pacific possible, and "had a profound effect on the future of California and the Northwest—an effect perhaps commensurate with the discovery of gold—for it was the use of this route by the emigrants that permitted the rapid settling and acquisition of Oregon, the early immigration to and subsequent conquest of California, and the settlement of Utah," wrote Charles L. Camp. "For almost fifty years, although other trails came into use, the South Pass route was *the* way west."[3]

Early travelers considered themselves in South Pass from the Last Crossing of the Sweetwater River until they reached the west-flowing waters of Pacific Springs west of the summit. Twenty-two miles to the northwest, fur traders (and eventually the Lander Cutoff) used an ancient Indian trail to cross the Continental Divide at a small ridge a few yards east of Little Sandy Creek. The Oregon, Mormon Pioneer, California, and Pony Express National Historic Trails crossed the Continental Divide at the southern edge of the gap in the

---

[3] Quoted in Utley, Memorandum on Sweetwater–South Pass Historic Sites, June 23, 1969, National Trails System Office files, Salt Lake City, Utah, 1.

mountains, just west of the magnificent Oregon Buttes and immediately north of Pacific Butte and the broken country of the Jack Morrow Hills.

The unimposing summit of South Pass meant that many overland emigrants failed to notice they had left the Mississippi River basin and entered the Colorado River drainage until they reached the spring at the head of Pacific Creek. As renowned geographer John Logan Allen observed, the topography of the pass is still so confusing that the exact location of South Pass is hard to detect on the wide rolling plain. "Modern travelers passing through the region today depend entirely on a Bureau of Land Management sign to alert them they have crossed the continental divide."[4]

A surprising amount of confusion exists about the altitude of South Pass. Master historian Dale L. Morgan gave its elevation as 7,550 feet above sea level, a popular figure that reflects the highest nearby elevation but not the actual summit of South Pass. The U.S. Geological Survey Pacific Springs 7.5-minute quadrangle (and many reference works) gives the elevation as 7,412 feet. The Meeker monument at South Pass stands "twenty feet west of the actual culminating height of the Pass where the old trail crossed the divide line," wrote trail expert Paul Henderson, without explaining how he determined the exact location. According to trail historian Gregory Franzwa, USGS engineers surveying the Continental Divide in 1946 found that Meeker had missed the exact location of the divide "by less than fifty feet."[5] During a June 2006 field survey, archeologist Colleen Sievers of the BLM Rock Springs Office took a global positioning system (GPS) reading of 7,440 feet above average mean sea level at the monument.

South Pass owes its immense significance to the geological processes that created the Rocky Mountains. Beginning about seventy-five million years ago, tectonic forces compressed the earth's crust and lifted the Foreland Ranges, the ancestral Rocky Mountains that became the Medicine Bow, Laramie, Bighorn, and Wind River ranges. During the Laramide Orogeny, these massive blocks of the Earth's crust "were hoisted upward, earthquake by earthquake, along massive fault lines." The Sweetwater Valley and South Pass did not exist, but water began forming channels through the ancient summits even as they rose, continuing the endless cycle of erosion. The building process was

---

[4] Allen, "The Invention of the American West," 152.
[5] Pritchard, *The Overland Diary*, 155n47; "A Tour along the Old Oregon Trail," June 1955; Franzwa, *The Oregon Trail Revisited*, 273–74.

complete by forty-five million years ago, creating a continuous high-elevation barrier across what became Wyoming, and "a towering mountain range lay where the Sweetwater River flows today." Erosion continued wearing down the massive peaks, "shedding the broken debris of the mountains into the adjacent basins, where it piled up as layer upon layer of sand and gravel."

About five million years ago, only the highest peaks rose above this gravel plain, where meandering rivers slowly wandered over the buried ranges. Then the mountains began to rise again, and "the hungry rivers bulldozed away the valley fill," exposing the buried ranges and creating today's river basins. "The result is one of the oddest sights in North American geology: rivers that cut right through ridges rather than going around them," geologist Keith H. Meldahl noted. "Nearly every Wyoming river cuts through one or more ridges—a reflection of this unique history of mountain burial and exhumation."

The once-mighty Sweetwater Range gradually collapsed and dropped between two large faults, forming the Sweetwater Valley. "The Sweetwater Hills are its exposed tips; the rest of the mountain lies buried below the valley floor." The former summits formed the valley's northern edge, the Rattlesnake Hills, and the Beaver Divide. The "orphaned foothills of the range still stand high" above the valley, while the Granite Mountains—Sentinel Rocks and the Crooks-Green-Ferris-Seminoe-Shirley mountain complex, along with Continental Peak—define the valley's southern border, creating the "elongated trough down which the Sweetwater River flows today."[6]

The valley of the Sweetwater provides the only gradual and well-watered natural gateway through the Rocky Mountains. At its headwaters, the river comes to within less than a quarter-mile of the Continental Divide. South Pass forms a unique passage through the massive cordillera stretching from Mexico into Canada, dividing the waters of North America between the Atlantic and the Pacific. It is not surprising that an Irishman who crossed the pass in 1849 could scarcely believe he was on the summit of a mountain range—his geographical lessons were "wont to consider one of the great marvels of creation."[7]

History is geography over time. Since ancient hunters first followed their prey across the Great Plains and the Rockies, rivers have determined how humans traveled. Three great river systems—the Missouri, the Platte, and

---
[6] Meldahl, "Wyoming's Rivers and the Overland Trails," 161; *Hard Road West*, 108–10.
[7] Kelly, *An Excursion to California*, 190.

the Arkansas—flow east across the Great Plains, but only the Platte River Valley leads to an easily crossed gap in the stony spine of the Rocky Mountains: South Pass. The Lewis and Clark Expedition never came close to the spot, but the landmark took its name from its relation to the "North Pass," where the explorers crossed Lemhi Pass in 1805, some four hundred miles to the northwest on today's Idaho-Montana border.

From the heights of South Pass, a sweeping view would have greeted bands of Shoshones, Arapahos, or Absarokas (the people also known as the Crows) traveling west in the summer of 1800. Directly north of the pass, Rennecker Peak rises to an elevation of 10,053 feet amid the snow-clad Wind River Range, but some identify Mount Nystrom (12,356 feet) or Mount Washakie (12,524 feet) as the northern boundary of the corridor that constitutes South Pass.

The Wind River Range—the "Winds"—runs to the northwest and includes Gannett Peak, at 13,804 feet the highest spot in Wyoming. Along the corridor's southern boundary, the sage-covered Antelope Hills fall away, terminating with a final thrust at Pacific Butte, which rises more than four hundred feet above the floor of the pass. This gap forms a broad valley: looking west from the pass, every creek and stream flows into today's Green River, which the Absarokas and the mountain men called the Seeds-ke-dee-agie, the River of the Prairie Hen. The Shoshones and Utes called it the Bitter Root River, "from a great abundance in its valley of a plant which affords them one of their favorite roots," John C. Frémont reported. Granville Stuart said they called it Can-na-ra o-gwa, "poor river," for its lack of trees and grass. But English swashbuckler Richard F. Burton said the Indians, "in their picturesque way, term this stream Wágáhongopá, or the Glistening Gravel Water."[8]

Less than three miles west of the pass on a gently declining sagebrush plain lies the green oasis now known as Pacific Springs, where Indians could water their horses and let them graze on the boggy acres of grass that surrounded several strong springs. Those who camped there probably noticed that on the east side of the pass, most watercourses flowed toward the rising sun, while west of the pass, running water usually followed the setting sun.

---

[8] Spence and Jackson, *The Expeditions of John Charles Frémont*, 1:466–67; Stuart, *Discovery of the Oregon Trail*, 172n67; Burton, *City of the Saints*, Aug. 21, 1860, 168/184. Mountain trader Joseph Gebow, the Utah Indian superintendent's interpreter in 1859, gave *Pe-ah-o-goie* as the Shoshone name for Green River, which sounds suspiciously like Popo Agie, a river on the Atlantic side of divide.

The True Northwest Passage:
The Geography of South Pass

The open plain between the Wind River Range and the Oregon Buttes, and the gap reaching ninety miles south to the Uinta Mountains, form a singular break in the North American Cordillera. As mountain men and explorers learned from hard experience, until the invention of the locomotive and the automobile, wheeled vehicles could not penetrate the high and wide barrier of the Rocky Mountains. To this day, no roads cross the Wind River Range except at Union Pass, which rises to an elevation of 9,210 feet at the northern terminus of the range.

As Meriwether Lewis and William Clark discovered, the Bitterroot and Beaverhead mountains form an even more daunting barrier. The passes that pierce the Continental Divide along today's Idaho-Montana border—Targhee, Monida, Bannock, Lemhi, Chief Joseph, Lost Trail, Horse Creek, Nez Perce, Lolo, Hoodoo, Lookout, and Thompsons—are almost all lower in elevation than South Pass, but none offers a practical crossing for a transcontinental wagon road. Ninety miles below South Pass, the Uinta Mountains and the Sierra Madre rise to close this gap in the Rocky Mountains, and to the south the cordillera forms a barrier to wagon roads that stretches to the Mexican border at Guadalupe Pass.

To Americans today, the notion that a nation-spanning Continental Divide separates the waters of the Atlantic and the Pacific seems entirely natural, almost intuitive. This has not always been so. "The conceptual geography of the western interior presented many puzzles to the minds of nineteenth-century Americans," observed John Logan Allen. "Paramount among them was the mystery of the 'division of the waters,' the dividing line or lines which separated the waters of the Gulf of Mexico, the Gulf of California and the Pacific proper."

The first solutions to the puzzle were based on "the geography of hope and logic" rather than on reliable reports from the actual terrain. The hope was largely wishful thinking related to the European quest for a Northwest Passage around or through North America that would provide a shortcut to the treasures of Asia. The logic supporting the belief in such a corridor was thoroughly Aristotlean, in the sense that the Greek philosopher theorized that the female of the species has fewer teeth than the male, a conclusion he reached based on his belief in the superiority of males that made it unnecessary to actually look in a female's mouth.

As the nineteenth century began, American geographers believed in "a pyramidal height-of-land, the centre of a symmetrical continent, from which rivers flowed in four cardinal directions," a theory with medieval roots presented in Jonathan Carver's 1781 *Travels through the Interior of North America*. This concept helped inspire President Thomas Jefferson's hope that Lewis and Clark would find a navigable passage from the Missouri to "the Oregon or River of the West, on the other side of the summit of the lands that divide the waters."

Lewis and Clark disproved Carver's notion that the sources of America's great rivers were relatively close. Much to Jefferson's disappointment, the Corps of Discovery learned that there were hundreds of miles of rugged mountain country between the navigable waters of the Missouri and the Columbia. Clark's master map of the West, however, perpetuated another myth: that the headwaters of the Columbia, Missouri, Yellowstone, Big Horn, Platte, Colorado, Arkansas, Rio Grande, and the legendary Multnomah (today's Willamette) were all located in a relatively small area in the height-of-land pyramid. In truth, the Arkansas, Rio Grande, and some of the sources of the Colorado rose more than three hundred miles to the south. Until 1815 the maps of such well-regarded experts as German naturalist Alexander von Humboldt incorporated the illusion of a common headwaters for all the great rivers of the West.

Even American explorers such as Zebulon Pike, who should have known better, perpetuated the myth. Pike returned from the Central Rockies in 1807 convinced that somewhere in the mountains was "a grand reservoir of snows and fountains" where he could visit the sources of the Arkansas, Yellowstone, Columbia, Platte, Colorado, and Rio Grande in a single day. That two great cordilleras, the Sierra/Cascades and the Rockies, divided the American West was slow to catch on.[9]

The significance of "the great South Pass" was clear to early explorers and travelers. The first man to report seeing it, Robert Stuart of the Pacific Fur Company, "fully recognized the significance of locating a feasible wagon route to the Pacific," historian David A. White observed. He had crossed the Rocky Mountains "through a defile not previously known; but which relieves adventurers from a great proportion of their toil and hazard," Stuart told Dr. Samuel Mitchell in 1815.[10] After his men showed him the route

---

[9] Allen, "Division of the Waters," 357–60.
[10] White, *News of the Plains and the Rockies*, 1:140.

they had rediscovered at South Pass, fur-trade mogul William Ashley told a newspaper that the trail was better than any turnpike in the United States, and "the elevation is exceedingly small where the passage of the mountains was effected—so small as hardly to affect the rate of going of the caravan."[11] For John C. Frémont, South Pass was "the great gate" between the Mississippi Valley and the north Pacific.[12]

The wide plain and easy ascent of the pass gave it "an immense importance, as being the great thoroughfare through which the commerce and traveling between the Mississippi valley and the shores of the Pacific must pass," J. Quinn Thornton wrote in 1846. "This remarkable depression, therefore, renders it comparatively easy to take loaded wagons over the Rocky Mountains."[13] Richard Burton thought the Sweetwater Valley appeared to be "a line laid down by nature to the foot of the South Pass of the Rocky Mountains."[14] South Pass provided the key to a continent and made possible the transformation of the American West in a single generation.

Historians have been keenly aware of South Pass's impact on the course of American history. Robert Stuart's discovery of a practical passage over the Rockies contributed more to the American people than just an awareness of new rivers, mountains, and plains, Kenneth A. Spaulding argued. South Pass provided a way to "transfer their families, their tools, and their beliefs to an area that promised to reward them with better lives than the ones they had put behind."[15] Jedediah S. Smith, Thomas Fitzpatrick, and James Clyman made the Oregon Trail possible when they rediscovered "the historic portal," Bernard DeVoto concluded, for South Pass was "the one opening through which wagons could cross the mountains, the door to Oregon and California, the true Northwest Passage."[16]

For historian William H. Goetzmann, "South Pass was the all-important gateway, and without it the commerce of the Rockies could hardly have existed at all." Goetzmann compared the significance of its location to that of the Cumberland Gap: "half a continent's worth of people would pour through this gap, making it as famous and important as the one discovered by Virginia

---

[11] Morgan, *The West of William Ashley*, 154.
[12] Spence and Jackson, *The Expeditions of John Charles Frémont*, 1:464.
[13] Thornton, *Oregon and California in 1848*, 1:158–59.
[14] Burton, *City of the Saints*, 39/45.
[15] Stuart, *On the Oregon Trail*, 17.
[16] DeVoto, *Across the Wide Missouri*, 54; DeVoto, *The Year of Decision, 1846*, 53.

hunters back on the Cumberland."[17] David Lavender called South Pass "the broad gateway to the West" and "the key to the West," because "a land of thirsty deserts" surrounded the streams that led to it.[18] David J. Wishart summed up the consensus: South Pass was "the most important gateway in the early settlement of the West."[19]

Defining exactly what constitutes the "great gate" was not as simple as it might seem. South Pass "is more than a hundred miles long, or wide, as it is usual to designate it," topographical engineer John W. Gunnison wrote murkily in 1852. He was referring to "Greater South Pass"—that is, the entire opening in the Rocky Mountains between the Wind River Range and the Uinta Mountains, as became clear when he described "the proper track for the Pacific Railway." Gunnison believed the railroad should leave the South Platte at Lodgepole Creek near today's Julesburg, Colorado, swing south of Wyoming's Black Hills and across the Laramie Plains, "leaving the Medicine-Bow Mountains on the south, and crossing the North Platte into the South Pass, over the Coal Basin," skirting the Bear River Mountains near Fort Bridger, through the canyons of the Bear and Weber rivers and then down to "the Valley of Lake Utah."[20] (This definition lets distinguished historians such as Henry Steele Commager and Samuel Eliot Morison get away with saying that the first transcontinental railroad crossed South Pass.)

Most modern experts take a less expansive view. "Although its name suggests a dramatic gap in the Rocky Mountain barrier," wrote historian Howard R. Lamar, "South Pass is actually a saddle between the southern extremes of the Wind River Range and the Antelope Hills to the south."[21] Three contemporary Wyoming historians argued for a more specific definition. "South Pass is the entire saddle between the summit of Mount Nystrom in the Wind River Mountains and the massive Oregon Buttes which dominate the southern horizon," they concluded. "The linear distance between these features is about twenty-five miles, though the Continental Divide between the two peaks actually winds along ridgelines for some forty miles."[22]

---

[17] Goetzmann, *Exploration and Empire*, 117, 146.
[18] Lavender, *Westward Vision: The Story of the Oregon Trail*, 165, 185.
[19] Wishart, *The Fur Trade of the American West*, 212.
[20] Gunnison, *The Mormons*, 151–52.
[21] Lamar, *New Encyclopedia of the American West*, 1069.
[22] Guenther, Hammer, and Chaney, "The Women Who Carried the Star of Empire," 149.

The oxen that trod down the sagebrush on the Oregon Trail created a vital wagon road, but engines driven by steam and internal combustion have different priorities. Transcontinental railroads and interstate highways bypassed South Pass. Since it is now far off the beaten track, South Pass has escaped most of the ills that have ravaged so much of the rest of the West. From its summit, the sweeping view appears almost eternal. Buttes—some ranchers today call them "sky islands"—knobs, hills, dunes, and creeks still fill the broad and broken expanse of the Green River Valley. In the far distance, the Wyoming Range still frames the horizon. And at a green oasis not far to the west, Pacific Springs is still "boiling up through the sod as cold as ice itself," just as it did on the first of August in 1852 for Miss Parthenia Blank.[23]

The history of the American West and its peoples—Indians of many nations, the "majority of scoundrels" who conducted the fur trade, missionaries and emigrants to the Oregon Country, government explorers who captured the country on maps, Latter-day Saints seeking a refuge across the Rocky Mountains, gamblers bound for El Dorado, mail couriers and Pony Express riders, and fifty thousand families seeking a new life in the West—converged at this quiet spot. It is a timeless place, and its simple grandeur evokes so many American memories that its landscape might prove the most enduring legacy of South Pass.

---

[23] Blank, "Twin Sisters on the Oregon Trail," 5:278.

SOUTH PASS TRAIL TODAY
A two-track road that now marks the passage of the Oregon, California, and Mormon Pioneer National Historic Trails through South Pass. Pacific Butte rises in the distance. *Courtesy Kay Threlkeld, 2005.*

CHAPTER I

"Daring and Intrepid Actions"
Discovering South Pass
1812

Long before the dawn of recorded history, humans used the natural gateway through the Rocky Mountains now known as South Pass for trade and travel. Paleolithic hunters have camped here for at least ten thousand years, and the entire area is rich in Plains Archaic and Late Prehistoric artifacts.[1]

The first written reports from the region are barely two centuries old, but they make clear that this key corridor between the streams and rivers that flowed to the Atlantic or Pacific ocean was contested ground when Europeans first saw it. The earliest descriptions of this elevated plain depict a paradise for bison on both sides of the pass. The large herds that ranged through the Green River Basin represented a great prize for the hunters whose lives depended on the shaggy beasts. The most successful of these people of the buffalo were clearly the Absarokas, better known as the Crows, who battled for control of this rich country with their ancient enemies, the powerful Blackfeet and the more vulnerable Shoshones. As the trade in firearms and horses expanded, however, the balance of power shifted. By the time the bison disappeared from the country west of South Pass during the 1840s, the Shoshones controlled it all.

Later travelers on the Oregon-California Trail told of meeting Absarokas, Arapahoes, Bannocks, Cheyennes, Nez Perce, Lakotas, and Utes at or near South Pass, but during the golden age of overland migration, the Shoshones

---

[1] Guenther, "The Burnt Ranch Saga," 29n4.

dominated the region and used the pass most heavily. Fur trader Osborne Russell knew the Shoshones well during the 1830s. When he left for Oregon in 1842, Russell reported that with the death of Pahdahewakumda (or Pahdasher-wah-un-dah) and his brother Moh-woom-hah, three men—Inkatushepoh, Fibebountowatsu, and Whoshakik had become "the pillars of the Nation and at whose names the Blackfeet quaked with fear."[2]

John Wilson, the first Indian agent to arrive at Fort Bridger, wrote, "The principal chiefs of the Sho-sho-nies are Mono, (about 45 years old) so called from a wound in his face or cheek from a ball that disfigures him; Wiskin (Cuthair) [and] Washikick, (Gourd Rattle) with whom I have had an interview, and Oapiche, (Big man.)"[3] Ultimately, it was Washikick (soon known as Washakie) who led the Shoshone through the most trying years in their long history.

As Mormon mail carriers traveled east from Salt Lake in mid-May 1850, they met a Shoshone village on the move. "They had wintered on the Wind river; had much fur, peltry, skins &c., which they were taking to [Fort] Bridger to exchange for ammunition, blankets, &c. &c.; all were on horseback, young and old; colts unable to travel, packed; dogs and eagles, packed," courier Robert Campbell reported. "We espied a rooster (which now they had packed up) and that had got so used to Indian life that we thought he seemed as graceful and dignified on horseback as if setting on the old barn yard fence at home."[4]

Appleton Milo Harmon, a Mormon, thought their horses "looked extremely well for haveing winterd in those lattitudes & altitudes." The animals were loaded with "Heavey and Bulkey burthens of undressed skins of Elk Deer Buffalo &c, on the top of which set their little papooses." He said the party's warriors "could be seen off some miles to the right and left in Search of game," and one of them occasionally returned to the moving village with blacktail deer, antelope, sage hen, goose, or duck, with which the country abounded. The Shoshones treated the Mormons with great civility and even helped them round up their cattle. "Some exchanges ware made with them by way of amunition for furs and we separated."[5]

P. L. Williams, who became South Pass City's district attorney, met Washakie in 1869. The Shoshone leader described his tribe's yearly cycle for the young attorney. It was their custom, he said, "to spend most of the year

---
[2] Russell, *Journal of a Trapper*, 115.
[3] Wilson to Ewing, Aug. 22, 1849, in Morgan, *Shoshonean Peoples and the Overland Trail*, 132.
[4] Campbell, July 7, 1850, "Interesting News from the Plains." *Frontier Guardian*, July 24, 1850, 1–2.
[5] Harmon, Diary, May 14, 1850, 67–68.

in the Wind River region, but about the 1st of June, the whole tribe, men, women and children, with all their belongings, ponies, tents, camp equipment, etc., would start on a trip to the Uintah Mountains in northeastern Utah, where they remained during the summer, returning about the latter part of September," Williams recalled. "The journey to and from this hunting and fishing ground was made by way of South Pass City, over the 'South Pass' of the mountain divide, across the broad valley of the Green River and by Fort Bridger. Thus they passed South Pass City twice each year."[6] Some say the Shoshone called South Pass "the place where God ran out of mountains."[7]

A Handsome Low Gap: The Astorians Find South Pass

So it was that Native peoples had used South Pass to cross the Rocky Mountains long before one of them told an American fur trader about this natural corridor in August 1812. John Jacob Astor started this chain of events in 1810 when he founded the Pacific Fur Company to extend the reach of his American Fur Company. Astor put up all the capital—two hundred thousand dollars—but kept half of the initial one hundred shares of stock in reserve and used it to form formed working partnerships with nine veteran fur traders, notably chief manager Wilson Price Hunt, Robert Stuart, and Ramsey Crooks. Except for Hunt, they all knew "the hardships of the Indian trade."[8] Astor quickly dispatched both land and sea expeditions to the Columbia River.

Robert Stuart never liked Jonathan Thorn, the furloughed Navy lieutenant whom Astor picked to command the ship *Tonquin* on its voyage to the Columbia River, but he was on deck when the U.S.S. *Constitution*, soon to earn her nickname "Old Ironsides," escorted *Tonquin* out of New York Harbor in September 1810.

Like many Scots in the fur trade, Robert Stuart had little use for officious potentates. When Thorn abandoned eight tardy crewmen after a stop in the Falkland Islands, including Stuart's "Old Uncle" David, he put a pistol to the lieutenant's head and persuaded him to return for them. *Tonquin* finally reached the Columbia in March 1811, and the party quickly built an outpost named Fort Astoria. By the summer of 1811 Astor's agents were building

---

[6] Williams, "Personal Recollections of Wash-A-Kie," 101–107.
[7] Heilig, "Director's Message," Wyoming Outdoor Council.
[8] Ross, *Adventures of the First Settlers on the Oregon*, 38.

trading posts at the confluence of the Snake and Columbia and along the Willamette, Spokane, and Okanogan rivers.[9]

Meanwhile, Wilson Price Hunt left St. Louis in October on a remarkable overland journey. After wintering on the Nodaway River, he headed west with four partners, a clerk, fifty-six *voyageurs*, eighty-two horses, and Wihmunke-wakan, best remembered as Marie Aioe Dorion, and her two children with Métis expedition member Pierre Dorion. Hunt ascended the Missouri and Grand rivers, then traveled overland to the Wind River, across the Continental Divide at Union Pass, and finally down the Hoback River to its confluence with the Snake, where he dispatched four trappers to collect furs. In mid-October 1811 he left his horses behind and set out with fifteen dugouts to descend the "Canoe River," which was actually one of the West's most treacherous watercourses, the Snake River. The voyage came to a disastrous end among the rapids of Caldron Linn, below today's Minidoka Reservoir in southwest Idaho. The westbound Astorians divided into smaller parties that made their way down both banks of the Snake to the Columbia and the Oregon Country. Hunt reached Fort Astoria, the company's headquarters at the mouth of the Columbia, in mid-February 1812 after traveling "2,073 miles since leaving the village of the Arikara. July 18th to February 15th—7 months."[10]

All had not gone as Astor and his traders had planned: the previous summer, the *Tonquin* "blew up in the air with a fearful explosion" on a trading voyage to Vancouver Island, which Stuart learned about in August from an Indian visitor to Fort Astoria. In October 1811 Lamazu, a half-British Chinook pilot known as George (or Jack) Ramsay, told how back in June Thorn had insulted a Nootka chieftain and provoked an attack in Clayoquot Sound, inspiring a surviving crewman to detonate Tonquin's magazine in defense. Lamazu was the sole survivor of "terrific and overwhelming" explosion.[11] The surviving partners confirmed the news after the company's second supply ship, the *Beaver*, appeared in May 1812 and began to reshape their strategy.

Upon his arrival, as the senior partner Hunt assumed command of the expedition. Fort Astoria's officers decided to send a five-man express overland party under John Reed to deliver the bad news to Astor and request supplies and reinforcements. The expedition did not get far. Robert Stuart

---

[9] Laton McCartney, a descendent of Robert Stuart, wrote *Across the Great Divide*, the best account of the Returning Astorians.

[10] Ronda, *Astoria and Empire*, 117–95, 232, 240–41; Stuart, *Discovery of the Oregon Trail*, 308.

[11] Ross, *Adventures*, 164.

"DARING AND INTREPID ACTIONS"

ROBERT STUART
Born in Scotland in 1785, the tough and resourceful Stuart led the first known party to cross South Pass before his thirtieth birthday. A brilliant and determined leader, Stuart later directed the American Fur Company's Northern Department from Mackinac Island and served as Michigan state treasurer before his death in 1848.
Courtesy the Collection of the Marquette Regional History Center.

had spent the winter scouting trading post sites and, while returning down the Columbia River to Astoria, he rescued a badly wounded John Reed. Reed had lost his "shiny metal dispatch box" of messages for Astor in a melee with Wishram Indians at The Dalles. The partners decided to send another express to New York "to inform Mr. Astor and the other persons connected with the expedition of the loss of the Tonquin." Stuart volunteered to lead it.[12]

The guns at Fort Astoria saluted Robert Stuart, Benjamin Jones, François LeClerc, André Vallé, John Day, Ramsay Crooks, and Robert McClellan when they set out on the afternoon of June 29, 1812. Day, Crooks, and McClellan had come west with Wilson Hunt and so knew some of the challenges that lay before them. The next morning they joined a larger band of traders and trappers bound for the Spokane and Okanogan rivers and "the interior parts of the country above the forks of the Columbia."[13] Stuart sent John Day back to Fort Astoria after Day tried to kill himself near the mouth of the Willamette River, but the others pushed on to the Walla Walla River. Here Stuart and his five companions parted ways with the other Astorians and bought horses from the Indians to continue the trek with packsaddles.

---
[12] "Letter by Elisha Loomis," April 2, 1831, in Stuart, *On the Oregon Trail*, 177.
[13] Ibid., 27. François LeClerc's name was also spelled Leclaire, Leclerc, and LeClaire. "LeClerc" follows the spelling used in Stuart's journal.

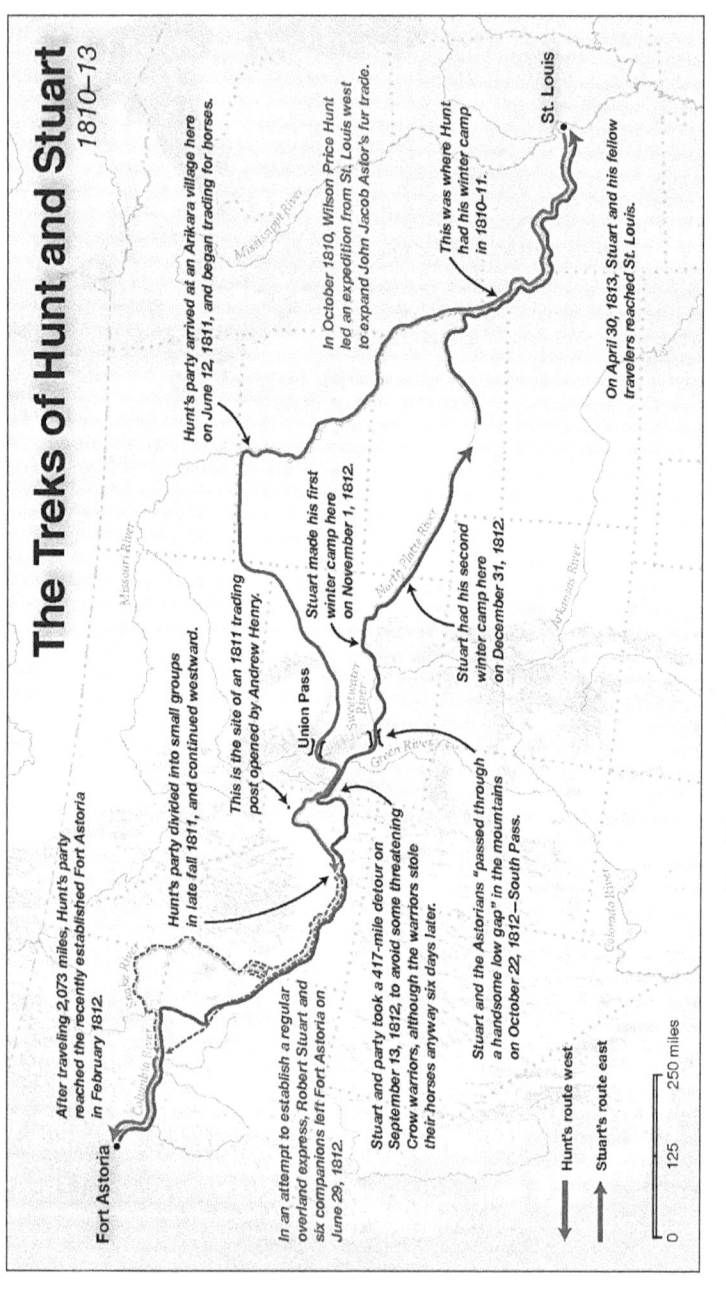

The Treks of Hunt and Stuart, 1810–1813

Courtesy Joan Pennington.

"DARING AND INTREPID ACTIONS" 39

After a difficult crossing of the Blue Mountains and Grande Ronde Valley and an equally tough trip down the left bank of the Snake River, Stuart reached the Bruneau River in mid-August.[14] That night the "innumerable hosts" of mosquitoes were so bad, Stuart wrote, that they "completely deprived our eyelids of their usual function," leaving the men nearly blind. The next morning the Astorians met the Indian who had guided Wilson Price Hunt's outfit "over the Mad River Mountain last Fall." The Absarokas had raided the Pacific Fur Company caches, the Shoshone reported, "and carried off every thing," but he also had more important news—history's first mention of South Pass. "Hearing that there is a shorter trace to the South than that by which Mr. Hunt had traversed the R. Mountains," Stuart wrote the next day, "and learning that this Indian was perfectly acquainted with the route, I without loss of time offered him a Pistol a Blanket of Blue Cloth—an Axe—a Knife—an awl—a Fathom (*of blue*) Beads a looking glass and a little Powder & Ball if he would guide us to the other side, which he immediately accepted." Two days later, the erstwhile guide disappeared with Stuart's horse.[15]

As far as records show, this was the first hint of the existence of South Pass in the annals of the American West. Andrew Henry of Missouri had opened a post northwest of the pass near today's St. Anthony's, Idaho, in 1811. As historian Dale L. Morgan observed, Henry's men "may have learned of the existence of, and even traversed, South Pass, but little evidence and not even a reasoned argument has been set forth in support of this view."[16] French, Spanish, and American fur traders had been wandering the northern Rockies since before the return of the Lewis and Clark Expedition. Only days before he crossed South Pass, Stuart heard from Shoshones that a trader named Jean Baptiste Champlain and three men had possibly used the pass on their way to Green River the previous summer, but Arapahos "murdered them in the dead of night and took possession of all their effects." Ezekiel Williams's "Lost Trappers" might have even crossed South Pass—and a recently discovered grave marked "Died 1814 Roy" not far from Aspen Peak and the Great Basin Divide near the Hastings/Mormon Trail suggests they did.[17]

Yet no reliable source shows anyone of European extraction knew about

---

[14] Most sources place the encounter on the Owyhee River, but Dale L. Morgan put the meeting near the mouth of the Bruneau. Morgan, *The West of William Ashley*, xxxix.
[15] Stuart, *Discovery of the Oregon Trail*, 83–84. A fathom was about six feet.
[16] Morgan, *Jedediah Smith*, 389n25.
[17] See John Eldredge's remarkable report in "Who Was Roy?" 21–29.

South Pass before that fateful day in August 1812. It is possible that an unknown but far-ranging French *voyageur* or an unrecorded but ambitious Spanish trader was the first non-Indian to see the corridor, but the arguments historian, collector, and former cowhand Philip Ashton Rollins presented in 1935 are still difficult to refute: French adventurers, Rollins noted, had ascended the Platte and traveled south to Santa Fe, "but there seems to be no record or tradition of their being near South Pass." Canadians had made "salient thrusts" toward South Pass, but none of these "intrepid folk reached its vicinity." Finally, there was "no trustworthy proof that the Spaniards were ever in Wyoming" before 1812.[18]

Stuart's men pressed on up the Snake, battling the heat and mosquitoes and keeping a much more careful watch on their horses. Near Salmon Falls on August 20, they met John Hoback, Edward Robinson, Jacob Rezner, and Joseph Miller, the men Wilson Hunt had left behind to trap the Snake River country. Arapahos had robbed the men twice, and their former partner Martin Cass had made off with the last of their horses, leaving the fur hunters to survive—barely—on fish. These half-famished friends, whose "terrific appearance beggars all description," accompanied Stuart to Caldron Linn. The contents of six of the caches Hunt had left behind the previous fall had vanished.

Stuart outfitted Hoback, Robinson, and Rezner for a two-year hunt from the surviving three caches, but Joseph Miller had seen enough of the West. "Mr. Millers curiosity and desire of traveling thro' the Indian countries being fully satisfied he has determined to accompany us." A new problem now confronted the expedition: like the lost trappers, if their skill as hunters failed them, they faced starvation, or what Stuart described as having "nothing for that very desirable operation: *the wagging of the jaws*."[19]

Miller had trapped on the Bear and Green rivers, and based on his reports, Stuart set an eastbound course "by which we proposed crossing the Rocky Mountains." The party ascended the Snake to its confluence with the Portneuf River, where they headed east to reach Bear River at Soda Springs and followed an Indian trace up the Bear to a camp near today's Dingle, Idaho. Here they fell in with an Absaroka war party whose threats, Stuart said, "indicated an evident intention to steal if not to rob" the Americans. Stuart gave them some gunpowder to prevent an open conflict "and left them happy at getting off on no worse terms."[20]

---

[18] Stuart, *Discovery of the Oregon Trail*, cxxxi.
[19] Ibid., 87, 109, 112–13.
[20] McCartney, *Across the Great Divide*, 190–94.

Since leaving the Columbia River, the party had essentially followed what later became the Oregon Trail, but the Absaroka warriors made them nervous. Stuart abandoned his plan to cross directly from Bear River to the Green. The Absarokas later became great friends of the whites, particularly American mountaineers, and they long boasted that their tribe had never killed a white man. They were, however, fiercely proud of their skill as raiders. "Trust to their honor," advised fur-trade entrepreneur Robert Campbell, "and you are safe: trust to their honesty, and they will steal the hair off your head."[21] Bill Gilbert of the Missouri Fur Company said the Absarokas admitted that "if they killed [us], we would not come back, & they would lose the chance of stealing from us."[22]

Cautiously, Stuart turned north and led his hungry men up Thomas Fork, starting on a wandering detour that would take 417 miles, by his own estimate, to reach the Big Sandy, which was less than a hundred miles away. The expedition leader's fears were not misplaced. Six days later, not long after dawn on September 19, 1812, the warriors returned and made off with all the party's horses, "not withstanding their being tethered & hobbled," in what Stuart called "one of the most daring and intrepid actions I ever heard of among Indians."[23]

Elisha Loomis retold "a brief but interesting account" of the trek Stuart recounted for him in 1831. Stuart provided no details of the theft of his party's mounts in his journal, but after the "Arapahai indians" ran off the horses, they turned to mock the dismayed trappers, "laughing heartily at the success of their plan," Loomis reported. "One of them took pains to turn his backside towards them in an insulting manner." An "old Kentucky hunter"—Ben Jones—raised his rifle "to shoot the villain." Stuart stopped him, fearing the killing would provoke the Indians to murder them all. The hunter "begged hard" to be allowed to take "*one crack at the Indian*." Stuart refused, even when the man offered to give up a considerable part of his wages for the privilege of killing the man who had apparently "mooned" the distraught fur traders. "Destitute of horses," Loomis wrote, "the party hardly knew what to do." Some of the men were ready to "die where they were, as it seemed hardly possible to cross the immense prairies on foot, weak as they had become and destitute of provisions."[24]

---

[21] Irving, *Adventures of Captain Bonneville*, 111.
[22] Morgan, *Jedediah Smith*, 87–88.
[23] Stuart, *Discovery of the Oregon Trail*, 131–32, 134–35, 141.
[24] Stuart, *On the Oregon Trail*, 170, 178–79. The "Araphais," who Stuart called "a southern band of Snakes," may have been Bannocks.

Now afoot and basically lost, the men burned whatever gear and supplies they could not carry and threw the rest into the Snake. "We find our Bundles very heavy as the road is by no means level," Stuart wrote. To make matters worse, the men now had "just food enough for one meal."[25]

"Some idea of the situation of those men may be conceived, when we take into consideration, that they were now on foot, and had a journey of two thousand miles before them, fifteen hundred of which was entirely unknown," a newspaper reflected next spring.[26] Seeking to avoid the Absarokas and the Blackfeet, Stuart and his men roamed across the mountains along today's Idaho-Wyoming border, "a country, in Mr. Stuart's own words, 'more fit for goats than men.'"[27]

Barely surviving on trout, duck, beaver, elk, and grizzly bear meat, the party rambled up Thomas Fork and up and down the Salt, Greys, Teton, and Hoback rivers, and even took a raft trip down the Snake. (Had they headed east from Greys River, the Astorians would have struck La Barge Creek and then South Piney Creek, the route the Lander Cutoff later followed.) Ramsay Crooks fell desperately ill, and though some of the men wanted to abandon him, Stuart refused. Pressing on, the party finally "reached the drains of the Spanish River"—the Green River Valley—on October 12, 1812, near Black Butte and the North Fork of Beaver Creek.[28]

The starving men had hoped to find plenty of bison in the valley, but the tracks of an old bull "was all we had for hope," Stuart wrote. The few antelope lurking along the ridgetops looked "so wild as to preclude any hope of getting near them." Next morning, the trap they set to catch breakfast "had nothing in it except the forepaw of a large Beaver—which has greatly damped our spirits." That night, François LeClerc said he "was determined to go no farther, but that lots should be cast and one die to preserve the rest." Stuart did his best to dissuade him, but when it became clear LeClerc was winning over some of his comrades, Stuart wrote he "snatched up my Rifle cocked and leveled it at him with the firm resolution to fire if he persisted." The next

---

[25] Stuart, *Discovery of the Oregon Trail*, 134–35, 141.
[26] "American Enterprize," *Missouri Gazette*, May 15, 1813.
[27] Ross, *Adventures*, 230.
[28] Philip Ashton Rollins's analysis of Stuart's route is detailed and stands up to scrutiny, but Wyoming native O. Ned Eddins has proposed a plausible alternate interpretation of the party's trek from Salt Creek Canyon to Green River. See O. Ned Eddins's "Mountain Man" website at http://www.thefurtrapper.com [Sept. 3, 2013].

afternoon, to their great joy, the starvelings discovered "an old run down Buffalo Bull" and killed it after considerable trouble. The men devoured part of the tough flesh raw.

The party followed the Green River south and on October 15 found buffalo skeletons scattered in every direction, evidence of a tribe's fall hunt. They "crossed a large Indian trail, about 15 days old," which Stuart attributed to the Absarokas. The next day they forded the New Fork River, Willow Creek, and Pine Creek in the shadow of the Wind River Range, stopping at or near today's Pinedale, Wyoming, where they found an abandoned Indian hunting camp.

The next morning they pushed on past Boulder Creek and the East Fork River and then camped at the point where it veers southwest to make a sharp turn around the northern fringe of Fremont Butte. They were still desperately short of food: "Our living has been and is of the meanest kind of poor Bull meat or Buck Antelope, both too bad to be eat[en] except in cases of starvation," Stuart mourned. On October 18 they met six poor but friendly Shoshones and accompanied them to their brush huts, possibly on Pocket Creek. They traded with the Indians for a six-day supply of buffalo meat and managed to buy the band's only horse, the last survivor of an Absaroka raid that had made off with all the rest of their animals and a number of women.[29]

By sunrise, the ragged adventurers had loaded their new old horse with "meat for six days and everything except our bedding." Stuart later called her "our good old Rozinante" after Don Quixote's noble steed. For her hard work, survival skills, and contribution to the exploration of the West, Rozinante ranks with the West's great horses, right up there with Little Bighorn survivor Comanche, Buffalo Bill Cody's Isham, and Midnight the Devil Horse, a Cayuse "Champion Bucker" of National Western Stock Show fame.

The mare and her seven companions headed south, soon striking a "large Crow trace" left by at least sixty lodges. "We followed this road 12 miles S.E. by S. to a Creek coming from the East"—the Big Sandy River—where a bitterly cold northeast wind persuaded them to camp, and their hunters finally brought down a young bison bull "in very good order." Fearful of the Absarokas who had done them so much harm, the next day they marched about eighteen miles to the southeast "through a beautifully undulating country" but "abandoned the Crow trace early in the day" as it headed toward the

---

[29] Stuart, *Discovery of the Oregon Trail*, 155–61, 178n107.

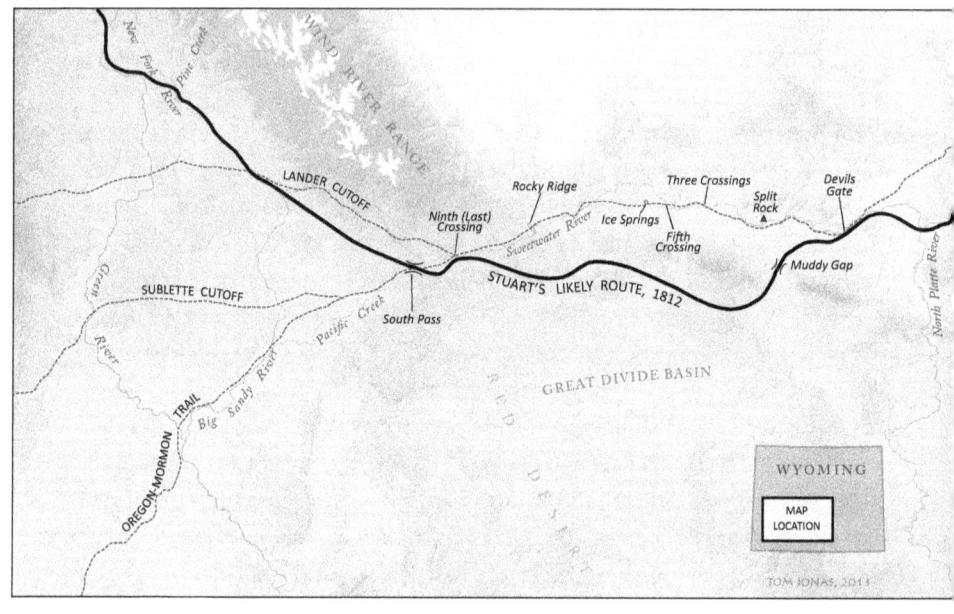

STUART'S LIKELY ROUTE, 1812
Map by Tom Jonas, 2013.

northeast.[30] More than a decade after Stuart used it, the trace would become the road to Green River that fur-trade caravans followed to the annual trading fair known as the rendezvous. Three decades later, it became the Oregon-California Trail alternate known as the Lander Cutoff.[31]

Stuart's justified apprehension shaped his course as he traced the future route of the Oregon-California Trail. The Astorians' trek brought them to a camp at or near the spot where the wagon and Pony Express trails later crossed the Dry Sandy. Here they struggled to get warm in a piercing nor'easter with only the help of a sagebrush fire, obliging the ragged men "to take refuge in our nests at an early hour." But as his journal makes clear, Stuart and his men could see the broad plain of South Pass looming before

---

[30] Ibid., 162–63.
[31] Thanks to BLM archeologist David Vlcek for pointing out that Stuart uses the word "road" to describe this historic Indian route.

them. "The ridge of mountains which divides Wind river from the Columbia and Spanish waters ends here abruptly," Stuart wrote in his journal that bitterly cold evening. The next day, he later recalled, the party had "made the best of our way" toward an opening in the mountains they could see to the southeast, and after a hard tramp the beleaguered Astorians "passed thro a handsome low gap"—South Pass.[32]

MUDDY WATERS OF THE MISSOURI: SOUTH PASS REVEALED

Stuart's men left camp on October 21, 1812, having waited to collect the meat of a bison that Robert McClellan had killed the previous evening. By the time they set out, it was snowing, but Stuart's journal indicates that they could see the open prairie of South Pass ahead of them. Not far from camp, they "crossed a large lodge trace steering little to the right of the point of the mountain we suppose made by another Band of the Absarokas who may have been hunting down on the Spanish River." The fresh evidence of the Indian threat apparently prompted the Astorians to seek an unknown and unused route that would avoid contact with them. Stuart's hunters "found a little bad water" a mile and a half from camp, so the thirsty men got a drink at last.[33]

Stuart's party—now made up of Ramsay Crooks, Benjamin Jones, François LeClerc, Robert McClellan, Joseph Miller, and André Vallé—made a dry camp in an aspen grove. Stuart's description of the day's march suggests his party camped on the slope leading to the corridor through the Rockies they had sought for so long, but his accounts make it difficult to determine the camp's specific location.[34] His journal and travel memorandum for the next day pose more problems, but these accounts show that these seven men made history when they accomplished the first recorded crossing of South Pass on October 22, 1812.

---

[32] Stuart, *Discovery of the Oregon Trail*, 162–63, 255–56. Stuart's "Spanish River" was the Green River. Rollins located this camp on Dry Sandy Creek, "some 11 miles southeast by south" of the crossroads at Elkhorn Junction, Wyoming.

[33] According to Rollins, Stuart camped at N42° 20' W108° 56' on the slope "immediately northeast of present-day Pacific Springs and one mile due south from the extreme headwaters of present-day Pacific Creek"—locations not easy to correlate with Stuart's description or identify with a single spot on the 7.5-minute USGS Pacific Springs Quadrangle. Stuart, *Discovery of the Oregon Trail*, 163–64, 181n148.

[34] William Clayton's guidebook gave the distance between Pacific Springs and the Dry Sandy as ten and a half miles. Stuart's estimated fifteen miles would put his October 21, 1812 camp several miles east of Pacific Springs. He should have found water at the springs, so it seems the day's travel fell short of Stuart's figure. The "small stream of excellent water" they found in the morning was perhaps Pacific Creek.

The men set out by daylight and headed to the gap in the mountains opening before them. After a hard tramp in a snowstorm, the beleaguered Astorians "passed thro a handsome low gap" to reach the east side of the Rocky Mountains. Veering south of the Twin Mounds and the Oregon Trail, they hiked several miles to a small stream, or perhaps Oregon Slough, where they breakfasted. Ten more miles brought them "to the head drains of a watercourse running East among banks and low Hills." It quit snowing, and they pushed on for five more miles along this creek until at last they "found a little water oozing out of the earth, it was of a whiteish colour and possessed a great similarity of taste to the Muddy waters of the Missouri."

They made camp about seven and a half miles due south of the confluence of Rock Creek and the Sweetwater, having come some twenty miles east by southeast, over broken ground "covered with but little Grass, some Sage and a good deal of Saltwood." Instead of their usual fare of bull bison beef, they feasted on two "Ibex"—big horn sheep—"which we find excellent eating," as a well-fed but chilly Stuart noted in his journal. They pushed on through the piercing cold the next day, happily "supposing this is a water of the Missouri."[35]

The "Travel Memorandum" Stuart wrote sometime before 1821 provides an alternate (and confusing) account of the day's events. The most puzzling description is of "the top of the mountain which we call the *big horn*, it is in the middle of the principal chain." Stuart said the flat summit of the peak, apparently volcanic in origin, formed a plain more than three square miles in size, "in the middle of which is a considerable Lake, which from every appearance was formerly the crater of a volcano." Historians have tied themselves in knots trying to interpret this. Philip Rollins dismissed Stuart's reference to a lake, which, "if not created by a mirage or a mistaken recollection as to the site, was doubtless a shallow ephemeral product of torrential rain or snow."[36]

Fear of another encounter with the powerful Abrasokas led Stuart to avoid "the Crow trace," which followed the future course of the Oregon Trail to the Sweetwater River. Yet he "recognized the South Pass for exactly what it was, the main boulevard over which 100 Crow lodges had just been dragged," historian David A. White observed. "Preferring not to meet the owners of those

---

[35] Stuart, *Discovery of the Oregon Trail*, 163–65, 181–82, 255–56. Sand Creek, the stream Stuart probably followed, disappears into the sands of the Great Divide Basin.

[36] Stuart, *Discovery of the Oregon Trail*, 164, 183.

DEVILS GATE
For many overland travelers, the long ascent of South Pass began at Devils Gate. This Charles Kelly photograph shows the landmark looking west from the Dumbell Ranch in about 1932. *Courtesy Utah State Historical Association.*

lodges, he detoured through a back alley."[37] In taking his southwest course, Stuart unknowingly left the Missouri headwaters to return to the interior basins of today's Wyoming, whose complicated geography was beyond his comprehension. The day after the party crossed South Pass must have been discouraging, for they marched some twenty-three miles, perhaps around Cyclone Butte, and then climbed a hill they dubbed Discovery Knob. Stuart looked out to see Lost Creek disappear into the Great Divide Basin—"a Plain bounded only by the Horizon." He resolved "to make the best of our way" north toward the Granite Mountains, hoping to find a wintering place as soon as possible. The Astorians turned northeast and hiked twenty-two miles over "tolerably level ground of *very* indifferent quality" to a camp somewhere near today's Lost Creek Reservoir.

For days the men and the "almost done out" Rozinante trekked across the alkaline flats south of the Green Mountains, down Lost Soldier Creek,

---

[37] White, *News of the Plains and the Rockies*, 1:140.

and north through Muddy Gap between Green and Ferris mountains. Late in October the party finally reached the banks of the Sweetwater River, not far upstream from Devils Gate, once again rejoining the future path of the Oregon Trail. They left the future wagon road to struggle down the river to the North Platte, where they turned north to rejoin the Oregon Trail, whose line they followed east for the rest of the trek. Near Red Butte Stuart's men raised a cottonwood log house—Wyoming's first building—and went into winter quarters.

A visit from an Arapaho war party convinced the men (with Rozinante) to move on after a month in their comfortable log house and make an arduous—and cold—descent of the North Platte. With most of the grass buried under snow, Rozinante survived on cottonwood bark and willows. On the last day of 1812, the men built their second shelter near today's Torrington on the Wyoming-Nebraska border. Here they hunkered down to hollow out cottonwood canoes and wait for the long winter to end.

The ice began to melt early in March 1813. On the eighth the men cast off in their new canoes, but the Platte was too shallow to float the heavy dugouts. After "considerable labour in wading and dragging," they abandoned their awkward craft and pressed on with their lone "quadruped," the resilient Shoshone horse, which had somehow survived the winter.

Near today's Yutan, Nebraska, the party found a large Oto village. Two resident French traders swapped the Astorian's "faithful four-footed companion" for a bullboat made of elk and bison hide, which Stuart's men used to float down to the Missouri and Mississippi rivers. Not long before sunset on the last day of April, the weary travelers reached St. Louis "in perfect health." They had completed "a voyage of ten months from Astoria, during which time we underwent many dangers, hardships, & fatigues, in short I may say, all the privations human nature is capable," wrote Robert Stuart.[38]

---

[38] "American Enterprize," *Missouri Gazette*, May 15, 1813; Stuart, *On the Oregon Trail*, 142–43, 158–59, 164.

By information received from these gentlemen, it appears that a journey across the continent of North America might be performed with a waggon, there being no obstruction in the whole route that any person would dare to call a mountain, in addition to its being much the most direct and short one to go from this place to the mouth of the Columbia river. Any future party, who may undertake this journey, and are tolerably acquainted with the different places where it would be necessary to lay up a small stock of provisions, would not be impeded, as in all probability, they would not meet with an Indian to interrupt their progress, although on the other route, more north, there are almost insurmountable barriers.

"American Enterprize"
Missouri Gazette, May 15, 1813

We packed up and moved down to the Aspin grove whare we remained some two or three weeks Subsisting on Mountain sheep. . . . We did not leave this camp until the Mountain Sheep began to get scarce and wild. . . . On leaving sweet water we struck in a South westerly direction. . . . We packed up our meat & traveled on until in the afternoon in hopes of finding water but did not succeed but finding large clumps of sage brush we camped all eav[en]ing & part of the night. Continuing on we found we had crossed the main ridge of the Rocky mountan. . . . 15 days without water or only such as we got from melting snow our horses eating snow and living fairly when beaver ground was found although we struck Sandy about noon some of the men went immediatly to cutting the ice with thier Tomahauks. Called out frose to the bottom. I walked down. They had got down the length of thier arms and was about to give it up. I pulled out one of my pistols and fired in to the hole up came the water plentifull for man & horse.

JAMES CLYMAN
FRONTIERSMAN, 24–25

CHAPTER 2

"Marshalling the Way"
Rediscovering South Pass
1824

As Dale Morgan wrote, "Stuart's arrival in St. Louis constituted something of a sensation."¹ The *Missouri Gazette* quickly announced the news and in a little more than a fortnight published the first description of their astonishing journey. A brief report printed on May 8, 1813, predicted, prematurely, that their story would show "the world that a journey to the Western Sea will not be considered (within a few years) of much greater importance than a trip to New York." A longer article appeared a week later and ended with an announcement of the discovery that would eventually transform the American West.

The article was widely reprinted in newspapers and even books, but Stuart's discovery was quickly forgotten. Some have speculated that John Jacob Astor suppressed the news of the existence of South Pass, hoping to keep it a trade secret. Stuart's journal remained unpublished for more than a century, but a translation of his "Travel Memorandum" appeared in a leading French journal in 1821. More importantly, the October after Stuart's return, Astor himself informed Thomas Jefferson that Stuart had left his journal with President James Madison.

Ramsay Crooks visited Washington City in 1820 and met congressmen Thomas Hart Benton of Missouri and Dr. John Floyd of Virginia at his hotel, where he provided these ardent western boosters with information about his overland adventure.² Floyd called for congressional hearings to "inquire into

---
¹ Morgan, *The West of William Ashley*, xl.
² Stuart, *Discovery of the Oregon Trail*, lxviii.

the expediency of occupying the Columbia River" country, Oregon. "The route to the mouth of the Columbia is easy, safe and expeditious," Floyd orated. "As to distance, I have already shown that in point of time the mouth of the Oregon or Columbia is not farther distant than Louisville was 30 years ago from New York, or St. Louis was 20 years ago from Philadelphia."

In his formal report to the House, Floyd claimed, "The practicability of a speedy, safe and easy communication with the Pacific is no longer a matter of doubt or conjecture; from information not to be doubted, the Rocky Mountains at this time in several places is so smooth and open that the labor of 10 men for 20 days would enable a wagon with its usual freight to pass with great facility from the navigable waters of the Missouri to that of the Columbia." There can be little doubt that Ramsay Crooks was the source of his "information not to be doubted." Floyd's geography and timetable were awful, but his vision would eventually capture the imagination of a nation.[3]

Secret or not, there was nothing anyone in Missouri could do in 1813 with the news that a natural wagon road led through the heart of the Rocky Mountains. Missouri itself was still largely unsettled, and Independence, the town that eventually served as the state's outfitting depot for expeditions to the Far West, would not even exist for another fourteen years. Coming in the middle of the War of 1812, which drove Americans from the upper Missouri River and halted the nation's western trade and exploration for ten years, the announcement of Stuart's discovery had no practical consequences. For all of Dr. Floyd's blustering about the Columbia River, during the 1820s, Americans were preoccupied with settling the midwestern Indian lands they had seized during the War of 1812.

Enterprising Young Men: Reviving the American Fur Trade

Ironically, just as the moribund American fur trade finally began to reawaken, Congress passed a law in July 1822 banning the sale of alcohol to Indians. Liquor had long been the main medium of exchange at trading posts, but without whiskey, it became harder for traders to persuade Natives to do the hard work of hunting and trapping fur-bearing creatures. William Henry

---

[3] Marshall, *Acquisition of Oregon*, 155–57. Floyd was the cousin of Sgt. Charles Floyd, the Lewis and Clark expedition's only casualty, and father of Sec. of War John B. Floyd.

Ashley, an ambitious Missouri entrepreneur, politician, and militia general, was ready to wager a small fortune that he could make a much greater one by seizing his share of the of the upper Missouri River trade in beaver fur. Early in 1822 he and his partner, Major Andrew Henry, formed the Rocky Mountain Fur Company. They planned to have their own men trap beavers and advertised in the *Missouri Gazette* that they were looking for one hundred "Enterprising Young Men" who were ready "to ascend the river Missouri to its source" and spend as much as three years risking their lives seeking their own fortunes in the fur business.[4]

So began the company that transformed the American Rocky Mountain fur trade. The men who answered this help-wanted ad became known as Ashley's Hundred. Its ranks included Jedediah Smith, the four Sublette brothers, Thomas Fitzpatrick, John H. Weber, David Jackson, Daniel T. Potts, Louis Vasquez, Mike Fink, and Lindsay Applegate. Henry set out with two keelboats, hoping to establish a post at present-day Great Falls, Montana. But before leaving the state of Missouri, one of his boats sank, along with ten thousand dollars in trade goods. Ashley pressed on with his remaining keelboat, while a mounted contingent followed on land. Upriver a band of Assiniboines ran off the party's horses, and Major Henry had to stop and build a post at the mouth of the Yellowstone. The next spring he headed upriver again, but the Blackfeet drove the Americans out of the Upper Missouri country, which by now was becoming a tradition.[5]

Not one to acknowledge defeat, Ashley recruited another hundred men, outfitted two more keelboats, and again set off in pursuit of "the wealth of furs not surpassed by the mines of Peru" that was waiting to be taken from the Three Forks country of the Upper Missouri. He headed upriver in March 1823, hoping to purchase horses from the Arikara Indians and send a mounted party overland to the Yellowstone River. Disaster struck at dawn on June 2, when the Arikaras attacked and killed half of the men they caught on the shore. Standing on a bare and open sandbar while the Indians shot at the trappers from their picketed village, James Clyman concluded such adventures were more than he had contracted for: the experience "some what cooled my courage." More than one-sixth of Ashley's party died in the attack.[6] The

---
[4] *Missouri Gazette & Public Advertiser*, St. Louis, Missouri, Feb. 13, 1822.
[5] Chittenden, *The American Fur Trade*, 1:262.
[6] Morgan, *Jedediah Smith*, 53–55.

Americans spent most of the summer avenging their losses, but by fall it looked like the firm of Ashley & Henry was headed for utter financial ruin.

Ironically, the ambush at the Arikara villages set in motion events that led to the practical rediscovery of South Pass. In desperation, William L. Sublette, Jedediah Smith, and Thomas Fitzpatrick set out up the White River about the first of October with some sixteen men, hoping to reach the rich beaver country along "the Spanish River"—the Green River—to recoup the company's fortunes. It was late in the year when they set out, and the Great Plains, Badlands, and Rocky Mountains stood between the American fur hunters and their goal.[7] Smith's striking talents earned him the title of captain of the brigade, and he took his men to the south fork of the Cheyenne River, where they traded for horses with a band of Lakotas. They traversed the Pierre Shale beds, a badlands that James Clyman called "this pile of ashes": he thought "the whole of this region is moving to the Misourie River as fast as rain and thawing snow can carry it."[8]

James Clyman (1794–1881) was one of the most resilient and remarkable of America's frontiersmen. Clyman's father had been one of George Washington's tenant farmers. After retiring from the fur trade in 1827, Clyman served in the Black Hawk War in the same Illinois militia company as Abraham Lincoln, making him one of the only Americans besides John Quincy Adams to have known both Washington and Lincoln. His diaries and recollections provide our only firsthand account of many major historical events.

After emerging from the Black Hills, Smith sent the "strange, half savage" Edward Rose to find the Absarokas and arrange for winter quarters. A "mixed-blood, part negro, Cherokee, and white" frontiersman, Rose had been in the mountains since 1806 and had spent years living with the tribe. The Absarokas knew Rose as *Chee-ho-carte*, The Five Scalps, for a ferocious victory in which he had killed five Minnetaree enemies. "Powerful in frame and fearless in spirit," Rose's daring quickly won him "rank among the first braves of

---

[7] Everything we know about these events comes from James Clyman's account, written in 1871, an 1847 John S. Robb letter based on what Thomas Fitzpatrick told him, and Washington Irving's *The Rocky Mountains*. Clyman credited Jedediah Smith with being the expedition's leader, while Robb's letter touted Thomas Fitzpatrick as the discoverer of South Pass, claiming Smith stayed in the Crow village. Irving was probably close to the mark when he said the brigade "was conducted by Smith, Fitzpatrick, and Sublette." Clyman reported the party consisted of eleven men, while Robb said they numbered sixteen. Dale Morgan concluded it must have initially been larger but probably never exceeded sixteen men. Morgan, *Jedediah Smith*, 80–83.

[8] Clyman, *James Clyman, Frontiersman*, 17–18. See also Charles Camp's sketch "James Clyman," in Hafen, *The Mountain Men*, 1:233–58.

the tribe," Washington Irving reported. When Rose chose to, he could be an invaluable guide and interpreter for those who needed help from the proud and powerful Absarokas. Rose was a valuable ally but a tricky friend. He had helped Wilson Price Hunt find Union Pass in 1812, yet Hunt considered him "a very bad fellow and full of daring." Smith found Rose willing to give him critical assistance.[9]

In the Powder River basin, a grizzly bear attacked Captain Smith and laid his "skull bare to near the crown of the head leaving a white streak whare his teeth passed," ripping one ear practically off his head. Smith told James Clyman how to sew him back together, then climbed on his horse and rode a mile to a stream-side campsite, where his men put up their only tent "and made him as comfortable as circumstances would permit." The experience gave the trappers a lesson "on the charcter of the grissly Baare which we did not forget," Clyman wrote. It also taught them something about the character of Jedediah Smith.[10]

A few men stayed in camp for about two weeks waiting for Smith to recover, Clyman recalled years later, and then made "easy travel west ward and Struck the trail of Shian Indians." Charles Keemle, an agent of the Missouri Fur Company, told a different story: he claimed the trappers were forced to leave Smith behind "in the care of two men, in a very hostile country," where Keemle and his party "fell in with Smith and his companions, and accompanied them to the village of a roving band of Cheyennes." They met Fitzpatrick and the rest of Ashley's men at the Cheyenne village, journalist John S. Robb wrote twenty-four years later in one of the first reports of these events. The reunited band "proceeded to the Big Horn, thence on to the waters of the Yellow Stone."[11]

WE COULD GO TO GREEN RIVER:
THE QUEST FOR THE SEEDS-KE-DEE

With winter closing in, the trappers needed to find shelter from the blizzards that would soon sweep the country. "Undertook to go to the territory of the Crow Indians, found them encamped on the Big Horn and staid with them [for the] most part of the winter," Clyman remembered. Two days after the

---

[9] For all that is known about Rose, see Irving, *The Adventures of Captain Bonneville*, 30–34, 111; Holmes, "The Five Scalps"; and Blenkinsop, "Edward Rose," in Hafen, *The Mountain Men*, 9:335–45.

[10] Clyman, *James Clyman, Frontiersman*, 17.

[11] Ibid., 19; SOLITAIRE, "Major Fitzpatrick, The Discoverer of the South Pass!" *St. Louis Weekly Reveille*, March 1, 1847, in Hafen, *Broken Hand*, 339.

trappers parted with the Cheyennes, Edward Rose rode into camp with fifteen or sixteen Absaroka warriors who had tracked the Americans for two days to make sure they had no Cheyennes with them. The Absarokas "relieved our Broke down horses and gave us a chance to ride," Clyman recalled. To ensure their friendship, Smith sent their fast-traveling benefactors ahead with "what they could pack." After an arduous trek "crossing several steep and high ridges that in any other country would be called mountains," the exhausted fur hunters found the tribe as November 1823 came to a close. Their camp was on the Wind River, probably near today's Dubois, Wyoming, but perhaps farther downstream at Riverton.[12]

The trappers spent an interesting ten weeks or so in the shelter of the Wind River Valley. "Snow did not fall deep and every Clear day it thawed whare the sun struck fairly," James Clyman said. The mountaineers passed much of the time hunting buffalo with the Indians; everyone estimated the Native hunters and their guests slaughtered a thousand bison in one "grand chase." The Absarokas dried the meat "on a grand scale and wood was in demand," so no doubt their axes helped the American trappers earn their keep. By February the guests and their insatiable appetites had worn out their welcome, and their moody mediator had run through a substantial part of their trade merchandise—when Edward Rose got them among the Absarokas, "he was exceedingly generous with their goods; making presents to the braves of his adopted tribe, as became a high-minded chief." Thus, though the northern Rockies were still locked in the grip of the Cold Maker, Smith and his men set out on their quest to find the beaver paradise said to exist across the mountains on the Spanish River. Rose probably gave them directions to Union Pass, and they tried to cross the mountains, as Clyman recalled, "but found the snow too deep and had to return."[13]

Rose interpreted for Thomas Fitzpatrick, but he seems to have been gone when the fur hunters returned to the Absaroka camp from their assault on the snowbound Union Pass. Somehow, an Absaroka chief told Fitzpatrick that "a pass existed in the Wind river mountains, through which he could easily take his whole band upon streams on the other side," John Robb said. Beaver were "so abundant upon these rivers that traps were unnecessary to catch them—they could club as many as they desired," the chief added.[14]

---

[12] Morgan, *Jedediah Smith*, 86; Clyman, *James Clyman, Frontiersman*, 19–20.
[13] Clyman, *James Clyman, Frontiersman*, 20–21; Irving, *Adventures of Captain Bonneville*, 215–16.
[14] Hafen, *Broken Hand*, 339.

As Clyman observed, "the whole employment" of the Absaroka men was hunting and war, and "at least one third of the warriors ware out in war parties in different directions they being in a state of warfare with all the neighbouring tribes." This complicated communications, since Rose was the only available translator. "We could not talk with them, but wanted information about the country West of there, but it seemed impossible to obtain it," Clyman recalled. He came up with an ingenious solution: "I spread out a buffalo robe and covered it with sand, and made in it heaps to represent the different mountains, (we were then encamped at the lower point of the Wind River Mountains) and from our sand map with the help of the Crow Indians, finally got the idea that we could go to Green River, called by them the Seeds-ka-day." So it was that Ashley's men learned about South Pass and how to find it from Indian sources, just as Robert Stuart had in 1812. "We undertook it in February," Clyman said.[15]

Eleven men left the safety of the Absaroka village early in 1824. Charles Camp identified Jedediah S. Smith, Thomas Fitzpatrick, William L. Sublette, James Clyman, Thomas Eddie, and two mysterious characters named Branch and Stone, perhaps Alexander K. Branch and S. Stone.[16] Based on the names of the men who were with Smith when he met Alexander Ross and Peter Skene Ogden of the Hudson's Bay Company that fall, Dale L. Morgan added three names to the "possible" list: Arthur Black, of Blacks Fork fame; Robert Nutt, who died in St. Louis in 1828; and Stephen Terry, the most mysterious of the lot.[17] Terry left no trace at all in the historical record.

Bitter cold and the Wyoming wind made the search for a passage through the mountains an arduous undertaking. Clyman's 1871 narrative provides the only detailed report on exactly how Ashley's men reached the Sweetwater River from the Absaroka winter camp. The Americans set off up the Popo Agie River, he recalled, passing "an oil springe neare the main Stream whose surface was completely covered over with oil resembling Brittish oil." Historians believe the trappers visited what became the first oil well drilled in Wyoming at the Dallas Oil Field about eight miles south of Lander, Wyoming, but this route would have taken them west of where they eventually bivouacked on the Sweetwater.[18]

---

[15] Clyman, *James Clyman, Frontiersman*, 264–65.
[16] Ibid., 30, 311n24.
[17] Morgan, *The West of William Ashley*, 93–94, 256n6, 245n169, 270n112, 294n232, 294n233.
[18] Clyman, *James Clyman, Frontiersman*, 310n21; Morgan, *The West of William Ashley*, 256n8.

That traditional interpretation may well be correct, but local topography suggests two alternatives. One would follow the Popo Agie to its headwaters, up Beaver Creek, and past the Beaver Creek Oil Field, which would lead to a divide on whose southern side lay the Seventh and Eighth Crossings of the Sweetwater near today's Sweetwater Station. A second would climb the Little Popo Agie, up Cottonwood Divide, across Beaver Creek, and on to the Sweetwater.

On his way to Oregon in 1844, at a campsite west of Rocky Ridge, Clyman noted that a short distance to the north, "a considerable branch of Popo Azie the most Southern water of the Wind River" rose from "an uneven high ridge which forms the dividing ridge" between the Yellowstone and Platte rivers. Beaver Creek is the only "considerable branch" of the Popo Agie River that fits all these particulars: Clyman could not have known of its existence in 1844 if he had not seen the creek in 1824.[19]

Petroleum was abundant along the Popo Agie but food was not. "Buffaloe being scarce our supply of food was Quite scanty," Clyman recalled, so he and his companions were both cold *and* hungry. Sublette and Clyman mounted up one morning and set out in quest of game. "We rode on utill near sundown when we came in sight of three male bufalo in a verry open and exposed place." Clyman managed to wound and finally kill a bull, but it was dark by the time he and Sublette were able to recover the animal, which "fell dead in a steep gutter." To make matters worse, "the North wind arose and grew stronger and stronger and a cold frosty snow commenced falling before [we] finished our suppers." Both men nearly died of exposure during the night, but Clyman's heroic efforts the next morning managed to get them to timber where they found an abandoned Indian lodge. Clyman built a fire and revived Sublette, who apparently suffered from an almost fatal case of hypothermia.

The entire party now moved over a low ridge, probably the Beaver Divide, and struck the Sweetwater River, where they camped on a cold and clear evening "close to the East foot of the wind River mountain." During the night a hurricane swept down "direct from the north and we had [to] Keep awake and hold on to our blankets and robes to keep them from flying away," Clyman recalled.

The blizzard got worse the next day. Branch killed a mountain sheep, and he and Clyman "packed him to camp whare efforts were made to broil small pieces but soon gave it up the wind still keeping up such a continual blast as

---

[19] Clyman, *James Clyman, Frontiersman*, Aug. 23, 1844, 97.

to prevent even a starving mountaneer from satisfying his hunger." The men took to their blankets to keep from freezing to death, but Clyman woke up during a lull in the wind and set to broiling thin slices of meat. "After a short time my comrades began to arise and we talked cooked eat the remainder of the night," he remembered. In the morning they renewed their search for game and "for more comfortable Quarters." Clyman went down the Sweetwater four or five miles "to whare the Kenyon opened out into Quite a valley and found plenty of dry aspin wood in a small grove at the Lower end of the Kenyon and likewise plenty of Mountain Sheep on the cliffs."

Based on Clyman's mileage estimates in his 1844 overland journal, the trappers camped seventy miles west of Independence Rock at the mouth of Sweetwater Canyon, upstream from what was later known as St. Marys Station.[20] The trappers hunkered down for two or three weeks and "did not leave this camp until the Mountain Sheep began to get scarce and wild."[21]

On leaving their winter refuge, the men "made a cash of Powder Lead and several other articles supposed to be not needed in our Springs hunt," Clyman recalled. On his first trip to the mountains in 1830, Warren Ferris described how mountaineers constructed a cache near the same spot: "A proper place being selected, which is usually near the border of some stream, where the bank is high enough to be in no danger of inundation, a round hole two feet in diameter is carried down to a depth of three feet, when it is gradually enlarged, and deepened until it becomes sufficiently capacious to contain whatever is destined to be stored in it." They covered the bottom and sides "with sticks to prevent the bales from touching the ground, as otherwise they would soon contract moisture, become mouldy, and rot." When everything was "snugly deposited and stowed in," the trappers sealed the cache with "valueless skins." They covered the surface with beaten earth to prevent the ground from settling or sinking. The displaced soil was "carefully gathered up and thrown into the stream, and the cache finally completed, by replacing stones and tufts of grass, so as to present the same uniform appearance." Goods stowed in such a cache in a hard clay bluff would "keep [for] years without damage"—provided the cache was truly waterproof.[22]

---

[20] See L. C. Bishop's "Aspen Grove" camp on his map of Fort Caspar, Independence Rock and South Pass, *Historical Emigrant Road Series*.

[21] Clyman, *James Clyman, Frontiersman*, 23–24, 95–96. On Aug. 21, 1844, Clyman "passed several fine groves of Aspin the first seen of any consequence," which dovetails with the "plenty of dry aspin wood" found near his 1824 campsite.

[22] Ferris, *Life in the Rocky Mountains*, 110–11.

WE HAD CROSSED THE MAIN RIDGE

Smith's men agreed to reunite at the cache or at some navigable point on the Sweetwater by the first of June. The trappers' camp became a popular spot to cache furs and trade goods, since the clay banks seemed impervious to water. Traveling west with William Sublette in 1834, William Marshall Anderson identified the spot as "Fitzpatrick's Cache."[23]

The trappers "struck in a South westerly direction this being some of the last days of February," Clyman remembered. They struggled over the wind-blasted terrain for almost a week. They sought shelter at night in clumps of sagebrush, drank melted snow, and quickly ran through their short stock of mutton—"many not having tasted food for four days & none of us from two to three"—when Clyman and Sublette shot a bison. Some of the desperate men devoured the meat in large, raw slices.

After making another camp in the sagebrush and surviving another bitterly cold night, the trappers realized the next day they "had crossed the main ridge" of the Rocky Mountains, Clyman recalled.

For days or weeks, the trappers had been without water "or only such as we got from melting snow." Now one of their first priorities was finding drinking water. About noon they reached Little Sandy Creek. The parched fur hunters "went immediatly to cutting the ice with thier Tomahauks," Clyman said. After hacking their way through an arms-length of ice, the disappointed and thirsty men concluded that the stream was frozen to the bottom. "I pulled out one of my pistols and fired in to the hole," Clyman recalled, and "up came the water plentifull for man & horse."[24] So ended the first documented east-to-west crossing of South Pass. It immediately proved worth the effort to the men, who reached the Green River not long after the Ides of March in 1824.

Some believe that one of Andrew Henry's brigades under John Weber followed Smith that spring to the Green, whose valley was filled with beaver dams.[25] The Hudson's Bay Company's Snake River expeditions had been trapping the Green River basin for years, but the Rocky Mountain Fur Company's agents hauled a fortune in beaver fur back to civilization that year. In addition, Gordon B. Dodds argued Etienne Provost discovered the true South Pass in 1824, while "Smith and Clyman crossed to the south of the pass," but Provost

---

[23] Morgan, *The West of William Ashley*, 256n9; Anderson, *Rocky Mountain Journals*, June 9, 10 and Aug. 12, 1834, 122, 180. Fitzpatrick again cached goods here in 1832 and 1833.

[24] Clyman, *James Clyman, Frontiersman*, 24–25.

[25] Utley, *A Life Wild and Perilous*, 72–73.

JEDEDIAH S. SMITH CROSSING THE MOHAVE DESERT
Like many (if not most) Rocky Mountain fur traders, Jedediah Smith was clean-shaven. When Frederic Remington painted this image of Smith and his men crossing a desert for "The Great Explorers" series, he had no reliable information about Smith's appearance. But the image, which appeared in *Collier's Illustrated Magazine* on July 14, 1906, captured the spirit of these bold mountaineers.

never worked for Ashley. How Smith's party could have missed the yawning gap of South Pass is hard to understand. As Dale Morgan observed, "There has been much idle discussion about the discovery of South Pass, as though it were twenty feet rather than twenty miles wide."[26]

Smith and six men went south along the river the American trappers called the Seeds-ke-dee to make their spring hunt, probably along Blacks Fork. Fitzpatrick and three men headed up Green River "to trap on the branches of the stream as soon as the ice gave way." Within days flocks of wild geese filled the sky, and Fitzpatrick's men "found beaver plenty and we commenced trapping," James Clyman recalled. Their spring hunt along the Green and its

---

[26] Lamar, *New Encyclopedia of the American West*, 226; Morgan, *Jedediah Smith*, 388n25.

JAMES CLYMAN
Utah artist and political cartoonist Pat Bagley used the only surviving photograph of an ancient Colonel Clyman to re-imagine the remarkable frontiersman as a young man. *Courtesy Pat Bagley.*

northern tributaries, notably Horse Creek, was remarkably successful, even though it almost ended in disaster when a band of Shoshones made off with all their horses and mules.

After completing their hunt on foot, Fitzpatrick, Clyman, Branch, and Stone managed to recapture their animals and set out to keep their promise for "all who were alive to meet at our cash on Sweet Water" in mid-June 1824. There was no sign of Smith or his companions near the cache. Clyman and Fitzpatrick went downstream about fifteen miles to see if they might be able to ship their bulging packs of beaver pelts to the Missouri by water. The Sweetwater proved to be too broad and shallow for even a bullboat to negotiate, so Fitzpatrick sent Clyman ahead to find "some navigable point" where he would wait for his comrades. Fitzpatrick returned to the camp, opened the leaky cache, and dried out its sodden contents. He was about to pack up the gunpowder when Smith arrived, his packs loaded with the furs taken during his spectacular spring hunt.[27]

Smith and his companions quickly recognized the advantages of the Platte River, the Sweetwater, and South Pass as a supply route for the Rocky Mountain fur trade. The brigade leaders decided that Fitzpatrick and his men would take the furs and news of their good fortune to St. Louis. They would arrange for supplies for next year's hunt, while Smith remained in the mountains and

---

[27] Clyman, *James Clyman, Frontiersman*, 25–26.

spent the next winter and spring collecting beaver pelts and exploring the country. Before returning west, Smith went downstream looking for Clyman but found nothing except an empty campsite and evidence that a war party had rubbed him out.[28]

The spring thaw transformed the Sweetwater from a trickle to a torrent, so the trappers built a bullboat and tried their luck as boatmen. It was an unfortunate gamble. The men hauled "the boat down stream untill it was nearly worn out and the water still falling," Clyman recalled. Both he and Robb indicate the bullboat sank in the canyon now submerged beneath Pathfinder Reservoir, where John C. Frémont met a similar disaster in 1842. But Dale Morgan concluded the venture probably came to grief in the North Platte, in the narrows right below the mouth of the Sweetwater, when the spring flood swamped the vessel. Two of the trappers' rifles and all their lead disappeared into the turbulent waters near Goat Island. With much hard work, the trappers recovered and cached their furs, and then Fitzpatrick, Branch, and Stone began their long walk to the Missouri River.[29]

Late that summer, four ragged specters staggered through the gates of Fort Atkinson at the mouth of the Platte River. The first was James Clyman, who began his solitary journey to the Missouri not knowing if he was on the Platte River or the Arkansas. He had endured hunger, mosquitoes, exposure, and the disappointed "hope of meeting some white men in this Indian world" during his almost seven-hundred-mile trek. Near the Loup Fork, Pawnees had appropriated his knife, blankets, rifle balls, and fire-making flint and steel, and would have taken his life, too, but his courage impressed one of the older warriors, who befriended and protected him. Clyman had not cut his hair in more than two years, and he let his benefactor who "wanted the hair for a memento of me" barber him with a dull butcher knife. ("I bearly saved my scalp," he recalled, "but lost my hair.") When he finally staggered over a hill and saw the American flag waving over Fort Atkinson, Clyman was so overpowered with joy that he fainted. "How long I lay unconcious I do not know," he recalled. "Certainly no man ever enjoyed the sight of our flag better than I did."[30]

The army provided the bedraggled trapper with rations, and the post sutler supplied him with shoes, a change of clothing, and a soldier's cap. To Clyman's

---
[28] Morgan, *Jedediah Smith*, 94–95.
[29] Morgan, *The West of William Ashley*, 96.
[30] Clyman, *James Clyman, Frontiersman*, 28–29.

astonishment, ten days later "Mr Fitzpatrick Mr Stone & Mr Brench arived in a more pitible state if possible than myself." Fitzpatrick sent William Ashley a letter "relating to him the discovery of the South Pass, their successes in trapping on the newly found streams, and their disasters." The letter did not survive but reported "that the new route would easily admit of the passage of wagons."

Fitzpatrick then did something characteristically remarkable. Having only recently returned from his adventures in the Rocky Mountains, Fitzpatrick left Council Bluffs after the first week of September to guide John Swizler and mules hired by Lucien Fontenelle of the Missouri Fur Company to his cache of furs on the North Platte. After an exceptionally quick trip, they brought the furs back to the Missouri about October 25, 1824.[31]

The previous summer, William Ashley had taken a drubbing in the Missouri gubernatorial election, while Andrew Henry had returned to St. Louis from his post at the mouth of the Big Horn River with too few furs to pay the partnership's enormous debts. The two men's fortunes were at low ebb, and their struggling enterprise's only hope lay with the brigades they had sent across the mountains. If John Weber and Jedediah Smith could trap enough beavers in the Green River country, it might cover their huge financial losses during the last three years and balance out the six dead trappers Henry had left on the upper Missouri. But Andrew Henry was finished with risking his life chasing an elusive fortune on the Upper Missouri, a country Indian agent Benjamin O'Fallon said was "stained with the innocent blood of the most daring and enterprising portion of our people and shut against us."

Not only had Ashley's ventures on the upper Missouri brought him to the verge of financial disaster, but the Indians had effectively bankrupted his rivals in the Missouri Fur Company. Prospects for the entire fur business looked grim. American traders now had no posts north of Forts Kiowa and Recovery—above where today's Interstate 90 crosses the Missouri River—and no security above Fort Atkinson near the mouth of the Platte. Col. Henry Leavenworth proposed that the army send an expedition up the river, not to secure the region for commerce but because "this *trapping* business should be fully and completely suppressed" to avoid conflict with the tribes.[32] In a very real way, the nation's future in the West depended on a handful of men

---

[31] Hafen, *Broken Hand*, 341; Morgan, *The West of William Ashley*, 96–97, 257nn15–17.
[32] Utley, *A Life Wild and Perilous*, 62–64.

determined to find a way to exploit the fortunes they knew were waiting for them in the Rockies.

The information Fitzpatrick and Clyman brought east from South Pass offered a ray of hope for the fate of the American fur trade in the Far West. The newspapers credited Henry with bringing the intelligence, but by early fall someone had delivered Fitzpatrick's letter alerting Ashley to the rediscovery of South Pass. The report of Smith's success countered a long string of bad news and galvanized William Ashley into action. By September he had secured a license to trade with the Snake Indians on "the Buonaventure and the Colerado of the West" from Superintendent William Clark. The audacious Ashley decided to lead a winter expedition to the Rocky Mountains, and on November 3, 1824, he headed up the Platte River from Fort Atkinson to overtake his "party of mountaineers (twenty-five in number), who had in charge fifty pack horses, a wagon and teams."[33]

Not long after Ashley disappeared into the West, the *Arkansas Gazette* printed the first known report of Fitzpatrick's news. "By the arrival of Major Henry from the Rocky Mountains, we learn that his party have discovered a passage by which loaded wagons can at this time reach the navigable waters of the Columbia River. The route lies south of the one explored by Lewis and Clark, and is inhabited by Indians friendly to us." The *Gazette* hoped that the discovery would replace "the prejudices of our Eastern Brethren" with "more enlightened views of general policy" toward the West. It hoped the news would win the "persevering and intelligent" Doctor Floyd more respect, especially for his proposal that the United States should establish a colony on the Columbia River, "a project, which a few years past was ridiculed as visionary."[34]

Congressman Floyd lost little time in pressing the West's case. By December he was extolling the easy (if non-existent) passes at the headwaters of the Yellowstone and Big Horn rivers as a transcontinental highway to the Pacific. More accurately if not precisely, Floyd described an even better pass that could be reached by "falling on to the river Platte, thence entirely up that river to its source, where the Oregon or Rocky Mountains sink into a bed of sand, without water or timber for the space of eighty miles, smooth and level."[35]

Jedediah Smith's rediscovery of South Pass and the quick integration of

---

[33] Morgan, *The West of William Ashley*, 83, 87, 97, 100.
[34] *Arkansas Gazette*, Nov. 16, 1824, 115, in Morgan, *The West of William Ashley*, 97–98. *Niles' Weekly Register* credited the *Missouri Herald* in a similar announcement in "The West," Dec. 4, 1824, 224.
[35] Marshall, *Acquisition of Oregon*, 69–70.

that knowledge into a revitalized American fur trade linked the pass to "the lines of force along which the American people were sweeping to the Pacific," wrote Dale Morgan. "To this wide depression along the continent's spine, missionaries followed the mountain men, settlers and gold seekers coming in their turn, thousands on thousands pursuing a vision or driven by need. Much was to come of Jedediah Smith's discovery of a way west." And as John S. Robb observed in 1847, Ashley's men were "marshalling the way for that tide of emigration which now is treading towards a new land once thought unapproachable from this side of the Rocky Mountains."[36]

---

[36] Morgan, *Jedediah Smith*, 92; Hafen, *Broken Hand*, 340.

CHAPTER 3

"Two Fortunes Apiece"
The Rocky Mountain Fur Trade

THE HEYDAY OF THE ROCKY MOUNTAIN FUR TRADE, ONE OF the most romantic of all American eras, lasted only from 1825 to 1840 but had a dramatic impact on the nation's expansion into a continental nation. The number of men employed in the trade at best totaled no more than a few thousand. When the enterprise's glory days ended only a decade and a half after they began, the characters who proudly called themselves mountaineers and freemen had explored the American West from the Missouri River to the Pacific Coast, from the Upper Missouri and the Columbia Basin to the Rio Grande and the Gila River.[1] They had blazed wagon roads up the Platte River and across the southern plains and had crossed the continent to California using a web of trails through New Mexico and the Great Basin.

"No doubt there will be two fortunes apiece for us," Warren Ferris wrote as he recalled the hopes he shared with his companions upon joining an expedition to the Rocky Mountains in 1830. Ferris claimed it was not the money but "the strong desire of seeing strange lands, of beholding nature in the savage grandeur of her primeval state" that persuaded his active, vigorous, resolute, daring, independent, and high-minded colleagues "to adventure with the American Fur Company in a trip to the mountain wilds of the great west."[2]

By 1830 Jedediah Smith, David Jackson, and William Sublette could report that the 180 men in their employ had "traversed every part of the country

---

[1] Hiram Chittenden estimated the Rocky Mountain fur trade employed fewer than a thousand men, while the yearly "average was nearer half that." *The American Fur Trade*, 1013. Robert Utley guessed the number of fur hunters in the Rockies in the 1820s and 1830s was a "thousand or so," with three-fourths of them claiming "French, French Canadian, or Creole blood." *A Life Wild and Perilous*, 87.

[2] Ferris, *Life in the Rocky Mountains*, 81.

west of the Rocky mountains, from the peninsula of California to the mouth of the Columbia river."[3] The mountaineers who survived these years became skilled frontiersmen who served as guides to the missionaries, emigrants, explorers, and soldiers who followed them across the Far West.

The men primarily responsible for creating the supply system that made this golden age possible—William Ashley, Jedediah Smith, and Thomas Fitzpatrick—did so with considerable risk and hardship. In early November 1824 Ashley overtook his "party of mountaineers (twenty-five in number)" who were heading up the Platte River with fifty packhorses, a wagon, and teams. (No record mentions how far west that wagon traveled or what happened to it.) Ashley's winter venture included both Fitzpatrick and Clyman, in addition to the equally talented Zacharias Ham and James Beckwourth, one of the most colorful characters in the annals of the West. Ashley hoped to secure provisions from the Grand Pawnee on Loup Fork, but their villages "were entirely deserted, the Indians having, according to their annual custom, departed some two or three weeks previous for their wintering ground." Instead of finding food and shelter, Ashley's men spent two weeks living on horsemeat while enduring the "intense cold and violence of the winds, blowing the snow in every direction," advancing only about a dozen miles. The winter was, Beckwourth recalled, "no fun."[4]

Back on the Platte, the expedition found feed for their starving horses and game in abundance. A hundred miles upriver at Plumb Point, near today's Lexington, Nebraska, they caught up with the Grand Pawnees, bound for their winter camps on the Arkansas. Their principal men encouraged the trappers to spend the winter at the confluence of the north and south forks of the Platte, the only spot between Plumb Point and the mountains with game and firewood. If he pressed on, they warned Ashley, he would endanger the lives of his entire party. The trappers moved out and soon fell in with the Skidi (or Loup) Pawnees and followed them to their winter quarters at the confluence, but despite the extreme cold and the intense suffering of both his men and animals, Ashley decided to press on. He persuaded the Pawnees to sell him twenty-three horses "and other necessary things"—buffalo robes and meat—and on Christmas Eve he set out up the South Platte.[5]

---

[3] Jackson, "The State of the Fur Trade," Sen. Doc. 39 (21:2), Serial 203, 21.
[4] Morgan, *Jedediah Smith*, 157; Morgan, *The West of William Ashley*, 101, 261.
[5] Morgan, *The West of William Ashley*, 101, 261.

One of the ironies of the rediscovery of South Pass is that the nature of the trail up the North Platte meant that the man who had bankrolled the exploration and his trappers were not able to take immediate advantage of their new route. The first of the three essential elements of early overland travel—wood, water, and grass—was sorely lacking all the way to the Laramie River, some two hundred miles up the virtually treeless North Platte. Parties traveling in summer could cook with buffalo chips, but soggy bison dung was entirely inadequate to fuel a trek in the heart of winter. "The south fork of the river being represented as affording more wood than the north," Ashley reported, "I commenced ascending that stream." At first the weather was merciful and the valleys filled with buffalo: all the portents "seemed to promise a safe and speedy movement to the first grove of timber on my route, supposed to be about ten days' march."

On the day after Christmas, it began to snow. Three days later, four of Ashley's horses were too weak to stand and had to be left behind. His men soldiered on over the paths that buffalo had trampled through the snow, without which the trappers "could not possibly have proceeded." On New Year's Day 1825, they found refuge on an island that provided firewood and sweet bark for their mounts. They huddled down "until the cottonwood fit for horse food was nearly consumed, by which time our horses were so refreshed as to justify another move forward."

The bitterly cold weather made the expedition's progress up the South Platte "slow and very labourious" until January 20, when at the mouth of Bijou Creek they "reached another small island clothed with a body of that wood sufficient for two days subsistence." Here they "had a clear and distant view of the Rocky mountains bearing west, about sixty miles distant." The pack train advanced slowly, reaching the foothills in early February. Ashley's men left the South Platte and followed an Indian trail up either Big Thompson Creek or, more probably, the Cache la Poudre before crossing the Front Range, even though "the mountains seemed to bid defiance to my further progress." The "exceedingly difficult and dangerous" undertaking took three days.

Heading northwest on the line of today's Highway 287, the trappers reached the Laramie Plains, where "the country presented a different aspect," its broad valleys "filled with numerous herds of buffaloe, deer, and antelope." After crossing the gap between the northern Medicine Bow Mountains and Elk Mountain, the party struck the upper North Platte River. Ashley's men headed west through southern Wyoming using the corridor later followed by the northern branch of the Cherokee Trail, the overland stage, the transcontinental railroad, and Interstate 80.[6]

As March ended, the trappers "were employed in crossing the ridge which divides the waters of the Atlantic from those of the Pacific ocean," Ashley wrote. He had entered the Great Divide Basin over Sage Creek Pass, just north of Bridger Pass and east of today's Rawlins, Wyoming. On the first of April, the Wind River Range appeared to the northwest, but even Clyman and Fitzpatrick were not sure where they were. The Absarokas, however, knew exactly where to find the Americans and expertly ran off seventeen of Ashley's best horses, leaving behind a Shoshone arrowhead to divert suspicion. The men sent after them followed the warriors to the Sweetwater. They failed to recover a single animal, but at last, as Dale Morgan observed, the whole geography of South Pass and the central Rockies fell into place.

The expedition turned north toward Wind River, followed Jack Morrow Creek almost to its confluence with Pacific Creek, and camped on the Dry Sandy, intersecting Jedediah Smith's trail of the previous year west of South Pass. On April 19, 1825, Ashley's men at last reached Green River, the legendary Spanish River and renowned Seeds-ke-dee, also spelled Shetskedee, Shetkedee, Shetkadee, and Shetskadee.[7]

Ashley divided his company into four hunting brigades and selected "one of the most intelligent and efficient of each party to act as partizans." He sent Clyman and six men north to the headwaters of the Green; Ham and seven men to the west; and Fitzpatrick with six men to the south, directing them to try to contact the brigades under Jedediah Smith and John Weber who had spent the winter "beyond the range of mountains appearing westwardly." Ashley would descend the river forty or fifty miles and there "make such marks as would designate it as a place of general rendezvous for the men in my service in that country," where they should all assemble by the tenth of July. The general and seven men loaded his merchandise aboard a newly made sixteen-foot bullboat and set out on adventures that included descending the turbulent Green River and exploring the Uinta Basin.[8]

Ashley made his way down the Green and picked the mouth of "Randavouze creek," today's Henrys Fork, as the site for his planned summer

---
[6] Ibid., 102–103, 262–63.
[7] Morgan, *Jedediah Smith*, 161; Morgan, *The West of William Ashley*, 106–107, 266–67.
[8] Ashley to Atkinson, Dec. 1, 1825, in Dale, *The Ashley-Smith Explorations*, 138–39.

gathering. On returning to the fork in June, he picked a better site twenty miles upstream at the confluence of Burnt and Henrys forks to hold the first annual trading fair in the central Rockies. By July 1, all of Ashley's brigades had assembled at the site, including the parties who wintered in the mountains under Weber and Smith.

Etienne Provost's expedition from Taos, plus twenty-nine trappers who had "recently withdrawn from the Hudson Bay company," joined them. The deserters, mostly Iroquois veterans of the fur trade, brought with them most of the furs taken during Peter Skene Ogden's Snake Country spring hunt. Altogether, some 120 men, many with their Native wives and children, assembled in two camps, trading their beaver skins for Ashley's supply of sugar, coffee, tobacco, powder, lead, fishhooks, flints, scissors, knives, cloth, blankets, and buttons. With this event, Robert Utley observed, William Ashley "almost incidentally set the foundation for the most dazzling institution of the fur trade": the rendezvous.[9]

FROLIC: THE RENDEZVOUS

Ashley's innovation revolutionized the Rocky Mountain fur trade. It also revived American expansion into the West, which had threatened to wither or even die with the demise of commercial operations on the upper Missouri. Before 1825 the fur trade had operated on a classic business model that was centuries old: companies built and supplied trading posts along navigable rivers in Indian country using canoes or flatboats. Indians brought furs to the posts, which were shipped downriver to depots at places such as New York, St. Louis, Mackinac Island, Montreal, York Factory on Hudson's Bay, Astoria, and Fort Vancouver.

The old ways did not work in the central and southern Rocky Mountains, which could not be reached by rivers like the Platte and Arkansas, choked by sandbars or rapids. It was hard work to get the region's Indians to trap small fur-bearing animals: they preferred to hunt big game. "The Indians in the Snake Country are inclined to be indolent in working beaver or other furs," chief trader Richard Grant wrote shortly after taking command at Fort Hall in 1842. "The Indians find it to their advantage, to hunt large Animals, which supply them and their families more food," Grant later observed.[10]

---

[9] Gowans, *Rocky Mountain Rendezvous*, 15–19; Utley, *A Life Wild and Perilous*, 79.
[10] Grant to Simpson, March 15, 1844, D.5/1, 425–28; and Feb. 22, 1850, D.5/27, 335, HBC Archives.

Donald MacKenzie, a former partner in Astor's Pacific Fur Company, had shown what the North West Company could do in the Snake country with independent trapping brigades. Smith and Ashley adopted and adapted MacKenzie's model with a new twist: unlike all previous fur companies, their roaming annual trade fair replaced the traditional fixed posts.

For the next fifteen years, the roving supply store, swap-meet, liars' festival, and blowout known as rendezvous provided a marketplace for free trappers to sell their furs and buy supplies. Bands of Shoshone, Bannock, Ute, Crow, Nez Perce, Salish, Iroquois, and Cayuse Indians came to exchange handicrafts, meat, buffalo robes, buckskin, and furs with the several trading companies that came to exploit the opportunity. Frontier venture capitalists organized supply caravans that initially used pack animals to haul their trade goods to market. After 1830 they employed wagons and carts whose wheels cut the first tracks in what became the Oregon, Mormon, and California trails. Their destination shifted among a half-dozen sites in today's Utah, Wyoming, and Idaho, and played a critical role in the development of roads over South Pass.

The arrangement freed trappers from hauling their catch to market and let them stay in the mountains fulltime, but it forced them to sell their furs at a low price and buy their supplies at an incredible markup. The fairs were the scene of wild carousing and involved pageantry, gambling, drunkenness, "barbarous music," duels, and even a pitched battle with the Gros Ventres at Pierres Hole. They provided the setting for the first cannon salute and the first Protestant sermon and Catholic Mass celebrated in the Rocky Mountains. They were, as Hiram Chittenden wrote, "one of the most picturesque features of early frontier life in the Far West." Rendezvous was, as Fred Gowans observed, a monumental event.[11]

At the first rendezvous, Ashley's goods vanished in a single day, but he apparently took orders from the trappers who wanted to stay in the mountains. The general left the fair on July 2, 1825, with about fifty men, his packhorses burdened with fifty-pound packs of beaver pelts. The party crossed South Pass about the middle of July, probably digging up the forty-five packs of beaver that Jedediah Smith had cached on the Sweetwater in 1824. They turned north to the head of navigation on the Missouri River near today's Thermopolis, Wyoming, where the Wind River emerges from the mountains and becomes the Bighorn. Ashley fell in with an army treaty-making

---
[11] Gowans, *Rocky Mountain Rendezvous*, 11.

expedition at the mouth of the Yellowstone in mid-August and loaded his furs on three government flatboats. By early October, he was back in St. Louis with furs worth almost fifty thousand dollars.[12]

General Ashley married Miss Eliza Christy shortly after returning to St. Louis, but his newly won fortune may not have been enough to both pay off his debts and provide for his new bride in the style he wanted. He needed a new partner to help run his radically reinvented enterprise. Ashley picked Jedediah Smith, the most talented of his extraordinary employees. Smith was, said Robert Campbell in a classic understatement, "a very efficient man." In late October, Jedediah Smith left for the mountains with sixty or seventy men (including fur-trade stalwarts Hiram Scott, Moses "Black" Harris, Louis Vasquez, and James Beckwourth), 160 mules and horses, and trade goods worth some twenty thousand dollars.

Despite his hard experience the previous year, Ashley had not learned the futility of sending a trade caravan across the Great Plains in the dead of winter. The weather trapped Smith and his men, who "wintered all along the Republican Fork, and suffered very much for want of provisions," Robert Campbell recalled. "One third of our mules died that winter, and we sent back for more mules to St. Louis."[13]

Harris and Beckwourth carried the word back, and next spring Ashley set out from St. Louis with a reinforcement of twenty-six men and horses purchased around Franklin, Missouri, then the outfitting place for the Santa Fe Trail. On April 1, 1826, Ashley's caravan found Smith's camp on Platte River at the head of Grand Island. Most of Smith's men had deserted. They were, Robert Campbell said, "sick of the trip, having suffered like the rest, almost to the verge of starvation." Ashley sent Smith and Harris to carry an express to the mountains and arrange for a rendezvous at Cache Valley in today's Utah, while the main company followed them to the forks of the Platte. Little is known about Ashley's expedition, but Beckwourth provided a few details about the caravan's route over the Rockies. "On arriving at the forks of the Platte, we held a council, and resolved to follow up its north branch to its source, thence over to Green River," he recalled. General Ashley had apparently learned to appreciate the natural road up the Sweetwater and over South Pass.[14]

---

[12] Morgan, *The West of William Ashley*, 148; Gowans, *Rocky Mountain Rendezvous*, 18–23.
[13] Morgan, *Jedediah Smith*, 175–76; Morgan, *The West of William Ashley*, 142.
[14] Beckwourth, *Life and Adventures*, 21, 60; Morgan, *The West of William Ashley*, 142–45, sorts out Beckwourth's confusing chronology.

Ashley's men marched to Hams Fork, Robert Campbell remembered, "meeting with few adventures." Sixty or seventy trappers came out to meet them before the party continued on to Cache Valley, probably establishing the rendezvous camp at the mouth of Blacksmith Fork near today's Hyrum, Utah.[15] The well-watered vale had been the "chief place of rendezvous and wintering ground" of a number of mountaineers who called it Willow Valley. It was "surrounded by stupendous mountains which are unrivalled for beauty and serenity of scenery," Daniel T. Potts reported after the gathering. "You here have a view of all the varieties, plenty of ripe fruit, an abundance of grass just springing up, and buds beginning to shoot, while the higher parts of the mountains are covered with snow, all within 12 or 15 miles of this valley."[16]

The arrival of "a vast amount of luxuries from the East" ignited a general celebration of "mirth, songs, dancing, shouting, running, jumping, singing, racing, target-shooting, yarns, frolic, with all sorts of extravagances that white men or Indians could invent were freely indulged in," recalled James Beckwourth. "The unpacking of the *medicine water* contributed not a little to the heightening of our festivities."[17] The trappers "brought in plenty of Beavers," Robert Campbell remembered, enough for Ashley to return to St. Louis with 123 packs of fur estimated to be worth sixty thousand dollars. Campbell recalled the blow-out lasted at least "a couple of weeks, long enough to complete the traffic with the trappers." The trade fair probably began in June, as Jedediah Smith reported. Daniel Potts wrote, "We celebrated the 4th of July, by firing three rounds of small arms, and partook of a most excellent dinner, after which a number of political toasts were drank."[18]

"Mountaineers and friends! When I first came to the mountains, I came as a poor man," William Ashley said, at least "as nearly as I can recollect," quoted Beckwourth decades later. "You, by your indefatigable exertions, toils, and privations, have procured me an independent fortune." Ashley's spectacular success freed him from ever again needing to risk his life in an enterprise as dangerous as the fur trade. "I now wash my hands of the toils of the Rocky Mountains," he said.[19]

Ashley dissolved his partnership with Jedediah Smith. Somewhere on

---

[15] Gowans, *Rocky Mountain Rendezvous*, 27–29. The rendezvous site may have been much farther north, Gowans suggested, along the Utah-Idaho border on Cub Creek, near today's Cove, Utah.
[16] Morgan, *The West of William Ashley*, 148–49.
[17] Beckwourth, *The Life and Adventures*, 70–71.
[18] Morgan, *The West of William Ashley*, 148–52, 152–53, 305n323; Gowans, *Rocky Mountain Rendezvous*, 30.
[19] Beckwourth, *The Life and Adventures*, 73.

"TWO FORTUNES APIECE"

Bear River on July 18, 1826, Smith, David Jackson, and William Sublette organized a company to buy out Ashley and take over the contracts for the forty-two men employed by Ashley and Smith. Ashley agreed to become their supplier and dispatch another caravan of trade goods in spring 1827, while the partners promised to confirm their order by the first of March. After making these arrangements, Smith set out on his first South West Expedition, which made the first overland crossing to California from the United States, while Jackson and Sublette led their brigades north to the Columbia River drainage and Yellowstone country.[20]

Through a Level and Open Country: The News

"The recent expedition of General Ashley to the country west of the Rocky Mountains has been productive of information on subjects of no small interest to the people of the Union," trumpeted the *Missouri Herald* on Ashley's return to St. Louis in September. "It has proved that overland expeditions in large bodies may be made to that remote region without the necessity of transporting provisions for man or beasts."

The newspaper gave a resounding affirmation of the most important information Ashley had learned in all his years in the West—the existence of South Pass. "The whole route lay through a level and open country, better for carriages than any turnpike road in the United States. Wagons and carriages could go with ease as far as Gen. Ashley went, crossing the Rocky Mountains at the sources of the north fork of the Platte." The long, gradual climb to the Continental Divide was two degrees less than the steepest ascent on the road to Cumberland Gap, the trail that tens of thousands of Americans had followed on their way to Kentucky and points west.[21]

Upon returning home, William Ashley arranged with B. Pratte & Co., better known as the French Fur Company, to provide about twelve thousand dollars' worth of trade goods for the outfit he had promised to send to Smith, Jackson, and Sublette in 1827. John Jacob Astor's American Fur Company absorbed Pratte's firm in December 1826 as the western department of Astor's expanding monopoly. Bill Sublette and Black Harris left the Salt Lake Valley on New Year's Day to confirm that their order with Ashley would be sent.

---

[20] Morgan, *The West of William Ashley*, 150, 161.
[21] *Missouri Herald and St. Louis Advertiser*, Nov. 8, 1826, in Morgan, *The West of William Ashley*, 153–54, which confirms that the 1826 caravan crossed South Pass.

After a spectacularly arduous trek over South Pass and down the Sweetwater and Platte rivers, they reached St. Louis in early March 1827. At the end of the month Sublette and Hiram Scott left with a supply train bound for that summer's rendezvous at Bear Lake, which opened with a stirring battle in which the mountaineers and their Shoshone and Ute allies drove off a party of Gros Ventres raiders.[22]

General Ashley "mounted a heavy 4 pounder on a carriage & sent it with his expedition westward. It was drawn by two stout horses to the vicinity of the great salt lake, & back to Lexington," Ashley wrote.[23] "I fitted out a party of sixty men, mounted a piece of artillery (a four-pounder) on a carriage which was drawn by two mules," Ashley recalled later. "The party marched to or near the Grand Salt Lake, beyond the Rocky Mountains, remaining there one month, stopped on the way back fifteen days, and returned to Lexington, in the western part of Missouri, in September." Ashley's 1828 outfit, worth $22,447.14, was ready and waiting at Lexington, and the caravan returned to the mountains using the same livestock. Ashley believed it arrived safely by the end of November, but it appears the supplies did not reach the mountains until the next spring.[24]

Ashley's cannon gained immortality as the first wheeled vehicle to cross South Pass. It greeted Jedediah Smith when he reached the rendezvous at Bear Lake on his return from California in 1827. Equally significant was the rival trading expedition that headed up the Platte that year, demonstrating that knowledge of the South Pass route was spreading. After experiencing the "full share of the accidents and miscarriages" that were part and parcel of the perilous business of the Indian trade, Joshua Pilcher of the Missouri Fur Company "determined in 1827 on more extensive operations," he reported late in 1830. Along with veteran mountaineers Lucien Fontenelle, William H. Vanderburgh, and Andrew Drips, Pilcher left Council Bluffs in September "with a party of men, forty-five in the whole, and an outfit of merchandise suited to the object"—the object being to get as rich as William Ashley.

"My route lay up the river Platte to its forks, and thence up its north branch to its source in the Rocky Mountains," Pilcher wrote. Absaroka raiders made off with most of the expedition's 104 "indispensable" horses, so the party was

---

[22] Ibid., 163–66; and Gowans, *Rocky Mountain Rendezvous*, 33–35.
[23] Ashley Memoranda, Feb. 20, 1828, in Morgan, *The West of William Ashley*, 178.
[24] Ashley to Macomb, March 1829, in Jackson, "The State of the Fur Trade," Sen. Doc. 39 (21:2), Serial 203, 7.

forced to cache its merchandise east of South Pass and "make the transit of the mountains" with only a few pack animals. The venture was a disaster, but Pilcher left behind one of the best early descriptions of South Pass: "The snow was deep, but the ascent and descent easy, being a depression of the mountains to such a degree that a carriage could cross without the least difficulty. The depression was not only low, but wide, something like a valley through the mountains, say thirty or forty miles wide, the river Colorado taking its rise on the opposite side."[25]

"The pass over the mountains, which I have found to be quite Smooth & easy is immediately on the direct route, & it is, I presume, the only place where the mountains can be crossed with great Ease and facility," William Ashley told Congressman Edward Bates in February 1828. Despite the spreading awareness of the existence of South Pass and its significance as the gateway to the vast lands that lay beyond, even the most zealous promoters of the West thought the Oregon Country was excessively remote.

The challenges associated with founding settlements in the Rocky Mountains appeared overwhelming. "I see no object which would induce any civilized man to locate himself in that Region, except those in pursuit of furs," Ashley advised. There was much rich land around and about the Great Salt Lake, he noted, but the region was "so divided by rough mountains that no Settlement could be made upon them sufficiently dense & Extensive to defend them against the depredations of the numerous tribes of Indians that inhabit that Country," a problem that Ashley described as "insurmountable."[26]

Only a month after the rediscovery of South Pass, T. S. Jesup, quartermaster general of the U.S. Army, independently concluded in April 1824 that "the enterprise of more than one of our citizens" had proven that an overland route from Council Bluffs to Oregon was practicable. Jesup thought a line of posts up the Missouri River (not the Platte) "extending from Council Bluffs entirely across the continent" was essential to American security. "It, no doubt, presents difficulties," he wrote, "but difficulties are not impossibilities."[27] As Joshua Pilcher observed after visiting Oregon, "The man must know but little of the American people who supposes they can be stopped by any thing in the shape of mountains, deserts, seas, or rivers."[28]

---

[25] Pilcher to Eaton, ibid., 7–8.
[26] Ashley to Bates, Feb. 20, 1828, in Morgan, *The West of William Ashley*, 179.
[27] Marshall, *Acquisition of Oregon*, 158.
[28] Pilcher to Eaton, circa Dec. 1830, in Jackson, "State of the Fur Trade," 7.

The Unusual Sight of a Train: First Wagons across South Pass

On April 10, 1830, William L. Sublette left St. Louis with ten mule-drawn wagons and two Dearborn buggies, bound for the annual rendezvous on the Wind River. "Our route from St. Louis was nearly due west to the western limits of the State, and thence along the Santa Fe trail about forty miles," his associates informed Secretary of War John H. Eaton that fall. The caravan turned northwest and headed "across the waters of the Kanzas, and up the Great Platte river, to the Rocky mountains, and to the head of the Wind river, where it issued from the mountains."

The train reached the great trading fair, just short of the Continental Divide, on July 16. That was as far as the partners "wished the wagons to go," since the trappers themselves brought the furs to "the great rendezvous of the persons engaged in that business. Here the wagons could easily have crossed the Rocky Mountains, it being what is called the *Southern Pass*, had it been desirable for them to do so," they reported. "This is the first time that wagons ever went to the Rocky mountains; and the ease and safety with which it was done prove the facility of communicating over land with the Pacific ocean. The route from the *Southern Pass*, where the wagons stopped, to the Great Falls of the Columbia, being easier and better than on this side of the mountains, with grass enough, for the horses and mules; but a scarcity of game for the support of the men."[29]

After the caravan returned to St. Louis in October, the *St. Louis Beacon* agreed: "The wagons did not cross the mountains;" Charles Keemle wrote, "but there was nothing to prevent their crossing," except, of course, the fact that there was no wagon road. Keemle saluted the partners' accomplishment—they were "the first ever that took wagons to the Rocky Mountains"—but discounted the difficulty of the feat, since the road was bad enough that they left the Dearborns behind in the mountains. They did, however, get all ten of the wagons back to Missouri, which handed promoters of the West a new argument. As Keemle wrote, this showed "the folly and the nonsense of those '*scientific*' characters who talk of the Rocky Mountains as the barrier which is to stop the westward march of the American people."[30]

Smith, Jackson, and Sublette sold their partnership to the Rocky Mountain

---

[29] Morgan, *Jedediah Smith*, 21–22. A Dearborn was a four-wheeled carriage.
[30] Ibid., 321–23.

B. L. E. BONNEVILLE
Benjamin Bonneville as a Civil War general, thirty years after taking the first wagons across South Pass. *Courtesy Library of Congress Prints and Photographs Division, LC-B814-1968.*

Fur Company—Thomas Fitzpatrick, Milton Sublette, Henry Fraeb, Jean Baptiste Gervais, and Jim Bridger—and no one tried to repeat their wagon experiment the next year. (William Sublette may have learned a hard lesson: he returned to using pack animals instead of wheels.) It took a novice to take wagons back to the mountains and, while he was an experienced frontier military officer, Capt. Benjamin L. E. Bonneville knew practically nothing about the fur business when he set out for South Pass with twenty wagons in 1832. An air of mystery still surrounds the captain's motives in taking leave from the army to go west. Some suspect he was actually on an intelligence mission, but the evidence indicates he simply hoped to beat his rivals—Astor's American Fur Company and the trappers doing business as the Rocky Mountain Fur Company—and get rich.

Historian, diplomat, and bestselling author Washington Irving recast Bonneville's journal as the adventures of Captain Bonneville, but his chronicle provides details of the passage of the first wagons over South Pass that would otherwise be lost. Bonneville believed wagons could more efficiently haul supplies to the free trappers of the Rocky Mountains than pack trains, since the vehicles "would save the great delay caused every morning by packing the horses, and the labor of unpacking in the evening." In theory, wagons required fewer horses and reduced the risk of their wandering away "or being frightened or carried off by the Indians." Plus, they could be easily defended by forming "a kind of fortification in case of attack in the open prairies." Bonneville apparently used oxen or teams of four mules or horses to draw the wagons, which were divided into two columns protected by outriders. The captain selected two outstanding lieutenants, Santa Fe Trail veteran Michel Cerre and frontier sheriff, trader, and Indian fighter Joseph R. Walker.

Bonneville left the frontier with high hopes. Even Washington Irving found it was "not easy to do justice to the exulting feelings of the worthy captain at finding himself at the head of a stout band of hunters, trappers, and woodmen; fairly launched on the broad prairies, with his face to the boundless West."

Bonneville introduced a major technological change. His theory was splendid, but the reality of blazing a wagon road up the Platte proved challenging. Even before reaching the Kansas River, the wagon wheels "sank deep in the mire" of the spring-soaked prairie. The "unusual sight of a train of wagons caused quite a sensation" among Kaw people at their agency on the Kansas River. They "thronged about the caravan, examining everything minutely, and asking a thousand questions: exhibiting a degree of excitability, and a lively curiosity." Irving described how the long train of wagons and oxen astonished a band of Absaroka warriors. (The sight of a cow and calf intrigued them even more.) "Wagons had never been seen by them before," Irving wrote, "and they examined them with the greatest minuteness." Getting the wagons to where the war party could see them was no easy task. "The chief difficulty occurs in passing the deep ravines cut through the prairies by streams and winter torrents," Irving wrote. "Here it is often necessary to dig a road down the banks, and to make bridges for the wagons."

Captain Bonneville knew nothing about the Platte's North Fork, but he could see "its direction was in the true course, and up this stream he determined to prosecute his route to the Rocky Mountains." To cross the South Fork, the teamsters removed their wagon boxes, covered them with buffalo hides, and smeared the boxes with a compound made of tallow, "thus forming rude boats," which ferried the fast-flowing river safely.

Beyond the hundredth meridian and on the "great steppes of the Far West," too little rather than too much moisture became a problem for the wagons. "The wood-work shrunk," and so did the hubs, so "the wheels were continually working out, and it was necessary to support the spokes by stout props to prevent their falling asunder." Aridity, Irving concluded, made the country unfit for cultivation. Bonneville went all the way to the mountains, "but with much difficulty," wrote John Ball, who passed the wagons on the Blue River while traveling with Bill Sublette's pack train. The packers stopped briefly to salute (or mock) Bonneville's caravan and then left it behind in the dust, "traveling with double the speed."[31]

The wagons forded the Sweetwater River for the last time on July 24, 1832, probably at the spot where the Lander Cutoff later left the main trail. After a march of seven hours, the fur hunters climbed over a low ridge and came to "a small clear stream, running to the south, in which they caught a number of fine trout." The trout alerted them to the fact that they had crossed the Continental Divide, "for it is only on the western streams of the Rocky Mountains that trout are to be taken." Captain Bonneville realized he had, as Irving put it, "fairly passed the crest of the Rocky Mountains; and felt some degree of exultation in being the first individual that had crossed, north of the settled provinces of Mexico, from the waters of the Atlantic to those of the Pacific, with wagons." The summary that Washington Irving made of Bonneville's now-vanished diary indicates the "small clear stream" they found west of the divide was Little Sandy Creek.

After making this historic crossing, Bonneville's enterprise did not prosper. His wagons made a hard trek across the barrens between the Big Sandy and Green River. On the march, the American Fur Company's pack train under Lucien Fontenelle overtook Bonneville's party, and he learned they were on their way to rendezvous at Pierres Hole. The wagons did not reach water until noon, and "the sufferings of both men and horses had been excessive, and it was with almost frantic eagerness that they hurried to allay their burning thirst in the limpid current of the river." Fontenelle lured away many of Bonneville's men, and the captain's livestock were in no condition to do anything harder than grazing: "the weary journey up the mountains had worn them down in flesh and spirit; but this last march across the thirsty plain had nearly finished them." To make matters worse, the Blackfeet and Gros Ventres were raising hell all over, and the captain had little choice but to fortify his camp.

"Fort Bonneville," as it was politely known, stood on rising ground, about three hundred yards from the Green River and two miles from Horse Creek,

---

[31] Irving, *Adventures of Captain Bonneville*, 8, 9, 11, 17, 22, 24; Ball, *Autobiography*, 66.

"commanding a view of the plains for several miles up and down that stream," Warren Ferris reported. The spot was too cold and exposed to be a practical winter quarters, and it was abandoned not long after it was built. "This establishment was doubtless intended for a permanent trading post," Ferris observed. "From the circumstance of a great deal of labor having been expended in its construction, and the works shortly after their completion deserted, it is frequently called 'Fort Nonsense.'" The location, about a mile south of today's Daniel, Wyoming, was not entirely without its attractions, for six of the last eight rendezvous were held nearby.

Benjamin Bonneville would strive mightily to make his investment in the fur trade a success, and he directed such far-seeing operations as sending Joseph R. Walker to California in search of beaver (or, some said, easily stolen horses). He eventually had to give up in 1835, having overstayed his leave. Bonneville's greatest accomplishment was bringing the first wagons across South Pass, but he managed to recoup some of his losses by selling the manuscript account of his experiences to Washington Irving for a thousand dollars. His trek had not been easy, but the adventures of Captain Bonneville began a new era in the opening of the West.[32]

Business Is Closed:
The Demise of the Rocky Mountain Fur Trade

The British Hudson's Bay Company, the most powerful economic force in western North America, had long been aware of the danger American enterprise posed to its business. The corporation might well have abandoned the money-losing operations in the Oregon Country that it inherited with its acquisition of the North West Company but for a desire to keep the United States from taking such an economic prize without competition. Instead, under George Simpson, the monopoly's new director, the company sent in new management and founded an impressive and efficient headquarters at Fort Vancouver on the lower Columbia. Here Simpson set in motion a policy aimed at stopping the American threat in its tracks. The corporation had the resources to do it: by 1835, the HBC had a steamboat, the *Beaver*, operating on the Columbia River.

---

[32] Irving, *Adventures of Captain Bonneville*, 31–36.

NATHANIEL J. WYETH
A successful and determined Massachusetts businessman, Wyeth fell in love with the idea of Oregon and hoped to make a second fortune from trading in furs and salmon. He failed, but his two overland expeditions helped transform the Far West. *Harper's Magazine* (November 1892), 836.

Not long after he broke a bottle of rum over its flagpole in March 1825 and christened the new fort, Simpson gave his famous order to trap out the beaver and create what historians have called a fur desert to keep the Americans at bay. "The more we impoverish the country," Simpson wrote, "the less likelihood is there of being assailed by the opposition." The HBC—wags in the West said the acronym stood for "Here Before Christ"—implemented the policy with ruthless efficiency, ignoring their ability to sustain a productive fur trade. Their American competitors assisted the effort by trapping whenever it was cold.[33]

Outside of the HBC's headquarters in London and beyond the halls of Congress, the news that the Rocky Mountains posed no serious obstacle to taking a wagon from the Missouri to Oregon produced no identifiable reaction. The knowledge did attract the attention of promoters like New England schoolteacher Hall Jackson Kelley, who in 1831 founded the American Society for Encouraging the Settlement of the Oregon Territory. Kelley's knowledge of the Pacific Coast was entirely theoretical, but his writings "operated like a match applied to the combustible matter in the mind of Nathaniel J. Wyeth."

An ingenious New Englander who had made a fortune shipping pond ice to the Caribbean, Wyeth now dreamed of building a trading empire in the Far

---

[33] Utley, *A Life Wild and Perilous*, 74; Newman, *Caesars of the Wilderness*, 276–79, 291–92; and Morgan, *Jedediah Smith*, 131–32.

West. He recruited twenty-one men to join his band of Oregon adventurers, bought a stock of trade goods "calculated for the Indian market," dispatched a supply ship to meet him on the Columbia River. Wyeth designed and built three amphibious wagons that "we may call by that name a *unique* contrivance, half boat, and half carriage," his skeptical cousin John B. Wyeth wrote. They were thirteen feet long and four feet wide, "of a shape partly of a canoe, and partly of a gondola," and "anatomically constructed like some equivocal animals, allowing it to crawl upon the land, or to swim on the water." The wagons made it only to St. Louis, where Wyeth sold them for less than half their original cost.[34]

Wyeth and his men wound up traveling to the 1832 rendezvous with William Sublette's pack train. Sublette and Bonneville had shown it was possible to take wagons over South Pass, but that did not mean it was practical, especially in a business as ruthless as the fur trade. After his 1830 experiment, Sublette went back to using pack animals, and no one in 1833 or 1834 tried to take wagons over the trail. Even packing required an extraordinary amount of work. "Was constantly engaged in repairing halters fixing the horse shoes &c. until time to pack up," Jason Lee complained. "There is more to be done on such an expedition as this [than] any one could possibly think who has never tried it." When Thomas Fitzpatrick took charge of the 1835 caravan at Fort Laramie, he left six wagons behind and packed all the supplies and trade goods on mules after the wagons suffered the usual accidents, such as breaking an axle.[35]

Gradually, fur companies turned to a more effective vehicle: the Red River cart, which Canada's Métis had been using since 1803. These carts had a light, open-frame box, a single axle, and two enormous wheels that were well adapted to crossing streams. They could transport as much as half a ton of cargo—one expert calculated they could carry ten times as much as a packhorse—and when drawn by mules, usually harnessed in a single line, they were much faster than a wagon. Historian Francis Parkman called carts mule-killers, and despite their many advantages, overland emigrants seldom used them. Mountain man Joe Meek recalled that the 1836 caravan left the settlements with nineteen carts and a light wagon owned by the American Fur Company. The company sent four carts west in 1839, each drawn by two mules and loaded with eight to nine hundred pounds. "The rest put their

---

[34] Wyeth, *Oregon*, 4, 10–12, 24.
[35] Lee, "Diary," June 11, 1834, 132; Parker, *Journal*, July 1, Aug. 1, 1835.

packs on mules or horses, of which there were fifty to sixty in the caravan," reported Dr. Frederick Wislizenus.[36]

Meanwhile, Nathaniel Wyeth had apparently left all his good luck behind at his Massachusetts ice enterprise. He played a small part in the famous battle at the 1832 rendezvous at Pierres Hole, but his men had little luck trapping beaver in the Great Basin. When he reached Fort Vancouver in October, Wyeth learned that his supply ship had been lost at sea, and his men began to disappear. Casting about for some way to salvage his fortunes, he tried unsuccessfully to strike a bargain with the Hudson's Bay Company or with Captain Bonneville. At last, he arranged with the struggling Rocky Mountain Fur Company to deliver supplies to their 1834 rendezvous. Wyeth pirouged down the Missouri to St. Louis with two Indian companions, and with Milton Sublette's help he raised a new round of capital in Boston that winter.

Wyeth left Independence with his supply caravan at the end of April 1834, but he was not the only trader bound for rendezvous that year. Bill Sublette had sold his Upper Missouri outfit to the American Fur Company that winter with the understanding he would have no competition in the Rocky Mountains for the next two years. He learned about his brother's agreement with Wyeth and led his own caravan west in May. A week later Sublette passed Wyeth's camp near the Blue River in Kansas. The race to the rendezvous was on.

When Wyeth crossed Laramie Fork, he found Sublette had left men behind who were busy building a fort. After searching up and down the tributaries of the Green, Wyeth's caravan reached the rendezvous at Hams Fork.[37] "On arrival the Rocky Mountain Fur Co. refused to receive the goods alledging that they were unable to continue business longer, and that they had disolved," Wyeth told his partners. The defunct fur company agreed to pay the advances Wyeth had made to Milton Sublette and forfeited the $500 bond that had secured the contract. "These terms I have been obliged to accept altho they would not even pay the interest on cash advances for there is no Law here," he complained.

Wyeth told Sublette he did not believe that he or Fitzpatrick had intentionally defrauded him, but he felt Fitzpatrick had "been bribed to sacrifice my interests by better offers from your brother. Now Milton, business is closed

---

[36] Vrooman, "The Métis Red River Cart," 8–20; Lamar, *The New Encyclopedia of the American West*, 952; Parkman, *The California and Oregon Trail*, 21; Victor, *The River of the West*, 1:203; Wislizenus, *Journey to the Rocky Mountains*, 29, 31.

[37] Gowans, *Rocky Mountain Rendezvous*, 96–104.

between us," Wyeth wrote. Ruthless competitors would make Sublette "a mere slave to catch Beaver for others," he warned, and turned his remarkable energies to trying to salvage something from the debacle. "If I do fail," Wyeth had written his wife early in 1834, "they shall never say that it was for want of perseverance."[38] He ended his career in the fur trade five years older and twenty thousand dollars poorer but, despite his hard luck, Wyeth never lost his enthusiasm or affection for the West.

"The American Fur Company must soon abandon the mountains," Cornelius Rogers wrote from the rendezvous in 1838. "The trade is unprofitable, and the men are becoming dissatisfied; besides, the Hudson's Bay Company will break down all opposition."[39] Rogers was right: by the late 1830s, the Rocky Mountain fur trade was on its last legs. It was not, as many long believed, that silk replaced beaver as the fashionable material for making hats or that or the fur market had collapsed: beaver pelts actually sold for more in 1840 than they had in 1825. The free trappers of the West were simply victims of their own success: the mountaineers had trapped too many beavers, and by the time the last major rendezvous was held in 1840, there were not enough animals left in the Rockies to sustain the business.[40]

The legacy of the Rocky Mountain fur trade proved more significant than its colorful legends. During its brief golden age, the freemen and mountaineers of the Rocky Mountains discovered all the major routes that wagons would soon follow to the Pacific Ocean. By the late 1830s, cartographers such as Albert Gallatin and David H. Burr incorporated Jedediah Smith's discoveries in their influential maps. Smith's own map has disappeared, and his unfortunate death on the Santa Fe Trail at age thirty-two cut short his spectacular career. Despite his tragic loss, Smith's explorations and reports "became the core of the new and more accurate image of the division of waters," John Logan Allen observed. By 1840 "the mountain men had literally demolished the geographical fantasies of Clark and Pike and Humboldt regarding the common source region."[41] The wealth they sought eluded most fur hunters, but the knowledge they gained created a better understanding of the geography of the American West. The passage they had found through the Rocky Mountains at South Pass would open the region to all those who followed their trails.

---

[38] Wyeth, *The Journals*, March 31, 1834, 123–25.
[39] Rogers to My Dear Friends, July 3, 1838, in Drury, *First White Women Over the Rockies* (cited as *Over the Rockies*, 3:274.
[40] Hanson, "The Myth of the Silk Hat," 2–11.
[41] Allen, "Division of the Waters," 361, 364, 365.

CHAPTER 4

"Unheard-of Journey"
Missionary Couples Cross South Pass
1834–1840

H ISTORY SOMETIMES SEEMS TO FOLLOW A LOGICAL PROCESS, with an event, invention, or social transformation triggering certain predictable results that, in hindsight, seem inevitable. But sometimes a wildcard appears in history's deck that changes everything. The wildcard in the annals of South Pass was religion.

A love of adventure may have drawn more young men to the fur trade and "a life more wild and perilous" than anything described in the annals of chivalry, as Francis Parkman put it, but the driving force behind the first American presence in the Far West was purely economic. Without the fortunes to be made in the fur trade, there would have been nothing to attract Americans to such a strange, distant, and dangerous country. Once the mountaineers—and the fur barons whom they made rich—effectively eliminated the region's beaver population, there appeared to be nothing, as William Ashley had observed in 1828, to induce any rational person to live there. "The trappers often remarked to each other as they rode over these lonely plains that it was time for the White man to leave the mountains as Beaver and game had nearly disappeared," wrote Osborne Russell about 1841, watching the fur trade die after his nine years in business.[1]

George Simpson's creation of a fur desert in the Snake River Basin as a barrier to American expansion appeared entirely successful. Geography alone would frustrate whatever dreams the United States might have about an empire on the Pacific, the Hudson's Bay Company mastermind concluded

---
[1] Russell, *Journal of a Trapper*, 125.

87

after meeting Jedediah Smith. Oregon was protected by "Mountains which even Hunters cannot attempt to pass, beyond which, is a Sandy desert of about 200 miles, likewise impassable, and from thence a rugged barren country of great extent, without Animals, where Smith and his party were nearly starved to Death," Simpson wrote in 1829. "So that I am of opinion, we have little to apprehend from Settlers in this quarter, and from Indian Traders nothing." Unless the U.S. government made a determined effort to settle the Pacific Northwest, the Hudson's Bay Company had nothing to fear from the Yankees.[2]

Americans who had seen the Rocky Mountains had an even lower opinion of the region's potential. The face of the country from the North Platte at the Red Buttes to the Big Sandy was "barren in the extreme; it is sand and nothing but sand," mountain man William Marshall Anderson wrote after his hard march to rendezvous in 1834. It was one immense desert, "a true American 'Sahara.'" He thought "such a waste and barren region could only have been intended for the gregarious prairie dog, or the migratory buffalo."[3]

As the Rocky Mountain fur trade began its precipitous decline, American prospects beyond the Missouri River did not look promising. Only something as unexpected as the discovery of a new source of wealth or an influence as compelling as economics seemed capable of shifting the balance of power in the Far West. This new force came to the Pacific Northwest with the 1864 expedition of Nathaniel Wyeth, who established Fort Hall on the Snake River to confound his rivals in the fur trade, but instead initiated an unexpected and revolutionary change.

This transformative influence was the power of religious faith, whose inspiration ultimately had more enduring consequences on the fate of the American West and its inhabitants than did the struggle to control the Rocky Mountain fur trade. It arrived in the form of three missionaries who set out for Oregon in 1834 under the command of a broad-shouldered Yankee lumberjack turned preacher.

A HARD AND MOST TOILSOME MARCH: JASON LEE

Indians from the Pacific Northwest had set these events in motion when they asked for someone to teach them the secrets of the white man's powerful

[2] Simpson, *Part of Dispatch from George Simpson*, March 1, 1829, 66–67.
[3] Anderson, *The Rocky Mountain Journals*, June 12, 1834, 127.

magic. In October 1831 fur-trader Lucien Fontenelle brought four Salish and Nez Perce emissaries from the Oregon Country to meet with Indian Superintendent William Clark in St. Louis. The veteran explorer understood that they had come to find a minister who could explain the Bible to them. An account of the request appeared in the Methodist *Christian Advocate* in March 1833, which issued the call, "Let the Church awake from her slumbers and go forth in her strength to the salvation of these wandering sons of our native forests."[4] Dr. Wilbur Fisk asked the Methodist Mission Board to send missionaries to answer the call, and the board provided three thousand dollars to fund the effort. Fisk recommended a former pupil at the Wilbraham Academy to lead the effort, and thus the board sent the Rev. Jason Lee to Oregon.

Along with naturalists and adventurers, Lee, two missionaries, and two hired hands joined Wyeth's second venture to the West to deliver supplies to the Rocky Mountain Fur Company in spring 1834. Lee and his companions were the vanguard of a small but devoted band of Christian evangelists who would accomplish something that had seemed entirely impossible, for by 1838 six determined American women—Eliza Hart Spalding, Narcissa Prentiss Whitman, Myra Fairbanks Eells, Mary Richardson Walker, Mary Augusta Dix Gray, and Sarah Gilbert White Smith—had proven there was nothing to stop a member of the supposedly weaker sex from crossing South Pass on horseback and reaching Oregon.[5] Their achievement changed everything.

A tall and powerful man, Jason Lee looked "as though he were well calculated to buffet difficulties in a wild country," one of his companions wrote. Lee had worked as a lumberjack until his deep religiosity led him to the ministry. At age thirty he answered the call to take the gospel to the Indians of Oregon.[6]

As strict as he was devout, Lee considered Nathaniel Wyeth "a perfect infidel"—American missionaries seldom had much good to say about fur trappers and traders. As Wyeth wrote from rendezvous in 1832, "There is here a great majority of Scoundrels."[7] Jason Lee, his nephew Daniel Lee, and fellow missionary Cyrus Shepard were true pioneers. The missionaries who followed them to Oregon transformed how Americans saw the West and

---

[4] Clark, *Eden Seekers*, 68–72; Lavender, *Westward Vision*, 250, from the *Christian Advocate and Journal and Zion's Herald*, March 1, 1833.
[5] For these women's lives, see Drury, *Over the Rockies*, 1:22.
[6] Townsend, *Across the Rockies*, 28.
[7] Gowans, *Rocky Mountain Rendezvous*, 117; and Wyeth to Ermatinger, July 18, 1833, in Wyeth, *The Journals*, 111.

viewed the possibilities of overland travel. Lee and Shepard also wrote the first detailed descriptions of the primitive trails through South Pass.

A confused Nathaniel Wyeth led his caravan up the Sweetwater River as it wound "its way through the cragged Mountains." Milton Sublette had told him that Fitzpatrick's men would gather at the mouth of the Big Sandy, but Wyeth had his doubts. He sent a message to Fitzpatrick on June 10 asking if the location had changed. The party's pack animals were failing fast as it approached South Pass, for the bison had eaten most of the grass. When the company camped for the last time on the Sweetwater, "alcohol was handed out freely by the Capt. which soon made the crew quite merry," Jason Lee commented dourly. "Some quarreled in the night from the effects of it." The next morning, Wyeth went ahead "to see if he could ascertain where he passed when he went out before," while his men headed southwest "to Sandy river, a branch of the Colorado of the west," wrote naturalist John Townsend. (Most fur-trade caravans headed to the northwest over what later became the Lander Cutoff, so Townsend's description seems to provide the first documented crossing of South Pass along the line that became the Oregon-California Trail.) It was, he recalled, "a hard and most toilsome march for both man and beast."[8]

Lee stayed behind the main company to help butcher a buffalo. About sunset, somewhere near the Continental Divide, he overtook his fellow missionaries, who had fallen behind the main party. The caravan was now scattered along the trail for several miles. The rough, uneven, and arid plain was "barren in the highest degree and extremely difficult to pass either for man or beast," Cyrus Shepard complained.

After sunset, a quarter moon crossed the late spring sky above the wide prairie at South Pass. "Night drew on fast and no water nor grass," Lee wrote. He hoped "to keep the trail after night should come on but it [was] impossible as we are in a country of wild sages which are so large that they impede the progress of the horses and also covered with Buffaloe paths which we sometimes mistake for the trail even in daylight." The missionaries "were soon overtaken by darkness and lost the trail of those that had gone on before and not knowing where to camp concluded to stop for the night and soon found a place," Shepard wrote. The men camped at ten o'clock "on the dry channel of a creek where our animals could get a little stunted verdure," but cooked no

---

[8] Lee, "Diary of Rev. Jason Lee," 133–34; Townsend, *Across the Rockies*, 77.

supper, "because we were in a dangerous part of Indian country and a light might attract them," Lee wrote.

The main party camped at about nine o'clock, not more than a mile and a half ahead of the missionaries. The Lee, Shepard, and Townsend accounts provide interesting details of the day's trek, but their inconsistencies make it difficult to sort out exactly how the different clusters of men crossed the divide. "We found no water on the route," Townsend recalled, "and not a single blade of grass for our horses." Lee wrote, "Dined on a spring of as good a water as I ever drank." (He agreed that the buffalo had swept the early grass crop from the prairie.) "Stopped at noon by two springs of clear cold water the best I ever tasted," Shepard noted, apparently describing Pacific Springs, but given later complaints about the quality of water there, this excellent spring may have been closer to the Sweetwater.

Lee's report shows there was not yet a single clear trail through South Pass. The contradictory accounts suggest that Townsend and the main party followed a different path than Lee and the missionaries. But as Shepard said the next day, they all realized "we have now passed the great dividing ridge which separates the waters of the Atlantic and Pacific." Lee observed, "Here we are on the height of Land [at] the dividing ridge between the Atlantic and Pacific."[9]

By mid-June, Wyeth had found the rendezvous and its collection of scoundrels on Hams Fork, where he learned that the Rocky Mountain Fur Company was out of business and had no need for his trade goods. The missionaries became acquainted with all the splendors of the annual mountain carnival. William Marshall Anderson estimated not fewer than fifteen hundred Indians flocked to the trading tents. By the twenty-sixth there was nothing in the camps "but drunken songs & brawls days or night." The mountain men gathered along the river were "as crazy a set of men as I ever saw," wrote Wyeth's subaltern, Joseph Thing. Jason Lee at least pretended to be oblivious to it all: from the rendezvous he wrote a letter to the *Christian Advocate* that he felt "perfectly safe" in the Shoshone camps, and asserted he would not hesitate to go among the dreaded Blackfeet, if Providence opened the way.[10]

Subsequent events suggest this was all brave talk. The missionaries and

---

[9] Lee, "Diary of Rev. Jason Lee," 134–35; Shepard, Diary, June 14, 1834; Townsend, *Across the Rockies*, 76–77.
[10] Anderson, *The Rocky Mountain Journals*, June 18, 26, 29, 1834, 27, 31, 137, 146.

Scots nobleman William Drummond Stewart joined Thomas McKay's small Hudson's Bay Company brigade, and the combined party managed to drive the mission's cows across the Blue Mountains and down to the Columbia. At Fort Vancouver, Lee and his companions were happy to accept Chief Factor John McLaughlin's advice not to go back to the mountains. Their efforts to Christianize the rapidly disappearing Native population were not even marginally successful, but they quickly recognized Oregon's tremendous potential and launched a number of economic enterprises in the Willamette Valley.

White for the Harvest: Parker and Whitman Go West

With the Methodists opening the way to Oregon, other Protestant congregations soon followed. The American Board of Commissioners for Foreign Missions (ABCFM), an alliance of the Congregational, Presbyterian, and Dutch Reform churches, sent the Rev. Samuel Parker on what he called "an exploring mission" to Oregon. He proposed to evaluate "the condition and character of the Indian nations and tribes, and the facilities for introducing the gospel and civilization among them."

Parker arrived on the Missouri frontier too late to go west in 1834 as he originally intended, but a year later he set out from Council Bluffs on June 22 with the American Fur Company's supply caravan under Lucien Fontenelle. Assisting Parker was his young associate, Dr. Marcus Whitman, a man "of easy, *don't care* habits, that could become all things to all men, and yet a sincere and earnest man, speaking his mind before he thought about it the second time," recalled William H. Gray, a carpenter who went on Whitman's second trip west 1836. As Gray observed, when he set his mind to doing something, Whitman was capable of unflinching tenacity. The refined Reverend Parker, on the other hand, was rather fastidious, and "his particular habits were not adapted to Rocky Mountain travel in those early days." At first, the caravan's rough crew had little use for either missionary: Whitman complained about the "very evident tokens" the company used to display their displeasure, such as "the throwing of rotten eggs at me."[11]

Thomas Fitzpatrick took command of the train at Fort Laramie. The traders and missionaries left their wagons "at the fort of the Black Hills, and all our goods were packed upon mules," Parker wrote. Being "exceedingly set in

---

[11] Parker, *Journal of an Exploring Tour*, 13; Gray, *History of Oregon*, 107–108; Drury, *Over the Rockies*, 1:31.

his opinions and conclusions of men and things," the dour reverend did not win many friends among the mountain men, but the unpretentious doctor quickly earned the esteem of these hard-bitten fur-trade veterans. After the missionaries thanked Fontenelle for his kind attentions and offered to pay for his services, the retiring captain said, "If any one is indebted, it is myself, for you have saved my life, and the lives of my men," referring to several cholera cases Whitman had treated.

The doctor astonished the mountaineers at rendezvous when he extracted a three-inch iron arrowhead that the Blackfeet had buried in Jim Bridger's back in 1832. "The Indians looked on meanwhile, with countenances indicating wonder, and in their own peculiar manner expressed great astonishment when it was extracted," Parker wrote. After Whitman successfully removed a second arrowhead from another trapper's shoulder, calls for his "medical and surgical aid were almost incessant." As the debauchery raged around him, Parker could only look on the mountaineers' demoralizing influence on the tribes with disgust. He despised their antics, such as selling an Indian a pack of cards at a high price and telling him it was a bible.

The Nez Perce and Salish (or Flathead) Indians seemed to offer a promising field, "white for the harvest" of missionary work. Whitman proposed that he return to the States with the caravan, recruit more evangelists, and raise enough funds to open a mission among them, which would "save at least a year, in bringing the gospel among them." Parker readily agreed, with the understanding that he would follow the Nez Perce and survey their homeland, and they would escort him to Fort Walla Walla on the Columbia River.

In the waning days of August, Parker went north with the Indians and Jim Bridger's brigade, while Whitman headed back to the Missouri with the returning caravan. "My anxious desire was, that the Lord would go with him and make his way prosperous, and make him steadfast to the object of his return, until it should be accomplished," Parker wrote. His young associate would do more than he had promised, but after conducting an extensive survey of the Oregon Country and its resources, Parker decided he would learn little more in once again "traversing the route to Rendezvous." Contrary to his agreement with Whitman, he seized the opportunity to take up the Hudson's Bay Company's offer of a free passage to Hawaii, "in the hope of a speedy opportunity would present to return to the United States."[12]

---

[12] Parker, *Journal of an Exploring Tour*, 63, 76–78, 80–83, 312–13.

Wonder and Astonishment: Women Cross South Pass

Not everyone in the United States during the 1830s thought colonizing Oregon was an inspired idea, but the best authorities (who were all men, of course) considered it pure lunacy to send American women overland to the Columbia River. "Only parties of men could undergo the vicissitudes of the journey," W. J. Snelling wrote in the *New England Magazine* in February 1832. "None who ever made the trip would assert that a woman could have accompanied them." The artist George Catlin, who knew as much about the West and its inhabitants as anyone at the time, said in 1836 he would not take a "white female into that country for the whole continent of North America." Two devout New Yorkers, the vivacious Narcissa Prentiss of Amity and the talented Eliza Hart Spalding of Holland Patent, did not accept the collective wisdom.

Narcissa Prentiss had heard Samuel Parker preach about his mission and was soon "very anxious to go to the heathen," Parker reported. In December 1834 he asked the mission board if they had any use for such a volunteer. Parker learned that there were no openings for unmarried females, but he apparently told Marcus Whitman about the young woman. Before he set out for the West, Whitman had proposed to Miss Prentiss, perhaps on the same day he met her.[13]

Eliza Hart had married Henry Harmon Spalding, a young Presbyterian studying for the ministry, in 1833, and the next year the couple decided to join "the band of missionaries for foreign missions." (At the time, the American Board of Commissioners for Foreign Missions considered Oregon a foreign mission.) "What object can we engage in that will compare with the cause of missions?" she asked in 1834. "For this object I wish to exert my powers and spend my strength."[14]

Aware of the challenges the women would face keeping up with a fast-paced trade caravan while riding sidesaddle, Marcus Whitman paid special attention to the evidence that a wagon could offer a viable alternative for a trip across the Rockies. He had heard rumors about the army's future plans: as Whitman and Parker were heading west in 1835, a regiment of dragoons had marched up the Platte River and its South Fork to the Rocky Mountains under Col. Henry Dodge. In an addendum to the journal he sent to the mission board,

---

[13] Drury, *Over the Rockies*, 1:28–29, 32.
[14] Ibid., 1:175–78.

Whitman somewhat obliquely presented his case to David Greene, secretary of the ABCFM, to take a wife and another couple on his return to the Rockies.

"If Col. Dodge should go to the Pacifick and transport cannon as he did last summer, we could cross the mountains with a waggon," Whitman wrote. Captain Bonneville had taken vehicles over South Pass, which suggested that it could be done again. Ironically, he pointed out that due to heavy rains and high water, the most difficult part of his second trip had been from Liberty, Missouri, to Council Bluffs, and "females can avoid this by being in time for the Company's boat."[15]

Secretary Greene must have questioned the doctor's sanity. "Have you carefully ascertained & weighed the difficulties in the way of conducting females to those remote & desolate regions and comfortably sustaining females there?" he asked, before Whitman had explicitly asked for permission to take women with him. Even before receiving Greene's letter asking the question, Whitman had sent an answer: "We can go as far as the Black Hills with a waggon for the convenience of females, and from that to rendezvous," he wrote. Not long after New Years 1836, the board approved sending women on the mission—"But families of children cannot be taken."[16]

Few missionaries had any interest in accepting an assignment in a place as remote and strange as Oregon, but ultimately Eliza and Henry H. Spalding agreed to go. Teacher and cabinetmaker William H. Gray signed on as the party's general handyman. Neither Henry Spalding nor William Gray was an inspired choice: Narcissa Prentiss had once turned down Spalding's marriage proposal, while Gray's pastor said he had none of the qualifications "desirable for such a station." They did share one attribute no one else had: they were willing to go to Oregon. In addition, Eliza Spalding contributed a light Dearborn carriage with wooden springs, a covered top, and wheels painted yellow with blue stripes, which her father had given the couple as a wedding present.[17]

Narcissa Prentiss wed Marcus Whitman in an emotional service at Angelica, New York, on February 18, 1836. As the closing hymn, the bride sang Samuel Smith's "Missionary Farewell" in her soprano voice, which one witness recalled was "as sweet and musical as a chime of bells":

---

[15] Whitman, "Journal," Oct. 26, 1835, 255–56.
[16] Drury, *Marcus and Narcissa Whitman*, 1:144–45, 148–49; Drury, *Over the Rockies*, 1:32–33.
[17] Drury, *Marcus and Narcissa Whitman*, 1:150–52, 154–56, 174.

In the deserts let me labor,
On the mountains let me tell
How he died—the blessed Savior—
To redeem a world from hell!
Let me hasten, Let me hasten,
Far in heathen lands to dwell.

After visiting the Whitmans' old home at Rushville and having a pair of men's boots made for Narcissa, the couple embarked on one of the most remarkable honeymoons in history.[18]

Narcissa Whitman "was a lady of refined feelings and commanding appearance," William Gray recalled. This "noble-looking" woman was definitely the star of the 1836 trek to Oregon, and her brutal murder in 1847 would elevate her to the pantheon of America's heroes. "She was not a beauty, and yet, when engaged in singing or conversation there was something in her appearance that was very attractive," recalled the Rev. Joel Wakeman, who knew her in New York. Another old neighbor, Levi Waldo, thought she was "a beautiful blonde, of fair form and well rounded features, dignified and stately, yet modest in her bearing." She was delighted with her marriage. "Jane, if you want to be happy get as good a husband as I have got, and be a missionary," Narcissa advised her sister. "The way looks pleasant, notwithstanding we are so near encountering the difficulties of an unheard of journey for females."

With her "course" voice and features, the darker Eliza Spalding tends to get lost in her famous companion's shadow, but she was the best educated of all the six women who went overland to Oregon before 1839. Her amazing ability to master Indian languages helped her accomplish the most before her death in 1851. "She never appeared to be alarmed or excited at any difficulty, dispute, or alarms common to the Indian life around her," William Gray remembered. "She was considered by the Indian men as a brave, fearless woman, and was respected and esteemed by them all."[19]

Both women wrote excellent letters and diaries describing their adventures on the way to the Pacific. Mrs. Whitman feared that Eliza Spalding was not quite healthy enough for the missionary enterprise. "Riding affects her differently

---

[18] Ibid., 1:162–63. "Missionary Farewell" appeared as hymn no. 328 in composer William Walker's popular *Southern Harmony and Musical Companion*.

[19] Drury, *Marcus and Narcissa Whitman*, 1:152, 158; Gray, *A History of Oregon*, 111.

from what it does me," she wrote. "Everyone who sees me compliments me as being the best able to endure the journey over the mountains." But Narcissa Whitman recognized character when she saw it: "Sister S. is very resolute—no shrinking with her. She possess[es] much fortitude. I like her very much. She wears well upon acquaintance." The same could not be said for Henry Spalding: simply being able to put up with her petulant husband marks Eliza Spalding as a saint, a fact her sister missionary recognized. "She is a very suitable person for Mr. Spaulding," Narcissa wrote, and had the right temperament to match him.[20]

The evangelists assembled a party that included William Gray, another hired hand named Dulin, plus Richard Tak-ah-too-ah-tis and John Ais, two Nez Perce Indians who had traveled east with Marcus Whitman. Another member of the tribe, Samuel Temoni, joined them on the frontier. On the third day on the trail near Fort Leavenworth, a nineteen-year-old boy who looked no older than sixteen wandered into Spalding's camp (the Whitmans had been delayed and were trying to catch up with the rest of the caravan). The ragamuffin wore "an old torn straw hat, an old ragged fustian coat, scarcely half a shirt, with buckskin pants, badly worn, but one moccasin, a powder horn with no powder in it, and an old rifle," Gray recalled. Though thin and spare—he had not eaten for two days—the boy was healthy and spirited and on his way to the Rocky Mountains. "He was really cold, wet, nearly naked and hungry," Gray wrote. He refused to turn back, "and said if we would allow him he would go with us to Council Bluffs, and then go with the fur company to the mountains." The young man, Miles Goodyear, "made an excellent hand."[21]

As usual, the missionaries traveled to the rendezvous with the annual trade caravan. Sir William Drummond Stewart brought along two mule-drawn wagons to support his latest hunting expedition, while the missionaries had a four-horse freight wagon and the Spaldings' two-horse Dearborn. Some say the American Fur Company sent nineteen carts and a light wagon west from Council Bluffs to the 1836 rendezvous, but Narcissa Whitman provided different numbers when she wrote home from the Platte River. "We are really a moving village—nearly four hundred animals, with ours, mostly mules and seventy men. The Fur Com. have seven wagons drawn by six mules each, heavily loaded, and one cart drawn by two mules, which carries a lame man, one of the proprietors of the Company." The lame man was Milton Sublette,

---

[20] Drury, *Over the Rockies*, 1:46–47.
[21] Drury, *Marcus and Narcissa Whitman*, 1:176; Gray, *A History of Oregon*, 113–14.

who was going west despite his amputated leg. Captain Thomas Fitzpatrick and the pilot led the way, followed by the pack mules, the wagons, and the missionaries, who brought up the rear.[22]

It was astonishing how well they got along "with our wagons where there are no roads," Narcissa Whitman wrote at Fort Laramie. "I may say [it is] easier traveling here than on any turnpike in the States."[23] The trail up the Platte River was one of the best natural roads in the world, but beyond Fort Laramie it became more difficult. Thomas Fitzpatrick left the caravan's carts behind at the post, and the missionaries abandoned their heavy wagon.

Eliza Spalding blamed her dysentery on a steady diet of meat and tea and tea and meat. But she was tough: thrown from her horse twice, after one fall she was dragged a considerable distance but somehow survived. "Although it was somewhat fatiguing to Mrs Spaulding," Marcus Whitman wrote, "Mrs Whitman endured it well." The missionaries' hardest task was keeping up with the trappers' "Forced march." Fitzpatrick set a brutal pace for the caravan, which needed to reach the rendezvous by early July to beat the increasing competition.

When the trappers who were gathered at the rendezvous site heard of the approaching caravan and its remarkable composition, the "exhilarating news" inspired a band of Nez Perce and mountaineers to ride for two days to meet them, "especially to salute the two white women who were bold enough to invade a mountain camp," trader Joe Meek recalled. The yelling and whooping welcoming committee greeted the astonished caravan, "dashing forward with frantic and threatening gestures" that seemed so completely savage that the train thought it was under attack until someone spotted a white flag. The crazy cavalcade continued its charge, "riding faster and faster, yelling louder and louder, and gesticulating more and more madly," and fired a volley over the heads of the company.

That evening Eliza wrote of the Nez Perces who had come to greet them: "They appear to be gratified to see us actually on our way to their country." The proud Indians she met on the Fourth of July in 1836 must have seemed as alien to a young woman born in Connecticut and educated at the Chipman Female Academy in Clinton, New York, as the vast landscape she encountered in the shadow of the Wind River Range. "Crossed a ridge of land, today called

---

[22] Drury, *Over the Rockies*, 1:51.
[23] Drury, *Marcus and Narcissa Whitman*, 1:185.

the divide, which separates the waters that flow into the Atlantic from those that flow into the Pacific, and camped for the night on the head waters of the Colorado," Eliza Spalding recorded that evening at a campsite on Little Sandy Creek, the only contemporary record of what happened on that historic day.[24]

Some twenty-two miles southeast of the Little Sandy, on the Oregon, California, Mormon Pioneer, and Pony Express National Historic Trails, a marker at the summit of South Pass commemorates Narcissa Whitman and Eliza Spalding as the "First White Women to Cross This Pass." For almost a century historians assumed the missionaries made the crossing using the trail that led to Pacific Springs. But the caravan was heading to the rendezvous at the Green River's confluence with Horse Creek, so it is clear the missionaries crossed the Continental Divide along the line of what later became known as the Lander Cutoff.

Here the Continental Divide follows a ridge at the headwaters of Lander Creek that rises less than sixty feet above Little Sandy Creek. Today the state of Wyoming owns the "ridge of land" that Eliza Spalding described crossing just west of Jensen Meadow between Lander Creek, a tributary of the Sweetwater, and the Little Sandy. Across the ridge, the Little Sandy flows along the very foot of the divide and into the Big Sandy, Green, and Colorado rivers on its way to the Sea of Cortez.[25]

Two days later the caravan arrived at the rendezvous, held near Bonneville's abandoned Fort Nonsense. Many of the Nez Perce men, women, and children greeted the missionaries. "The women were not satisfied, short of saluting Mrs. W and myself with a kiss," Eliza Spalding wrote. "All appear happy to see us." The Indians "were greatly interested with our Females cattle & waggon," Marcus Whitman reported.

"The two ladies were gazed upon with wonder and astonishment by the rude Savages they being the first white women ever seen by these Indians and the first that had ever penetrated into these wild and rocky regions," noted one veteran mountaineer, Osborne Russell. The ladies were of no less interest to his fellow mountaineers. "The tents of the white ladies were besieged with visitors, both civilized and savage," Joe Meek recalled. In particular, Mrs. Whitman "shone the bright particular star of that Rocky Mountain encampment, softening the hearts and the manners of all who came within

---

[24] Victor, *The River of the West*, 1:201–202; Drury, *Over the Rockies*, 1:189, 191, 195n32.
[25] Guenther et al., "The Women Who Carried the Star of Empire Westward," 148. This excellent article places the crossing at T30N, R104W, Sec. 36 NW, as shown on the Pinedale 1:100,000-scale USGS quadrangle.

her womanly influence." Both women began to study the Nez Perce language, but Eliza Spalding "perhaps succeeded better than Mrs. Whitman in the difficult study of the Indian dialect," Joe Meek recalled. She "seemed to attract the natives about her by the ease and kindness of her manner."[26]

As Reverend Spalding wrote from the rendezvous, the trip was exhausting, but the women "endured the fatigues of the march remarkably well," especially after riding "on horseback from morning till night day after day for 15 or 20 days, at the rate of 25 and 30 miles a day." He did not, however, consider the trip a success. "Never send another mission over these mountains if you value life and money," he said in a second letter to the mission board. Eliza Spalding had felt so wretched that she doubted she would live to see the end of the journey, even though she thought her miserable diet had "affected my health favorably." Once they left rendezvous and began eating jerked bison meat, she revived.

An Immense Fund of Determination

Thomas McKay invited the missionaries to accompany his Hudson's Bay Company brigade to the Columbia. The combined party left the rendezvous on July 18, 1836. "It seems a special favour of Providence that that Company has come to Rendezvous," Narcissa wrote, since otherwise the missionaries would have had to go with the Indians over a more difficult route. The trail that lay before them—over the Bear River Mountains to Soda Springs, out of the Great Basin and down to the Snake River at Fort Hall and Fort Boise, and across the Blue Mountains—would be arduous enough.[27]

To complicate matters, "Dr. Whitman refused to leave the light wagon, although assured he would never be able to get it to the Columbia, nor even to the Snake River," Joe Meek recalled. "The good Doctor had an immense fund of determination when there was an object to be gained or a principle involved." The only people who did not oppose taking the wagon farther west were the Indians, who admired the doctor's determination and helped him. "The wagons, the domestic cattle, especially the cows and calves, were always objects of great interest with them," Meek said.[28]

---

[26] Drury, *Over the Rockies*, 1:194; Russell, *Journal of a Trapper*, 41; Victor, *The River of the West*, 1:206–207.
[27] Drury, *Over the Rockies*, 1:58, 73, 195; 3:311.
[28] Victor, *The River of the West*, 1:209.

Getting the vehicle the hundreds of rugged miles from South Pass to Fort Hall was no small feat. It wore out Miles Goodyear, the party's roustabout, who quit when Whitman refused to leave the wagon at Fort Hall. A mountaineer named Hinds, "a colored man who came with us from Rendezvous on account of his health, being far gone with the dropsy," as Narcissa Whitman described him, took Goodyear's place.[29]

The resolute doctor pressed ahead with his wagon, determined to take it all the way to the Columbia. Never before had a wheeled vehicle crossed an inch of the rugged terrain. On the trek down the barren Snake River plain, Whitman could not remember "a single fertile spot to the amount of an acre on the River for the whole distance." The traders shared a bit of rice and an occasional fried cake with the missionaries, helping to vary the constant diet of dried meat. They were delighted to reach the camps at Salmon Falls, where Shoshonean bands had gathered for the annual run. Beyond the falls, Dr. Whitman converted his chariot to a cart. When they at last reached Fort Boise, "The waggon we left," he wrote, but "subject to future order," since he hoped to retrieve it later. As Narcissa observed, "Our animals were failing & the route in crossing the Blue Mountains is said to be impassable for it." Two Indians on horseback towed the missionary wives across the Snake River in a "snug little canoe" made of "bunches of rushes tied together, and attached to a frame made of a few sticks of small willows," she wrote. "It was just large enough to hold us and our saddles."[30]

The party had crossed its last major river, but the trip over the deserts and mountains of Oregon got no easier. The missionaries and their cattle climbed the steep, narrow trail up the Burnt River going single-file, and on August 25 they reached the Powder River Valley.

The spectacular Blue Mountains overwhelmed Narcissa Whitman—"I do not know as I was ever so much affected with any scenery in my life"—but the descent demanded her attention as "we began to descend one of the most terrible mountains for steepness and length I have yet seen. It was like winding stairs in its descent and in some places almost perpendicular," she wrote. "We had no sooner gained the foot of this mountain, when another more steep and dreadful was before us." When the ragged party reached

---

[29] Dropsy is edema, swelling usually associated with congestive heat failure due to an accumulation of excess fluid. Goodyear would go on to establish Fort Buenaventura in 1846 at today's Ogden, Utah.
[30] Whitman to Greene, Sept. 5, 1836, in Drury, *Marcus and Narcissa Whitman*, 1:207; Drury, *Over the Rockies*, 1:79–87.

Fort Walla Walla on the first of September, the post commander, Pierre Chrysologue Pambrun, received the missionaries "in the kindest manner & the great hospitality we received almost made us forget the fatigues of our long journey," Marcus Whitman reported.[31]

"The ladies have borne the journey astonishingly," wrote naturalist John Townsend, who greeted them at the fort. They looked "robust and healthy." Dr. Whitman could see "no reason to regret our choice of a journey by land." Did she "regret coming by land?" Narcissa asked that fall. "I answer NO! by no means." She had, she said, enjoyed living outdoors and "the healthful effects of a horseback ride" over two thousand miles.[32]

Thirty-four years after crossing the Continental Divide, Henry Spalding told a grandiose tale of how the first female American citizens crossed South Pass. "Mrs. Spalding and Mrs. Whitman, alighted from their horses, themselves in great weakness," at high noon on the Fourth of July "with the banner of the cross in one hand and the stars and stripes in the other." They took formal possession of Oregon "in the name of their Saviour and their country, in the name of American mothers and the American church, and being immediately confronted by the British lion, they instantly bearded the royal beast in his lair."[33] His story had variants. "The moral and physical scene was grand and thrilling. Hope and joy beamed on the face of my dear wife, though pains racked her frame. She seemed to receive new strength," Spalding allegedly recalled. "'Is it reality or a dream,' she exclaimed, 'that after four months of hard and painful journeyings I am alive, and actually standing on the summit of the Rocky Mountains, where yet the foot of white woman has never trod?'"[34]

Henry Spalding told these stories as he was busily re-imagining the past to support an evolving mythology about how America acquired the Pacific Northwest. Spalding, whose love of country was exceeded only by his hatred of Catholics and the Hudson's Bay Company, made them the villains of his legend. Nothing in the historical record supports these stories: in a letter written from the rendezvous shortly after crossing South Pass, Spalding said simply, "When we left the waters of the Atlantic we struck those of the Pacific in six or seven miles, without passing any mountain." He did not even realize

---

[31] Drury, *Over the Rockies*, 1:88–92.
[32] Ibid., 3:308; Townsend, *Across the Rockies*, 245.
[33] Drury, *Marcus and Narcissa Whitman*, 1:193n28.
[34] Eells, *Marcus Whitman, Pathfinder and Patriot*, 34–36. Grace Hebard, "First White Women in Wyoming," 30, attributed the statement to Eliza Spalding's diary.

it was the Fourth of July, for he wrote, "we struck the water of the Colorado, 2d of July."[35] A noted historian dismissed Spalding's account as "nothing more than the embellishments of an old man's fertile imagination."[36]

The truth was more compelling than Spalding's fables. At the dawn of the twenty-first century, it is hard to commemorate what Eliza Spalding and Narcissa Whitman accomplished without using terms that sound both racist and sexist—and the annals of the West are filled with tomes that proudly celebrated them in exactly that way. History is too complicated to abide such narrow prejudices. The identity of the first woman to cross South Pass is buried in the mists of prehistory, but Isabel Craig, Virginia Meek, and Kittie M. Newell—the daughters of Nez Perce chief Kowsoter and wives of three noted American frontiersman—all accompanied their husbands over South Pass before settling in Oregon in 1840. Robert "Doc" Newell's manuscript record places the birth of his first child, Francis Ermatinger Newell, at "Green River, South Pass, June 14, 1835"—the first recorded birth in the area. This makes Kittie Newell the first woman known to have crossed South Pass.[37]

As the "First White Women Over the Rockies"—the title Clifford Drury chose for his 1963 collection of their diaries—the accomplishments of Eliza Spalding and Narcissa Whitman still deserve appreciation. When Spalding and Whitman climbed over that short hill and reached the Little Sandy on the Fourth of July in 1836, they stood the assumptions of their contemporaries on their heads. Their achievement needs to be considered for its broader consequences, which proved disastrous for the Indian peoples living in the lands they crossed but ultimately liberating for their gender. After they arrived in Oregon, no one could argue credibly that women were incapable of facing the hardships and challenges of transcontinental travel.

Over the next thirty years, tens of thousands of members of their sex would follow these two dauntless women to the Pacific. Wyoming Territory gave women the right to vote in 1869. Only thirty-four years later, after Spalding and Whitman had passed within three miles of her future home at South Pass City, in 1870 Esther Hobart Morris became the boomtown's justice of the peace and the first woman to hold political office in the United States.

---

[35] Spalding, "A Letter," July 11, 17, 1836. Spalding apparently thought he had crossed the divide upon reaching Lander Creek.

[36] Drury, *Marcus and Narcissa Whitman*, 1:189.

[37] Anderson, *The Rocky Mountain Journals*, 339, citing Alvin M. Josephy, Jr., for the Newell family record.

In a Dangerous Country: The 1838 Missionary Band

When they crossed South Pass in 1836, Eliza Spalding and Narcissa Whitman "were in the vanguard of a great procession of men, women, and children, who were to travel that same way" over the next three decades, Clifford Drury wrote. "They proved it was possible for women to cross the Rockies." Whitman and Spalding had shown that women could meet whatever challenges the West could throw at them. If there were any remaining doubts, the next four American women to ride to Oregon should have dispelled them. Myra Fairbanks Eells, Mary Richardson Walker, Mary Augusta Dix Gray, and Sarah Gilbert White Smith and their husbands formed the missionary band that trekked to Oregon in 1838.

Only a handful of Americans had ever ventured west of the Missouri River, and Samuel Parker was the only one who had both crossed the continent by land and sailed around Cape Horn. He informed Mary Walker's husband Elkanah that the land route was much preferable. "By all means go across the continent by land. I had rather go across the continent three times than go around the Cape once, and probably it would not take more time," Parker advised. "A lady can go with far more comfort by land than by water."[38]

William Gray had returned from Oregon in 1837 to find a bride. The mother of his first fiancé reportedly asked him about the two bullet holes in his hat. The Sioux had put them there when they killed his Indian companions at Ash Hollow, Gray explained. The woman wisely decreed that no daughter of hers was going to make the dangerous trip to Oregon. Gray (who Mary Walker found "exceedingly fractious") had to find a new bride. According to family tradition, he met Mary Augusta Dix at a church social on Valentine's Day in 1838 and proposed to her that very evening. Whatever the case, she had accepted his proposal within a week.[39]

Pierre Chouteau sent a small caravan to the rendezvous in 1838. It probably consisted of no more than seventy men—but with familiar hands such as William Drummond Stewart, Moses Harris, and an ambitious and unscrupulous European emigrant, John Augustus Sutter, whose trading post on the Sacramento River later became the destination of the California Trail. Cornelius Rogers was the only bachelor among the nine members of the "mission band" of 1838, who all shared a single one-horse wagon. Stewart had his wagon drawn

---
[38] Drury, *Over the Rockies*, 1:62, 2:41.
[39] Ibid., 1:237–40, 239, 2:85

by four mules, while the fur company had a small fleet of carts. "The wagons are all covered with black or dark cloth," Myra Eells wrote. "When we are fairly on our way we have much the appearance of a large funeral procession in the States."[40] The missionary wagon only made it to Fort Laramie, but the four women proved to be remarkably adept at riding their sidesaddles.

Hoping to fend off competition from the Hudson's Bay Company, the American Fur Company secretly moved the rendezvous to the Wind River. Francis Ermatinger, the HBC's man at Fort Hall, learned the trade fair would be held near today's Riverton, Wyoming, from a note scrawled in charcoal on the old storehouse door at Fort Nonsense. Mary Walker's journal said it read, "Come on to the Popeasia; plenty of whiskey & white women."[41] Ermatinger had guided Jason Lee to the trade fair, and Lee was on his way east to recruit additional support for the Methodist mission. Ermatinger visited "the American rendezvous chiefly for the purpose of gathering information," according to his boss, John McLaughlin. Coincidentally, the Hudson's Bay Company's pack train now escorted the missionaries to Fort Hall.[42]

The rendezvous had been held on the east side of the mountains, so the missionaries still had to cross the Continental Divide. According to Sarah Smith, their pack train traveled twenty miles on June 12, fording both the Popo Agie and Little Popo Agie. They moved sixteen more miles the next day "over hills of red rocks & earth," as Mary Walker wrote. "Mr. Ermatinger says we are on the back bone of America," Myra Eells recorded on the fourteenth. She called the scenery romantic and described the "red sand stone piled on Mts on every side of us, so steep we can only go up and down them sideways."

The company covered almost thirty miles "over the height of land between the Popcasia to the Sweet Water," Sarah Smith wrote. "Have passed over frightful places of which you have no idea." She heard in the States that the ascent of South Pass was so gradual she would hardly know she had reached the mountains before she was over them, but Francis Ermatinger took her over the great divide by quite an entirely different trail. "For my part I thought we were rising today," she observed. "We ascended & again descended strong mountains where I could hardly sit upon my horse. I walked down one mountain where I had to catch by the stones to keep me from falling." But Mrs.

[40] Ibid., 2:75, 3:297.
[41] Drury, *Over the Rockies*, 2:101, 3:301.
[42] Gowans, *Rocky Mountain Rendezvous*, 180.

Smith was adjusting to life in the Far West. "All this I enjoy much compared to a ride upon the prairie," Sarah wrote. "I am not at all afraid."[43]

Myra Eells was bearing up well, but her husband was "fatigued and almost discouraged." That night, a bison herd passed so close to the campsite they could hear them pant, and for the first time, Mary Walker felt the child she was carrying move. The next day was the Sabbath, July 15, 1838, but Ermatinger assured them "that we are in a dangerous country and we must travel," Myra wrote. Five hours and twenty miles later, the party camped with a band of Shoshones on Little Sandy Creek on the southern slope of the Wind River Range. Sarah Smith's red hair intrigued the Native men. "They are talking & laughing, greatly pleased to see a white squaw as they call me," she wrote. "I suspect they would like my scalp."[44]

After two day's rest on the Little Sandy, the women rode "over high mountains and through deep ravines, crossed two creeks, nooned on the last, then rode across a long plain, 35 miles, without coming to any water where we could encamp," Myra Eells wrote. "Pretty well tired out, all of us," Mary Richardson Walker thought. "Stood it pretty well myself." She had almost fainted when she dismounted, but revived after drinking some tea. Still, Walker admitted, "45 miles to ride in one day is hard."[45]

At the end of August, the missionaries arrived at the primitive station the Whitmans had built about twenty-five miles east of Fort Walla Walla at Waiilatpu—the place of the rye grass. "I can not describe its appearance," Myra Eells wrote of the rough adobe cabin, "as I can not compare it with anything I ever saw."[46] The first women to cross the continent on horseback had met a difficult challenge, but life on the remote Oregon frontier would prove no easier.

Hardships and Perplexities: Women and South Pass

When Narcissa Whitman and Eliza Spalding crossed from the Missouri to the Columbia River in 1836, their achievement transformed the American West. The safe arrival in 1838 of four more missionary wives over what would soon

---

[43] The sources indicate the packers climbed over the eastern shoulder of Mount Nystrom to the headwaters of the Sweetwater.
[44] Drury, *Over the Rockies*, 2:102–104, 3:95–96.
[45] Ibid., 2:102–104.
[46] Ibid., 2:116.

be called the Oregon Trail confirmed that women could make the 2,000-mile trek successfully. Two more women—Desire C. Smith Griffith and Sarah Elizabeth Hoisington "Eliza" Munger—completed the journey in 1839. "You can judge something of Eliza's health and strength if she is able after riding almost constantly for 4 months, to get on to a horse & ride 25 miles in less than half a day," Asahel Munger wrote after he and his wife crossed the Rockies.[47] The next year, Emeline Clarke, Adeline Sadler Littlejohn, and Abigail Raymond Smith crossed South Pass on their way to the Columbia. By the end of 1840, eleven women had accompanied their missionary husbands overland to Oregon.

Despite what these women accomplished, many skeptics still doubted that the Wild West was an appropriate place for a woman, including some of the women and their husbands who had crossed South Pass. Narcissa Whitman called it "a dreadful journey." As much as she wanted to see them again, she told her family, "I cannot think of ever crossing the mountains again—my present health will not admit of it."

Several husbands who had brought their wives overland to Oregon thought sending *any* more missionaries across the continent was a bad idea: "I cannot think it proper for any company to come in the manner we did," Elkanah Walker concluded in October 1838. "I hope it will never be done again. The more I think of our journey, the more fully satisfied I am that it is improper for missionaries, especially females, thus to travel," wrote Asa B. Smith in 1840. "The trials, hardships, and perplexities of such a journey no one can realize but those who have undertaken it." His wife, Sarah, agreed. "When I look back upon it, I tremble at what we have passed through," she wrote in the last entry of her 1839 diary. "It does seem to me that it is improper for a female to undertake" what she called this "tremendous journey."[48]

People learned that the first women from the United States had reached Fort Vancouver in 1836 from a Henry Spaulding letter published in the October 1837 number of *The Missionary Herald*. The news that women had survived the long and perilous journey to Oregon had an immediate impact. "Thus has vanished the great obstacle to a direct and facile communication between the Mississippi Valley and the Pacific Ocean," Missouri's Lewis F. Linn proclaimed on the Senate floor.[49] The notion that two women could prosper on

---

[47] Munger, "Diary," Sept. 10, 1839; Drury, *Over the Rockies*, 3:316–17.
[48] Whitman, *Letters*, Sept. 29, 1842, 138; Drury, *Over the Rockies*, 3:313, 314.
[49] Drury, *Marcus and Narcissa Whitman*, 1:187.

JOSEPH LAFAYETTE MEEK
Mountain man and "Minister Extraplenipotentary of the Republic of Oregon" to the United States in 1848, Joe Meek helped secure territorial status for Oregon and a job as the territory's first marshal. *From Frances Fuller Victor, The River of the West (1870).*

a journey that few men had made defied all accepted notions about female frailty and a woman's place in society. It challenged the stereotype of women as helpless creatures and shattered the illusion that only men could ride two thousand miles on horseback.

Narcissa Whitman and Eliza Spalding crossed the Oregon Trail as a response to their deeply held religious beliefs at a time when most Americans felt there was no good reason to go to the Far West. By completing their unheard-of journey, they had done something that most Americans thought was simply impossible. Their achievement showed that even in the wilds of the West, a determined woman could do anything she set out to do. For Marcus Whitman, it became one of his life's great accomplishments. "If I never do more than to have been one of the first to take white women across the Mountain," he wrote in his last known letter, "I am satisfied."[50]

After Narcissa Whitman's death, an anonymous admirer put the achievement of the eleven women who had crossed the long trail before 1841 in perspective. "The simple act of these two females, sustained by others who have followed them on a similar enterprise, has contributed more to the present occupancy of Oregon than all the fine-spun speeches and high-sounding

---

[50] Hulbert and Hulbert, *Marcus Whitman*, 2:103, 330.

words that had yet issued from the executive branch at Washington," wrote one Oregonian. Before Eliza Spalding and Narcissa Whitman "ventured to try the perils of a journey across the mountains," such a project was considered "presumptuous in the extreme, and doubtless has contributed to dispel the fears and remove the dread of a passage from the Mississippi to the Columbia, more than all other adventures."[51]

The missionaries' success seemed to revive interest in using wagons to haul goods to the mountains. The fur companies had, as Henry Spalding observed in 1836, "made bridges and prepared roads" that helped pioneer the way to Oregon.[52] Thomas Fitzpatrick led a train of thirty wagons and two carts to Fort Laramie in 1837 and continued to Green River with some twenty carts, a venture brilliantly captured in the notes, sketches, and paintings of Alfred Jacob Miller.[53] Andrew Drips left Westport, Missouri, in 1839 with seventeen carts and wagons. William Drummond Stewart took along a four-mule wagon, while Pierre Chouteau sent four carts to Green River under Moses Harris. The Rocky Mountain fur trade had a last hurrah in 1840, when Andrew Drips, with help from Jim Bridger and Henry Fraeb, led a caravan of thirty carts and forty men to Green River.

Robert "Doc" Newell and Joe Meek made a breakthrough in the fall of 1840 when they bought the first "horse canoes"—the Indian term for wagons—over the Rockies and the Blue Mountains to the Columbia.[54] Meek's biographer told a classic tale of her hero giving up his free-ranging ways. "Come, we are done with this life in the mountains—done with wading in beaver-dams, and freezing or starving alternately—done with Indian trading and Indian fighting. The fur trade is dead in the Rocky Mountains, and it is no place for us now, if ever it was," Newell said to Meek. They should move their families to the Willamette and take up farming. "What do you say, Meek? Shall we turn American settlers?" he asked.[55]

Thirty years after coming to the Rocky Mountains, Newell still showed the determination that brought the first wagon to Oregon. "Doc" ended his days as a respected pioneer and Indian agent in Idaho. The trappers bought the missionaries' wagons at the last rendezvous in 1840. The next spring

---
[51] "Oregonian," *Oregon Spectator*, Feb. 5, 1848, quoted in Drury, *Marcus and Narcissa Whitman*, 1:188.
[52] Spalding, "A Letter," July 11, 1836.
[53] Gowans, *Rocky Mountain Rendezvous*, 145, 150.
[54] Tobie, *No Man Like Joe*, 86–87.
[55] Victor, *The River of the West*, 2:25–26.

Newell proudly noted in his memorandum book, "This is to be remembered that I Robert Newell was the first who brought waggons across the rocky mountains."[56]

The First Train of Emigrants to Oregon: The Walker Family

Veteran Santa Fe trader Joel Pickens Walker, the older brother of the renowned fur hunter and explorer Joseph R. Walker, arrived in the Willamette Valley in mid-September 1840 with something no one had ever before brought overland from the United States: a family. Along with his wife's unmarried younger sister, Martha, Mary Young Walker and their four children, John, Joe, Newton, and Isabella, "formed the first train of emigrants to Oregon," Walker recalled. Unlike all the other Americans who had preceded him to Oregon, he went not to get rich in the beaver trade or to convert the heathens: Walker came to settle.

At the last rendezvous, the family joined Bill Craig's small party and went to Fort Hall and then on to Oregon with the Hudson's Bay pack train that was taking the year's "returns"—furs—to Fort Vancouver. The fort's head trader, Dr. John McLaughlin, treated the new arrivals very kindly, "charging for nothing we got, and offering to outfit me for a year, for which I should return stock and wheat when I succeeded in raising it," Walker later wrote. He visited Jason Lee's Indian school in the Willamette Valley but found the missionaries were not as generous as the Hudson's Bay Company. "There I had to pay for everything I got," Walker remembered. He settled down and got on with "making just about a living."[57]

The Walkers were the first family to come to Oregon to put down roots. Over the next thirty years, tens of thousands of families would cross South Pass and complete the revolution that mountaineers and missionaries had started in the American West.

---

[56] Newell, *Memoranda*. The vehicle Newell got to Oregon was not exactly a wagon. Asa Lovejoy, in "Lovejoy's Pioneer Narrative," 250, reported the men "cut the wagon in two, and used a pair of wheels," indicating that they converted the wagon into a cart or simply brought the running gears without the wagon box over the mountains.

[57] Walker, *A Pioneer of Pioneers*, 12, 18. Mary Young Walker gave birth in Jan. 1841.

CHAPTER 5

"Treading Unknown Paths"
Emigrants and Explorers
1841–1848

WITH THE DEMISE OF THE ROCKY MOUNTAIN FUR TRADE, the fact that women had successfully completed the journey to Oregon and that wagons could probably cross the continent changed the way the American people thought about the Far West. But hordes of people did not immediately begin lining up on the Missouri frontier each spring with "Oregon or Bust" painted on their wagon covers. "The *agitation* for Oregon migration and the awakening of interest in that country forms one story; the *actual result* (men on the ground) forms another," observed Archer Butler Hulbert, a perceptive chronicler of western settlement.

Boosters such as Hall Jackson Kelley had already been promoting emigration to the Pacific Northwest for a decade, and the Oregon Provisional Emigration Society was organized in Massachusetts in August 1838 "to prepare the way for the Christian settlement of Oregon." The society published "the interesting, if short-lived," *Oregonian and Indian's Advocate* in Boston from October 1838 to August 1839, but it does not appear to have inspired a single American farmer to migrate to Oregon. Neither did the many bills introduced into Congress before the War with Mexico become law or do much to encourage the settlement of the far-distant territory or produce much noticeable popular enthusiasm. "What the average American in the East saw in his daily or weekly newspaper, or in the congressional record, was one thing," Hulbert pointed out. "What the Whitmans saw coming down the stony slopes of the Blue Mountains to the Walla Walla River was another thing."[1]

---
[1] Hulbert and Hulbert, *Marcus Whitman, Crusader*, 2:84–85.

About six miles from our encampment brought us to the summit. The ascent had been so gradual, that, with all the intimate knowledge possessed by Carson, who had made the country his home for seventeen years, we were obliged to watch very closely to find the place at which we had reached the culminating point. This was between two low hills, rising on either hand fifty or sixty feet. . . . I should compare the elevation which we surmounted immediately at the Pass, to the ascent of the Capitol hill from the avenue, at Washington. It is difficult for me to fix positively the breadth of this Pass. From the broken ground where it commences, at the foot of the Wind River chain, the view to the southeast is over a champaign country, broken, at the distance of nineteen miles, by the Table rock [the Oregon Buttes]. . . . It in no manner resembles the places to which the term is commonly applied—nothing of the gorge-like character and winding ascents of the Alleghany passes in America; nothing of the Great St. Bernard and Simplon passes in Europe. Approaching it from the mouth of the Sweet Water, a sandy plain, one hundred and twenty miles long, conducts, by a gradual and regular ascent, to the summit, about seven thousand feet above the sea; and the traveler, without being reminded of any change by toilsome ascents, suddenly finds himself on the waters which flow to the Pacific ocean.

JOHN C. FRÉMONT
JOURNAL, AUGUST 8, 1842, 1:253–54

There was, however, a growing awareness in the United States that it probably was possible to take a wagon over South Pass and on to the Columbia River. Adventurer Thomas Jefferson Farnham followed the Santa Fe Trail and ascended the Arkansas River with the "Oregon Dragoons" of Peoria in 1839 and then reached the Pacific Northwest by way of Browns Park, a remote spot near present-day Utah's northeast corner.

After visiting Oregon and California, Farnham returned to the United States well informed about the significance of the Platte River Road and the anomaly of South Pass, even though he had not seen them. He realized that the Platte River might be useless as a navigable waterway, but it had "an unequalled importance among the streams of the Great Prairie Wilderness!" The route was destined to be of great value, for "overland travel from the States to Oregon and California will find its great highway along its banks." A promoter and visionary who may have gone west as a government agent, Farnham foresaw a time when fortified posts would protect "countless caravans of American citizens."

"Even now loaded wagons can pass without serious interruption from the mouth of the Platte to navigable waters on the Columbia River in Oregon, and the Bay of San Francisco, in California," Farnham claimed. Neither statement was true when his book appeared in 1843, and his secondhand description of the trail to California was almost comical, but Farnham grasped the significance of South Pass. "Upon the headwaters of the North Fork is the only way or opening in the Rocky Mountains at all practicable for a carriage road through them," he knew. "But the Great Gap, nearly on a right line between the mouth of the Missouri and Fort Hall on Clark's River [sic]—the point where the trails to California and Oregon diverge—seems designed by nature as the great gateway between nations on the Atlantic and Pacific seas."[2]

The fact that a family had reached Oregon safely in 1840 using roads and trails developed by fur traders and missionaries was not widely known in 1840, but Joel and Mary Walker had shown what was possible. That fall, some five hundred people pledged to head west, but almost none of them showed up at the designated departure point the next spring. Yet in 1841, the Bidwell-Bartleson party, the first wagon train headed for California, set out from Independence, Missouri, though some of its eighty-odd members had set their sights on Oregon. Over the next eight years, this trickle of overland

---

[2] Farnham, *Travels in the Great Western Prairies*, 21 22.

emigration would grow first to a rivulet, then swell to a brook that become a considerable stream and finally a mighty river of families, wagons, and cattle.

As the 1840s drew to a close, a new people had settled by the Great Salt Lake and founded a city. The great trail historian John Unruh, Jr., calculated that by 1848, 18,847 Americans had crossed South Pass on their way to new homes in the West.[3]

The events of 1849 transformed not only South Pass but the entire American nation. A flood of migration surged up the Platte and Arkansas rivers, around Cape Horn, and across Mexico and Panama to reach the goldfields of California. This began the golden age of wagon travel to Utah and the Pacific and, by the time the gold rush drew to a close in 1850s, California had achieved statehood and Oregon was on the verge of joining the Union. Unruh estimated that by 1860, almost three hundred thousand men, women, and children had crossed South Pass.

The increasing use of the trails and the end of the gold rush opened a new era of conflict and violence on the road west. The Mormon people resented the federal government's interference with their attempt to build the Kingdom of God in the Great Basin, and the Indian peoples of the central plains and Rocky Mountains began to understand the disastrous impact of what they called "Great Medicine Road of the Whites." The Mormon conflict ended before it could become a holocaust, but as the nation relentlessly slipped into civil war, the road across South Pass became the scene of a war of survival.

Fifty Roads: Evolving Trails over South Pass

Along with his heady prophecies, T. J. Farnham's promotional prose shows that South Pass did not yet have a popular name as the 1840s began, nor was anyone sure whether this gateway to the continent lay in the United States or south of the forty-second parallel—in Mexico. There was not yet even a clearly defined wagon road across the landmark. The earliest reports indicate travelers followed several traces from the Ninth or Last Crossing of the Sweetwater at today's Burnt Ranch to the Little Sandy, depending on where they were bound. The main road through the pass had not yet settled on what became the most popular trail, the direct route from the Last Crossing to Pacific Springs. The first overlanders found Indian roads headed in all

---

[3] Unruh, *The Plains Across*, 119–20.

directions and only occasional signs of the old fur-trade trails, perhaps because the most heavily used road headed to the northwest and the old rendezvous sites at Horse Creek on Green River. By 1843 South Pass was "already traversed by several different roads," John C. Frémont reported.[4] The number of roads across the open plain increased with the intense traffic that arrived with the California gold rush as travelers sought out campsites that had not been stripped of grass. Jim Bridger told one Forty-niner, "he could make fifty roads through the South Pass," and today it sometimes seems that he did.[5]

Western trails were a series of overlaid pathways. They began as game trails and evolved into the hunting and trading routes adapted by the West's first human inhabitants for their own purposes. The use of dogs and then horses to drag travois—basically two-pole sleds used to haul supplies, lodges, trading goods, and other property and camping gear—created the first trails that American Indian nations used for hunting, seasonal migration, and trade. These drag-ways crisscrossed the West: the day before he reached the Continental Divide, Robert Stuart reported seeing "a large Lodge trace"—and as early as 1812, Stuart called the Absarokas' route over South Pass a road.[6] These Indian trails became the West's first highways, which were well established when wagons first followed them.

These first trails had a variety of uses and characteristics. As emigrant John Bidwell's party wandered across the deserts of the Great Basin, they "intersected an Indian trail, which we followed directly north towards the mountains, knowing that in these dry countries the Indian trails always lead to the nearest water."[7] These traces proved extremely helpful in creating a wagon road, but wagons required a fundamentally different track. "In some places we found an Indian trail and in other places not," Nineveh Ford recalled when he described how he and his companions pioneered the wagon road down the Snake River in 1843. "The Indians would take a straight course up and down where wagons could not go. We had to go around to get on to divides which we could travel from one place to another. We seldom followed the trail."[8]

Fur caravan carts and missionary wagons had left a trail in their wake, but it was not yet a true wagon road. Father Pierre-Jean De Smet reported in

---
[4] Spence and Jackson, *The Expeditions of John Charles Frémont*, 1:464.
[5] Lorton, Diary, July 31, 1849, Bancroft Library.
[6] Stuart, *On the Oregon Trail*, Oct. 21, 1812, 122.
[7] Bidwell, *A Journey to California*, Aug. 26, 1841.
[8] Ford, Recollections, Bancroft Library, 9.

1840, "we traveled over immense plains, destitute of trees or shrubs, except along the streams, and broken by deep ravines, where our voyageurs lowered and raised the carts by means of ropes," indicating that even the supposedly flat and level road up the Platte posed substantial challenges to the wheels of early travelers.[9]

The broad Santa Fe Trail had been "beaten out by the caravans," Frederick Wislizenus observed when he went west in 1839, but the nascent Oregon Trail was only "a narrow wagon road, established by former journeys to the Rocky Mountains, but often so indistinctly traced, that our leader at times lost it, and simply followed the general direction." According to Wislizenus, the road beyond Fort Laramie was no highway: "The road was growing daily more difficult. Steep ascents and deep clefts and ravines often made it necessary to lower the carts with ropes and pull them up again, or else make a wide circuit," he wrote. "We were visibly ascending."[10]

Almost fifty years after he crossed the trail in 1841, John Bidwell remembered that "William Subletts, an Indian fur trader" had taken wagons to the Rocky Mountains. He mistakenly believed the wagons Sublette had brought to the Popo Agie were the only ones that had made the trip. But Bidwell made a revealing remark about the fur-trade trace: "sometimes we came across the tracks, but generally they were obliterated, and thus were of no service."[11]

One of the hardest tasks in blazing the Oregon Trail was cutting a path. "We traveled about ten miles a day, much impeded by the thickets of sage and greasewood," Joseph Williams of the Bidwell-Bartleson party wrote on Blacks Fork.[12] "Breaking our road through sage brushes all the way," Samuel Hancock recalled, "was rather tedious and fatiguing to our animals."[13] "Had the sage been as stout and hard as other shrubbery of the same size, we should have been compelled to cut our wagonway through it, and could never have passed over it as we did, crushing it beneath the feet of our oxen and the wheels of our wagons," wrote Peter Burnett.[14]

Nineveh Ford gave a vivid description of what it was like in 1843 to cut a new trail through sagebrush, "which was very hard to get over. We could

---

[9] De Smet, *Life, Letters and Travels*, 201.
[10] Wislizenus, *A Journey to the Rocky Mountains*, 31, 72.
[11] Bidwell, in Nunis, *Bidwell-Bartleson Party*, 108.
[12] Williams, *Narrative of a Tour*, July 27, 1841, 31.
[13] Hancock, *The Narrative of Samuel Hancock*, 22.
[14] Burnett, *Recollections and Opinions*, 118.

FATHER PIERRE-JEAN DE SMET, S.J. A Belgian-born Jesuit priest who came to the United States in 1821, De Smet devoted his life to missionary work among the American Indians from Missouri to Montana. He may have been the most charming character in the history of the West, and his laughter, he said, made "people love the good Lord." *From* Western Missions and Missionaries: A Series of Letters, by Rev. P. J. de Smet *(1859)*.

not stop to chop it out. The wagons would bend it down but the ground was sandy and the wagons would sink deep into the sand and then rise high on the sage brush. The foremost wagons would mash it down." As Ford pointed out, it was especially hard on the draft animals. "It tired the foremost teams very much. We had to change the foremost teams back every day, and use the strongest teams and the strongest wagons to mash the sage brush down. We could do it however so that the next wagon could follow more easily." The trains often sent horseman ahead to scout the best route through the tangled undergrowth for wagons to follow. If they found any obstacle, such as a ravine or an impassable rock barrier blocking the way, "they would turn back and notify the train and turn them in [the] right direction where they should go."[15]

John C. Frémont reached the Sweetwater River west of Devils Gate from the south via Muddy Gap in 1843. He described "the road to Oregon; and the broad smooth highway, where the numerous heavy wagons of the emigrants had entirely beaten and crushed the artemisia"—the sagebrush. A year earlier, Frémont wrote that "the artemisia continue[d] in full glory" near the divide, but South Pass itself appears to have been relatively free of sagebrush in the early 1840s, at least compared with the parts of the Green River Valley covered with "sage brush as thick as the hair on a dog's back," as Richard Ackley said almost two decades later.[16]

---

[15] Ford, Recollections, Bancroft Library, 9–10.
[16] Spence and Jackson, *The Expeditions of John Charles Frémont*, Aug. 11, 1843, 1:253, 464; Ackley, "Across the Plains," Aug. 21, 1858, 206.

From its beginning, the road over South Pass was a work in progress. John Bidwell was twenty-one when he joined the first wagon train to ever set out for California in 1841. The man eventually hailed as the "Prince of California Pioneers" had supposedly come west "fearlessly treading unknown paths and blazing the wilderness for generations yet to be," yet he was actually a former schoolteacher whose land in Platte County, Missouri, had been "jumped" by a local bully. He decided to go west after hearing an old trapper—probably Antoine Robidoux—sing the praises of California's climate, fertility, healthfulness, and oranges. Bidwell was soon elected secretary of the small wagon train that assembled in spring 1841 at Sapling Grove, west of Independence, Missouri.

"Our ignorance of the route was complete," Bidwell admitted later. "We knew that California lay west, and that was the extent of our knowledge."[17] Fortunately, the small band of emigrants joined forces with Father Jean-Pierre De Smet, who had gone west the previous year and was now returning with a band of missionaries bound for the Bitterroot Valley in today's Montana. The missionaries had hired probably the best wagon train guide in the annals of overland emigration, Thomas "Broken-Hand" Fitzpatrick, one of the men who had rediscovered South Pass in 1824.

As Bidwell indicated, of all the men and women in the party, only the missionaries and their guide had the slightest notion of what lay ahead. Adapting the faint trace that constituted the trail west into a road fit for wagons was hard work. "We had to make the road, frequently digging down steep banks, filling gulches, removing stones, etc.," Bidwell wrote. "In such cases everybody would take a spade or do something to help make the road passable."[18] Nicholas Dawson recalled, "We had a great deal of work to do in digging down banks to cross ravines, and fuel becoming scarce we had to resort to buffalo chips."[19]

Father De Smet described how these true pioneers "directed our course more and more toward the heights of the Far West, ascending, sometimes clambering, until we reached the summit, from which we discovered another world"—what De Smet appropriately called "the immense Oregon Territory."[20] A definitive description of exactly which route the Bidwell-Bartleson train followed over South Pass would help us better understand how the

---

[17] Bidwell, "First Emigrant Train to California," 101–103.
[18] Ibid., 106.
[19] Nunis, The Bidwell-Bartleson Party, 148.
[20] De Smet, Life, Letters and Travels, 298.

Oregon Trail finally settled on the road to Pacific Springs, but it remains something of a puzzle. None of the contemporary records are very helpful: the diary of Joseph Williams, for example, jumps from July 16 to the day the company crossed the pass—two days later. He says simply, "Sunday. July 18th. We lodged on Little Sandy Creek, a beautiful stream."[21]

Bidwell's journal provides helpful details: "Left Sweet Water this morning, course sw. Crossed the divide which separates the water of the Atlantic and Pacific oceans, and after a travel of 20 miles reached Little Sandy, a branch of Green River—1 buffalo was killed."[22] This would seem to indicate the party took what became the main trail over the Continental Divide, but when he told the story almost fifty years later, Bidwell muddied the waters, remembering that they "crossed the Rockies at or near the South Pass, where the mountains were apparently low."[23]

Despite a disclaimer to the contrary, Father De Smet left the most dramatic report of the first emigrant train to cross the Continental Divide: "I will not presume to add to the many pompous descriptions which have been given of the spectacle now before us. I shall say nothing either of the height, the number or the variety of those peaks, covered with eternal snows, which rear their heads with menacing aspect to the heavens. Nor will I speak of the many streams descending from them and changing their course with unexpected suddenness; nor of the extreme rarification of the air with the consequent effect upon objects susceptible of contraction, at so great an elevation. All this is common; but to the glory of the Lord, I must commemorate the imperious necessity I experienced of tracing his holy name upon a rock, which towered preeminent amid the grandeur around."[24]

A THOROUGH FARE FOR NATIONS: JOHN C. FRÉMONT

Ironically, for thirty years after its discovery, no one was quite sure exactly where South Pass was located—or even whether the critical corridor lay within Mexico or the United States. Powerful Missouri senator Thomas Hart Benton, the frontier's leading advocate, hoped French scientist Joseph N. Nicollet, who had conducted the newly created U.S. Army Corps of

---
[21] Williams, *Narrative of a Tour*, July 18, 1841, 30.
[22] Bidwell, *A Journey to California*, July 18, 1841, 36.
[23] Bidwell, "First Emigrant Train," 108.
[24] De Smet, *Life, Letters and Travels*, 298–99.

COL. JOHN C. FRÉMONT
This 1856 image capitalized on the first Republican presidential candidate's international renown as an explorer. *Courtesy Library of Congress Prints and Photographs Division, LC-DIG-pga-03112.*

Topographical Engineers' first expeditions and had surveyed the upper Mississippi and Missouri rivers, would lead an expedition to South Pass. But as the Corps began to organize such a venture late in 1841, Nicollet's health rapidly declined and even his most ardent supporters doubted his ability to do the job. At a Christmas dinner at his Washington City mansion, Senator Benton told several powerful western politicians that Lt. John C. Frémont, one of Nicollet's protégés who happened to have recently become the senator's son-in-law, would lead the expedition.[25]

Col. John J. Abert received a letter from Benton early in 1842. "I think it would be well for you to name, in the instructions to Mr. Fremont, the great pass through the Rocky Mountains, called the South West Pass." Benton described it as "the gate through the Mountains" from the valley of the Missouri that would "be a thorough fare for nations to the end of time. In the mean time we only know it from the reports of hunters & traders, its lon. & lat. unknown, its distance & bearings from navigable water equally unknown." Such orders, the senator suggested, would define a worthy object:

[25] Chaffin, *Pathfinder: John Charles Frémont*, 96–97.

the exploration of the great Platte River, which Benton considered "the most striking and interesting point in the communication with the country on the Columbia river."[26]

So it was that a year after the first organized wagon train of American settlers left the Missouri River bound for the Pacific, Lieutenant Frémont of the Topographical Engineers headed west to conduct a scientific survey that would solve the critical mysteries of South Pass. At St. Louis he assembled a band of experienced frontiersmen "who were nearly all of French origin," Frémont reported, with the exception of his chief scout, Christopher "Kit" Carson.

Frémont's objective, Carson recalled, "was to survey the South pass and take the height of the highest peaks of the Rocky Mts." The army's first topographical survey of the Oregon Trail left the frontier on June 10, 1842. About a week later, into their camp rode a hunter who had met a party of emigrants bound for "the Columbia river, under the charge of Dr. White, an agent of the government in Oregon Territory." (Elijah White, one of the company's captains, had secured the odd title "Sub-Indian agent for Oregon," but Congress never confirmed his appointment.) The hunter estimated the emigrants were about three weeks ahead of Frémont's party. "They consisted of men, women, and children. There were sixty-four men and sixteen or seventeen families. They had a considerable number of cattle, and were transporting their household furniture in large, heavy wagons." As became his habit, the man later hailed as "Pathfinder" was following a wagon train.[27]

The emigrants, now under the leadership of Lansford W. Hastings, a young and ambitious Ohio attorney, had some of their most interesting adventures as they climbed the Sweetwater River to what Hastings later called "the well known great southern pass, through which companies of emigrants and others, are annually passing, from the United States to Oregon and California."[28]

Thomas Fitzpatrick was once again guiding this party of lucky but inexperienced emigrants. In July 1842 the White-Hastings train saw a sight that few later emigrants would see: thousands of Indians gathered in the Sweetwater Valley. The overlanders ran into a massive camp of Lakota and Cheyenne families. Some of their young men were part of "a war party of Sues & Shians who had been to fight the Snakes," their enemies' name for the Shoshones, who

---

[26] Benton to Abert, 1842, in Volpe, "Origins of the Fremont Expeditions," 254.
[27] Carson, *Kit Carson's Own Story*, 50–51; Spence and Jackson, *The Expeditions of John Charles Frémont*, 1:174, 175.
[28] Hastings, *The Emigrants' Guide*, 24.

camped with the emigrants near the Three Crossings. Medorem Crawford, the party's best chronicler, reported, "Mr. Fitch Patrick judged they were a village of Crows, Shians & Sues between 4 & 5000"—an unlikely mix and number. Two days after climbing "a long rocky hill"—Rocky Ridge—the emigrant party left the Sweetwater River at seven o'clock on July 28, 1842, Crawford recorded, and "crossed the dividing ridge. Camped at 10 o'clock on a little stream running westward," clearly Pacific Creek. Here they left a cart, keeping only a single wagon. "Snowy mountains constantly in sight," Crawford wrote.[29]

Eleven days later, Frémont and his men left their campsite on the Sweetwater River early on the cloudy morning of August 8, 1842. They rode over South Pass amid intermittent showers. "Our general course was west, as I had determined to cross the dividing ridge by a bridle path among the country more immediately at the foot of the mountains, and return by the wagon road, two and a half miles to the south of the point where the trail crosses." The rest of his narrative leaves little doubt that he followed emigrant wagon tracks along what became the main wagon road.

Frémont was "obliged to watch very closely to find the place at which we had reached the culminating point." The summit of the pass proved so elusive that he incorrectly placed the divide between the Twin Mounds, "two low hills, rising on either hand fifty or sixty feet," some two and a half miles east of the actual summit. He famously compared the climb to the pass to the ascent of Capitol Hill along Constitution Avenue in Washington, D.C.—an analogy later repeated in many overland narratives.[30]

The 1842 expedition produced much useful knowledge and the first scientific maps of the interior west. His charts of the wagon road to South Pass proved especially important. Unfortunately, Frémont lost much of his scientific equipment, which "consisted of a sextant, artificial horizon, &c., a barometer, spy-glass, and compass," before he reached the divide, and without a barometer he was unable to measure its altitude accurately. (His estimate of about 7,000 feet was not a bad guess.) The venture helped make the young lieutenant a national celebrity, but as historian Vernon L. Volpe observed, "Not surprisingly, perhaps, the public's acclamation for Fremont's exploits largely overshadowed the original scientific motivations for the initial 1842 project."[31]

---

[29] Crawford, "Journal," 12–13.
[30] Spence and Jackson, *The Expeditions of John Charles Frémont*, 1:253–54.
[31] Volpe, "Origins of the Fremont Expeditions," 254.

MYSTERIOUS MARKER AT SOUTH PASS
This image captures the vast sweep of the landscape at the most critical gateway on the wagon roads to Oregon and California. Historian Charles Kelly believed John C. Frémont's men built this monument to mark what the explorer believed was the summit of South Pass. The cairn, however, bears a suspicious resemblance to the rock piles that bored Wyoming shepherds had raised for years when Kelly took this picture in 1941. *Courtesy Utah State Historical Society.*

On his second expedition, in 1843, Frémont followed the emigrant road "at the southern extremity of the South Pass, which is near twenty miles in width." His men awoke on the clear and cold morning of August 13, 1843, to find white frost covering the grass, and the thermometer reading almost six degrees below freezing. This time when he reached "what might be considered the dividing ridge in this remarkable depression in the mountain," he was able to take a barometrical observation that put the elevation of the pass at 7,490 above sea level. He hailed the spot "as the great gate through which commerce and traveling may hereafter pass between the valley of the Mississippi and the north Pacific." It was 962 miles from the mouth of the Kansas River and 882 miles from the mouth of the Great Platte, and about 1,400 miles from the mouth of the Columbia, "so that under a general point of view, it may be assumed to be about half-way between the Mississippi and the Pacific ocean, on the common traveling route," or "the emigrant road to Oregon."[32]

John C. Frémont literally put South Pass on the map. Americans finally knew that South Pass lay within their nation's borders—and the young explorer gave it a name most of his fellow citizens would soon recognize. Between 1842 and 1847 Frémont's three topographical expeditions made him a national celebrity and won him worldwide fame. Two subsequent disastrous privately financed railroad explorations did little harm to his reputation. In 1856 he became the first Republican candidate for president of the United States. A campaign biography promoted him as the discoverer of South Pass and called him the "Pathfinder"—an accomplishment and title he never claimed for himself. Richard F. Burton praised "his eloquent descriptions of the magnificent scenery" and his admirable reports for doing as much as any other single influence to promote the settlement and transformation of the American West.[33]

A STERN REALITY TO FULFILL: THE OREGON TRAIL

When overland migration to the Pacific began in the 1840s, the United States divided its claim to the Oregon Country with Great Britain, based on the discoveries of James Cook and George Vancouver of the Royal Navy in 1778 and 1792 and American merchant seaman Robert Gray in 1791. The two nations shared sovereignty over the Pacific Northwest under a joint occupancy agreement negotiated in 1818, but neither nation had the resources to establish a government or appoint officials to manage the territory. Britain delegated that task to the Hudson's Bay Company, which for all practical purposes governed all the country west of the Rocky Mountains, south of Alaska, and north of Mexico's border on the forty-second parallel. Yankee sea captains and fur-trade speculators such as Nathaniel Wyeth occasionally traded in the territory, but except for a few itinerant fur hunters and missionaries, until 1840 there were no American settlers west of the Rockies to support their nation's territorial claim to Oregon.

As noted, the notion that by 1840 a great multitude of Americans were

[32] Spence and Jackson, *The Expeditions of John Charles Frémont*, 1:464–65.
[33] Burton, *City of the Saints*, 164.

lining up on the country's western border with a burning desire to go to the Oregon Country is an illusion. U.S. citizens could stake a claim to land in the Pacific Northwest, but they held no legal title, and despite considerable agitation, Congress did nothing to resolve the situation. The number of people who chose to bypass the vast amount of unsettled fertile land in the Midwest to gamble on an uncertain future in a distant territory on the Pacific initially was not large, but it grew from slightly more than one hundred in 1842 to eight or nine hundred in 1843 and almost fifteen hundred in 1844, to about four thousand in 1847. By the end of the decade, more than twelve thousand people had crossed South Pass on their way to Oregon.

"The road is good, much better than we expected," Jesse Looney wrote after reaching Oregon in 1843, "but is long."[34] When that year's "Great Migration" set out, the pattern of covered wagon life was already established. Wagon trains usually began as large operations with a complicated political organization and elected officers that quickly fractured and broke up into more manageable parties. Days began early, with the men catching and hitching up their teams while women cooked breakfast and generally enough food to provide for dinner, as most people called the midday meal. Trains got underway as early as possible and stopped in the heat of the day to "noon," which gave people and animals a welcome rest.

The company would then roll on until mid- or late afternoon, or whenever they found a campsite with wood, water, and grass. The train would circle or corral its wagons for the night. This was not so much for defense from hostile attacks—which seldom happened in the trail's first decades—as to provide a place to pen livestock during the night, protecting the animals, especially horses, from young Indian raiders and white desperadoes eager to steal them. Families usually camped in tents outside the corral or slept in or under the wagons. Men and boys tended the grazing livestock, children collected wood or "buffalo chips" to fuel cooking and campfires, and women continued the endless cycle of work that dominated their lives. Despite the exhausting routine, when the day's labor at last came to an end, many people would gather around campfires to talk or make music or even dance.

Western waters proved to be great trout streams, as overlander Benjamin S. Lippincott found in 1846. "Oh! the fishing, speckled trout & the

---

[34] Looney to Bond, Oct. 27, 1843, Oregon Hist. Society.

salmon trout were my daily prey—with a yankee rod & reel I astonished the Hoosiers," he wrote. Lippincott observed a singular fact, that "not a trout [is] to be taken in the streams east of the South pass, but in every brook in the west I caught trout."[35]

Hollywood later depicted wagon trains fighting their way through swarms of hostile Indians, but the first wagon companies had few violent encounters. More often the tribes offered invaluable help. "The Indians were at that time very friendly, and looked with wonderment upon the white settlers," recalled Alexander Blevins thirty-six years after he came to Oregon with the "Great Migration" of 1843. He told how the Zachary family's wagon sank while crossing the Kaw River in 1843, "immersing the whole family as well as their provisions and all in the water." The crowds of peaceable Indians on the shore "boldly plunged into the water to their rescue," he reported. A small boy, apparently six-year-old Alexander Zachary, Jr., floated off clinging to an ox yoke. "The river ran very rapid at this place and the little fellow perched on his frail raft hung on without a cry of fear. Several savages fleet of foot ran down the bank, and after getting a few rods ahead of the boy, went out and brought the young Moses ashore."[36]

For the first wagon trains, crossing the Great Divide had political as well as symbolic significance. As master overland journalist Alonzo Delano commented, "We were now in Oregon—the ridge of the Rocky Mountains being its eastern boundary—and fifteen hundred miles from our homes."[37] South Pass also marked the approximate midpoint of a journey to Oregon, the spot where emigrants like A. H. Garrison recognized "that we had passed over one side of the Continent, and were just at the edge of the other half. We realized that we were then in Oregon Territory."[38]

The perception that the first Americans to settle in Oregon and California were heroic yeomen and brave pioneers is not a complete illusion. Certainly, by any measure, the people who made up the first wagon trains to cross the West were a remarkable collection of men, women, and children, but their ranks included a sizeable contingent of scoundrels and ne'er-do-wells. Francis Parkman found many "very sober-looking countrymen" among the emigrants

---

[35] Lippincott to John L. Stephens, Feb. 6, 1847.
[36] Blevins, Reminiscence of 1843, 1879. Thanks to Stephanie Flora for young Zachary's name.
[37] Delano, *Life on the Plains*, 116.
[38] Garrison, Reminiscences, 20–21.

who thronged the streets of Independence in 1846, but he also met "some of the vilest outcasts in the country."[39]

Many American emigrants arrived in Oregon "destitute both of clothing, and even the necessaries of life, and are not in general what may be called enlightened Citizens, but in most cases, the scum and refuse of the back States," John Kennedy of the Hudson's Bay Company complained early in 1844. Near Fort Laramie, Edwin Bryant met a man returning from California who swore "there was not a man in the country, now that he had left it, who was not as thoroughly steeped in villany as the most hardened graduate of the penitentiary."[40] Those who pioneered America's transcontinental wagon road were often marginalized people infected with generations of wanderlust, and untold men went west to escape debt, the law, or their families. They were an impatient lot, observed William Ide, soon to be president of the short-lived Bear Flag Republic, and neglected the present "in consequence of great anticipations of the future—they long to see what the next elevation hides from their view."[41]

There are few universal truths about the settlement of the West, but one of them is that everyone who made the trek did so in hopes of finding a better life. A fortunate few found it—and those who came as children to settle this new country often did very well—but many remained as marginalized in Oregon or California as they had been in Kentucky or Missouri. Those who lived to great old age recalled their trip across the plains with justifiable pride, for they had changed the fate of the nation at great personal risk.

"It was men of the character and disposition to face such dangers accompanied by their heroic wives, mothers and sisters, who severed all connecting them with home and civilization and struck out boldly upon a trackless desert, known to be inhabited by howling wolves and merciless savages, surrounded by dangers, seen and unseen, who I undertake to say, were the chief event to save Oregon to the United States," David Arthur recalled forty-six years after he crossed the plains in 1843. "Hence, I was a pioneer from necessity and in fact, and have ever looked at it without romantic coloring, but as a stern reality to fulfill a duty or destiny."[42] Many of those who had been among the

---

[39] Parkman, *The California and Oregon Trail*, 15.
[40] Bryant, *What I Saw in California*, 114.
[41] Ide, "From Our Oregon Correspondent," June 25, 1845, in *Sangamo Journal*, Sept. 4, 1845.
[42] Arthur, "Across the Plains in 1843," 1889.

first to make the long and perilous journey found themselves no better off than they had been in the States and faced an impoverished old age, Arthur complained. But despite this, he did recall the past in heroic terms and with plenty of romantic coloring.

Destiny or not, American fur traders, missionaries, and pioneers transformed a network of Indian hunting and trading paths into a transcontinental highway in a single generation. When Col. Stephen W. Kearny led the first military expedition to South Pass in 1845, the road from the Missouri to South Pass "was as well marked as Pennsylvania Avenue."[43]

We'll Find the Place: The Mormon Trail

About eight thousand men, women, and children had crossed South Pass on their way to Oregon or California by 1847, and a new people with a closer destination joined the migration that year to swell the rising time of emigration to the West. Once again, as when missionaries began using the trail over South Pass during the waning days of the fur trade, religion played a major role in western history as the Church of Jesus Christ of Latter-day Saints—abbreviated as LDS and popularly called the Mormons, but known among themselves as "the Saints"—left its former headquarters in the Midwest to find a new home in the Great Basin.

After their charismatic prophet, Joseph Smith, founded the religion in upstate New York in 1830, Mormons had experienced bitter opposition and outright persecution in their settlements in Missouri and Illinois. The young prophet's murder in 1844 convinced their new leader, Brigham Young, that the Saints would never be able to live in peace with their American neighbors and resolved to seek a new home in Mexico. By the time the movement's advance guard left the faith's camps on the Missouri River in 1847, the United States was at war with Mexico, and Mormon leaders knew the Great Basin would soon become American territory. In what became the religion's most popular hymn, William Clayton expressed the hope his fellow Saints would find the refuge they called "Zion."

> We'll find the place which God for us prepared,
> Far away in the West,

---

[43] DeVoto, *The Year of Decision, 1846*, 22.

Where none shall come to hurt or make afraid;
There the Saints will be blessed.
We'll make the air with music ring,
Shout praises to our God and King;
Above the rest these words we'll tell—
All is well! all is well!

In April 1847 Brigham Young led "the Pioneer Camp of the Saints" west from Winter Quarters, the Mormon camp on the Missouri. As historian Richard E. Bennett noted, the trace that became the Mormon Trail was "a pathway laid at considerable sacrifice and breathtaking risk." Brigham Young was gambling that the Latter-day Saint religion could survive in a region where American farmers who had seen it thought agriculture would be impossible—Forty-niner George McKinley Murrell told his father he would not give one good acre in old Kentucky for all the land from the Sacramento River to within two hundred miles of the Missouri line. "The more a man would have of it the poorer he would be," he wrote.[44] Young knew that the very survival of his young religion depended on finding a safe and arable refuge in the Rocky Mountains.

After enduring the hard winter of 1846–47 in the log huts and dugouts at their Winter Quarters near today's Omaha, Brigham Young led the advance guard of the Mormons west along the north bank of the Platte River. The Pioneer Camp reached the Last Crossing of the Sweetwater in late June and enjoyed a rousing snowball fight.[45] The company camped that night on the banks of the Sweetwater near Twin Mounds, a quarter-mile north of the trail, "a good place to camp, there being plenty of grass and willows," William Clayton observed.

The party had sent Orson Pratt, their best scientist, "ahead with the barometer to try to find the culminating point or highest dividing ridge of the South Pass."[46] Pratt found it was a difficult task. "This country called the South Pass, for some 15 or 20 miles in length and breadth, is a gentley undulating plain or prairies, thickly covered with wild sage, from one to two feet high," he wrote. "On the highest part of this plain over which our road passes, separates the waters of the two oceans, is a small dry basin of 15 or 20 acres,

---

[44] Bennett, *We'll Find the Place*; Murrell to Dear Father, Sept. 17, 1849.
[45] Bullock, *Pioneer Camp of the Saints*, June 26, 1847.
[46] Clayton, *Intimate Chronicle*, June 26, 1847, 267.

destitute of wild sage but containing good grass." Two gentle ridges bordered the basin to the east and west, and either one could be "considered as the highest on our road in the Pass," Pratt concluded. He measured the western elevation and calculated it stood 7,085 feet above the sea. Pratt camped at Pacific Springs that night with fur-trade veteran Moses Harris and "obtained much information from him in relation to the great interior basin of the Salt Lake, the country of our destination."[47]

The Mormons crossed South Pass the next day with little fanfare. They were delighted with the Salt Lake Valley and the mountains that surrounded it—and relieved to learn that mountain man Miles Goodyear had raised corn north of the valley at the confluence of the Weber and Ogden rivers. More than two thousand Latter-day Saints followed the Pioneer Camp to Salt Lake that fall, and the hardship and sacrifices that were typical of such treks marked their passage. "Passed a number of graves [during] the last few days, mostly children," Peter Decker observed the day he crossed South Pass in 1849. "Graves along the road mostly of 1847 of Mormon Emigrants. Generally a board or stone at the head with either initials or names on."[48]

That fall Brigham Young returned to Winter Quarters, the Mormon refugee camp on the west bank of the Missouri River, to organize the evacuation of the rest of his followers to the Rocky Mountains. His party met the "Second Division" of the 1847 Mormon emigration on the Big Sandy on September 3. The next day they found apostle Parley P. Pratt and many Saints at the Little Sandy. On the seventh, Young's company crossed South Pass in a snow storm and camped with Apostle John Taylor, who staged a surprise feast of "Roast & boiled Beef, Veal (they had killed the fatted Calf to make merry), Pies, Cakes, Biscuits, Butter, Peaches, with coffee, Tea, Sugar, Cream & a variety of the good things of life."[49] After the returning pioneers met the last of the westbound Mormon companies on September 9, an Indian raiding party made off with fifty of their horses.[50]

The heroic pioneer epic of 1847 often overshadows the Mormon emigration of 1848, which was actually larger and arguably more difficult than that of

---

[47] Pratt, *Journal*, June 26, 1847. Using the odometer William Clayton designed, Pratt said, "the distance of this Pass from Fort Laramie, as measured by our mile machine, is 275½ miles."
[48] Decker, *The Diaries*, June 16, 1849, 98–99.
[49] Roberts, *Comprehensive History*, 3:295–97.
[50] Bullock, *The Pioneer Camp of the Saints*, 278–81.

1847. Brigham Young's 1848 company reached South Pass in late August and spent almost two weeks in the area reorganizing and dealing with illnesses and an epidemic that afflicted many of their oxen.

Few of the hard-pressed travelers had much to say about the landscape, but from the top of the divide between Rock Creek and Willow Creek in 1848, George Alley thought he could "see the land of five Nations": Missouri and Indian Territory to the east and southeast, Texas and Mexico to the south with Alta California to the west, and the mountains of Oregon on the north. "We are now at the South Pass," he wrote, "a Space of about 20 miles where the mountains are levelled down apparently, into smooth gentle swales & in some places for 4 or 5 miles nearly level, notwithstanding we are gaining up higher & higher, till we got to the sumit of the pass where we now are, but one would hardly think they were over 7000 feet above the level of the Sea. The mountains on the right hand & on the left rise in majestic grandeur with their white caps of Eternal Snow. The scenery in many places is verry grand. These mountains are rightly named the rocky mountains for they are indeed rock, or rocky, & nothing else in many instances."[51]

Over the next twenty years, almost seventy thousand Mormons crossed South Pass on the way to their new Zion. Their exodus encompassed some of the most inspiring and heartbreaking stories in the history of the American West. "The Mormons," as E. P. Whipple said in 1849, "have at last found a resting place."[52]

Altogether Most Impressive:
Travelers Admire the Scenery

"We have hitherto never had anything like a correct description of the country we have passed over," Forty-niner Samuel R. Smith complained after reaching California. In an age when people learned about the world around them largely through newspapers and books with very limited graphics, most Americans had no more idea about the landscape of the Far West than they did about what the surface of the moon might look like. "There are but few who do not know

---

[51] Alley to Geo. H. Alley, Aug. 24, 1848, Pacific Springs, 2–3. Thanks to the late Gail Robinson of Green River, Wyoming, for this letter.

[52] Whipple, "The Mormons in California," Feb. 16, 1849.

There are occasionally some narrow strips of bottom along the river which are covered with a luxuriant growth of grass and dense thickets of willows amongst which is seen the sweet wild rose in full bloom perfuming the air with its rich fragrance, and the ground thickly matted with the wild strawberry vine, whilst upon the cliffs at intervals were beautiful shady groves of the quaking asp in pleasant contrast with the otherwise barren country around. . . . We are now fairly in the South Pass, the Rocky Mountains in full view, their rugged peaks capped with glittering snow. . . . We are now within a few miles of the summit of the pass which we are all eager to see. . . . Two miles more brought us to the Pacific Springs whose waters flow to the Pacific Ocean, the fountain head of the great Colorado of the west. . . . Previous to reaching the springs, I climbed a mountain [Pacific Butte] of about two thousand feet elevation to the south of the road from which I had a magnificent view of the gigantic Rocky Mountains whose lofty and rugged peaks capped with eternal snow glittered in the rays of the sun and seemingly pierced the sky. Beneath my feet gushed the crystal waters augmenting in volume, pursuing their winding way westward towards the setting sun, receiving tribute from every little rill and brook until lost in distance.

CALVIN TAYLOR
"OVERLAND TO CALIFORNIA," 320–22

"TREADING UNKNOWN PATHS" 133

the route, so far as mere descriptions can convey an idea of it," the *Missouri Republican* noted. Even those who "had read much, and had heard much about it" had almost no idea of what to expect on the road west. So the first people to follow the trail over South Pass had little notion of what it looked like.

Few have suggested that a desire to see the landscape motivated many pioneers to head west, but Nineveh Ford said while reading the journals of the Lewis and Clark Expedition, "The scenery described in that took my fancy; and a desire to see that and to explore the country" inspired him to move to Oregon in 1843.[53]

Beginning with the very first wagon train to leave the frontier, emigrants commented on the Continental Divide's astonishing landscape. "This morning we came in sight of Wind River Mountains; their snow-enveloped summits were dimly seen through the misty clouds that obscured the western horizon," John Bidwell wrote on his way up the Sweetwater in 1841. The snow banks that easterners encountered on their way over South Pass and the glaciers that were visible on the slopes of the Wind River Mountains, plus the "view of many lofty peaks glittering with eternal snow and frost under the blaze of a July sun," amazed travelers. Almost fifty years later, Bidwell recalled the range "gleaming under its mantle of perpetual snow." It was the first time he had ever seen snow in summer. "Some of the peaks were very precipitous," he wrote, "and the view was altogether most impressive."[54]

After climbing Pacific Butte at sunset to take "a farewell look of the scenery towards the Atlantic," Edwin Bryant described the inspiring panorama. "The sun went down in splendor behind the horizon of the plain, which stretches its immeasurable and sterile surface to the west as far as the eye can reach. The Wind River Mountains lift their tower-shaped and hoary pinnacles to the north. To the east we can see only the tops of some of the highest mountain elevations. The scene is one of sublime and solemn solitude and desolation." He described the Oregon Buttes as "a spiral elevation, resembling a Gothic artificial structure." The next day, he gave a similarly eloquent account of the country west of South Pass: "Rising solitary from the face of the plain, are elevated buttes, of singular configuration," while the formations "far to the northwest, present castellated shapes. Others resemble vast structures,

---

[53] Smith, "From California," Sept. 2, 1849; Wilkins, *An Artist on the Overland Trail*, 3–17; Ford, Recollections, Bancroft Library.
[54] Bidwell, *A Journey to California*, July 8, 16, 1841; and Bidwell, "First Emigrant Train to California," 108.

surmounted by domes." Bryant found the bed of the Dry Sandy as dry as ashes, and at the Little Sandy, he "came in view of a plain of white sand or clay, stretching to the southeast a vast distance."[55]

Bidwell and Bryant considered the scenery inspiring, but the alien landscape and far horizons intimidated others—especially when the weather turned bad. Dark clouds frequently rolled over South Pass, recalled J. Quinn Thornton. "Every thing seemed to have undergone a change. There was a gloomy vastness in the distant prospect, and an awful solitude in the immediately surrounding scene; a sense of which, when associated with the conviction that we were about to drink of the waters that flowed into the great Pacific, made the day one of the most melancholy of my life." When the gloomy clouds parted, "far below we beheld scenery sublime and grand, that appeared to gleam up awfully through wild depths of azure. High, rugged, cold, blue mountains towered far up on either side, into a region where all save the voice of the storm is hushed, where all is cold and chill; and where the mountains wrap around them the drapery of the clouds, and cover their heads in mist." The scene made him realize "we had indeed ascended to the region of the clouds."[56]

For a few hardy souls like Charles T. Stanton, crossing South Pass fulfilled a lifelong dream. The day after passing the "culminating point" on July 18, 1846, Stanton wrote to his brother, "Thus the great day-dream of my youth and of my riper years is accomplished. I have seen the Rocky mountains—have crossed the Rubicon, and am now on the waters that flow to the Pacific! It seems as if I had left the old world behind, and that a new one is dawning upon me. In every step thus far there has been something new, something to attract."[57]

---

[55] Bryant, *What I Saw in California*, 134.
[56] Thornton, *Oregon and California in 1848*, 1:138.
[57] Stanton to Sidney Stanton, "South Pass," July 19, 1846, 615. After achieving his dream, Stanton would sacrifice his life in the Sierra Nevada trying to rescue his friends in the Donner party.

On the Big Sandy we were detained whilst Col. Landers was concluding a treaty with the southeastern band of Shoshonee Indians, which occupied about three days, during which time we were occupied by hunting, fishing, exploring, &c., as suited the tastes of the different individuals. Our encampment was made at the foot of Fremont's Peak, which is the highest mountain in the Rocky Range. Its melting snow and numerous springs form the head waters of Big Sandy. I could not refrain from making it a visit for many reasons, some of which was that we had been in sight of it for six or eight days' travel. Its top and much of its sides, especially that of the north, is covered with perpetual snow. In climbing to the top of this peak, I think one comes as near experiencing the effect of the four seasons in a few hours, as any place I know or ever read of. The scenery from the top of this peak is most lovely indeed. An attempt to describe [it] would and could only end in a miserable failure, unless a more experienced writer than myself should undertake the task. Nothing short of a visit can give any one a correct idea of the grandure [sic], sublimity and liveliness of the scene.

JOHN BOWLES
"CALIFORNIA—THE TRIP OVER THE PLAINS"
SEPTEMBER 9, 1859

THE VIEW AT SOUTH PASS
The Oregon Buttes, seen to the southeast from Pacific Butte. For overland emigrants, the Oregon Buttes marked their passage from an old world to a new world in the West. Visible for dozens of miles on the wagon road to South Pass, the formation seems to change shape continually. *Courtesy Lee Kreutzer, 2005.*

CHAPTER 6

"The Other Side of the World"
The Gold Rush
1849–1855

THE 1848 DISCOVERY OF GOLD IN CALIFORNIA BEGAN AN international frenzy that changed the nature of overland travel. The subsequent rush to "the new El Dorado" revolutionized every aspect of life in the American West. Before the great rush for riches ended, tens of thousands of gold seekers would cross South Pass in pursuit of their dreams of wealth. At first, the news seemed too good to be true, but the nugget James Marshall found in the foothills of the Sierra Nevada was only the first manifestation of the vast mineral wealth hidden in the foothills and mountains of California and Oregon and what became Nevada, Utah, Idaho, Arizona, Colorado, Montana, and Wyoming. "I pledge my honor to you as a brother, that I will tell you only what is true," Donner party survivor James F. Reed wrote home. "I have seen the gold; I have handled it; I have it now in my possession to the amount of thousands of dollars; and what is most cheering, the quantities appear to be inexhaustible."[1]

In the States the *New York Herald* reported the discovery in August 1848. That fall a flood of letters, military reports, and rumors tantalized the East Coast. "California has at last proved to be the long sought for 'El Dorado' of the Spanish adventurers," San Francisco resident William P. Reynolds wrote not long after Christmas 1848. "Gold is here in great abundance." Since the discovery of the first flakes on the South Fork of the American River in January, "there has been, at the least calculation, 7,000,000 dollars taken from the mines. Its Extent is all

---

[1] Reed to Dear Brother, Aug. 11, 1848, "From California. A Letter from James F. Reed," *Illinois Daily Journal*, June 29, 1849, 2.

of 1000 square miles, and new veins are being discovered every day each richer than the other," he guessed. Reports of the gold discovery soon emptied the white population of the Sandwich Islands—Hawaii—and thousands of men were pouring in from South America and Mexico. "There will no doubt be thousands from the Atlantic States, if they credit it, for it is certainly almost incredible, were it not for the gold to speak for itself," Reynolds concluded.[2]

Reynolds was more than right: the great rush to El Dorado would transform the overland trail and the entire American West. "From 1812 to 1848 travel up the Platte was only minimal to moderate," historian Merrill J. Mattes observed, "with a grand total of around 5,000 to Salt Lake, 10,000 to Oregon, and 2,000 to California." Between 1849 and 1852, about 120,000 people—mostly men—would flock to the gold fields over the California Trail, while some 35,000 more men, women, and children would cross South Pass on their way to Oregon or the Great Basin.[3]

From the beginning of the great rush, the sheer number of people and animals on the trail complicated overland travel. "The immense crowd that was on the road made the trip much more difficult and disagreeable than usual. If you tried to pass other trains, you were breaking down your team in doing so. If you laid by to recruit, hundreds of teams were passing daily, making it more difficult to procure grass. This gave occasion for much contention among men of the same party," wrote A. H. Houston from the gold fields. "The great mania of every one, as they got farther on the road, was to get through as fast as possible, at no matter what sacrifice."

Crowds overwhelmed even the most remote and desolate regions. "On all sides I see multitudes of people, wagons, cattle and horses at all times throng the way. The road, from morning till night, is crowded like Pearl Street or Broadway. In the evening, fires are seen in all directions, gleaming from a city of white tents," overland journalist Franklin Langworthy wrote at South Pass in 1850. It was a noisy assembly: "We hear on all sides the lowing of cattle, the neighing of horses, the braying of mules, and barking of dogs, mingled with the clack of human voices. To this is added the sound of the viol, bugle, tamborine and clarionette. To fill up the chorus, rifles and pistols are almost constantly cracking, responsive to the rumbling, grinding music of carriage-wheels still passing along."[4]

---

[2] Reynolds to John Reynolds, Dec. 27, 1848, Huntington Library.
[3] Mattes, *Platte River Road Narratives*, 2; Unruh, *Plains Across*, 119–20.
[4] Houston, "From California," Oct. 16, 1849; Langworthy, *Scenery*, June 19, 1850, 62.

"THE OTHER SIDE OF THE WORLD" 139

During the height of the gold rush migrations from 1849 to 1852, the campgrounds around South Pass were as crowded as today's Yellowstone Park on the Fourth of July. German goldseeker Hermann B. Scharmann recalled "the countless crowds of emigrants" on the road between Fort Laramie to the South Pass stripped the country of forage. He claimed he "found five thousand oxen and numerous mules and wagons, besides their human owners" camped at Pacific Springs in 1849. "The encampments on the plains are as one immance city as far as we can see," journal keeper David Carnes wrote west of Ice Spring in 1849, but general good order prevailed and he was "surprised that there is no more difficulties considering the multitude of emigration."[5]

"This morn we arrived at South Pass after which all water we see will be running to the Pacific," Lucy Rutledge Cooke wrote on her way from Iowa to California in 1852. "So we are now on the other side of the world." Almost everyone recognized the significance of crossing the Continental Divide, but gold-rushers found South Pass disorienting, disheartening, and cold. "Last night and this morning is as cold as it is in the States in December," diarist Thomas Christy wrote after reaching Pacific Springs in mid-June 1850. The road through the pass was still choked with snow—"Sometimes the road runs through it," he wrote. "Today has been unusually cold, so much so that at 3 PM it commenced raining and snowing, and continued for 2 hours. This goes hard on men that is not used to the like," Christy commented after crossing the pass in the rain. Guidebook author James Abbey found "the air as cold as in the depth of winter at home" as he approached the pass a day behind Christy, while "a violent wind blowing from the snowy mountains" made the atmosphere raw and uncomfortable. "A person wants lungs like a balloon," gasped twenty-one-year-old Forty-niner William B. Lorton.[6]

SOUTH PASS TRAILS, 1849–1855

"Throughout history the trail through the pass varied from one year to the next," historian Dale L. Morgan observed, "as the availability of grass and the absence of dust suited individual convenience."[7] The shallow drainage that the Oregon Trail followed west of the summit of South Pass was shaped like

---

[5] Scharmann, *Overland Journey*, 24–25; Carnes, Journal, July 1, 1849, 44.
[6] Cooke, "Letters on the Way," 251; Christy, *Road across the Plains*, June 14, 1850, 42; Abbey, *California*, June 15, 1850, 32–33; Lorton, Diary, July 27, 1849, Bancroft Library.
[7] Morgan, *Jedediah Smith*, 388n25.

an hourglass, narrowing to a choke point a little more than one-quarter mile west of the divide. The host of wagons that arrived with the California gold rush created a need for an alternate road that avoided the traffic jams that occurred at the peak of the emigration season. The resulting detour might be called "South South Pass," a passage that left the historic trails not far from where they intersect with the modern gravel road. This alternate crossed the Continental Divide about a quarter-mile south of the old road through the pass and returned to the main trail about a mile and one-half after leaving it.

Irish adventurer William Kelly, one of the first Forty-niners to cross South Pass, noted the continuing influence of the area's Indian trails: "We had the horse-tracks and lodge-pole trails still ahead of us on our path, making, no doubt, for the pass too."[8] The massive migrations of the gold rush meant the trails to and over South Pass developed new alternates and ways to get around obstacles such as Rocky Ridge and the narrows at the actual summit of the pass. "Several roads can be made through here," William Lorton commented, an indication that the road evolved constantly.[9]

Mormon John D. Lee spent two weeks at South Pass in 1848. After burying his mother-in-law at the ninth crossing of the Sweetwater, he "Took the River Road & reached the Pacific spring," he wrote, indicating there was already a network of wagon roads around the pass. A year later, Lee left the Salt Lake Valley "on a Picking up Expedition" with one of his wives, five yoke of oxen, and a pair of horses. Back on the Sweetwater on August 1, he found "the Road was lined with waggons from the Vally to this Point [so] that one would scarecly ever be out of Sight of Some Train." Mormon packers had told him they had seen feed in abundance when going out that spring, but now the country was "a dreary waste, having been Measureably burned off. Wood or Timber shared the Same fate," he reported. "Every Camp Ground presented one continual Scene of distruction." The massive influx of oxen, loose cattle, horses, and mules, plus the passage of thousands of wagons, carts, and carriages, had expanded the region's already complicated road system. He found the trails confusing, since the Forty-niners had made a desperate search for grass. "I will here mention the Traveler would not be at a loss to find Roads & yet be puzzled to keep the main one," Lee wrote. "For out of necessity, every creek, River or Vally for (10 ms.) at lest from the Road was penetrated in search of feed."[10]

---

[8] Kelly, *An Excursion to California*, 190.
[9] Lorton, Diary, July 25, 1849, Bancroft Library.
[10] Lee, *A Mormon Chronicle*, 75, 111, 113.

"For 100 miles or more our road follows the meanderings of this river of the desert. A high and lofty range of mountains border the north side of this stream; to the left of the road lies the outstretched desert as bare of vegetation as the mountain rock to our right," wrote master diarist John Hawkins Clark as he contemplated the road up the Sweetwater in 1852. He meant the trail was bare of *useful* plants—like grass: "the whole country is covered with the everlasting sage except the narrow strip of verdure bordering the Sweetwater. The road is dusty and we every now and then pass pools of alkali which make it very interesting to those who have loose cattle to drive." His campsite that night had poor grass, indifferent water, and no wood, but there were plenty of hungry teams, while "many graves line the road we have traveled to-day."[11]

The waybill of Platt and Slater in 1852 described Pacific Creek as "a small stream but a little miry." This influential and reliable guidebook also mentioned a new development: "Persons traveling to Salt Lake will find a new route turning to the left here, and following down the Pacific Creek to its entrance into Green river. This is some farther, but has more grass and water than the other road towards Salt Lake," they advised.[12]

The classic trail left Pacific Creek a few miles beyond the pass and headed west-northwest at Hay Meadow, tempting ambitious emigrants to simply follow Pacific Creek to the Southwest. "At this point the trail turns off to Salt Lake, and we took it, glad to escape the monstrous throng in which we have been moving for two weeks past," wrote diarist and future jurist Addison Moses Crane. He knew there was another, older trail that headed for Salt Lake at the Parting of the Ways—where emigrants had to decide whether to go southwest toward Fort Bridger on the main road or take the Sublette Cutoff to save time—but the new trail down Pacific Creek "was thought to be the best. It goes down the valley of Pacific Creek to its entrance into Green River—we found comparatively few emigrants on this route—but enough for protection." The next day, "the trail down pacific creek was quite indistinctly marked & full of roots—hence we concluded to wheel back—about a mile on to the regular California & Oregon trail, until we came to the regularly traveled Mormon trail." Crane celebrated completing the trek to Green River "by shaving—washing all over with warm water and soap, and finishing with clean shirt and socks."[13]

---

[11] Clark, "Overland to the Gold Fields," 263.
[12] Platt and Slater, *The Travelers' Guide*, 15.
[13] Crane, in Herbert, *Overland Trail*, 185–87.

Mormon journals allow us to track the development of this important alternate trail west of South Pass, which opened late in the summer of 1851. After camping for two days at Pacific Creek, Mormon overland captain Preston Thomas "took a new road leaving the old road to the right & going down Pacific creek & after traveling some 16 miles camped where we had very poor grass." The next day his train negotiated "a heavy sandy road through a bottom." Thomas repeated his complaint: "after traveling some 16 miles we camped on big Sandy where we had very poor grass." Judge Elias Smith, who later won fame as "Pious Elias" among the non-Mormons of Utah, and British convert Jean Rio Griffiths Baker (who was hauling a piano across the plains) accompanied Thomas. "The country we travelled to day was very barren," Smith complained. "Came down the Pacific creek about sixteen miles and turned off the road to camp a mile or more." At Pacific Creek, Baker found "the wolves very troublesome all night with their howling, which was accompanied by the barking of all the dogs in camp."[14]

"The road we now travel is a new road—following down Pacific Creek to near its junction with Green river," Jotham Newton, a reformed whaler on his way to California, wrote early in July 1853. "About 7 miles brought us to an Alkali Marsh & springs. The water has the appearance of being very strongly impregnated with Alkali." Newton provided one of the most detailed reports of the route, but his account hardly makes it sound attractive. "In about 9 miles more crossed Pacific Creek—4 miles and we come to it again, and here we camped. The water of this creek is very bad water, but it is the best that can be obtained. Grass very thin, but nutritious what there is of it—no wood."[15]

The "deceitful meadow" was a "morass of twenty acres, vividly green and with a sluggish stream running through it" when diarist Thaddeus Kenderdine nooned at Pacific Spring in 1858. His party was able to drag its floundering livestock out of the swamp, but the many carcasses polluting the bog made the water unfit to drink. They left in the afternoon and followed Pacific Creek, camping near another swamp. "About midnight the hungry cattle got into this, and we worked an hour or more in the cold water and mud getting them out. Some we were obliged to leave there to die."[16]

---

[14] Thomas, Journal, Sept. 9–12, 1851; Smith, Journal, Sept. 11, 1851; Baker, "By Windjammer and Prairie Schooner," Sept. 11, 1851.
[15] Newton, Trip to California, July 2, 1853.
[16] Kenderdine, *A California Tramp*, 86–87.

To Cross the Devil's Backbone: Seminoe's Fort and Cutoff

All through the summer of 1852, overland travelers saw a new trading station take shape west of Devils Gate. "We passed here a trading post, they kept quite an assortment of goods, which were all brought from St. Louis; they had enormous waggons, serving as a kind of shop, & store house," Lodisa Frizzell wrote in her journal. They had eight tons of freight brought from St. Louis and their teams thrived on the excellent pastures. "Some of them were fat, for here the grass was excellent; they offered them for sale, one of our company bought 3 yoke, for from 45 to 60 dollars per yoke," Frizzell said. "This is a romantic place, & a good place for a post, for there is [an] abundance of grass, & water; & some considerable pine & cedar timber on the mountains."[17]

Early in July, diarist William H. Hart "reached a trading shanty of brush wood and canvass belonging to a French man who had established himself here to buy furs of the Indians, and weakly and sickly stock of the emigrants and to sell provisions to those who needed. He had located himself a little to the west of the Gate and appeared to be doing a good business. He kept an indian herding his cattle on a little pasture that he had discovered a few miles off and recruited a great many broken down valuable oxen and cows."

The trader told Hart about a campsite four miles south of the road where the train would celebrate the Fourth of July, starting with a "'few de joie' of double barrelled guns rifles + pistols." Soon the Stars and Stripes "taken from sundry garments supposed to form parts of female wearing apparel" floated in the breeze. The women prepared and the men ate a feast. The party "all joined in a grand game of ball (the ball was found amoung the childrens play things) and at sunset a national salute of 100 guns (more or less) ended our fourth of July and as pleasant a one as ever I spent," Hart wrote. It truly was "a Fourth of July on the plains never to be forgotten."[18]

Within a month, Oregon-bound Chloe Terry "passed a house where a trader lived. He had everything to sell that emigrants want—two ladies here."[19] Next June, the Dinwiddie brothers found a full-fledged trading post under construction: "a very fine hewed log house built in a square [with] three sides being built," apparently with a sod roof. The fort was about 120 feet long, and

---
[17] Frizzell, *Across the Plains to California*, June 21, 1852, 27–28.
[18] Hart, Diaries, July 2–4, 1852, 101–10; Conyers, "Diary," July 2–4, 1852.
[19] Terry, Diary, Aug. 4, 1852, typescript, punctuation added.

as one brother noted, "quite a number of French about here."[20] By late summer, James Farmer described "about 10 houses all neatly built of wood" at the outpost.[21] A year later, nineteen-year-old Mary Burrell of Plainfield, Illinois called the fort "quite an establishment. Hewed logs & shingled with mud."[22]

This outpost, now known as Fort Seminoe, was named after its main proprietor, whose name was variously spelled Cimineau, Seminoe, Simmeno, Semineau, Semenole, Seminole, Siminoes, and Sendriose. "Seminoe" was actually Charles Lajeunesse, "*dit* [called] Simond (Simino)." His nickname perhaps came from his younger brother, Basil Cimineau Lajeunesse, the skilled partisan who Frémont called "my favorite man." (Klamath River Indians buried a hatchet in Basil's skull after the Pathfinder failed to post a guard one night in May 1846.)[23]

The Lajeunesses were prominent fur traders, and Charles had long experience in the business. He was working on the upper Missouri in 1823, already a polished linguist and interpreter. By 1830 Lajeunesse was a *voyageur* at the American Fur Company post among the Yanktonais. He acquired the nickname "Bad Hand" in a tussle with a bear in 1833, during which he rammed his arm down the bruin's throat while Emanuel Martin of Andrew Drips's party dispatched the beast. Lajeunesse left the mountains that fall with Etienne Provost. He returned next summer with William Sublette, for whom he acted as an interpreter with the Pawnees. William Marshall Anderson met him in August 1834 looking for Cheyennes and Lakotas to send to the newly established Fort William on the Laramie River. Lajeunesse apparently spent the last days of the Rocky Mountain fur trade working for the Upper Missouri Outfit.[24]

Lajeunesse began his long association with the Oregon Trail as early as 1843, when he traveled on the Sweetwater River with Joseph Chiles's California-bound wagon train. Diarist John Boardman reported that he "started hunting with Seminoe," apparently at Muddy Gap between Devils Gate and Rocky Ridge, "without coat or blanket." The two men killed two buffalo cows in poor condition and spent a cold August night camped on a creek.[25]

---

[20] Dinwiddie, "Overland from Indiana to Oregon," June 23, 1853, 8.
[21] Farmer, Journal, Sept. 4, 1853.
[22] Burrell, "Council Bluffs to California," 238.
[23] Rea, *Devil's Gate: Owning the Land, Owning the Story*, 67–68.
[24] Anderson, *The Rocky Mountain Journals*, 334; and family data in author's possession.
[25] Boardman, "The Journal," Aug. 3, 1843, 105.

He next appeared in Edward Smith's long-overlooked 1848 trail journal not long after Smith reported Joseph Chiles's arrival at Fort Laramie, where an encounter apparently took place between Lajeunesse and a member of a Brulé band camped near the fort. "To day occurred a singular trait in the Indian character. A young Indian had stolen a horse from one of the emigrants by the name of Simmeno. As soon as his brother found that he was the only Indian that was gone from the band he went with an interpreter to Mr Simmeno and spoke to him as follows: 'My brother has made me ashamed by stealing your horse but I will not make you ashamed. There is the best horse I have got. Take that for the one that was stolen.'"[26]

At the North Platte's last crossing, Smith and "Simmeno Layanesse (in English Chas Young) went to examine the ford. Found the water too deep. We crossed over about 1/3 [of our] wagons & quit for the day." The train got the rest of its wagons across the next morning. Smith at first identified Lajeunesse as an emigrant, but at Devils Gate he noted, "we came to another wagon which had been abandoned and Simmeno Lan[j]anesse a trader from Bridgers Fort took it to put in a part of his load of goods." Smith last mentioned Seminoe on July 18, 1848, when Chiles's train "crossed the divide between the Atlantic & Pacific and encamped at the Green Springs," noting that here "Chas. Young lost an ox."[27] It seems likely that Lajeunesse left the company at the Parting of the Ways and headed for Fort Bridger.

Emigrants met other traders at the new post besides Lajeunesse, including Hubert Papin, Moses and Charley Perat, and most notably, Seminoe's partner Auguste Archambault. In 1852, a French trader who "was with Colonel Fremont during his notable trip through this country" told Enoch Conyer how to cure an "alkalied" ox. Conyer said this "Schambau" was "building a trading post near the Devil's Gate with timber hauled from the mountains about six miles distant."[28] On April 28, 1852, the *St. Joseph Gazette* called the new post Archambault's Fort. Archambault had been in the fur trade since at least 1831 and perhaps for a decade longer. He worked for the Rocky Mountain Fur Company in 1837 and for Sir William Drummond Stewart in 1843. Frémont hired him as a hunter at Browns Hole in spring 1844. He joined the Pathfinder's third expedition in 1845 and returned from California to

---

[26] Smith, Journal of Scenes and Incidents, 129.
[27] Ibid., 131–33.
[28] Conyers, "Diary," July 2, 1852; Unruh, *Plains Across*, 487n62.

Missouri carrying dispatches with Kit Carson. Beginning in 1849, he served as the chief guide for the Stansbury Expedition to the Great Salt Lake. At the mission's conclusion in November 1850, Lt. John Gunnison left his horse at Archambault's farm at St. Ferdinand, Missouri.[29] He moved his operations to the Green River in 1856, the same year he reported a Cheyenne war party had killed Almon W. Babbitt, secretary of Utah Territory, at Fort Kearny. Archambault collected Babbitt's papers, which "were scattered about the prairie near the spot," including "treasury drafts and valuable notes."[30]

The twenty-eight-mile Seminoe Cutoff left the main trail at Warm Springs Creek, about six miles west of Ice Spring and some three miles southeast of today's Sweetwater Station. (The village now on Highway 287 should not be confused with the Civil War army post near Independence Rock, also known as Sweetwater or Lower Sweetwater Station.) The trace headed southwest to the Warm Springs, "one of the many alkaline pans which lie scattered over the face of the country," as Richard Burton commented. "From the road nothing is to be seen but a deep cunette full of percolated water."[31] Seminoe's route crossed the Antelope Hills, passed Wagon Tire Spring and Upper Mormon Spring, and touched the Sweetwater not far from its confluence with Rock Creek. It then skirted Oregon Slough and finally reunited with the main trail not far beyond the Ninth Crossing, about eight miles east of South Pass. Antelope Springs was some fourteen miles west of the Warm Springs mail station and perhaps a mile south of Cow Camp Spring: it might have been called Immigrant Spring. Variant trails connected the cutoff with to the main trail along the Sweetwater at both the Fifth and Ninth Crossings.[32]

"I can highly recommend Sendriose cut off, which is the left hand road, about 6 miles this side of Ice Springs," wrote Edward Stevenson, a Mormon missionary who left the best description of Seminoe's road. "As it may be beneficial hereafter, I will give the watering places; first about one mile, a sulphur creek and some grass, but not a desirable place to camp. Five miles to small stream, and tolerable good grass; then 6 miles to a spring and some grass right of road; 12 miles to Sweetwater, good feed, water, and fuel; about 8 miles to Old Road; 10 miles from South Pass." The road was "somewhat hilly, but much better than to cross the Devil's Backbone [Rocky Ridge] of the

---

[29] Madsen, *Exploring the Great Salt Lake*, 10n15.
[30] "The Indian Outrages—Confirmation of the Death of Col. Babbitt," *New-York Daily Times*, Nov. 7, 1856.
[31] Burton, *City of the Saints*, 158, 174–75.
[32] These springs are on the USGS South Pass 1:100,000 quadrangle.

Rock mountains." During the drought year of 1855, "Strawberry creek and other streams are dried up, and no water for 25 miles," Stevenson reported.[33]

Who found or first used what became known as the Seminoe Cutoff is unclear. Unlike the main trail, this alternate ran south of the Oregon-California-Mormon Trail, avoided four crossings of the Sweetwater (a big advantage during the highwater of the "June rise"), and the hard trek over Rocky Ridge. Like most cutoffs, the new trail was longer than the old. Its biggest disadvantage was lack of water, "but there were a few springs and small creeks along the way that could accommodate wagon trains of moderate size." Hard-driving freighters, military units, many Mormon emigrant and eastbound missionary companies, and Californians in a hurry favored the trail. By historian Melvin L. Bashore's preliminary and conservative count, more than five thousand Latter-day Saints used the route between 1854 and 1868, while thirty-eight Mormon companies traveled on the cutoff in eleven different years.[34]

Joseph Stratton and the legendary Mormon frontier scout Ephraim Hanks, sent from Salt Lake in 1850 "to search out new routes and where to obtain the best feed for cattle," may have made at least one unsuccessful cutoff during their mission "to look out camping places & feed" for Mormon emigrants. That year Mormon mountain man Barney Ward led a party over another shortcut that Mormon overlander Sophia Goodridge called "a new route to the pass made by Captain [Milo] Andrus," but Apostle Wilford Woodruff said he "travled 14 miles the whole Distance of Strattons new cut off or road" and found it "was 3 miles further & 5 miles worse without watering or feeding our oxen on the road." He concluded the new trail "ought not to be travled" in the future.[35] It wasn't.

The Seminoe Cutoff seems to have been used as early as 1852, when it was mentioned in a lost trail guide by one Walker—at least the Rev. George F. Whitworth noted in July 1853 that the road was "pretty accurately described by Walker, except as to the track to avoid rocky ridges. Too indefinite and not little used [so] we missed it."[36] The first Mormons to use the trail were nine missionaries and church leaders who left Salt Lake on March 27, 1854. The company included Brigham Young's cousin and Mormon apostle Franklin D.

---

[33] *Deseret News*, Sept. 5, 1855, 208.
[34] Bashore, "Avoiding Rocky Ridge: Mormons on the Seminoe Cutoff," 2–3.
[35] Woodruff, Journal, Aug. 24, 1850; and Goodridge, Journal, Aug, 24, 1850; and Minerva Stone to Dear Parents, Sweet Water River, September 11, 1850, all at LDS Archives.
[36] Whitworth, Diary, July 21, 1853, Whitworth College Archives.

Richards and Young's son-in-law, Edmund Ellsworth, both missionaries bound for England. (Two years later Ellsworth would return and lead the first handcart company to Utah via the cutoff.) This missionary band called the trail the Seminoe Cutoff, so Lajeunesse himself could have discovered it or followed an existing trail during his years in the fur trade. Some Mormons called it Hanks Cutoff—so Ephraim Hanks might have discovered the route on his 1850 scouting trip.

On his way back east to lobby Congress, Apostle George A. Smith camped near an alkali pond on the cutoff on May 3, 1856. During the night, "a dreadful storm commenced from the northeast and continued to increase until morning; the men turned out of their beds and tied blankets upon the animals, and thus preserved them from perishing." The party sought refuge in patch of willows on the Sweetwater and waited while the "storm continued with unabated fury for fifty-six hours." When the sun came out for a few hours after the storm broke, it left the entire party sunburned, while Apostle Orson Pratt and noted Mormon triggerite Orrin Porter Rockwell "were struck blind, and suffered the most excruciating torture for several days."[37]

Former dragoon Percival G. Lowe used "Semino's Cutoff" both going to and coming back from Utah with a mule train in 1858. William A. Carter, who later built a ranching and trading empire around Fort Bridger, made one of the last known references to the post when he "halted awhile at the Trading Post kept by Bisnett and Semino, in hope of getting some fresh beef" in late 1857, "but after waiting some time were disappointed."[38]

The Martin handcart company and the last of the church freight trains on the trail took refuge in the decaying outpost in 1856. "All the people who could, crowded into the houses of the fort out of the cold and storm," Mormon frontiersman Dan W. Jones recalled. "One crowd cut away the walls of the house they were in for fuel, until half of the roof fell in; fortunately they were all on the protected side and no one was hurt." Mormon trains stored their freight at the fort and left nineteen men with twenty days' provisions under Jones to guard the property. He "told them in plain words that if there was a man in camp who could not help eat the last poor animal left with us, hides and all, suffer all manner of privations, [and] almost starve to death" he should overtake the trains going to Salt Lake. "No one wanted to go," Jones

---

[37] Smith, "Captain A. O. Smoot's Company," *Deseret News*, June 11, 1856, 106.
[38] Lowe, *Five Years a Dragoon*, 255, 268; Carter, "Diary," Nov. 1, 1857, 100.

said. "All voted to take their chances." The men came close to eating their packsaddles but managed to hang on until relief arrived in the springtime.[39]

The next year, Mormons tried to revive the outpost as a station for the Brigham Young Express & Carrying Company, but they chose to destroy the fort when the U.S. Army marched to Utah. The location proved too attractive to remain empty for long and was soon reoccupied. Richard Burton stopped at the "muddy station kept by M. Planté, the usual Canadian," about five and a half miles west of Seminoe's fort.[40] A year later emigrant Bartlett Tripp mentioned "Merchants Ranche" at the west end of Devils Gate.[41] Merchant apparently had a partner named Wheeler, for at the end of May 1862 Dr. Harvey C. Hullinger camped immediately west of the gate, "a few rods below Wheeler's and Merchant's station." Militia officer Robert Burton named both "Plaunt's Fort" and Merchant's operation on his way east, but he found "Mr. Merchant's Station at Devil's Gate had been burned to the ground, supposed[ly] by Denver emigrants" in May 1862.[42]

Charles Lajeunesse served as a guide and messenger for the 1857 Utah Expedition. Several army units used the Seminoe Cutoff, and sutler William A. Carter recorded meeting "Semino the express man sent by Col. Cook from Independence Rock" to Blacks Fork.[43] When the expedition's new commander, Col. Albert Sidney Johnston, reached the main force at Hams Fork in mid-November, he sent orders to Lt. Col. William Hoffman at Fort Laramie to deliver thirty mule loads of salt to Fort Bridger as soon as possible via "the route up the Laramie River" popularly known as the Bridger Pass or Cherokee Trail. "As soon as Col. Cooke arrives, Janise, or some other reliable person, will be sent over that route to report to you the probabilities of success."[44]

Charles Lajeunesse ran his trading station for about four years before mysteriously abandoning it, reportedly due to conflicts with the Lakota, and he became hard to track after his service in the Utah War. According to family traditions, his Shoshone wife died of smallpox at Fort Seminoe. He subsequently wed a Cheyenne woman named Mi-Coo-Sah but called Lucy,

---

[39] This story is told in Jones's memoir, *Forty Years Among the Indians*, 73–74; and in Wallace Stegner's *The Gathering of Zion*, 260–74.
[40] Burton, *City of the Saints*, 151.
[41] Tripp, Journal, July 24, 1861, LDS Archives.
[42] Fisher, *Utah and the Civil War*, 50, 123, 127.
[43] Carter, "Diary," Nov. 16, 1857, 108.
[44] Hafen, *The Utah Expedition*, 165. Hafen identified "Jeanise" as Antoine Janise (variously spelled), but William A. Carter used the name Semino.

who gave birth to Lucy, Jules, and John between 1853 and 1859. Like Lajeunesse's previous children, they were raised as Shoshones. She is said to have died at Fort Laramie in 1867. Arapahos allegedly rubbed out Seminoe and a Frenchman known as Big Joe on Clarks Fork of the Yellowstone early in 1865. The two were collecting "some cattle and wagons they had purchased from emigrants who had abandoned them." They had camped with the Arapahos and fed them supper and breakfast. "While Seminoe and Joe were out yoking up their cattle, they brutally shot them down; at least this was the story the Indians told." Others claim Lakota warriors killed Lajeunesse on Powder Creek, scattering his freight train's tobacco, salt, guns, and ammunition and, to get the sacks, dumping the flour on the ground.[45]

Lajeunesse, his outpost, and his cutoff nearly disappeared from historical memory until the Church of Jesus Christ of Latter-day Saints purchased the Sun Ranch and authorized the Wyoming State Archaeologist's Office and the Department of Anthropology at the University of Wyoming to conduct an archeological investigation in 2001 to determine the site of the trading station. "It's really an unknown part of Wyoming's history," Assistant State Archaeologist Danny Walker told a reporter. Seminoe "was there for four years, and when you think about, a trading post in existence for four years back in the 1850s, 100 feet from the Oregon, Mormon and California trails—he made a profit, to put it mildly, I think."[46] Utah historian Lyndia Carter "spearheaded the search for the fort site." The project was particularly exciting, Walker said, because "it's been a totally undisturbed site, its exact whereabouts unknown for almost 100 years. Except for a handful of pioneer accounts, there was very little known about the fort."[47]

The investigation revealed the distinctive architectural style used to construct the trading post's nine buildings "consisted of vertical posts placed a minimum of two to three feet into the ground, flat foundation rocks placed between the posts and then logs cribbed up to form the walls, with nails holding the logs to the posts." Five of the cabins seem to have been built using this technique. "Foundations of the remaining four cabins were not as obvious in the archaeological record. During the early 1860s (probably 1863, according to some emigrant diaries), another cabin was built within the limits of one of

---

[45] Bryant, "Seminoe vs. Seminole," 237–38; Franzwa, "Reconstruction of Seminoe's Fort," 1–2.
[46] "Mormon Trail Landmark Unearthed," Associated Press, July 3, 2001.
[47] Barbara Jones, "Digging Up History at Cove," *Deseret News*, July 24, 2001.

"THE OTHER SIDE OF THE WORLD" 151

Seminoe's cabins, using foundation rocks from these four earlier cabins, an adaptive reuse of construction materials." The survey identified a blacksmith shop, storerooms, and living quarters.[48]

Artifacts recovered included hundreds of trading beads, and "more than 150 varieties of buttons, and pennies and dimes dating to the 1840s bear out that the fort was a trading post frequented by both pioneers and American Indians. A copper powder flask embossed with an English hunting scene and broken pieces of fine china and crystal could be remnants of other items sold at the fort or belongings left by European immigrants." The charcoal that blanketed the site and melted window and bottle glass provided evidence that the fort was burned.[49]

The LDS Church decided to rebuild the outpost near its original location as part of its Handcart Ranch operation at Devils Gate. "After a lapse of 146 years, Seminoe's Fort is once again up and running," historian Gregory Franzwa reported in August 2003. As local historian Levida Hileman said, "the reconstruction is first rate." The project showed the value of the archeological resources distributed throughout the Sweetwater Valley and South Pass region. "There is reason to believe that it looks just as it did when the handcart pioneers of 1856 struggled into its protection," Franzwa concluded.

Charles "Seminoe" Lajeunesse is no longer forgotten.

Hail Columbia: Celebrating South Pass

Confusion reigned throughout the trails era about the exact location of the summit of South Pass, but virtually everyone who left a record considered crossing the Continental Divide an event worth noting. Emigrants found a variety of ways to celebrate reaching South Pass, and those who had flags proudly displayed Old Glory.

Traveling at the forefront of the emigration, Forty-niner Peter Decker's company devoured a well preserved and "beautifully sugar ornamented Pound Cake," the best he ever ate. "I got out the 'Star Spangle banner' & planted it on the South Pass, a breeze waved it, our folks met around it & passed a cheerful evening, fiddling, singing, & dancing on a sheet of zink," Decker wrote that night. "Stan played Hail Columbia while going over the south pass," noted 1852

---

[48] Franzwa, "Reconstruction of Seminoe's Fort," 1–2.
[49] Jones, "Digging Up History," *Deseret News*, July 24, 2001.

overlanders Nancy Jane and Henry Bradley. The American flag flying at frontier entrepreneur James Madison Estill's private post office greeted overlander Margaret Frink when she reached Pacific Springs on a warm, hazy day in June 1850. "To see the old flag once more strongly reminded us of home. There was a hail-storm at noon, but that did not prevent having an off-hand celebration of our arrival at the summit. Music from a violin with tin-pan accompaniment, contributed to the general merriment of a grand frolic," she wrote.[50]

For some the mere existence of the pass was confirmation of America's "Manifest Destiny." On his way to California in July 1848, diarist Richard Martin May described the "Thousands of Wagons & Teams crossing the great ridge dividing the waters of the Atlantic & Pacific without an effort at the hight of near 8000 feet above the Gulf of Mexico and that too in the immediate vicinity and full view of the Snow Caped Mountains and you will come to the conclusion that this pass was washed out by natures hand for great and noble purposes in days and years yet to roll by."

Forty-niner Joseph Curtis Buffum agreed: "And it comes forcibly to mind that this passage in the great Rocky Mountains was fashioned by the supreme ruler to aid the progress of the American people in their westward march to the Pacific Ocean." Practical sojourners saw its importance more simply: "Nearly half of our long journey was accomplished," John Hawkins Clark journalized in 1852, "and we could now see the great halfway mile stone and would soon be resting within its shadow."[51]

The Forty-niners camped around South Pass on the Fourth of July were determined to salute the seventy-third anniversary of the Declaration of Independence with as much enthusiasm as they did at home. They awoke to find what deaf Forty-niner Elijah Allen Spooner called "a curiosity to us for the season of the year: Water was frozen in pails and other vessels a fourth of an inch in thickness this morning; and water exposed was immediately frozen over, even after sunrise." Spooner's train nooned at Pacific Springs, "which is considered about the summit though the water from them flows westerly as their name denotes," he wrote. "Here we took a glass of lemon punch, which we drank to the Health and Happiness of those Dearly Beloved ones that we had left far behind."

---

[50] Decker, *The Diaries*, June 16, 1849, 99; N. J. and H. Bradley, Journal, July 17, 1852, 58; Frink, "Adventures," June 24, 1850, 2:105.

[51] May, *The Schreek of Wagons*, July 18, 1848, 62–63; Buffum, The Diary, June 25, 1849, typescript; Clark, "Overland," June 28, 1852, 264.

On its way to El Dorado in 1849, David Shaw's party had crossed the pass on the third of July in a light snowstorm and camped at Pacific Springs, "full of patriotic zeal for the morrow's celebration. We were early awakened by one of our party firing his revolver and he was soon followed by others," he recalled. "Then came three cheers for the flag, three short speeches and the singing of 'America' and 'From Greenland's Icy Mountain.'"[52]

"We came to the south pass, the division of the Pacific and Atlantic waters," Forty-niner Henry Wiman wrote after reaching California. "We lay two days before entering [the] desert and celebrated the 4th of July. There were a good many trains encamped there on the night of the 3d. We serenaded all the camps, we had an excellent band of music." The parties camped in the pass greeted the rising of the sun with a thirteen-gun salute and "killed the fatted calf and barbecued it. There was 8 or 10 women who baked bread and pies and sweet cakes, stewed fruit, made coffee and tea. We had molasses and brandy all fixed off in style, a better dinner I thought I never ate any where," Wiman recalled. J. C. Morris gave a speech and read toasts before dinner, while someone else read the Declaration of Independence. "After eating we had music and dancing, the ladies joined us of course." Remarkably, Wiman reported that at four o'clock his train was "all on the desert moving through a cloud of dust."[53]

Like many other overland travelers, Charles Ross Parke found the renowned site did not meet his expectations. "We are now entering what is known as the South Pass of the Rockies, but a stranger would not know it as a pass if he had not read a description of it," he wrote after leaving Strawberry Creek on the eve of his nation's birthday. The next day, Parke laid over for the afternoon above the last crossing of the Sweetwater, camping virtually on the Continental Divide. "This being the nation's birthday and our clothing not as clean as we could wish, we commenced our celebration by 'washing dirty linen' or rather woolens, as we all wore woolen shirts," he wrote. "Washing done and shirts hung out to dry—we never iron—all hands set about enjoying themselves as best they could."

After such a prosaic beginning for a Fourth of July celebration, Parke concocted a unique treat for his companions: "Having plenty of milk from the cows we had with us," he wrote, "I determined to [do] something no other

---

[52] Spooner, Letters and Diary, 38–39; Shaw, *Eldorado*, 51–52.
[53] Wiman to Dear Parents, Oct. 25, 1849.

living man ever did in this place and on this sacred day of the year, and that was to make *Ice Cream at the South Pass of the Rockies*." Parke found a two-quart tin bucket, "sweetened and flavored" the cream with peppermint—"had nothing else," he noted—put the bucket "inside a wooden bucket or 'Yankee Pale' and the top put on." Nature provided a huge bank of coarse snow, "which was just the thing for this new factory. With alternate layers of this and salt between the two buckets and with the aid of a *clean* stick to stir with, I soon produced the most delicious ice cream tasted in this place." All his delighted companions "as a compliment drew up in front of our tent and fired a salute, bursting one gun but injuring no one."[54]

Ironically, Parke was not the only gold-seeker who was inspired to think of ice cream by the snow banks that surrounded South Pass, even in the heat of July. "Snow may [be] seen on the north side of all deep revines on the plaines, an uncommon thing," David Carnes wrote when camped at the Last Crossing and apparently shared Parke's bounty. "We enjoyed the luxary of ice cream on the fourth of July."[55] On Strawberry Creek later that month, William B. Lorton went down the stream "in search of an ice spring, and to my astonishment find huge piles of snow and ice within a few feet of green grass and willows." He put as much ice as he could carry into an old sack and brought it back to camp. "Everyone ran after a piece, for it was a novelty; 'twas now disbelievers believed that the white upon the mountains was snow. They had laughed at the idea of snow laying exposed to the sun's rays and not melt away. We now propose making ice cream," Lorton reported.[56]

Thirty miles away on the Big Sandy, other overlanders found their own way to celebrate the "day which fills every American patriot's heart with gratitude and love to our forefathers," wrote Oregon-bound Forty-niner William Watson. His party had crossed the divide two days earlier, but he felt he was still in the South Pass of the Rocky Mountains. He and his companions were determined to salute "the noble and daring deeds" their forefathers had "put into execution on this day." They took all the extra gunpowder they had "and put it in a keg, and wrapped it with two table cloths and three log chains" they found in the creek. The patriots carried the device up a hill, buried it in a hole two feet deep, put a slow match to it, and fired "a national salute three

---

[54] Parke, *Dreams to Dust*, July 4, 1849, 46.
[55] Carnes, Journal, July 4, 1849.
[56] Lorton, Diary, typescript, July [23], 1849.

times, with twenty rifles besides our pistols) when our magazine exploded seeming to make the neighboring mountains shake."[57]

South Pass and Pacific Creek saw their share of explosions. On their way to California in in 1849, Jonathan Manlove and his brother abandoned their wagon at "the celebrated South Pass" and spent a day at Pacific Springs where they "rigged up pack saddles." The brothers left behind a keg of powder. "Someone had been taking our powder and had spilled some around and under the keg and the keg was left open," Manlove recalled. "While we were sorting and packing, a green Missourian came along. He bothered around and asked questions and finally got some fire and touched off the spilled powder. It flashed over the ground and connected with that under the keg. The keg went rolling off across the plain at high speed. One mule bucked off his pack [in] the excitement. Mark told him that if he didn't leave he would kick him in half a minute," Jonathan wrote. "He left."[58]

Surpassing Grandeur: Gold Rush Views of South Pass

There was no shortage of talented writers among the tens of thousands of people who crossed South Pass during the California gold rush. Many left spectacular descriptions of the landscape of "this wonderful place," which goldseeker J. D. Mason found "covered with plenty of grass and wild flowers."[59]

"High and rugged mountains covered perhaps with snows of an eternal winter stand on our right. Elevations less bold lay at our left among the most prominent of which is Table rock," wrote journalist Joseph Curtis Buffum, using the name many emigrants gave to the Oregon Buttes. After camping at Pacific Springs at noon on a cold, windy day, diarist Joseph Warren Wood and a companion set out to climb the Oregon Buttes. They hiked about five miles and climbed over Pacific Butte—"a steep high bluff with snow on its side"—and found "a small cool stream of water pure & cold" running through a cottonwood grove on its far side. "The birds were singing in the branches, the grass was green & it was a beautiful spot to spend a little time." The men began climbing again and "went down into another valley & in 4 or 5 miles came to the foot of the rock," Wood wrote. "It was higher than I had

---

[57] Watson, *Journal*, July 2, 4, 1849, 24–25.
[58] Manlove, An Overland Trip, typescript.
[59] Mason, "Letter from California," undated letter of Aug. 1850, 1/1–3, courtesy Kristin Johnson.

anticipated." Another hour's climb brought the men to their goal. From the summit, the view "was grand & imposing. It seemed as though we could see 200 miles in almost any direction."[60]

"From our camp this morning the view is most beautiful," wrote Forty-niner Gordon Cone at Pacific Spring. "Our elevation enables us to view the country for a great distance to the westward of the Rocky mountains—The mountains that are in sight, present a most splendid appearance, as we behold them.... With the Rocky mountains on the east of us, we are completely surrounded by mountains of the first magnitude, and seen at so great a distance, they present a grand, and sublime appearance." As Cone observed, it could be a terrible beauty. "The snow capped mountains that we behold on every side, are beautiful to look upon—this beauty however can never be the means of begetting a feeling of admiration in any but the mind of the traveller, as the extreem barroness of the country, and its total inability to produce vegetation forever precludes the idea, that any other use can be made of it, than the foundation for a thoroughfare to a more lovely country, and congenial clime."[61]

"As we approach the South Pass, the scenery becomes more grand and imposing. An immense chain of mountains bound us on either side whose broken and rugged peaks tower aloft and seemingly pierce the sky," Calvin Taylor rhapsodized on his way to California in 1850. He had only had his first view of the immense Wind River Range, "stretching away to the north, their snowy peaks glittering in the sunbeams like burnished silver and presenting a scene of great beauty and sublimity." Like a few other adventurous souls, Taylor climbed Pacific Butte and was rewarded with "a magnificent view of the gigantic Rocky Mountains.... Beneath my feet gushed the crystal waters augmenting in volume, pursuing their winding way westward towards the setting sun, receiving tribute from every little rill and brook until lost in distance."[62]

At Rocky Ridge, Franklin Langworthy described his "climb up the steep side of a mountain three or four miles" to where the "high table land of vast extent, having snowy summits in sight to the west, south-west and north" opened up before him. "Upon this stupendous height I halted a moment, and looking back towards the east, the prospect was one of surpassing grandeur. An immense extent of country is visible, and from its expanded surface,

---

[60] Buffum, The Diary, typescript, June 25, 1849; Wood, Diary, July 3, 1849, 52–53.
[61] Cone, Journal, July 25–26, 1849, 58–59.
[62] Taylor, "Overland to California," July 16, 1850, 319–20, 321–22.

hundreds of summits shoot up, mingling with the clouds, many of them glimmering with snow, reflecting the beams of the declining sun." His party apparently camped on Strawberry Creek "in a delightful spot, in the midst of clumps of aspen trees, and near a fine spring of good water, not tinctured with the everlasting alkali." Even after he and his companions donned all their overcoats the "wintry blasts" of a cold front made them shiver.[63]

The altitude, the exotic landscape, and its alien appearance affected how people raised in humid woodlands described the scenery. Diarists often reported seeing mirages. Richard Burton said the "earth and air were both so dry that the refraction of the sunbeams" created mirages as perfect as the ones he saw in Persia. "The mirage has deceived us several times to-day," wrote James Abbey west of Little Sandy. "While worn with travel and thirsting for water, there might be seen, sometimes to the right, sometimes to the left, and then in front, representations of large rivers, lakes and streams of pure water; but as we would advance in the direction whence they would appear, they would recede or fade away, leaving nothing to view but the barren desert and the blighted hopes of the weary traveler."[64]

Some descriptions were so overwrought it is hard to tell if the chronicler had seen a mirage or was hallucinating. "My vision was all at once greeted with the sight of a city resting upon the crest of the mountains to my right," wrote John Hawkins Clark as the Wind River Range appeared on the western horizon. "This vision of beauty, of grandeur and magnificence, pervaded my whole being." Imperial Rome could not outshine "the grand picture before me. Palaces and dome-roofed churches, castles and towers, lofty walls and far reaching streets, standing clear cut against the blue sky, a phantom city, above a desert waste, heedless of all my surroundings." Clark could not remember how long "this wonderful apparition" detained him before "this capital city of delusion passed away and the rugged world, with its stern realities, I had again to contemplate."[65]

Again and again, these narratives reveal that their authors had never seen mountains like the ones they saw at South Pass. Almost everyone commented on the sight of snow in summer, something never seen east of the Mississippi River except at the highest elevations in New England. Two members

---

[63] Langworthy, *Scenery*, June 28, 1850, 60–61.
[64] Burton, *City of the Saints*, Aug. 21, 1860, 168; Abbey, *California*, June 18, 1850, 34.
[65] Clark, "Overland," June 27, 1852, 263–64.

of Abigail Scott Duniway's Oregon-bound wagon train climbed to the top of one of the Sweetwater Hills to settle a dispute "with regard to a white substance" on the summit was snow or "a species of white granite or white gravel": they found snow. "The view far surpasses anything seen east of the Mississippi river," David Shaw wrote. The prospect from the great elevation of his camp grounds at Pacific Springs "gave a magnificent view of the surrounding country for a long distance." Shaw felt that "the broad expanse of plain and river, made a picture that would satisfy the most ardent lover of the grand and picturesque in nature." "We are nearly surrounded by lofty bluffs and the scenery is grand and picturesque," reported diarist William Hoffman while camped on Willow Creek. "We have a most glorious sight before us," he wrote the next day after camping on the Sweetwater not far from South Pass, praising the peaks of the Wind River chain and "the most magnificent view of the snow clad Rocky mountains."[66]

The Loneliest Land for a Grave: South Pass Memorials

On her way to Montana in 1864, Kate Dunlap noticed the grave of an emigrant on the Sweetwater River "who had fallen by the way years ago." A thick mat of prickly pears covered the burial, "a good defence against intruders." She had passed many graves during the previous week, most of them old, and wrote, "How sad a thought it is to die so far away from one's friends and to be buried alone on these desert plains."[67]

Long before he became famous as Mark Twain, by the time Sam Clemens saw the trail in 1861, the road west was lined with graves. As his stagecoach "sped away, always through splendid scenery" while crossing South Pass, he noted the "long ranks of white skeletons of mules and oxen—monuments of the huge emigration of other days." The "up-ended boards or small piles of stones which the driver said marked the resting-place of more precious remains" amid the "desolation and utter solitude" left a deep impression on him. "It was the loneliest land for a grave!" Twain wrote.[68]

Nineteenth-century Americans had intense feelings about death and complicated funeral and burial traditions. For many overland travelers, burying

---
[66] Scott, "Journal," July 2, 1852, 5:80; Shaw, *Eldorado*, 54; Hoffman, Journal, July 26, 27, 1853.
[67] Dunlap, *Montana Gold Rush Diary*, July 5, 1864, 78.
[68] Twain, *Roughing It*, 103.

family and friends far from civilization, in what they considered a howling wilderness, was a heartbreaking necessity. "I would have been willing to have borne anything that came—but O how hard to leave my idol my treasure away in this lonely and dreary land," wrote emigrant Elizabeth Duncan after her daughter died. "It looks so sad and lonely, I should think of all things dread to lie here alone. It must be a sad heart-sickening task for a company of emigrants to thus leave one of their party," recalled overlander Delia Thompson Brown after passing a new grave in 1860.[69]

The knowledge that the survivors might never be able to visit the site again compounded the tragedy. Traveler Harriet Scott Palmer's mother died in the Black Hills in 1852, "a crushing blow to all our hopes. We had to journey on, and leave her in a lonely grave—a feather bed as a coffin, and the grave protected from the wolves by stones heaped upon it. The rolling hills were ablaze with beautiful wild roses—it was the 20th of June, and we heaped and covered mother's grave with the roses so the cruel stones were hid from view. Her grave is lost. No one was ever able to find it again."[70]

Between the August morning in 1844 at the Ninth Crossing of the Sweetwater when James Clyman buried Joseph Barnett, "the first white man that ever rested his bones on this stream," in "the most decent manner our circumstances would admit," and the final internment of a wagon train fatality at an unknown date, dozens if not hundreds of overland emigrants were laid to rest along the historic trails between Ice Spring and the Big Sandy. (Clyman thought he was digging the first grave at South Pass, but Peter Burnett described a burial near the Three Crossings the year before.[71])

The narratives of the survivors often mention burials near South Pass. "A little on the west of the summit of ridge are the Pacific Springs (and here is the grave of a young man named Dexter, in loose sand and short board)," wrote William Lorton. Diarist Caroline Richardson saw "three new graves and some old ones" when she camped on Pacific Creek in 1852. "We passed the grave of a child about 14 months old, buried to day near where the road crosses the creek, on the west side," one couple reported.[72] "Hundreds that

---

[69] Duncan, Diary, Sept. 25, 1867, 20; Brown, Diary, June 16, 1860.

[70] Palmer, *Crossing Over the Great Plains*, Oregon Hist. Society.

[71] Clyman, *James Clyman, Frontiersman*, Aug. 27, 1844, 98; Burnett, *Recollections*, 114–15. Charles Camp's notes indicate that the headstone Clyman carved for "Barnette" still stood in 1959.

[72] Lorton, Diary, July 25, 1849, typescript; Richardson, Journal, June 28, 1852; Bradleys, Daily Journal, July 17, 1852, 58.

have left their homes with the brightest anticipations are now mouldering upon the plains," reported Forty-niner Elmon S. Camp. "Were there no other marks, to guide the emigrant upon his way, the graves upon either side of the trail would be sufficient to direct him with unerring certainty for hundreds of miles."[73] Graves are eloquent reminders of the sacrifices of the thousands of men, women, and children who used America's wagon roads. Almost every emigrant narrative mentions deaths, funerals, burials, and graves encountered by the wayside. If he failed to note the graves lining the trail, "It would be a neglect of sympathy for those who have 'fallen by the way,'" wrote John Hawkins Clark. "I should not be doing my duty to those friends who will wait and wait, until the heart grows sick for news of absent ones who are scattered along this great highway, sleeping in unknown graves."[74]

Most trail graves are unidentified, and few are more than a collection of scattered rocks. Previously unknown graves continue to be discovered at sites like Rock Creek.[75] Most remain silent. A handful, however, have compelling stories to tell, such as the "Pioneer Grave," a multiple-burial site on a bench overlooking Pacific Creek.

Before dawn on September 21, 1862, Charlotte Rudland Dansie, 33, died "of a 'Miscarriage' and general debility" while giving birth to her eighth child at a camp a mile east of the Continental Divide. According to her descendants, Dansie told her husband "she could stand her suffering no longer and asked him to pray to God that she might be released and return to her maker." The infant lived only long enough to be given the name Joseph. John D. T. McAllister, who served as chaplain for the Ansil P. Harmon company, and a few companions "went ahead to dig a grave for the body of Sister Charlotte Dansie. . . . One mile brought us to the Summit or pass. Three more we made the Pacific Springs, one mile farther we crossed the Pacific Creek and dug the grave on the right of the road."

As the men were digging her grave, "Captain Harmon rode up and informed us that Caroline Myers, aged 25 was dead. She died of Bilious fever just after the wagons left camp. We widened the grave for both bodies," McAllister wrote. William Ajax, who was driving the train's loose stock, provided another account of this sad Sunday morning. "Started about 8, and nooned

---
[73] Camp to Dear Brother, July 8, 1849, in Cumming, *The Gold Rush*, 48.
[74] Clark, "Overland," June 29, 1852, 41.
[75] Brown, "The Grave of Ephraim Brown," 25–27.

CHARLOTTE DANSIE'S GRAVE
The graves of most emigrants who died on the road west are lost in the sagebrush, but the resting place that Charlotte Dansie shares with Caroline Myers is marked and revered near Pacific Springs. Russell L. Tanner photo. *Courtesy the Bureau of Land Management.*

about 1 mile beyond the Pacific Springs, where 3 persons were buried—2 grown up women, one that had died of a puerperal death, and a child that had been born in the morning." Twenty members of Harmon's train had died since they left the Missouri, Ajax estimated.[76]

Charlotte Dansie left behind her husband Robert, 37, and five surviving children: Robert, 12, Alfred John, 10, Charles Nephi, 8, Sarah Ann Elizabeth, 4, and William Heber, 1. According to local or family lore, several of Dansie's descendants returned to South Pass during the Great Depression to attempt to locate her grave. To their shock and surprise, they met a sheepherder who had Charlotte Dansie's burial necklace. To defuse the family's wrath, the sheepherder agreed to lead the descendants to the grave he had robbed.

---

[76] McAllister, Journal; Ajax, Journal, both Sept. 21, 1862.

Seventy-seven years after that tragic September morning, eight of Charlotte Dansie's descendants and relatives, including her 81-year-old daughter, Sarah Ann Elizabeth, visited South Pass to mark her grave with a handsome headstone. In 1958 President Dwight D. Eisenhower authorized the secretary of the interior to convey 1.25 acres of public land to the Dansie Family Organization to help preserve the site. The headstone tells a powerful tale:

> In loving memory of Charlotte R., daughter of Wm. and Susan Rutland born in Suffolk England. Died in child birth with infant son Joseph at Pacific Springs Wyo. Sept. 21, 1862, while crossing the plains to Utah. In Ansel P Harmon Co. leaving husband and five children. Caroline Moyers buried in the same grave. Died Sept. 21 1862 of Bilious fever age 25 years. Grave located July 3, 1939 by Joseph H. and Leroy Dansie. Erected in 1939.[77]

---

[77] Wyoming State Historic Preservation Office website.

CHAPTER 7

Conflict and Catastrophe at South Pass

1856–1860

TRANSCONTINENTAL WAGON TRAVEL WAS SAFER AND SPEEDIER in 1856 than it had been in 1846, but the trek was still a long and perilous journey. The "mountain and prairie Indians" continued to suffer from the vast number of emigrants passing "through their country, destroying their means of support, and scattering disease and death among them," Commissioner of Indian Affairs Luke Lea admitted. Indian agents D. D. Mitchell and Thomas Fitzpatrick (now known as White Hair), gathered ten thousand Sioux, Cheyenne, Arapahoe, Absaroka, Arikara, Mandan, and Gros Ventre tribal members near Fort Laramie in 1851 to "make an effective and lasting peace" among the tribes and have them recognize the right of the U.S. government "to establish roads, military and other posts, within their respective territories." Twenty-one "chiefs, headmen, and braves" signed the agreement, which divided the land into tribal territories but said nothing about Indian rights to these lands. Yet within weeks of signing the treaty, Mitchell proposed creating Nebraska Territory, to "give to the United States all the agricultural lands south of the Missouri river that are considered exclusively Indian territory."[1]

Utah Indian agent Jacob Holeman invited Jim Bridger, Washakie, and a delegation of the Shoshones to attend the conference with "the wild tribes of the prairies." Despite a purported armistice, Cheyenne warriors ambushed and killed a Shoshone and his son on their way to visit an emigrant camp and

---

[1] Commissioner of Indian Affairs, *Annual Report*, 1852, 9; *Annual Report*, 1851, 62; Prucha, *Documents of United States Indian Policy*, 84–85.

stole some of Holeman's horses. To "cover the body," the Cheyenne staged a feast when the Shoshones reached the treaty ground and gave them "blankets, bolts of red and scarlet cloth, knives, tobacco, and other articles." Washakie's placated but well-armed warriors put on an impressive display at the negotiations: "These are the finest Indians on earth," Bridger said of the Shoshones. "They live all about me, and I know all of them."[2]

Despite their dignified and impressive behavior at the council, Mitchell did not consider the Shoshones "embraced in his instructions," so they were "not parties to the treaty negotiated with the other tribes." Commissioner Lea inexplicably called them "a disaffected and mischievous tribe, infesting one of the principal routes of travel to Oregon." He thought their leaders "returned to their people with more friendly feelings towards the Government and the whites."[3] Perhaps they did, but when agents at Fort Laramie replaced Washakie a year later with "a quiet, unobtrusive man, who never had been a chief, nor was in the line of chiefs, and designated him as head of the Shoshones," the tribe derisively called him the White Man's Child.[4]

The other Plains tribes were even less impressed. At Fort Laramie in 1854, a Cheyenne spokesman listed his nation's demands. "He commenced by stating that the travel over the Platte road by emigrants should be stopped." The tribe wanted four thousand dollars in cash and the "balance of their annuity in guns and ammunition, and one thousand white women for wives." The rookie agent, John Whitfield, "found this band of Cheyennes the sauciest Indians I have ever seen."[5] To the west, the Shoshones saw the Mormons chase Jim Bridger, their old ally, away from his fort in 1853 and begin establishing their own settlement on Blacks Fork. Brigham Young wanted Washakie to give up hunting buffalo and take up farming in Browns Hole.[6] Young was simultaneously using his authority to intimidate non-Mormon federal judges and promote his religious and personal interests as Utah Territory's governor and Indian agent.

"This is my country, and my people's country," Washakie told a Mormon emissary in 1854. "The buffalo and elk came here to drink water and eat grass; but now they have been killed or driven back out of our land. The grass is all eaten off by the white man's horses and cattle, and the dry wood has been

---

[2] "Letter," Sept. 8, *Missouri Republican*, Oct. 29, 1851; Lowe, *Five Years a Dragoon*, 81–82.
[3] Commissioner, *Annual Report*, 1851, 10.
[4] Brown, *Life of a Pioneer*, 92.
[5] Whitfield to Manypenny, Sept. 27, 1854, in Commissioner, *Annual Report*, 1854, 94.
[6] Young to Wash-e-kik, Nov. 6, 1855, LDS Archives.

burned." When his young men got tired and hungry and visited white camps, they were "ordered to get out, and they are slapped, or kicked, and called 'd——d Injuns,' " he complained. Some of his young men had been "so abused that they have threatened to kill all the white men they meet in our land." He had always been the white man's friend, but "Now I can see that he only loves himself; he loves his own flesh, and he does not think of us." Looking at Green River, Washakie said, "Every white man, woman or child, that I find on this side of that water, at sunrise tomorrow I will wipe them out."[7]

The Most Dangerous War Grounds in the Rocky Mountains

By the mid-1850s, South Pass lay between the two centers of power on the trail west: the army post at Fort Laramie and the Mormon capital at Great Salt Lake City. On the Sweetwater in 1860, a Pony Express rider told Clara Downes the Indians "say they have two fathers the president & Brigham Young. One lies where the sun rises & the other where the sun sets."[8] The Shoshones who called South Pass home found themselves caught between the two entities, but their lands lay much closer to their father in the West. In the last years before the nation tore itself apart, South Pass stood at the center of growing conflict, not between North and South, but among three nations: the army and travelers representing the power of the expanding American Republic, the Mormon Kingdom of God, and the Native peoples who still technically owned the land. Divided into the Bannock, Shoshone, Ute, Lakota, Arapahoe, and Absaroka nations, these tribes used their considerable military power against their traditional enemies—each other—and watched from the sidelines as the Mormons engaged the army in mock warfare. At stake were "the most dangerous war grounds in the Rocky mountains"—the land north of the Yampa River, west of the Platte, and south of the Wind River Mountains in what *Horn's Overland Guide* called the "Indian Enchanted Ground."[9]

During the early 1850s, Utah's Mormon leaders were "satisfied to abide their time, in accession of strength by numbers, when they may be deemed fit to take a sovereign position," observed the perceptive topographer, John W.

---

[7] Brown, *Life of a Pioneer*, 339.
[8] Downes, Journal, June 23, 1860.
[9] Spence and Jackson, eds., *The Expeditions of John Charles Frémont*, 1:709.

CHIEF WASHAKIE AND HIS MEN

For most of his long life, which lasted almost a century or more, Washakie provided the Eastern Shoshones some of the most effective leadership enjoyed by any American Indian Nation. *Chief Washakie and His Men Near Tipis, All in Partial Native Dress, Some with Ornaments. Near South Pass, 1870*, by William Henry Jackson. *Courtesy Smithsonian Institution.*

Gunnison.[10] Those leaders saw recruiting new converts and transporting them to their new Zion as both a sacred duty and as essential to their survival. God had called the Latter-day Saints "to bring to pass the gathering of mine elect" in one place to prepare "against the day when tribulation and desolation are sent forth upon the wicked," Joseph Smith proclaimed 1830, for soon "all the proud and they that do wickedly shall be as stubble; and I will burn them up, saith the Lord of Hosts, that wickedness shall not be upon the earth."[11] Scholars have long recognized early Mormons believed in this doctrine "literally and fervently." The Latter-day exodus across the plains "reenacted the gathering of the Israelites to the Promised Land and was a necessary preparation for the coming of Christ in the 'Last Days.'"

There was more to "gathering of the poor" to Utah than historians have realized. Intensely millennial, the Latter-day Saints believed they would witness the end times, when the wicked would slay the wicked, and plague, famine, disease, and the judgments of Heaven would depopulate the earth. "The just will flee to Zion, learn the ways of the Lord" and "become qualified to rule on the earth as Kings and Priests unto God, having attained an endless dominion."[12] Brigham Young had other goals: "We calculate to be the kings of these mountains," he told an army quartermaster in 1857.[13]

As historian Polly Aird observed, "the gathering had earthly aims as well"— it was fundamental to building the Mormon Kingdom of God in the vast territory they claimed in the West. A larger population would bolster Utah Territory's application for statehood, "a status that would give them more control over political affairs." From its very beginning in 1847, a lack of resources made the Mormon gathering to Zion a difficult undertaking. Cooperation, organization, and discipline characterized the Latter-day Saints' move west, but it was consistently underpowered, underfinanced, and even underfed. To try to finance its massive migration program and bring thousands of European converts to its mountain Zion, the LDS Church incorporated the Perpetual Emigrating Fund Company (PEF) in 1849 to help bring the poor to Utah. To stretch its scarce resources, the faith developed strategies such as the Ten and Thirteen Pound Companies to expedite low-cost emigration to the Great Basin.[14]

---

[10] Gunnison, *The Mormons or Latter-day Saints, in the Valley of the Great Salt Lake*, 23.
[11] Smith, *Doctrine and Covenants*, 29:7–9.
[12] *Millennial Star*, Preface, Volume 15, 1854.
[13] Minutes, Aug. 23, 1863, in Anonymous, *Minutes of the Apostles*.
[14] Aird, "Bound for Zion," 300–25.

Utah's leaders needed something else—manpower. Having already appointed George D. Grant to raise a company of mounted men, on April 28, 1849, the legislature of the provisional state of Deseret reconstituted the Nauvoo Legion, a territorial militia that evoked the name and memory of Lt. Gen. Joseph Smith's Illinois volunteer unit.[15] Under Lt. Gen. Daniel Wells, the Mormons devoted scarce resources to drilling their irregulars in what proved to be a ragtag force, but some of the men gained considerable field experience in the Legion's campaigns against the Utes and Goshutes. Accompanied by many of the legion's senior officers, apostle and brigadier general Franklin D. Richards took command of the faith's European Mission in 1854. "Cannot the 30,000 British Saints do a great deal more than they are now doing to prepare the minds of those of whom is the kingdom of heaven, to become valiant soldiers of that kingdom?" his brother Samuel Richards had asked in The Latter-Day Saints' Millennial Star in January. "Depend upon it, on this earth, there is a struggle yet to come, or rather to be concluded, between the kingdom of God and the kingdom of Satan, in which the rising generation will act a most conspicuous part."[16]

In addition to General Richards's standard duties as mission president, the militia's "Order No. 1" apparently directed him to act as a recruiting officer. "We have the pleasure to Baptise every week many promising Soldiers," missionary William Warner Major informed Brigham Young.[17] Maj. William H. Kimball, who had served in an 1853 Indian campaign with Richards and Col. George A. Smith, reported to Apostle Smith from London in September that he was "with Generals, Colonels, Captains, Lieutenants, Serjeants, not forgetting Majors, and all recruiting officers sent out to enlist volunteers. We hope to select chosen battalions of sterling soldiers, and march them safely to Zions' standard, there to defend virtue, truth, & genuine liberty. Our drill is somewhat different now, yet [under] the same King, and same Commander; but I find tactics very different and much more difficult." Kimball was already "commanding upwards of 4,000 sterling volunteers, still enlisting for the great conflict," and he was eager to get back home to lead them in "surpressing the incursions of savages, white or red."[18] His commander-in-chief agreed:

---

[15] Morgan, The State of Deseret, 20–21.
[16] "Home Intelligence," Millennial Star, January 21, 1854, 40.
[17] Major to Young, June 7, 1854, Brigham Young Collection, LDS Archives.
[18] Kimball to Smith, Sept. 23, 1854, LDS Archives.

CONFLICT AND CATASTROPHE AT SOUTH PASS 169

"We want to give a heavy lift to the emigration of the poor, next season. We have brought out a considerable number this season, but it is hardly a beginning to what we wish to be brought out next season."[19]

DISASTER AT SOUTH PASS: THE FIRST HANDCART TRAINS

"Much has been written about the Pioneers, and the 'Mormon Battalion' crossing the plains, but I have never seen any thing like a history of the Hand Cart Emigration of the year 1856," wrote William Woodward many years after he made the trek to Zion as a captain in James G. Willie's ill-fated fourth handcart company. "It was a new scheme for the deporting of a numerous people to Salt Lake Valley," Woodward recalled. "This plan was to bring as many people as possible, for as small an amount of money as could be possible." Elder Woodward summarized the strategy behind the new scheme: "It was the constant desire of the authorities of the Church to plan for the people for their temporal & spiritual welfare."[20]

The inspiration for the handcart scheme was rooted in problems with the Perpetual Emigrating Fund. Despite much creative financing after its founding in 1849, the plan was quickly mired in debt, which even the 10 percent annual interest rate imposed on its patrons failed to mitigate. Utah's cash-starved frontier economy offered few opportunities for new emigrants to repay the principle, let alone the interest. As the 1850s progressed, such prospects grew worse. Deseret, as the Mormons called their community of faith, suffered a crushing drought in 1855 that devastated the already troubled economy, leaving the emigration fund in dismal financial shape. During the winter of 1855–56, Brigham Young reported the territory's loss of cattle was catastrophic, "probably two thirds of our entire stock."[21]

By early 1855, its 862 debtors owed the PEF more than one hundred thousand dollars. That summer, Brigham Young complained that Apostle Erastus Snow had used church credit to finance that year's emigration "without my consent, or without my knowing anything about it, and our agents have run us in debt almost fifty thousand dollars to strangers, merchants, cattle dealers,

---

[19] Brigham Young, *Journal of Discourses*, Oct. 6, 1853, 1:326. Young also complained that only two people had "paid one dime towards cancelling a [PEF] debt amounting to over $80,000, besides other notes, accounts, and obligations which we hold."
[20] Woodward to Joseph F. Smith, 1907, LDS Archives.
[21] Young to Rich, April 3, 1856, LDS Archives.

and our brethren who are coming here." Young refused to pay such drafts. "It is the poor who have got your money, and if you have any complaints to make, make them against the Almighty for having so many poor. I do not owe you anything." He later explained, "I cannot chew paper and spit out bank notes."[22]

The Mormons had considered using wheelbarrows as early as 1847. Mail courier Robert Campbell's eastbound party met "a man with a wheelbarrow (said to be a Scotchman)" in the Sweetwater Valley in 1850. Several companies had invited him to join them and offered to haul his provisions and bedding. This innovative, hard-charging Scot told the Mormon couriers he "thanked them kindly, but wished to be excused, as he could not wait on the tardy movements of a camp. He never was afraid of the Indians stealing his horses, and he never lost any rest dreading a stampede." One of the Mormons, John O. Angus, said on beholding the wheelbarrow man that he had "seen the fulfillment of a Mormon prophecy": Three years earlier Angus had heard a prophet declare Mormons would cross "the plains with wheelbarrows."[23]

Mormon leaders began seriously considering cheaper ways to cross the plains in 1851. "Some of the children of the world, have crossed the mountains and plains, from Missouri to California, with a pack on their back to worship their god—Gold. Some have performed the same journey with a wheel-barrow, some have accomplished the same with a pack on a cow," the First Presidency wrote. Their epistle observed that some Saints had made the trek with wagons or carts made "without a particle of iron, hooping their wheels with hickory, or raw hide, or ropes, and had as good and safe a journey as any in the camps, with their well wrought iron wagons." Faithful Mormons could do the same. "Families might start from Missouri river, with cows, hand-carts, wheel-barrows, with little flour, and no unnecessaries, and come to this place quicker, and with less fatigue than by following the heavy trains with their cumbrous herds, which they are obliged to drive miles to feed. Do you not like this method of travelling? Do you think salvation costs too much? If so, it is not worth having."[24]

Late in 1855, Mormons in Britain learned of the new plan to hurry up the gathering at the lowest possible cost. "We cannot afford to purchase wagons and teams as in times past, I am consequently thrown back upon *my*

---

[22] Arrington, *Great Basin Kingdom*, 101, 156.
[23] Campbell, July 7, 1850, in *Frontier Guardian*, July 24, 1850, 1–2.
[24] "Sixth General Epistle," *Deseret News*, Nov. 15, 1851.

old plan—to make hand-carts, and let the emigration foot it, and draw upon them the necessary supplies, having a cow or two for every ten," Brigham Young wrote to European Mission president Franklin D. Richards. "They can come just as quick, if not quicker, and much cheaper—can start earlier and escape the prevailing sickness which annually lays so many of our brethren in the dust."[25] Young was also planning an overland freighting operation that envisioned creating a string of supply stations along the trail, but without such a system in place, the handcart scheme offered little margin for blunders or bad weather.

At the end of October 1855, the LDS Church's First Presidency issued a general epistle that implemented its revolutionary new type of overland migration. It called on all the faithful who could to "gather up for Zion and come while the way is open before them; let the poor also come, whether they receive aid or not from the Fund; let them come on foot, with hand carts or wheel barrows." The handcarts would save "the immense expense every year for teams and outfit for crossing the plains." The new system would eliminate "the expense, risk, loss and perplexity of teams" so more Saints could "escape the scenes of distress, anguish and death which have often laid so many or our brethren and sisters in the dust." Faithful and experienced leaders with suitable instructions would be sent "to some proper out-fitting point to carry into effect the above suggestions." Those who wanted the PEF's help were "expected to walk and draw their luggage across the plains" and would be assisted in no other way. The decree also contained an implicit promise: "Let them gird up their loins and walk through, and nothing shall hinder or stay them."

The epistle reflected the First Presidency's belief that the road to Zion should be hard. "If any apostatize in consequence of this regulation, so much the better, for it is far better that such deny the faith before they start than to do so, for a more trifling cause, after they get here," the statement said. "If they have not faith enough to undertake this job, and accomplish it too, they have not faith sufficient to endure, with the saints in Zion, the celestial law which leads to exaltation and eternal lives."[26]

"I will give you my plan of building the carts," Brigham Young wrote in September 1855. The instructions reflected his early experience as a carpenter. "Take Iron Wood or Hard Hack for Hubs, turn them out about six inches

---

[25] Young to Richards, Sept. 30, 1855, "Foreign Correspondence," *Millennial Star*, Dec. 22, 1855, 813.
[26] "Thirteenth General Epistle," *Deseret News*, Oct. 31, 1855, 268–69.

long and five or six inches in the diameter." The axles should be about four and a half feet wide and made "of good hickory about 2 inches in diameter at the shoulder." The hubs and wheels should be lined with sole leather. The wheels "should be about four and a half, or five feet high" with hickory rims and spokes "set bracing in the hub and seasoned." The beds should be built of half-inch lumber to be as light as possible. "You will not need a particle of Iron and the brethren can come along with no trouble or perplexity of teams and save a great deal of expense."[27]

By late 1855 drought and grasshoppers had devastated Utah Territory. Despite Young's promises, church leaders in the East waited in vain for him to appoint someone "to superintend the emigration in the West," as was the custom. John Taylor expressed the frustration that Mormon authorities outside of Utah felt about the failure to make clear who was responsible for managing the 1856 operations: "I may be obtuse and so may those who were with me," Taylor later wrote, "but however plain your words might be to yourself on this matter, neither I nor my associates could understand them."

Sometime in late 1855, Apostle Taylor had received Young's letter ordering "the manufacture of Hand-Carts, their size, material, dimensions &c. and various instructions pertaining to the emigration, not only in relation to an early start, but also positive instructions that *no indebtedness should* be incurred." The appointment to oversee and manage the new and complex emigration system failed to come. Fortunately, Taylor, the most capable Mormon leader of his time, stepped in to fill the void as best he could. When he first learned of the handcart plan, the apostle admitted, "at first sight it looked rather like 'Jordan's a hard road to travel.'"[28]

Taylor initially expected someone "might be sent from the Valley to superintend the emigration in the West. In the absence of such persons, I have felt it a duty incumbent upon me to make all preliminary arrangements for the furtherance of the interests of the emigration." By late November 1855 Taylor had "carefully considered that matter" and took active steps to implement Young's visionary plan. He appointed a committee of missionaries who had walked across the plains to determine what supplies four people would need for their cart.

The committee recommended sending 60 pounds of breadstuffs and 60

---

[27] Dary, *The Oregon Trail*, 266.
[28] Taylor to Young, Jan. 18, 1856, Feb. 24, 1857, LDS Archives.

CONFLICT AND CATASTROPHE AT SOUTH PASS   173

of meat, a pound of tea and some sugar, 20 pounds of cooking utensils, plus clothing, bedding, and a tent, for a total of 449 pounds in supplies. In addition, there should be a cow for each two carts or eight persons and a wagon with three yoke of oxen for every ten carts. "The above is predicated upon the calculation of being met at the upper crossing of the Platte or the Devil's gate" with more supplies, Taylor cautioned. Young later told Taylor, "We expect to start teams with provisions to meet the emigration so soon as we can get flour from the present harvest."[29]

Taylor ordered one hundred carts built to Brigham Young's specifications out of seasoned wood at St. Louis. He had purchased a defective wagon wheel at Council Bluffs, and warned the prophet against having carts built by the shady contractors common on the frontier. "If the wheels should break down on the road," Taylor cautioned, "the company would be ruined." By late April 1856, Taylor felt "deeply solicitous for the welfare of the travelling Saints, and more especially am I anxious that everything shall be conducted properly, with due care and safety, and as far as may be practicable, for the comfort of those who may be going by hand-carts." It was "a new project, and will require our greatest attention and vigilance."

As directed, Taylor surveyed a new route from New York to the frontier and made preliminary arrangements for campgrounds. The plan's lack of clearly defined leadership responsibilities undercut all Taylor's valiant efforts and hard work. When no one was assigned to oversee the 1856 migration, Franklin D. Richards attempted to manage it from Liverpool. Richards asked Taylor to "make arrangements for the transmission in that way for 10,000 souls across the plains" that fall, Brigham Young happily reported.[30]

"We are pleased with the start the hand cart trains are making this season and have no fears but the plan will prove eminently successful," Brigham Young wrote in June. It would be a novel sight to see the Saints at Iowa City "starting out with their hand carts on foot for home, will it not prove another testimony to the world of the workings of the Lord with His people! and is the time far distant when the name of the people of God and their Zion & the fame thereof will cause the nations to tremble with fear."[31]

---
[29] Taylor to Young, Nov. 21, 1855; and Young to Taylor, June 30, 1856, LDS Archives. Young did not follow through.
[30] Taylor to Young, Jan. 18, 1856; Taylor to Richards, March 4, 1856; Young to Charles C. Rich, April 3, 1856, LDS Archives.
[31] Young to Taylor, June 30, 1856, LDS Archives.

Three months later, a large crowd, a brass band, and a company of militia lancers greeted the first two handcart companies to arrive in Salt Lake in late September 1856. The system was proclaimed a triumph. "Prest. Young has declared from the beginning that it was a practical safe operation, his sayings in this, as in all other cases have proven true," Wilford Woodruff wrote after witnessing the spectacle.[32] Some of the earliest participants painted a different picture. William Knox Aitken arrived with one of the vanguard handcart parties, "wearied and worn down, the bones almost through the skin, not only of myself but of all that were in the company, having walked from Iowa city to the Great Salt Lake city, a distance of 1,350 miles, and were half starved to the bargain, our whole allowance being 12 ounces of flour per day, and we did not even get so much."[33]

---

[32] Woodruff, "Correspondence from Utah," Sept. 30, 1856, *The Mormon*, Nov. 15, 1856.
[33] Aitken, "Adventures of a Mormon," *London Advertiser*, Aug. 9, 1857. Aitken fled Utah the next spring with three hundred souls "all determined to get off or die."

Mormons Crossing the Plains
One of the few contemporary images of Mormon handcarts appeared in *Ballou's Pictorial* on September 20, 1856.
Courtesy Rick Grunder.

We Are Bound to Be Caught in the Snow:
The Willie Company

The late start, the lack of a leader assigned to run the plan, the uncertainty about how large the migration would be, and the challenge of getting enough handcarts quickly built ensured a chaotic situation at Iowa City, the designated assembly spot for the handcart treks. Franklin D. Richards never should have sent the last two handcart companies west from the Missouri in late August, long after an overland party could expect to reach South Pass before winter began. "One prominent and sanguine gentleman proffered to eat all the snow the emigrants would find between the Missouri and Salt Lake," John Jaques recalled. The remark struck him as hasty, impulsive, and strange "when it was known that in the region of the South pass snow was capable of falling at almost any time of the year," he wrote. "The results of the determination to proceed were fraught with disaster and death."[34]

---

[34] Jaques, *Salt Lake Daily Herald*, Dec. 1, 1878, 1. William H. Kimball was the "sanguine gentleman."

Cascading mistakes led to a catastrophe for the last two handcart trains that played out between the Platte River and South Pass. Disaster struck on October 19 when a blizzard caught the last handcart train near today's Casper, Wyoming. Already desperately lacking supplies and still far from South Pass, the last handcart companies under James G. Willie and Edward Martin, along with the last wagon trains traveling near them, suffered incredible hardships. The blizzard stopped the march west in its tracks. Martin's company lost fifty-six souls while stalled for nine days near the Platte. They began moving after learning that help was on the way but were soon trapped near Devils Gate in a poorly sheltered "ravine" now known as Martins Cove, where their "ration of flour was reduced to 4 oz. and 2 oz for the children."[35]

After a swift carriage ride across the plains, Richards and his friends, all senior officers in the Nauvoo Legion, reached Salt Lake on October 4, 1856. The next day, Richards told a church conference he was confident that God would "over-rule the storms" and protect the handcart pioneers. When he caught up with the last two trains at Florence, Nebraska, Richards explained, he had asked the Saints to express their faith "and requested to know of them, even if they knew that they should be swallowed up in storms, whether they would stop or turn back. They voted, with loud acclamations, that they would go on." He said their faith would "bring the choice blessings of God upon them." Richards claimed the Saints still on the trail, "about one thousand with hand-carts, feel that it is late in the season, and they expect to get cold fingers and toes. But they have this faith and confidence towards God that he will over-rule the storms that may come in the season thereof and turn them away, that their path may be free from suffering more than they can bear."

Brigham Young took a much more practical view. "Many of our brethren and sisters are on the plains with hand carts, and probably many are now 700 miles from this place, and they must be brought here, we must send assistance to them," he said. He dismissed the meeting and ordered local bishops to send sixty mule teams, more than forty teamsters, a dozen or more wagons, and twelve tons of flour to relieve the people struggling in the mountains.[36]

Historian David L. Bigler called the subsequent two-month struggle against winter "the most desperate rescue operation in western history." By the time the relief wagons reached them, the handcart trains were in desperate

---

[35] Bleak, Journal, Nov. 5, 1856, LDS Archives; Rea, *Devil's Gate*, 90–92.
[36] Richards, "Discourse"; "Remarks by President Brigham Young," *Deseret News*, Oct. 15, 1856, 252–53.

shape. "Seventeen pounds of bedding and clothing proved inadequate to keep exhausted emigrants warm," Bigler wrote. "First to droop and die were the old and infirm. Soon the burial ritual each morning began to include the bodies of younger members, mainly men." The trek became, Samuel Jones remembered, "one long funeral march." Even after the first rescue wagons reached the Willie company on October 23, 1856, the ordeal continued. "The relief they provided was only temporary, just enough to get the company moving again, but inadequate to stop its suffering," the camp clerk wrote.[37]

The Willie company climbed Rocky Ridge through deep snow on "a Severe day. The wind blew awful hard, and colde," wrote Levi Savage, a returning missionary and a stalwart hero of the disaster. The few teams traveling with the handcarts hauled wagons "loaded down with the Sick, and children" so thickly stowed he feared some of them would smother. Long after dark, survivors staggered into camp, where "but few tents were pitched, and men, women, and Children Sit shivering with colde around their Small fires." Just before daylight a wagon arrived with more stragglers. "Some badly frozen; Some dying, and Some dead. It was certainly heartrending to hear Children crying for mothers, and mothers, crying for Childrin," Savage wrote.[38]

That morning, probably on Willow Creek, the Willie train "concluded to stay in camp today & bury the dead as there were 13 persons to inter." The company clerk recorded their names and ages: William James, 46; Elizabeth Bailey, 52; James Kirkwood, 11; Samuel Gadd, 10; Lars Wendin [Venden], 60; Anne Olsen, 46; Ella Nilson, 22 years; Jens Nilson, 6 years; Bodil Mortinsen, 9 years; Nils Anderson, 41 years; Ole Madsen, 41 years. "Many of the Saints have their feet & hands frozen from the severity of the weather," noted William Woodward.[39]

The Utah Pioneer Trails and Landmarks Association erected a monument on Rock Creek in 1932 to commemorate the event:

THE WILLIE'S [sic] HANDCART COMPANY

Captain James G. Willie's handcart company of Mormon emigrants on the way to Utah, greatly exhausted by the deep snows of an early winter and suffering from lack of food and clothing, had assembled here for reorganization by relief parties

---
[37] Bigler, *Forgotten Kingdom*, 111–13, 115.
[38] Savage, Journal, Oct. 23, 1856.
[39] Woodward, Emigrating Company Journal, Oct. 24, 1856.

from Utah, about the end of October, 1856. Thirteen persons were frozen to death during a single night and were buried here in one grave. Two others died the next day and were buried near by. Of the company of 404 persons 77 perished before help arrived. The survivors reached Salt Lake City November 9, 1856.

South Pass was at the center of this tragedy. It had already seen death and suffering among the first handcart trains that traveled in relatively clement weather. When William Knox Aitken returned to the United States in spring 1857, he saw the remains of an "old woman, whom we buried at the South Pass." As often happened, wolves had desecrated the woman's grave. "As I passed, her long brown hair were mingled with the tattered garments that covered her poor worn carcass. Some fell dead while pulling their hand-carts; one a little ahead of us was struck down by lightning."[40]

"The effects of our lack of food, and the terrible ordeal of the Rocky Ridge, still remained among us. Two or three died every day," John Chislett recalled. "At night we camped a little east by north from the South Pass, and two men in my hundred died." Chislett had to bury them, but the stench of their corpses made him sick and he "vomited fearfully." One of the dead men was wearing a pair of medium-heavy shoes. "I looked at them and at my own worn-out boots. I wanted them badly, but could not bring my mind to the 'sticking-point' to appropriate them," he wrote. Chislett asked for advice. "They will do you more good than they will him," William Kimball said.

In the midst of this suffering, the Willie company found part of the rescue party camped near South Pass "with several quarters of good fat beef hanging frozen on the limbs of the trees," Chislett wrote. "These quarters of beef were to us the handsomest pictures we ever saw." After surmounting the pass, "we soon experienced the influence of a warmer climate, and for a few days we made good progress," he recalled. "We constantly met teams from the Valley, with all necessary provisions. Most of these went on to Martin's company, but enough remained with us for our actual wants. At Fort Bridger we found a great many teams that had come to our help. The noble fellows who came to our assistance invariably received us joyfully, and did all in their power to alleviate our sufferings."[41]

The Willie company still faced more than a hundred miles of suffering.

---

[40] Aitken, "Adventures of a Mormon," *London Advertiser*, Aug. 9, 1857.
[41] Stenhouse, *The Rocky Mountain Saints*, 314–32.

Brigham Young was in deep denial about the extent of the disaster and thought the rescue effort, along with moderating weather, would solve the problem. "A portion of our emigration this year are very late, not having yet arrived— they have encountered severe storms on the Sweetwater," he wrote in early November. He had ordered his bishops to send them teams, wagons, provisions, clothing, and men and trusted "that their journey may be accomplished without any great degree of suffering or loss of life."[42]

Besides, Young had more important concerns than the handcart trains, most notably the machinery, hardware, personal property, and groceries loaded in the church's freight wagons. When Apostle Erastus Snow left Salt Lake in early April 1856, he carried detailed orders from Young. First, Snow was to "gather up all the articles left by you last season" and "attend to this business very carefully and strictly, particularly with regard to the steam engine, as I wish it brought on this season perfect in every particular." If Snow found "the least essential portion lacking it will be necessary for you to see that any such deficiency is made up." Snow's instructions also included a detailed specification and order for Deseret alphabet type but said not a word about the handcarts.[43] Young wanted a threshing machine, which filled one wagon, and the machinery for a woolen mill that James H. Hart said would weigh "as near as I can guess would be about 45 Tons." Hart thought about twenty "extra strong wagons" could get it to Utah.[44]

Young ordered overland veteran and Salt Lake mayor Abraham O. Smoot to take charge of the church's 1856 freight train. Smoot sent detailed reports to Salt Lake on his troubles, slow progress, and desperate need for supplies and fresh teams. The provisions that John Taylor had made clear would be essential for the success of the handcart trains instead reached Smoot at the North Platte on October 2 and two weeks later at the Little Sandy, delivering flour, "19 men, several span of horses & mules & wagons, also Beef, Flour & Vegetables." It wasn't enough, even for these veteran frontiersmen. "After travelling through a long & tedious snow storm, for the last 7 or 8 days I find myself at this place with a broken-down set of teams, with which I shall be unable to move all my train any farther," Smoot wrote from Fort Bridger in late October. His teams were too weak to haul half his freight

---

[42] Young to Cannon, Nov. 4, 1856, LDS Archives.
[43] Young to Snow, April 10 1856, Brigham Young Collection, LDS Archives.
[44] James H. Hart to Brigham Young, September 23, 1855, Brigham Young Collection, LDS Archives.

over the Wasatch Mountains, so he informed Young he had decided to "leave the Books, Thrashing machine, your Engine & fixtures & a part of the nails, glass & groceries & perhaps a portion of the Dry Goods" at Fort Bridger. The "Engine" referred to the massive steam engine Smoot had hauled from the Missouri River. At Echo Canyon, Smoot received orders from Young "to bring all the goods in and if he had not enough teams to call upon the brethren who were out in the mountains with ox teams to assist the hand cart emmigrations."[45]

Like many gifted men, Brigham Young often believed what he wanted to believe. Even in the midst of the handcart crisis, he dramatically underestimated the desperate circumstances of the hundreds of starving men, women, and children still freezing in the mountains. "As the weather has grown milder, there is no necessity for leaving any wagons and property at Bridger, hence I wish all brought in," he instructed Smoot, "and if you should deem it necessary for you to go back to see its being all certainly brought, I shall wish you to do so."[46]

Why Young attached such importance to Smoot's freight in the midst of such a human catastrophe is puzzling. They included his own "private supplies," but Smoot had already told him that "the boiler & other machinery is more or less rusted by exposure to the weather, & the books I fear, are some damaged also."[47] A winter at Fort Bridger would hardly leave them worse for wear, but it was not the machinery that worried President Young. Most likely it was not the six wagons loaded with machinery but a "Californian Wagon, marked 'Pacific Distillery,'" which Smoot found abandoned at Cottonwood Springs on September 7 and hauled to Salt Lake, along with the six tons of goods carried in Brigham Young's three private wagons. They contained his "large supply of Tobacco, Rum, Whiskey, Brandy, and other liquors, also tea and coffee," which camp clerk Caleb Green reported Smoot's train had hauled across the plains—items unlikely to survive until spring at Fort Bridger. Young, of course, publicly considered such luxuries "rather worse than useless to the Salt Lake community." Green thought the "'word of wisdom' which from B. Young is divine revelation was intended to make them as contented

---

[45] Smoot to Young, Oct. 28, 1856; Woolley, Autobiography, 15, LDS Archives.
[46] Young to Smoot, Oct. 31, 1856, LDS Archives.
[47] Young to Bernhisel, April 14, 1856; Young to Smoot, Oct. 31, 1856; Smoot to Young, Sept. 15, 1856, all LDS Archives.

as possible under the circumstances. Brigham in this case does not practice the doctrine that he teaches."[48]

After fording the Bear River on November 4, the survivors of James G. Willie's company learned "President B. Young had sent word that some freight still lying at 'Fort Bridger' was to be brought in this season & that some teams and men of our company were needed," wrote William Woodward in the camp journal. "Several teams & men were selected for the trip." Willie's party was still eighty miles from Salt Lake: seven more people, ages eight to sixty-six years, would die before they reached safety.[49]

STARVED FORMS, HAGGARD COUNTENANCES:
THE MARTIN COMPANY

Meanwhile, as November began, the Martin company was still trapped far east of South Pass in Martins Ravine after fording the intensely cold Sweetwater River near Devils Gate. Temperatures as low as eighteen degrees below zero and relentless hunger tormented the desperate emigrants. When the storm broke, the train began slowly crawling westward. "The sun was about an hour high when I spied somethin[g] in the distance that looked like a black streak in the snow. As I got near to it, I perceived it moved," rescuer Ephraim Hanks recalled. Near Ice Spring he realized he had found the long looked-for Martin company. "The sight that met my gaze as I entered their camp can never be erased from my memory! The starved forms and haggard countenances of the poor sufferers, as they moved slowly, shivering with the cold to prepare the evening meal, was enough to touch the stoutest heart. When they saw me coming they hailed me with joy inexpressible."[50]

Hanks, already a legendary frontier scout, "had left his wagon behind him and come on alone on horseback, and had managed to kill a buffalo," John Jaques recalled. "Some others of the relief parties, further this way, had come to the conclusion that the rear companies of the emigration had perished in the snow, but Eph was determined to go along, even though alone, and see for himself."[51] The bison that Hanks had killed gave the starving survivors

---

[48] Green, Journal Containing A Visit to the Great Salt Lake, Missouri Historical Society, 8–9. See also Caleb Grant [Green], Report, December 12, 1856, LDS Archives.

[49] Woodward, Willie Emigrating Company Journal, Nov. 4–9, 1856, LDS Archives.

[50] Kingsford, Leaves from the Life, 6.

[51] Jaques, Salt Lake Daily Herald, Dec. 22, 1878, 1.

their first taste of meat in weeks. "Many of the immigrants whose extremities were frozen, lost their limbs, either whole or in part. Many such I washed with water and castile soap, until the frozen parts would fall off, after which I would sever the shreds of flesh from the remaining portions of the limbs with scissors," Hanks recalled. "Some of the emigrants lost toes, others fingers, and again others whole hands and feet."[52]

The piercing cold grew colder as the terrible journey dragged on, John Jaques wrote. The Martin company crossed South Pass about 18 November, "a bitterly cold day. The snow fell fast and the wind blew piercingly from the north," making it so cold the travelers feared they would freeze if they rode in the wagons. "As the company was crossing the south pass, there was a sufficiency of wagons, for the first time, to carry all the people," Jaques remembered, "and thence forth the traveling was more rapid." When the company camped in the willows that night at Pacific Springs, about two miles west of the pass, the snow was "still falling furiously, and with one to two feet of it on the ground." Jesse Haven wrote simply, "It has been a hard days travel."[53]

The broken remnants of the Martin company, many of them unable to walk, hurried west from South Pass in mule-drawn wagons. They arrived in Great Salt Lake City on the last day of November, appearing on East Temple Street just as the Sunday congregation was leaving the old adobe tabernacle. "The meeting of the emigrants with relatives, acquaintances, and friends was not very joyous. Indeed it was very solemnly impressive. Some were so affected that they could scarcely speak, but would look at each other until the sympathetic tears would force their unbidden way," John Jaques recalled. Friends and relatives took the survivors to their homes and made them as comfortable as possible "while they thawed the frost out of their limbs and recruited their health and strength. And this ended this unfortunate expedition." Jaques concluded, "I think that none of the emigrants would be willing to endure another such a journey under any circumstances whatever. One in a lifetime is enough."[54]

How many people died in the 1856 disaster? "Censuses of the dead were never taken," historian Tom Rea observed, but handcart veterans reported about 225 souls perished in the Willie and Martin companies. The LDS

---

[52] Bigler, *Forgotten Kingdom*, 118.
[53] Jaques, *Salt Lake Daily Herald*, Dec. 22, 1878, 1; Haven, Journal, Nov. 19, 1856, LDS Archives.
[54] Jaques, *Salt Lake Daily Herald*, Dec. 22, 1878, 1.

Church's own experts estimate the ten handcart companies suffered between 252 and 340 deaths.[55]

Who was to blame for the debacle? Historians still argue about who was responsible. Even as the tragedy was unfolding, there was "a spirit of murmuring among the people, and the fault is laid upon br. Brigham."[56] In the Mormon kingdom, such dissent was intolerable. "If any man, or woman, complains of me or of my Counselors, in regard to the lateness of some of this season's immigration, let the curse of God be on them and blast their substance with mildew and destruction, until their names are forgotten from the earth," Brigham Young warned after word of the catastrophe reached Salt Lake. "I do not believe that the biggest fool in the community could entertain the thought that all this loss of life, time, and means, was through the mismanagement of the First Presidency," his fiery councilor, Jedediah M. Grant, agreed.[57]

Most Mormons appear ready to throw their own mother under a bus rather than hold accountable the man who conceived, designed, promoted, and finally lied about the handcarts. Most lay the blame on Franklin D. Richards, who made a convenient scapegoat. "Brigham attacked him in the tabernacle, held him up to ridicule and contempt, and cursed him in the name of Israel's God," wrote T. B. H. Stenhouse in the first detailed telling of the handcart story. Richards, at least, suffered for his role in the disaster. For years, he "could scarcely lift up his head; he absented himself from the public meetings and was rarely seen in times of rejoicing. His heart was crushed. He could not defend himself, for when once Brigham has spoken no man who values his favour dares to contradict him."[58]

For his part, Brigham Young was desperate to find someone to share the blame with Richards. He wrote two letters in late October and December 1856 holding his most talented subordinate, Apostle John Taylor, responsible. Young accused Taylor of "saving one and incurring three dollars expence" and asked, "Is it impossible to avail ourselves of the advantages arising from your position . . . without throwing the business, the means, the absolute dictation of this part of it into your hands?"

---

[55] Rea, *Devil's Gate*, 98; Black, "How Many Latter-Day Saints Died?" 40–44.
[56] Kimball, "Remarks," Nov. 2, 1856, *Deseret News*, Nov. 12, 1856, 282–83.
[57] Young, "Remarks"; and Grant, "Discourse," both Nov. 2, 1856, *Deseret News*, Nov. 12, 1856, 283–84.
[58] Stenhouse, *The Rocky Mountain Saints*, 842.

Taylor's response was to the point, expressing his loyalty to the cause but stoutly defending his integrity. "Why yes Brother Brigham, to be sure you can, you can have me do anything that you wish me to do, and without either coaxing or driving; all I wish is to know what that desire is," he wrote. Taylor made clear he would never, as Joseph Smith had instructed him years earlier, "resign any charge that was legally given to me." To Young's accusation that he had wasted church funds, Taylor responded, "You must have been misinformed—it is false in toto, and without any foundation or semblance in truth. I am prepared to meet any man on this or any charge, at any time or place. I have records of my acts which I am not afraid to have scrutinized."

Apostle Taylor challenged Brigham Young to consider his own role: "The Hand-Cart system was to me, and to us all, a new operation," he wrote. It was better for a small company to go "through safely than for a larger one to perish on the way." The experiment demanded the utmost care: when a train started, Taylor wanted "to know that it would go through. I knew of the weakness and infirmity of many women, children and aged persons that were calculated to go, I did not consider that a few dollars were to be put in competition with the lives of human beings."[59]

FOOLED, EVERYBODY: THE UTAH EXPEDITION

By 1857 tension between the U.S. government and the Mormon settlements in the Great Basin had been increasing for a decade. When a new president resolved in May to replace Brigham Young as governor of Utah Territory and send troops to make sure it happened, this long-simmering conflict almost exploded into war. James Buchanan's decision to dispatch the army was made too late in the spring to organize what became known as the Utah Expedition without risking winter catching it in the Rocky Mountains.

In late May, the army's senior officer, Maj. Gen. Winfield Scott, advised the secretary of war to wait until 1858 to launch the expedition. Two days later, the secretary ordered Scott to concentrate twenty-five hundred men—almost a quarter of the entire U.S. Army—at Fort Leavenworth "to march thence to Utah as soon as assembled." The units ordered to Utah, as well as the massive freight trains needed to support them, left the frontier in detachments: the Fifth and Tenth Infantry and the Fourth Artillery, totaling about half

---

[59] Taylor to Young, Feb. 24, 1857, LDS Archives, 5–6.

the force, were on the march by July 21, but the new governor, the expedition's commander, Col. Albert Sidney Johnston, and the six companies of the Second Dragoons, which should have led the parade, did not head west until mid-September. Strung out for hundreds of miles along the overland trail, the advance regiments lacked any cavalry support, and by default command fell to the senior infantry officer, Col. Edmund Alexander.[60]

Governor Young knew he was being replaced by early July, but the government failed to notify him formally until September 8, when an army quartermaster arrived to arrange winter quarters for the troops. The Mormon leader staged a dramatic announcement on July 24, 1857, the tenth anniversary of his arrival in the Salt Lake Valley. At a celebration high in a mountain canyon, Young told the by-invitation-only crowd of twenty-five hundred of his most devoted followers that the army was on its way. The Mormon people "constituted henceforth a free and independent state, to be known no longer as Utah, but by their own Mormon name of Deseret," Governor Young proclaimed. His first counselor, Heber C. Kimball, "called on the people to adhere to Brigham, as their prophet, seer, and revelator, priest, governor, and king." The Mormons denounced the approaching army as a "mob," yet another sign that their country would "grudge us an existence upon any part of God's footstool," as Young had said earlier. Over the next two months, Utah's leaders whipped up millennial enthusiasm "as fiery speeches predicted the nearness of God's kingdom and the fall of the United States government."[61]

He had been driven five times, broken up and robbed, and afflicted almost to death, President Kimball told a congregation. "Send 2500 troops here, our brethren, to make a desolation of this people? God Almighty helping me, I will fight until there is not a drop of blood in my veins," he vowed. "Good God! I have enough wives to whip the United States, for they will whip themselves."[62]

Determined to stop the army in its tracks, the Mormon leaders adopted a strategy centered around South Pass. They sent units of the Nauvoo Legion to reconnoiter the advancing army and cache supplies as far east as Devils Gate, where seventy of their irregular cavalry spotted the army's advance elements on September 22. Colonel Alexander ordered forced marches in an

---

[60] MacKinnon, *At Sword's Point*, 130, 295, 354. For another recent study, see Bigler and Bagley, *The Mormon Rebellion: America's First Civil War*.
[61] "Celebration of July Fourth," *Deseret News*, July 9, 1856, 140/3; Browne, "The Utah Expedition," 368; Poll, *Utah's History*, 167.
[62] "Remarks," *Deseret News*, Aug. 12, 1857, 179/2.

attempt to catch up with the unprotected supply trains already approaching the Green River. Mormon raiders struck the army's advanced units at Pacific Springs early on September 25, 1857.

"This morning about 2 o'clock several shots were fired immediately behind my tent, and immediately the whole herd of mules stampeded with a terrific rush," Capt. Jesse Gove of the Tenth Infantry informed his wife. The rapid gunfire surprised Gove, and the herders began crying, "soldiers turn out, we are attacked." Gove always kept a candle and matches by his bed, and his company was the first to assemble "under arms, rifles loaded, awaiting orders." Colonel Alexander had the presence of mind to have his bugler sound stable call, but a minor miracle saved the regiment's mules. "The herders always have one mule which wears a bell," Gove wrote. "By this all the herd is governed; they will follow it wherever it goes. Well, the bell mule by the merest accident got caught by the picket rope in a wild sage bush, stopping him, and with him most of the herd stopped." The sound of stable call meant oats to the mules, and they turned and stampeded toward the bugles, taking the mounts of the Mormons, who had dismounted to fight, with them. The herders collected all the stray mules, and the Mormon mounts, too. "I think the ball is about to open," Gove said.[63]

The high-water mark of the Mormon Rebellion took place at dawn on October 5, 1857, at Simpsons Hollow on the Big Sandy River a little more than forty miles west of South Pass. Lot Smith's Nauvoo Legionnaires captured Lewis Simpson's train and burned twenty-two wagons loaded with military supplies. Mormon raiders destroyed two additional freight trains loaded with 368,000 pounds of supplies, mostly provisions. Smith later joined forces with Porter Rockwell and ran off more than a thousand of the expedition's cattle. These adventures ended abruptly when federal cavalry arrived.[64]

The burning of the government supply trains created the response that Brigham Young had hoped for in the States, but the provocative action had unintended consequences. "Recent accounts from Utah confirm the declaration made by Brigham Young that he would resist the United States troops to the utmost and that he with his wives could conquer the entire army, an assertion of no trifling nature at the present time," wrote the *Missouri Democrat*. "The troops were reported to have retreated from the South Pass, then in possession of the Mormons." The newspaper inflated reports of the Nauvoo Legion's destruction of the supply trains into a military victory, but

---

[63] Gove, *The Utah Expedition*, 64–65.
[64] Furniss, *The Mormon Conflict*, 109, 116, 144–45.

lamented, "The Mormons have possession of the only accessible pass in the mountains" and would defend their position until reinforcements arrived.[65] Such reports generated considerable anger, for many Americans considered the attacks on government property as a declaration of war.

The Mormon strategy depended on forming an alliance with the Indian nations of the Great Plains and the Rockies, but this plan had little appeal to the tribes who had grown weary of Mormons settling on their best lands. Washakie met the army at the Green River in late September with an offer "to take 1200 warriors into the field. They are a splendid set of men," wrote Captain Gove. No American military commander was yet prepared to recruit Indian allies, especially to fight white people, but Gove thought Alexander's refusal to hire some of the Shoshones as hunters and guides reflected the incompetence of the "old woman." The young captain thought Alexander was "the most worthless old fogy in the world, frightened to death. He is in his dotage, and I really believe he is a little frightened."[66]

Colonel Alexander's lethargy wasted two weeks of beautiful fall weather marching up and down Hams Fork, trying to find a way to enter Utah without facing the Mormons manning the fortifications in the narrows near the mouth of Echo Canyon. The Nauvoo Legion commander issued orders that if the army stayed on the road to Fort Hall, the soldiers should not be molested, but if they marched west from Fort Bridger, they were to "pitch into their picket guards and sentinels, and among them all you can." If troops threatened to enter the northern settlements, Young ordered his soldiers to harass the army "both by night and by day, until they take their final sleep: pick off their guards and sentries & fire into their camps by night, and pick off officers and as many men as possible by day." Young also gave orders not to destroy any more wagon trains, for "we may need the articles they contain." If the troops attempted to enter Deseret, Young wrote, "we shall fall heir to the property in their possession."[67]

"I have informed Colonel Alexander that had his command been the men who have heretofore mobbed us, and the lying scribblers and the wicked rabble who have all the day long been trying to incite mobs against us," Brigham Young taunted the indecisive commander in October, "they never would have seen the South Pass." In the meantime, the Mormon commanders

---

[65] "From Kansas," *Deseret News*, Feb. 17, 1858, 397/3.
[66] Gove, *The Utah Expedition*, 66.
[67] Bigler, *Forgotten Kingdom*, 153; MacKinnon, *At Sword's Point*, 323, 359.

issued orders to employ lethal force if necessary. "You are already aware of our mode of warfare, to stampede animals, cut off scouting parties, and use every other means to wipe out our enemies," Young ordered one commander. "If we have to kill men pick off the officers when they least expect it. We wish to whip them without killing them except some contemptible wretch of an officer who is for a fight."[68]

The Mormons had a formidable ally waiting in the wings: the weather. "Our most potent enemy at present is the snow and constitutes at present our chief embarrassment," Colonel Johnston wrote on October 18, the day he crossed South Pass. The weather stopped the army's advance up Hams Fork, forcing Alexander to give up his "design of penetrating Salt Lake City." He plodded back to the wagon road, still paralyzed by indecision.

Johnston and his cavalry caught up with the Army of Utah on November 3 after a "slow and tedious" march from South Pass. Even though "the road was excellent and the weather fine," his party had averaged only eleven miles a day "on account of the broken down condition of the draught animals." A blizzard struck the command during their march to Fort Bridger, and the thermometer quickly dropped to sixteen degrees below zero. The lack of adequate forage west of South Pass had debilitated the army's livestock, and animals began dying rapidly. At least three thousand head of cattle perished during the arduous march. "The army under my command took the last possible step forward at Bridger, in the condition of the animals then alive," Johnston reported.[69]

The Army of Utah's rearguard faced its own crisis when the blizzard caught the last units east of South Pass. As the Second Dragoons under Col. Philip St. George Cooke struggled over the rugged terrain, the temperature dropped to twelve degrees below zero on November 8, and one historian reported the mercury read forty-four below. "Last night was an awful night, the most disagreeable I think that I ever felt. The wind blew a storm all night sweeping the snow in our direction—The piteous cries of the famished mules was heart rending. They crowd around our camp fire, and seemed to beg for food in the most supplicating cries but we had none to spare them," wrote army sutler William A. Carter. "The storm still raged furiously. We had 14 miles to make, but fortunately the wind blew in our backs most of the time all day. The wind

---

[68] Hafen and Hafen, *The Utah Expedition*, 193; Young to Merrill, Sept. 28, 1857; Young and Wells to Cummings and Burton, Sept. 25, 1857, Nauvoo Legion Letterbook, Arrington Papers, Utah State Univ.
[69] Hafen, *The Utah Expedition*, 155, 173; Furniss, *The Mormon Conflict*, 113–16.

CONFLICT AND CATASTROPHE AT SOUTH PASS 189

swept with wild fury drifting the snow around us and up across our road. At every half mile a mule was turned loose unable to proceed any further."[70]

Similar weather helped kill almost three hundred Latter-day Saints the previous fall. How many soldiers perished in 1857? "Because of Cooke's ability as a leader, only one man died during the arduous march," near Chimney Rock, "and he had been the victim of lockjaw," reported historian Norman L. Furniss. Historian John Eldredge identified an additional casualty of the blizzard, James Curran, a sleeping private killed by a ricochet. Beyond Cooke's sterling leadership, the fact that the army fed and sheltered its men made a critical difference to their survival—but "of the 144 horses in his original command, 130 lay dead on the thousand miles of Plains behind him."[71]

The army went into winter quarters at Fort Bridger and Camp Scott, the new post built two miles up Blacks Fork from the smoking ruins the Mormons left behind at the old trading station. Both sides hunkered down and prepared for a spring campaign. Johnston dispatched thirty-five volunteers under Capt. Randolph B. Marcy to New Mexico to procure additional supplies, mounts, and men. He sent others, notably the redoubtable B. F. Ficklin, north to the Flathead country to buy horses and cattle from the mountaineers.[72] When the Utah territorial legislature met in December, Governor Young charged that federal troops were sent to Utah to execute the government's plan "to deprive us of every vestige of Constitutional rights" and "destroy the inhabitants of Utah." He claimed the "prolonged howl of base slander" from the press was intended "to excite to a frenzy a spirit for our extermination."[73]

The Mormons had decided to burn their property and flee to the mountains if necessary, but they also planned an aggressive spring offensive. Gen. James Ferguson of the Nauvoo Legion proposed arming "mountain brigades" with bows and arrows. The legislature authorized creation of "the Standing Army of Deseret" or the "Standing Army of the Kingdom of God," a full-time military force of between 1,000 and 1,200 men. "Twelve squadrons of mounted riflemen of one hundred each were recruited and equipped in a few days," the earliest Mormon account of the conflict reported. "Each supplied with two horses, a revolver and carbine, and sufficient food for six months,

---

[70] Carter, "Diary," Nov. 10, 1857, 105.
[71] Furniss, *The Mormon Conflict*, 117–18. Eldredge identified six other soldiers who died during the march. See his *Utah War*, 9, 18–19, 35.
[72] Browne, "The Utah Expedition," 371–73.
[73] Young, "Governor's Message," Journal History, Dec. 15, 1857.

these twelve hundred cavalrymen, the cream of our youth, constituted an imposing body" of elite troops.

The Mormons planned to seize South Pass and "intercept any reinforcement of troops and supplies coming from the United States through this channel; assign two squadrons to the task of overtaking the horses and mules Captain Marcy was to bring back from New Mexico; then resume positions along Devils Gate, that steep mountain chasm straddling the road just ahead of the Sweetwater and offering a series of formidable strategic points," French convert Louis Bertrand wrote in 1862. "This plan, as simple as it was practical, would no doubt have been crowned with success." Despite his sixteen field guns and "three thousand heroes at Fort Bridger," General Johnston "would have found himself in the dire necessity at surrendering without even the satisfaction of having fired a single cap."[74]

Fortunately, none of this came to pass, and America avoided what would have been a disastrous religious war. Immediately after dismissing an unofficial emissary from President Buchanan in early March 1858, Brigham Young received word that Shoshone and Bannock raiders (perhaps with the encouragement of B. F. Ficklin) had attacked the northernmost Mormon settlement at Fort Limhi on the Salmon River in today's Idaho. Without the help of Indian allies, Young realized, the Mormons could not resist the military might of the United States. He sent word he was willing to send supplies to Camp Scott. That spring Buchanan issued a "full and free pardon to all who will submit themselves to the authority of the federal government," which Mormon leaders grudgingly accepted after two "peace commissioners" delivered it in June 1858. "Thus was peace made—thus was ended the 'Mormon War,'" reported Lemuel Fillmore of the *New York Herald*. He summarized the outcome: "killed, none; wounded, none; fooled, everybody."[75]

Jaded and Worn Out: The Last Handcart Trains

As the last wagon trains struggled to reach Salt Lake in 1856, LDS Church leaders proclaimed the handcart system a success and doggedly pressed on, eventually organizing two more handcart trains in 1857, one in 1859, and two

---

[74] Bigler, *Forgotten Kingdom*, 183–84; Stout, *On the Mormon Frontier*, 2:652; Homer, *On the Way to Somewhere Else*, 107–108.

[75] Bigler, *Forgotten Kingdom*, 157–58, 184–89; Gove, *The Utah Expedition*, 351.

in 1860. "This season's operations have demonstrated that the Saints, being filled with faith and the Holy Ghost, can walk across the plains, drawing their provisions and clothing on hand carts," the church's First Presidency announced in December 1856. "The experience of this season will of course help us to improve in future operations; but the plan has been fairly tested and proved entirely successful." The handcart system was "as easy as and indeed easier than that method hitherto practiced; and the women endured the trip quite as well, in comparison, as the men."[76]

To show that handcarts were better than wagons, Brigham Young dispatched about seventy "handcart missionaries" from Utah to the Missouri River in April 1857. Their redesigned handcarts were built of good lumber, and these young Mormon frontiersmen were well provisioned. Yet when westbound wagonwright Chauncey Webb, who had built some of the 1856 carts, met the handcart missionaries at Devils Gate, he "found them completely jaded and worn out."[77]

The first reports from the missionaries had hailed the trek as a great success. "We traveled with our hand-carts across the plains to Florence, Nebraska Territory, without horse, mules, cow, or any other animal to assist: drawing in them our provisions, bedding, cooking utensils, tents, &c." They reached the Missouri on June 10 "in the full enjoyment of health," having made "the entire trip from point to point in 48 days," reported the "Clerk of the Hand-Cart Company," Daniel Mackintosh, "but out of that number, we lay by to rest, repair carts, &c., 7½ days, which would make the total number of traveling days 40½, and we would remark that we are satisfied that the trip can be accomplished in a shorter period, say from 30 to 35 days."[78]

Private reports lacked such enthusiasm. "I will not attempt to relate to you all the incidents witch happned on our trip. Sufice it to say that in all our hardships the Lord was with us & blessed us and thank God it is over now," Salt Lake actor Philip Margetts told his wife. He praised the handcart system as "the prettyest way to travil that ever was but we traviled quick witch made it hard work for some." He and his two companions had hauled 150 to 200 pounds and "Consumed about 350lbs of provisions including every thing" by the time they reached Florence. "I thought of you when I have come into Camp

---

[76] *Deseret News,* Dec. 10, 1856, 313–14.
[77] Young, *Wife No. 19,* 226–27.
[78] Mackintosh, "Correspondence," 3. The author's great-great-grandfather, David Brinton, was captain of the fourth ten in the party.

with my feet all—all Blisterd & fatiged in body with no one to Console me but him witch is above all. Then as soon as we arrived in Camp the next thing was to do another half days work that was to get Chips & Cook supper."[79]

Ironically, Brigham Young had come up with another ambitious plan that might have made the handcart system successful: The Brigham Young Express & Carrying Company, or the Y.X. or B.Y.X. Company. Young began developing a series of "ranch forts" along the trail in 1856, where substantial settlements would provide way stations at such key locations as Loup Fork, Deer Creek, and Devils Gate. Young had gained control of the federal mail contract for Utah in 1856, and the Mormons established a mail station at the Last Crossing of the Sweetwater, near South Pass. The outbreak of the Utah War turned this promising operation into another financial debacle for the hard-pressed Mormon economy when the massive investment literally went up in smoke. Having expended so much capital on the B.Y.X. project, the church lacked the resources to properly finance the 1857 emigration. As a handcart train ran out of supplies on the Sweetwater River, surprising sympathizers came to their aid.

"We appreciated the fact that at one time when our company was nearly without food, almost like a miracle, the Army came to our rescue," recalled handcart veteran Carl Dorius. An army captain "approached us and said in a kindly way, that one of his oxen had a crushed foot. If we could use it we were welcome to have it. This came as a blessing, because the company had been without any meat for several weeks. It was a real treat," Dorius wrote. Christian Christiansen, captain of the seventh handcart company, sent to Salt Lake City for provisions, but they "came too late to help. One tenth of the company died for want of care and nourishment."[80]

Mormon James Jensen described the same event on the Sweetwater. "There, one of Uncle Sam's fat oxen had one of its feet crushed by a wagon which ran over it. In that condition it was of course thought unfit by the captain for the food of his men." He walked up, "and in a half-joking manner said, 'You may have that ox. I guess you need it.'" The soldiers "treated us kindly—and the Army was a Blessing to our people in Utah," Kersten Erickson Benson recalled. "We didn't have any trouble with the Indians," Sarah Hancock Beesley remembered. "In fact they saved our lives at various times, such as when they gave us food." California overlanders "often pitied us and

---

[79] Phillip to Elizabeth Margetts, June 14, 1857, punctuation added. Michelle Margetts graciously provided a transcription of her ancestor's letter.
[80] Dorius, Journal, *The Dorius Heritage*, 86–88.

gave us food," she remembered. "Yes, I crossed the plains with a handcart once but I am thankful I have never had to again."⁸¹

Hunger was a constant companion for all the handcart pioneers. "The standard ration was one pint of flour per day, children less;" wrote the leading authority on the topic, Lyndia Carter, "but frequently the ration had to be reduced to keep supplies from running out entirely."⁸² Every company suffered hunger and privation, so much so that it appears the failure to provide adequate provisions for Mormon trains was a matter of policy.

Before reaching Fort Laramie in 1857, the Israel Evans party's provisions were almost exhausted, Robert Fishburn recalled. "We had not the slightest idea where we were going to procure any. This gave us some uneasiness when we realized that we still had five hundred miles to travel before reaching our destination." Fishburn learned that Brigham Young had ordered large amounts of flour to be stored along the road to relieve emigrants. These supplies, however, were not free. After Fishburn's train "finished up everything we had in the company in the shape of provisions," Evans gathered the party together and asked how they felt about handing over all their personal property, "which consisted of our handcarts, teams and wagons, tents, cooking utensils, etc., to the Church when we arrived in Salt Lake City, if we were provided with provisions through the remainder of our journey," Fishburn remembered. "We very willingly agreed to hand them over rather than starve; and while we could not help but feel that somebody was at fault for the scanty supply of provisions furnished us, we could not do otherwise than acknowledge the hand of a kind and over-ruling Providence in blessing his servant Brigham with wisdom and foresight sufficient to cause such an abundance of provisions to be sent out and stored at different points expressly for the relief of any and all emigrants who might need such relief."⁸³

The failure to provide adequate provisions for handcart companies continued until the scheme ended. Both Henry Hobbs and Ann Jarvis Stickney described the suffering of the George Rowley company west of South Pass in 1859. "Many of the Saints are faint[,] worn & weary & comming in hours after the rest with their H.C.," Hobbs wrote. "Much of this weakness is caused through the lack of food." He also observed that "some who have not a sufficient

---

⁸¹ Jensen, Reminiscences, 12–41; Erickson, Recollections, 1–3; Beesley, Reminiscences, 34, all LDS Archives.
⁸² Carter, "Mormon Handcart Companies," 11.
⁸³ Fishburn, "Pioneer Autobiographies," 2:205–206.

quantity of clothes suffer the cold nights." One of the last two handcart trains went three days without food. Stickney recalled how Rowley's handcart train "suffered extremely for want of provisions." Her mother's very poor health made it impossible for her family to get her proper nourishment. "We were four days without bread or flour, with nothing to eat but what we could pick from the bones of an old ox," she remembered. "On the third day we were without bread, she died very suddenly." John S. Stucki remembered his party in 1860 had "just half as much as is considered an average person needs to live on."[84]

"The hand-cart scheme was perfectly feasible, if carried out under proper management," historian H. H. Bancroft wrote long ago. Many historians still consider the project an overall success. "Despite the drudgery and the tragic drama, most of the handcart emigrants felt they had reached their goal and that was what mattered, not what they had gone through to get there," Lyndia Carter concluded. The handcart plan "clearly proved its feasibility by the fact that eight of the ten emigrant handcart companies had made the trip as successfully as any wagon company," historian Howard A. Christy argued.[85]

Yet it is hard to find veterans of the eight allegedly successful handcart trains who would agree with this assessment. "Don't ask me anything about that," Sarah Hancock Beesley responded years later when someone asked about her experience as a handcart pioneer in 1859. "Those are dreadful stories and I don't see why we shouldn't try to forget them. I say 'Bury them with the dead who died on the plains.' My children have often tried to get me to write my handcart story but I will not." Danish handcart captain John A. Ahmanson called the vehicles *"tohjulede Menneskepiner,"* which has been translated as "two-wheeled man-tormentors" but might be better rendered as two-wheeled torture devices. "Of course it was a dreadfully hard journey and like the other companies we suffered from lack of food," recalled Hannah Lapish. She traded her jewelry for seven hundred pounds of flour that ran out before her train reached Green River. "Our company was one of the last companies to make the journey in that pathetic way," she said. "We handcart people will never outlive the memory of those experiences."[86]

---

[84] Hobbs, Journal, Aug. 19, 22, 1859, LDS Archives; Stucki, *Journal,* 42–46; Stickney, "Autobiography," 9:439.

[85] Bancroft, *History of Utah,* 430; Carter, "Mormon Handcart Companies," 14; Christy, "Weather, Disaster, and Responsibility," 9.

[86] Beesley, Reminiscences, in Handcart Stories, LDS Archives, 28–34; Matteson and Matteson, "Mormon Influence on Scandinavian Settlement"; Ahmanson, *Secret History,* 33; Lapish, Recollection, LDS Archives, 37–40. Ellipses omitted. Lapish was "very enthusiastic about" the handcart story, Sarah Hancock Beesley recalled.

CONFLICT AND CATASTROPHE AT SOUTH PASS 195

"To all, the journey, with its great and incessant toils, its wearing hardships, and wasting privations, was a hard and bitter experience, wholly unanticipated," wrote John Jaques in 1879. "But to many, and especially to women and children who had been delicately brought up and tenderly cared for, and who had never known want nor been subject to hardships previously, as well as to the weakly and elderly of both sexes, it was cruel to a degree far beyond the power of language to express, and the more so for the reason that the worst parts of the experience were entirely unnecessary, because avoidable by timely measures and more sagacious management." Jaques asked himself who he blamed for his "hard and bitter experience" as a handcart pioneer. "I blame nobody. I am not anxious to blame anybody," he wrote. "I am not writing for the purpose of blaming anybody, but to fill up a blank page of history with matters of much interest."[87]

During Brigham Young's lifetime, faithful Latter-day Saints seldom spoke about the handcart disasters, leaving the story to be told by dissenters and "apostates." Today, however, Mormons fondly embrace this tragic tale as a testament to their ancestors' faith or fortitude. Every year, thousands of people commemorate the handcart experience, and teenagers push and pull handcarts over the original tracks up Rocky Ridge. It is a worthy tribute to the sacrifice and suffering of their pioneer ancestors but all too often degenerates into a celebration of modern religious propaganda.

It is impossible to accurately estimate the handcart system's total casualties, since Mormon authorities "tried to keep the full horror of the disaster from becoming public, especially in England. But it would be safe to estimate the total at well over two hundred, or at least one in five of the last two companies, with many others maimed for life," wrote David L. Bigler. "One thing is certain—the handcart disaster of 1856 was the greatest single tragedy in the history of the nation's move west in the nineteenth century."[88]

"Oh it was so hard," said Sarah Hancock Beesley. The handcart system never resolved how to provide enough food for people who could not haul it themselves in their small human-powered carts. The system resulted in the largest loss of life in the three decades of overland wagon travel on the Oregon, California, and Mormon trails, killing in its first year at least five times as many men, women, and children as perished with the Donner party.

---

[87] Jaques, *Salt Lake Daily Herald*, Jan. 19, 1879, 1. Jaques suggested "freely and fully" canceling the remaining PEF debt.

[88] Bigler, *Forgotten Kingdom*, 118.

Ultimately, it was a system that replaced draft animals with human beings and put "a few dollars . . . in competition with the lives of human beings," as John Taylor wrote. "Truly," as Lyndia Carter observed, "the Mormon handcart pioneers went west the hard way."[89]

BETTER THAN THE SOUTH PASS:
THE CHEROKEE TRAIL AND THE OVERLAND STAGE

By 1843 the Oregon Trail over South Pass had become *the* overland wagon road, but frontier veterans such as James Beckwourth, Moses Harris, James Clyman, Louis Vasquez, and Jim Bridger knew about an alternate route to the south. They had all crossed the Great Divide Basin and "the ridge which divides the waters of the Atlantic from those of the Pacific ocean" during the winter of 1825 with William Ashley. Their recollection of that experience would eventually give birth to a more direct (if drier) road across the plains that ultimately replaced South Pass.[90]

In late June 1847, Moses Harris told Thomas Bullock, Brigham Young's clerk, that if the Mormons attempted to cross the Oregon Trail in winter and found snow blocking the road, when they "arrived 3 miles above 'Devil's Gate' on the Sweetwater, look to your left; you will see an open space in the Mountains; go thro' it." The opening Harris described is now known as Muddy Gap. Highway 287 uses it to reach the Great Divide Basin and Rawlins. "Then let your course be West, till you top the hill out of the Great Plain. Then look to the South and you will see a Square But[t]e. Leave it to the left. Go on and cross Green River, then let your course be West to Bridger's Fort, by the road."[91] Following Harris's directions today, Thomas Bullock could have taken Interstate 80 to his destination.

As geographer John Logan Allen noted, the knowledge that such an alternative existed was not new. Only three years after the rediscovery of South Pass, an anonymous mountaineer—perhaps Jim Bridger—had suggested another road across the Rockies could head east from Green River and ascend "the valley of the Bitter Creek, thence crossing the north fork of the Platte near the medicine Bow mountain, and the laramie River in Laramie plains. It would cross the Sherman Hills country, and the southern part of the Black Hills, and

---

[89] Carter, "Mormon Handcart Companies," 2.
[90] Morgan, *The West of William Ashley*, 106–107.
[91] Bullock, *The Pioneer Camp of the Saints*, 203–204.

probably descend the Lodge Pole Creek to its junction with the South Platte." This was the route the first transcontinental railroad would follow in 1868.[92]

Late in the summer of 1849, John Wilson, whose expansive federal job made him both the "Salt Lake Indian Agent" and the agent for most of California, sent the secretary of the interior important news from Great Salt Lake City about the overland wagon road. The Oregon-California Trail was a desert "in every sense of the term," he said. But there was already a road "opened by partial travel almost in a direct line from Fort Bridger to Fort Laramie," Wilson reported, "which will cut off more than 150 miles in the distance." Louis Vasquez of Fort Bridger said the trail was "a much better road & passes the rocky Mountains by a pass considerably *lower* than the South pass, & affords a better supply of both water & grass the whole road." As proof, Wilson said Vasquez was taking seven or eight ox teams to Fort Laramie to pick up the fort's fall supply of goods, "& he intends returning that way with his loaded wagons—thus avoiding a most barren & indeed to his cattle mules &c a disastrous road now traveled from Larame to the South pass."[93]

Nothing much came of this alternate until the Washington County Gold Mining Company left the Grand Saline River in the Cherokee Nation with forty wagons and some 130 Arkansans and Cherokees on April 24, 1849, to join the rush to California. The party included five slaves belonging to Cherokee members of the party and about ten free blacks. Under the leadership of Lewis Evans, the company blazed a trail north across today's Oklahoma, picked up the Santa Fe Trail east of the future site of McPherson, Kansas, and followed it up the Arkansas River to the trading post at Fort Pueblo. They came north along the Front Range to the South Platte River, where they buried a small brass cannon at Cherry Creek.[94]

Much of this route used the Trapper's Trail, an old pack train trace connecting Fort Laramie with Taos and Santa Fe. From today's Denver the trailblazers marched to Fort St. Vrain, an abandoned trading post on the South Platte about 140 miles north of Pueblo. "We had a good road and down the Platte to the mouth of another stream," the Big Thompson River, John Rankin Pyeatt wrote. The company ferried the South Platte below the mouth of the swollen

---

[92] *Niles' Weekly Register*, Oct. 6, 1827.
[93] Morgan, *Shoshonean Peoples*, 139.
[94] Madsen, *Exploring the Great Salt Lake*, 631–32; Fletcher and Fletcher, *Cherokee Trail Diaries*, 1:26; Whiteley, *The Cherokee Trail*, 3; "The Find on the Desert," *Salt Lake Tribune*, May 11, 1902, 31. Clem McNair's 1850 Cherokee Trail party included "105 men, 15 negroes and 12 females."

Cache la Poudre River. From here, the party was "without road, trail or guide through the plains" of today's northwest Colorado and southwest Wyoming.[95] The Cherokee train followed the Cache la Poudre "thro' the mountains to Laramie Plains; thence crossed Laramie river near the mountains, crossed Medicine Bow river, crossed Medicine Bow Mountains; crossed the North Park and North Platt, Green river, south of the South Pass, and intersected the Independence road on Black's Fork, about 14 miles west of Green River," as New Yorker Oliver Wack Lipe described their trek. Evans led thirty wagons to the North Platte River near present Rawlins, Wyoming. From here they crossed the Great Divide Basin and the Red Desert along the general line of today's Interstate 80. Near today's Granger, they joined the Oregon-California Trail east of Fort Bridger.[96] It was the first time westbound wagons had ever crossed the central Rockies using a different route than South Pass. Four more trains crossed the trail in 1850, and packers blazed a new trail to Fort Bridger sometimes known as the Southern Cherokee Trail.

Before he completed his survey of the Salt Lake Valley in 1850, topographical engineer Howard Stansbury decided "not to return by the beaten track, but to endeavour to ascertain the practicability of some more direct route than that now travelled to the waters of the Atlantic." He had heard about a route that headed directly for the North Platte near the Medicine Bow Mountains and skirted the southern edge of the Laramie Plains to reach the head of Lodgepole Creek, which descended into the South Platte. "A straight line would thus be accomplished from Fort Bridger," Stansbury reported, "and the detour through the South Pass and the valley of the Sweetwater, as well as all the ruggedness of the Black Hills, upon that line, be entirely avoided." Mountaineers considered such a trail "entirely practicable." Stansbury's claim that the practicality of the route was unresolved was disingenuous: he knew emigrant wagons had successfully crossed the trail for two years. He even called the wagon road east of Bitter Creek "'Evans' trail." On his return in September 1850, southwest of today's Rawlins between Muddy Creek and Sage Creek, Stansbury crossed Bridger Pass, which neither of the Cherokee routes had used.[97]

Cattlemen and emigrants from Arkansas and Mormons from Texas used the Cherokee Trail heavily throughout the 1850s. The government made a tentative

---
[95] Whiteley, *The Cherokee Trail*, 15–16.
[96] Ibid., 16; *Cherokee Advocate*, 21 Jan. 1850.
[97] Stansbury, *Exploration and Survey*, 229; Madsen, *Exploring the Great Salt Lake*, 631, 650.

CONFLICT AND CATASTROPHE AT SOUTH PASS 199

effort to develop the Bridger Pass route in 1856 when it sent Lt. Francis T. Bryan to survey a trail from the Platte up Lodgepole Creek to the Laramie Plains. Using Indian trails and advice from Arapaho leader Eagle Head, Bryan struck "the beaten track of the emigrant route" near Medicine Bow Butte. It was a very good road, he observed, but he saw so many worn out horse and mule shoes he advised trains using it to consider taking a forge along. The trail's fine, hard gravel "was very destructive to the feet of our animals." Bryan was unable to find Bridger Pass but claimed he had reached "the nearest practicable point to it as far as we could ascertain" before being forced to turn back "by fear of starvation of our animals, so little subsistence of any kind does this region afford." Perhaps to reduce his fear, the army sent Bryan out again in 1857, when he bridged Sage Creek, and in 1858 to improve the route.[98]

The Utah War made use of the road an urgent matter. Albert Sidney Johnston sent John Bartleson east in December 1857 to find a direct route from Fort Bridger to Fort Laramie, believing reinforcements for the Utah Expedition could use it to reach his post at Blacks Fork "a month earlier than by the Oregon and California Route, South Pass." Bartleson completed his trek in only three weeks. He crossed Bridger Pass on Bryan's wagon road on December 12, "the dividing ridge, which is so level that it is hardly perceivable; we still follow the wagon trail, which is very good." He thought that "this pass is better than the south pass." Next spring, Capt. Randolph B. Marcy brought provisions and fresh livestock from New Mexico to the Army of Utah over the trail.

The army developed the Bridger Pass route as a military road in 1858 when Company A of the Army Corps of Engineers sent an advance detail "to explore the country and prepare the road in advance of the main body." Lt. William Seville found the scenery at Bridger Pass "entirely too commonplace to satisfy our expectations of a pass through the Rocky Mountains." Despite the improvements to the road, no trains or commands should "be sent after us over this route," for the shorter distance did not compensate for the lack of grass, a senior officer warned.[99]

Despite such negative assessments, the Bridger Pass wagon road's shorter distance and lower elevation gave it distinct advantages over the South Pass road. The Cherokee Trail proved to be the road of the future.

---

[98] Bryan, "Road from Ft. Riley to Bridger's Pass," Aug. 6, 7, 15, 1856; Fletcher and Fletcher, *Cherokee Trail Diaries*, 3:197.
[99] Ibid., 3:221–25.

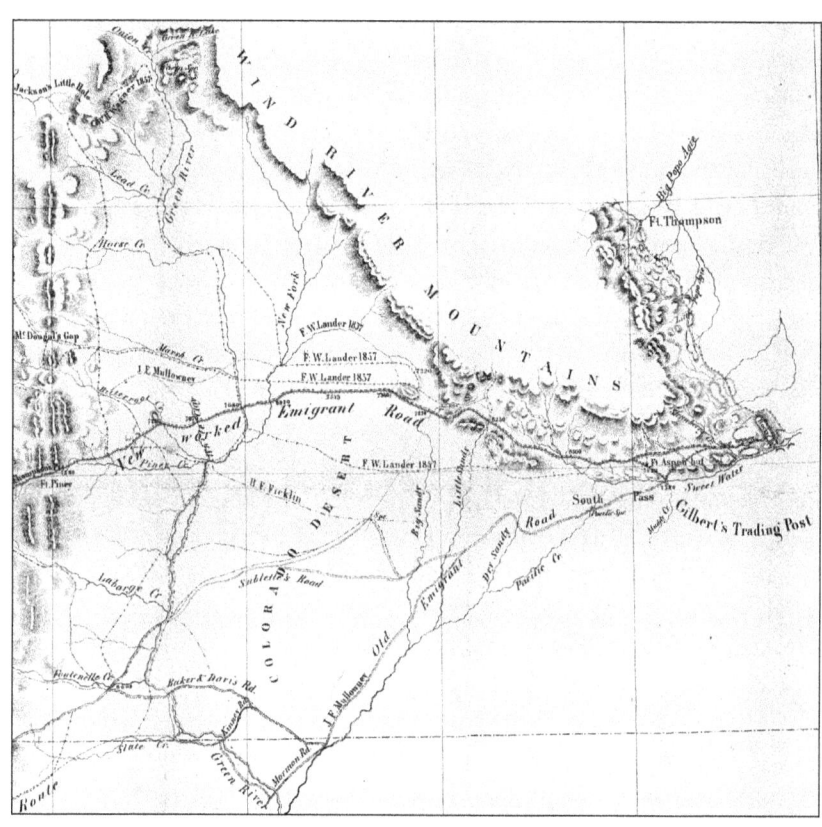

DETAIL FROM PRELIMINARY MAP
OF LANDER'S CENTRAL DIVISION, 1859
Expedition engineer William H. Wagner produced this map of the South Pass section and the "New worked Emigrant Road" of the Fort Kearney, South Pass, and Honey Lake Wagon Road in 1859. It remains one of the best maps of the Lander Cutoff and early emigrant roads over South Pass. *Author's collection.*

CHAPTER 8

"Emphatically an Emigrant Road"
The Lander Cutoff

FREDERICK WILLIAM LANDER WAS BORN TO A LONG LINE OF famous New England patriots, notably Nathaniel West, who made a fortune commanding the privateer *Black Prince* during the Revolution.[1] That the man who signed as simply "F. W. Lander" had his middle name "mysteriously changed from William to West long after he died" is not surprising.[2] It was natural, since this forgotten American hero, who lived a life as adventurous and romantic as any nineteenth-century American and died fighting to save the Union, should have made his most enduring mark in the American West. His name is widely honored in Wyoming, where it adorns his cutoff, a peak near South Pass, a creek, and the town of Lander, while Nevada named a county after him. Otherwise he has vanished from historical memory, despite his accomplishments as an engineer, explorer, diplomat, and general. One admirer said Lander had "more presidential material than a dozen Fremonts," leaving historians to wonder what he might have accomplished had he not died before his fortieth birthday.[3]

The Lander Trail's complex history was "thoroughly intertwined with the major issues confronting the United States during the 1850s," historian

---

[1] Jermy Benton Wight's *The Oregon Trail: Frederick W. Lander and the Lander Trail* contains the best recent research on the Lander Cutoff. Lander's middle name was William, not West. Douglas Branch seems to have introduced the error in 1929 in "Frederick West Lander, Road-Builder," 172.

[2] Ecelbarger, *Frederick W. Lander: The Great Natural American Soldier*, 5. Surprisingly little has been written about this remarkable American or his cutoff. Gary Ecelbarger's biography focuses on Lander's military career, but it and Peter T. Harstad's "The Lander Trail," 14–28, are the best summaries of Lander's work in the West. Leland, *Frederick West [sic] Lander* is useful. Houston and Houston's "The 1859 Lander Expedition Revisited" corrects several long-standing errors.

[3] Houston and Houston, "The 1859 Lander Expedition Revisited," 51.

Peter T. Harstad noted.[4] When California entered the Union in 1850, the West acquired a voice in Washington. Seventy-five thousand Californians petitioned Congress in 1856 "praying that a road might be built through the South Pass"—the largest petition "by many tens of thousands of names, ever introduced into that body," John B. Weller said when he submitted the appeal to the Senate.[5] The sectional politics of the time rendered Congress unable to choose a route for a transcontinental railroad. Southerners insisted such a vital transportation corridor use a snow-free route to the south, while northerners preferred a path that would serve their growing industrial might and the largest port on the Pacific, San Francisco.

To resolve the conflict, Congress appropriated $150,000 to identify the best route for a railroad to the Pacific in 1853. The army's Corps of Topographic Engineers surveyed five potential transcontinental routes "to ascertain the most practicable and economical route for a railroad from the Mississippi River to the Pacific Ocean."[6] Along with an additional expedition to identify the best prospective line between the Sacramento Valley and the Columbia River, these explorations lasted for two years. The hope "to locate scientifically the best route" and so diffuse the political conflict failed entirely, since Secretary of War Jefferson Davis wanted a snow-free route rather than the Oregon-California Trail over South Pass, which many of the leading experts considered the best.[7] Disgusted with the maneuvering, a talented young railroad engineer who had proved his mettle on the northernmost survey set out to identify the most practical route on his own.

As a civil engineer for the forty-seventh parallel survey, Frederick W. Lander operated independently with a band of "men of iron," gaining a reputation as "an inveterate horse-killer" for his hard-charging style. He managed to kill a 1,200-pound grizzly bear, emptying two Colt revolvers into the beast, which won him his enduring nickname, "Old Grizzly." Convinced the northern route across today's Minnesota, South Dakota, Montana, Idaho, and Washington was impractical, Lander persuaded the Washington Territorial legislature to pass a series of resolutions on March 8, 1854, endorsing his proposed independent survey of the more promising central route. Ten days later, Lander and five men headed east from Olympia. The party traced the

---

[4] Harstad, "The Lander Trail," 15.
[5] Lander, *Maps and Reports of the Fort Kearney, South Pass, and Honey Lake Wagon Road*, 7–8.
[6] This was the title of the War Department's multivolume *Reports of Explorations and Surveys*.
[7] Unruh, *The Plains Across*, 233.

Oregon Trail to South Pass, where Lander battled blizzards to explore the Great Divide Basin.

After almost starving, only Lander and John R. Moffet made it to a cabin west of Omaha, Nebraska, on July 9, where a young settler and former student of Lander, Grenville M. Dodge, greeted the gaunt sojourners. Lander assured Dodge the Pacific Railroad would run through his claim. Moffet was "Dead From Exposure" not long after reaching the frontier, but Lander pressed on to Washington City and published the report of his survey of the road over South Pass and the more direct route to the south over Bridger Pass.[8]

In the wake of its failure to select a railroad route and decades of lobbying for federal support of an overland wagon road, early in 1857 Congress passed the Pacific Wagon Road Act. The act appropriated three hundred thousand dollars to survey and construct the "Fort Kearney, South Pass, and Honey Lake Wagon Road." Having bitterly alienated the people of Utah while mismanaging the federal mail contract for the territory, William M. F. Magraw used his immaculate political connections to win appointment as the project's superintendent. Already a national celebrity for his western adventures, Lander became the expedition's chief engineer. Secretary of the Interior Jacob Thompson instructed him to move quickly to South Pass and search for a shorter line of travel to the City of Rocks. A notorious alcoholic, Magraw managed to squander much of the appropriation before leaving the frontier. With Tim Goodale, the expedition's guide and interpreter, he smuggled more than three tons of liquor to Fort Laramie in government wagons. Magraw's outrageous behavior alienated his best men. As a disgusted military officer wrote, the survey's officers concluded Magraw was "an ignorant blackguard, totally unfit for the head of such an expedition, while the chief engineer of the party is."[9]

Lander led fourteen men from Independence to South Pass in a single month, where he sent parties to explore the maze of cutoffs west of the divide. He examined the headwaters of the Big Sandy and the New Fork of Green River. The challenge of crossing the Little Colorado Desert provided one of the best opportunities to improve the overland trail. "A good road slightly to the north of this inhospitable sector would shorten the distance to the Pacific by almost two hundred miles," historian Turrentine Jackson observed.[10]

---

[8] Ecelbarger, *Frederick W. Lander*, 13–29; Lander, *Report of the Reconnaissance of a Railroad Route from Puget Sound via the South Pass*. Dodge later became chief engineer of the Union Pacific Railroad.

[9] Jackson, *Wagon Roads West*, 161–62, 197; Harstad, "The Lander Trail," 18; Phelps, "Diary," Sept. 3, 1857, 123.

[10] Jackson, *Wagon Roads West*, 191–93.

GEN. FREDERICK W. LANDER, 1861
As chief engineer and superintendent of the
Fort Kearney, South Pass, and Honey Lake
Wagon Road from 1857 to 1861, F. W. Lander
transformed the Oregon and California trails into
proper overland wagon roads. *Mathew Brady portrait.
Courtesy Library of Congress Prints and Photographs
Division, LC-B813-1314 B.*

By season's end, Lander had covered three thousand miles on horseback in ninety days. In two months, his men had explored sixteen mountain passes and "the whole country between the South Pass, the waters of the Great Basin, and the Pacific." The investigation identified excellent routes at the northern and southern limits of the survey. Lander said the southern line "would be excellent for winter mail, when furnished with forage stations, but would not avoid the Green River desert." The northern line, however, was "so abundantly furnished with grass, timber, and pure water, with mountain streams abounding with fish, plains thronged with game, and so avoids the deleterious alkaline deposits of the south, that it may be described as furnishing all that has been long sought for through this section of the country—an excellent and healthy emigrant road, over which individuals of small means may move their families and herds of stock to the Pacific coast in a single season without loss."[11]

Now all that seemed necessary was to build a wagon road over Lander's northern route, which traced much of the old fur trappers' trail between the Sweetwater and the rendezvous sites on Green River. With the development of the Oregon Trail, virtually all wagon traffic used the road to Pacific Springs along the south side of South Pass, and for almost two decades the old fur-trade route again became an Indian road. Only a handful of overland parties seem to have used the trace, notably when Joseph Thing led a train

---

[11] Lander, *Maps and Reports*, 9; Jackson, *Wagon Roads West*, 195.

over the general route in 1849. Thing, "an eminent navigator and fearless son of Neptune," had come west with fur trader Nathaniel Wyeth in 1834 to "measure the route across the Rocky Mountains by Astronomical observation."[12] Neither Thing's observations nor his memory were very good, because he failed to find the old fur-trade road and traveled somewhat south of what became the Lander Cutoff before becoming entirely lost.

Lander was exceptionally pleased with the trace he had surveyed along the north side of South Pass. "The passage of the line is located nearer to the base of the snow-capped mountains, in a more elevated region, richly grassed, and along the great summer trails of the Indians," he wrote. His new route would be favorable to the emigrants' health and "the preservation of their stock, and gives them abundance of pasturage, with water at short intervals from mountain streams."[13]

Ironically, by moving the overland wagon road from the dry sagebrush plain on the south side of South Pass to its northern foothills, Lander also shifted travel to what might justly be called "the scenic route." The older Oregon-California Trail had a certain stark grandeur, but the pine trees, aspens, and spectacular views of the Wind River Range on the Lander Trail matched the alpine country most Americans of the time considered inspiring scenery.

"It is a beautiful spot," wrote Kate Dunlap in 1864; "on the north of us stretch out the Bear River mountains whose summits are white with snow, while on the South lies a range called the Table mountains, covered with pine and quaken asp, at the base of which the Big Sandy winds its pure and rippling waters." Emigrant Jane Gould described the "several kinds of very pretty flowers" she found along the trail, and "a number of kinds of mosses. One has a very pretty white flower and is very fragrant like the fragrance of the grass pink." Gould "found several kinds of new flowers, some of them very pretty."[14]

Expedition politics complicated surveying the wagon road. First, the engineers with Superintendent Magraw's slow-moving column wrote to Lander from Fort Laramie saying that Magraw had forfeited his office due to his atrocious behavior and asked Lander to take command of the survey. Not to be outdone, Magraw announced the expedition would go into winter quarters and told the laborers that the engineers had asked him to lay them off

---

[12] Russell, *Journal of a Trapper*, 1.
[13] Lander, *Maps and Reports*, 7.
[14] Dunlap, *Montana Gold Rush Diary*, 82; Gould, *Oregon and California Trail Diary*, 47–48.

to insure the officers had sufficient supplies, a trick that successfully turned the laborers against the officers. Lander wisely refused to be drawn into the conflict. From seventy miles west of South Pass, Lander said only "small ambition or insane folly" would him make him do something so foolish as displace the superintendent. A few days later, Magraw finally arrived at South Pass, having waited at Independence Rock for U.S. troops on their way to Utah to protect him against his real or imagined enemies among the Mormons.[15]

When the long-brewing conflict between the federal government and the Mormons boiled over into a confrontation the wagon-road survey found itself embroiled in a potential war. As Magraw and Lander met in late September to decide what to do to wind up the season's survey, Mormon raiders struck U.S. Army infantry units camped at South Pass without any cavalry to protect them. "Small guerrilla parties are scattered throughout the mountains to cut off our supplies," dissenters from Utah had warned Capt. Jesse Gove.[16]

Lander, who had carefully nurtured good relations with Brigham Young for years, initially discounted reports that the Mormons were on the warpath. "At Soda Springs a messenger came into camp very much excited informing my men that a party of twelve mounted Mormons were following us to use his emphatic expression—'to wipe us out' because we were government surveyors," Lander reported. His guide, Thomas Adams, "paid no attention to the warning but completed his work with his party." Lander felt he and his men "were treated with great incivility and even rudeness by the settlers of Cache Valley and there may be some truth in these rumors, but I have not thought proper to credit them or to commit any overt act against the party." He was confident his mountaineers "could have struck them at great advantage."[17]

Lander gave Magraw a twenty-seven-page report outlining his survey of the wagon road, along with considerable detail on the tight political situation. Magraw and Lander agreed to send their men into winter quarters. B. F. Ficklin, a mountaineer named James Saunders, and James E. Bromley, a veteran mail rider, spent four days locating a site on the Popo Agie near the Eastern Shoshone winter camps at today's Lander, Wyoming. On October 3, the men began cutting hay and building the log cabins and corrals they dubbed "Fort Thompson." Lander returned east, promising Magraw he would report the

---

[15] Harstad, "The Lander Trail," 20; and Jackson, *Wagon Roads West*, 197–98.
[16] Gove, *The Utah Expedition*, 58, 67.
[17] Lander to Magraw, Oct. 7, 1857, National Archives.

expedition's internal conflicts fairly, though privately he intended to resign unless the Interior Department replaced Magraw. Meanwhile, Magraw volunteered the services of his men and eighteen wagons to the Utah Expedition. Forty-one men enlisted in a volunteer company and elected Magraw captain, while fifteen others stayed behind to man Fort Thompson.[18]

BETTER LEAVE THE OLD ROAD: THE LANDER CUTOFF, 1858
Lander returned to Washington and advised Jacob Thompson to hear both sides of the Magraw case, but the secretary viewed Magraw's enlistment in the army as a resignation and terminated his service as superintendent of the South Pass wagon road survey. Lander became Secretary Thompson's confidant and main advisor on the project. He submitted a preliminary report by the end of November, noting that if the Mormon conflict had not exploded, his new road over South Pass "could have been very cheaply and rapidly graded by the aid of the labor of Utah Territory." Should the clash with the Mormons who controlled the trails and resources in the Green River Valley intensify, Lander suggested using a route that turned north of the Wind River Range at Devils Gate and made its way to Fort Hall via the upper Snake River.

In January 1858 the secretary made Lander superintendent of the Fort Kearney, South Pass, and Honey Lake Wagon Road. He was soon appointed special agent to the Shoshones, "Eastern and Western, and the Pannachs [Bannocks]." By mid-June, Lander and his crew, including skilled lumberjacks and bridge builders from Maine, were camped at South Pass. Four days later they began building a wagon road along the northern alternate identified the previous season. "It was deemed important to open this route, in view of the large emigration which annually passes overland to Pacific shores, and in view of the unsettled condition of affairs in the vicinity of Salt Lake City at that time," wrote Albert Campbell, superintendent of the entire Pacific Wagon Road project.[19]

Lander's men built "Ft. Aspen hut," a storehouse three and a half miles west of the Last Crossing of the Sweetwater on the drainage now known as Slaughterhouse Gulch. On June 18 William H. Wagner began surveying the trail where the Oregon-California Trail left the Sweetwater River and

[18] Jackson, *Wagon Roads West*, 197–98.
[19] Harstad, "The Lander Trail," 22–23.

climbed Rocky Ridge, the point where Magraw's road to Fort Thompson left the Oregon-California Trail. As the road builders worked their way west, they picked up the tools Magraw had dumped on the prairie from the expedition's wagons on his way to Fort Bridger. (They may not have found all of them: four years later, the men in one Oregon-bound train "found two or three good wagons, some harnesses, scythes, a stove, and a great many things else in a ravine off half-a-mile from the road," Jane Gould reported in July 1862. "One man took two wagons and another a harness.") West of Strawberry Creek, the surveyors laid out a "New Road" that bypassed the Ninth Crossing of the Sweetwater and connected directly to the Lander Cutoff about two miles northwest of "Ft. Aspen hut" at what Lander called "Long's creek," now the site of an abandoned ranch known as the Erramouspe Place on Pine Creek.[20]

Lander said his men built fifteen miles of trail per day, from "the broad plain of South Pass to Piney cañon, of the Wahsatch mountains," progress that would have been impressive for a wagon train merely crossing the trail. The initial section between Aspen Hut and the Big Sandy required little work, having been used for decades if not centuries by Indians, fur traders, and missionaries. The division encountered its "first hard work" at Piney Canyon, sixty miles west of the Big Sandy. The crews were equipped with ploughs, shovels, two large saws, axes, crowbars, a scraper, scythes, pitchforks, and chains, plus four hundred pounds of blasting powder and five thousand percussion caps. By year's end, Lander's men had laid out and improved much of the 229-mile route that soon became known as the Lander Cutoff, Road, or Trail. "Over sixty-two thousand cubic yards of earth and rock have been removed, eleven miles of willow, and twenty-three miles of heavy pine timber cleared from the roadway," said the official report. The initial section of trail only required two and one-third miles of grading and 4,562 cubic yards of excavation, less than a third of the excavation required in the canyon alone—and the road between the Sweetwater and the Big Sandy comprised only 39.6 of the 99.86 miles to the mouth of Piney Canyon.[21]

Rather than being a new trail through the wilderness, Lander knew his cutoff followed a very old path. "The road was first laid out by the best explorers in the world—the old beaver-trappers and hunters of the fur companies," he

---

[20] Leland, *Frederick West Lander*, 108; Gould, *Oregon and California Trail Diary*, July 17, 1862; Wight, *The Oregon Trail*, 2:18–22.
[21] Campbell, *Pacific Wagon Roads*, 7, 48, 51; Harstad, "The Lander Trail," 24.

wrote. He relied heavily on frontier veterans, including famous and forgotten mountaineers such as Tim Goodale, Thomas Adams, James Baker, William Bodes, Johnny Grant, Peter Gabriel, Michael "Bad-Hand" Martin, Simon "Sol" Gee, Isaac Frapp (aka Shoshonee Aleck), Thomas Lavatti, the less-than-reliable Thomas Pembrun, and Ned Williamson, "an old mountaineer, a clever fellow, and fearless as a bull terrior." The new cutoff had many advantages over the old Oregon-California Trail and was about sixty miles shorter than the old trail to Fort Hall.[22]

"The new road in many instances follows the summer and fall trail of the Shoshone tribe," noted expedition guide Charles H. Miller, whom Lander praised as "the acknowledged best travelling conductor in the mountains." "The animals of the emigrants will destroy the grass of the valleys," Miller pointed out, and "it would be a very unjust and cruel course of action" for the government to use the Indian lands without payment. Early in the season, the expedition came in close contact with Washakie's Eastern Shoshones. Lander witnessed one of the "'antelope surrounds,' in which the whole tribe often engages," on the headwaters of Green River. The expedition had only five hundred dollars in trade goods to give to the Native peoples it met, and the train carrying them was still far behind on the trail, so Lander gave Washakie "a fine herding horse."

Peter Gabriel had a less friendly encounter with a party of Bannocks later that summer. The band had attacked the Mormons at Fort Limhi the previous winter, and they "debated whether we should be killed or not, the Indians believing us to be Mormons," Miller reported. Their leader, however, said "although his heart was very bad against the Mormons, he loved the children of his 'Great Father,' and should not allow any harm to come to them within the borders of his camp."[23]

Forty-seven workers from Utah, many of whom were former Cornish miners, did much of the construction during 1858. "They have given satisfaction," Lander told Brigham Young. "The strict Mormons have proved the best men of the party, civil, attentive & never profane." The men arrived in a destitute condition, Lander informed the Interior Department. He took "great pains to

---

[22] Lander, *Maps and Reports*, 8; Houston and Houston, "The 1859 Lander Expedition," 64. Lander's guide, page 61, gave the distance from the Sweetwater to Fort Hall as 252.72 miles. Haines, *Historic Sites Along the Oregon Trail*, 238, 305, gave the distance on the Oregon Trail as 312.3 miles.

[23] Campbell, *Pacific Wagon Roads*, 69–70; Leland, *Frederick West Lander*, 108–109.

explain to the foreigners the nature of our Government, which is imperfectly understood by them." "It is not difficult to imagine a camp scene," historian Peter T. Harstad wrote, "with Lander lecturing to his crew on the virtues of American democracy."[24]

Merchant Henry S. Gilbert had been freighting goods to Salt Lake since 1850. The stage station he opened in 1858 at the Ninth Crossing of the Sweetwater quickly became known as Gilberts Station. It was one of a series of overland mail outposts that John M. Hockaday, William Magraw's old partner, established at great expense between the Missouri and Great Salt Lake City. An 1859 guidebook identified it as "Gilbert's station at Forks of Lander Pacific Wagon Road, U.S. Mail Station No. 31." The "neatly and compactly built" log cabin was "but a regular form of trading house, adapted by the mail people," Capt. Albert Tracy wrote when he visited in April 1860. Gilbert impressed him as "a young, civil and quiet man, but with marks of a resolution and courage, needful to all inhabiting these wild, uncertain latitudes."[25]

Gilbert may have already been at the crossing when Lander arrived in mid-June. The station was located at the point where Lander began the emigrant guide he composed later that fall: "Gilbert's station, at the South Pass, (last crossing of the Sweetwater,) is the point at which you had better leave the old road, for fear of getting lost among the different camp trails. Gilbert will direct you." In his guide, Lander admitted some of his new cutoff's limitations: "You must remember that this new road has been recently graded and is not yet trodden down; and, with the exception of grass, water, wood, shortened distance, no tolls, fewer hard-pulls and descents, and avoiding the desert, will not be the first season as easy for heavily loaded trains as the old road, and not until a large emigration has passed over it." Ultimately the superintendent could not resist promoting his creation. "All stock-drivers should take it at once. All parties whose stock is in bad order should take it, and I believe the emigration should take it, and will be much better satisfied with it, even the first season, than with the old road."[26]

Lander's guide provided a rough description of the trail from Gilberts Station to the Big Sandy. After heading northwest for three and a half miles, the cutoff passed two hundred yards south of Aspen Hut. Longs Creek, 5.7

---

[24] Lander to Young, Sept. 23, 1857 [1858], LDS Archives ; Harstad, "The Lander Trail," 23.
[25] Allen, *Guide Book to the Gold Fields of Kansas*, 65, in Haines, *Historic Sites Along the Oregon Trail*, 237; Tracy, "Journal," April 1860, 103–104.
[26] Lander, "Emigrant Guide," in *Report and Map*, 6.

odometer miles northwest of Gilberts Station and known today as Pine Creek, offered travelers "a good camp, the grass on the hills being excellent. Willows on creek, aspen or mountain cottonwood to left, pine timber to left, crossing good gravel bottom." A little over two more miles brought travelers to Clover Creek, today's Fish Creek, with "Good grass and water."

A mile west of Fish Creek, today's trail crosses Highway 28. In two more miles it found good water, fine grass, and aspen timber at Garnet Creek, now known as Sharps Meadows Creek. "From this creek to the Sweetwater it is a rolling country, with fine bunch grass," the guide read, noting that after almost five miles the trail encountered pine timber as it approached the river. What the guide did not comment on were the fantastic rock formations abutting the cutoff at the top of Anderson Ridge before it made a steep descent to the Sweetwater. Today one of those rocks bears an inscription, "Lander Rd. 58," that might well be authentic. "You will find this a good camp," the guide said of the pleasant meadows surrounding the trail's last camp on the Sweetwater River. "Fine grass and heavy pine timber a short distance up the creek to right."

The trail climbed a steep quarter-mile over a ridge rising abruptly from the Sweetwater. At the top is a cairn perhaps built by the crew's surveyors. The trail made a sharp descent to what Lander called Poor's Creek, named for Richard L. Poor, an expedition engineer. Today the stream is known as Lander Creek. "Excellent grass and fine timber to the left of the road," the guidebook said. "Good camping places all the way along for nine miles, the road following up the creek for that distance." After fording the stream, the wagon road followed the south side of Lander Creek to the foot of the Continental Divide.

Four miles from the crossing, "the road descends into a large grass plain, called Antelope meadow. A great many antelope here. Camp near the rocks, where you can have cedar for fuel," the waybill recommended. Cattle have largely replaced wildlife at what is now known as Jensen Meadow, but antelope are still abundant. The guidebook did not mention that the unimpressive fifty-foot-tall rise at the head of the creek marked the divide between the waters of the Atlantic and Pacific, but less than a hundred yards from the crest of the hill, the headwaters of Little Sandy Creek flowed by on their journey to the Gulf of California. The guide gave the distance from Little Sandy Creek to the "Big Hole of Sandy" at 5.33 miles of road that wound over forested hillsides and rolling sagebrush plains. The last five miles to the Big Sandy River crossing was a "Hard pitchy road" with a "steep descent to go down to the river." The distance measured by odometer between the Big Sandy and Gilberts Station was 39.60 miles.[27]

A canny politician, Lander collected testimonials, "numerously signed by emigrants," praising his new wagon trace. The government road from South Pass to Fort Hall, "called Lander's Cut-Off," was "abundantly furnished with good grass, water, and fuel; there is no *alkali* and no desert, as upon the old road, and while upon it our stock improved and rapidly recovered from sickness and lameness," they said. "We were much surprised at the great amount of labor that had been done in cutting out the timber and bridging and grading the road, and in all respects it more than met our expectations, especially those of us who have heretofore travelled the other routes." All the thoroughfare needed, several thousand signers said, was a bridge over the Green River. In Utah the first issue of *The Valley Tan* praised Colonel Lander's energy and "go-aheaditiveness." The report said the route was "far superior to many California trails," for it passed "through a country of extensive meadows, largely timbered, and with no Alkali waters" and plenty of "those great essentials wood, water, and grass."[28]

Lander returned to Washington in December, having built his road in half the allotted time using only $40,260 of his $75,000 budget, which the *St. Joseph Journal* said justified having the engineer's name "emblazoned in gold and put up in the halls of Congress as an example to all generations." Lander acknowledged his route was not suitable for the overland mail. The cutoff was "especially and emphatically an emigrant road, so located as to avoid the tolls of bridges, alkali plains and deleterious and poisonous waters, and to furnish fuel, water, and grass to the ox-team emigration." It was calculated to avoid "the extreme dryness and heat of the artemisian deserts," which would solve the "chief difficulties and obstacles" travelers encountered on the trails west of South Pass in July and August. The report Lander submitted on January 20, 1859, included "a description of the new road from the South Pass to the City of Rocks and an emigrant guide." His exploits made him a national hero. The bloody brawl that Lander and Magraw engaged in the next spring at the fashionable Willard Hotel in Washington, D.C., did not detract from Old Grizzly's growing reputation.[29]

---

[27] Campbell, *Pacific Wagon Roads*, 58–59.
[28] Lander, *Additional Estimate*, 1, 2, 4; "South Pass," *The Valley Tan*, Nov. 6, 1858, 3/1.
[29] Lander, *Maps and Reports*, 7; Ecelbarger, *Frederick W. Lander*, 45–48.

"EMPHATICALLY AN EMIGRANT ROAD" 213

A Full Corps of Artists: The Lander Cutoff, 1859

Lander's March 1859 instructions directed him to proceed to South Pass and "go over the road opened last year, make such improvement upon it as might be necessary," identify a more efficient mail route, complete a continuous survey of the Pacific Wagon Road to Honey Lake, and locate a new wagon trace north of the Humboldt River, if possible. He was to conclude the survey, sell off the expedition's property, and prepare a final report. The road-building budget was limited to twenty-five thousand dollars, but he received an additional five thousand dollars to make "peaceful arrangements with the Indian tribes through which this road passes." Lander reported in July 1859, "The new road touches only the northern extremity of the Mormon Settlements at Blackfoot river, where the farms have been abandoned on account of the Pannack Indian hostilities," indicating that one of the advantages of his new cutoff was that it directed overland traffic away from the troubles in Utah Territory.[30]

Lander assembled a "full corps of artists, bearing their own expenses" to accompany his 1859 expedition. They included an American master, Albert Bierstadt, his student Frances Seth Frost, and the talented if forgotten Henry Hitchings. The sketches and paintings the expedition produced were among the first landscapes of the American West to be regarded as fine art. An unidentified photographer (perhaps Bierstadt) joined them, and his faint wet-collodion prints are among the very first photographic images of the overland trail.[31] "They have taken sketches of the most remarkable of the views along the route, and a set of stereoscopic views of emigrant trains, Indians, camp scenes, &c.," Lander reported, "which are highly valuable and would be interesting to the country." He noted he had no authority to purchase the images, and most of the photographs have since disappeared.[32]

In 1859 gold seekers crowded the road west, bound for Pikes Peak. An ebb tide of discouraged prospectors met Lander's expedition as it headed west, and he recruited some of them to work on the wagon road. The "efficient and energetic" engineer William H. Wagner led a small advance train to South Pass, arriving on May 27 and immediately setting out "to explore and

---

[30] Lander, *Maps and Reports*, 2; Campbell, *Pacific Wagon Roads*, 66.
[31] Houston and Houston, "The 1859 Lander Expedition Revisited," 50, 67, 69–70. This article rescues Hitchings from obscurity and shows that the artists accompanied the expedition much farther west than previously believed.
[32] Lander, *Maps and Reports*, 5. A few of these images survive at the Kansas State Historical Society. Snell, "Some Rare Western Photographs," 1–5.

map the entire country north and in the vicinity of the Humboldt River valley." The main corps of road builders reached South Pass on June 24, 1859. Lander left Edmund L. Yates, who resided in Tim Goodale's lodge, as the expedition's "road agent" at Gilberts Station with an express rider and several employees "to inform emigrants of the completion of the new road, to give them information about it, and to furnish guides to those who desired to adopt it." The Interior Department had not had time to print the guides, so Yates and his men hand-copied a thousand of them and gave the waybills to emigrants. The new cutoff threatened those who had long profited from traffic on the old trail, and Goodale had a "slight affray" with traders from Salt Lake, "who endeavored to prevent emigrants from taking the new road, and who gave them false reports in regard to it."[33]

Overland traveler John Bowles wrote home late that summer, describing how he "got on to the Pacific wagon road or Lander's Cut-off, which leaves the California road at the South Pass, and bears almost directly west until it intersects the old Soda Springs road, near Fork Hall." Bowles praised the road's many advantages. "First of all, there is an abundance of good grass and water, a superior road, 70 miles shorter than the old California road or Seblet's Cut-off; and by going the new road we avoid a desert of 60 miles, the crossing of which has been the death of thousands," he said. Bowles spent the Fourth of July camped on the Big Sandy with three hundred other emigrants who "were detained whilst Col. Landers [sic] was concluding a treaty with the southeastern band of Shoshonee Indians, which occupied about three days." Bowles spent the time hunting, fishing, and exploring, and even climbed to the summit of Fremont Peak. "The scenery from the top of this peak is most lovely indeed. An attempt to describe would and could only end in a miserable failure, unless a more experienced writer than myself should undertake the task. Nothing short of a visit can give any one a correct idea of the grandure [sic], sublimity and liveliness of the scene," he wrote.[34]

When overlander James Berry Brown's party showed up at Gilberts Station in July, he "learned from a mail agent and road agent stationed here that the new road from this point is opened through which avoids the desert by keeping well north and is nearer than either of the others." The new road ran "North West

---

[33] Lander, *Maps and Reports*, 2–4.
[34] Bowles, "California—The Trip over the Plains," Sept. 9, 1859. Bowles (misprinted as "J. Bowley") joined the nine thousand emigrants who endorsed Lander's new road. His 1892 novel, *The Stormy Petrel*, described his adventures.

"EMPHATICALLY AN EMIGRANT ROAD"

"Crossing the Platte"
Harper's Weekly used this sketch Albert Bierstadt made on F. W. Lander's 1859 Pacific Wagon road expedition to illustrate its article, "The Pike's Peak Gold Mines," August 13, 1859, page 516. It is one of the few eyewitness images of the risky business of fording the South Platte River. The man with the bucket appears to be the artist or Colonel Lander. *Courtesy Library of Congress Prints and Photographs Division, LC-USZ62-49128.*

around the west base of the mountains which can be seen from here, crosses the desert where it is only 18 miles wide then by a new route through the mountains west of Green river strikes the old Oregon road 14 miles south of Ft Hall and comes into Sublettes cut off at Raft River and joins the Salt Lake road at Steeple rocks." His party voted unanimously to try the new road. Despite the warning in Lander's guide that the trace and its sagebrush was a problem, Brown found the vegetation "pretty well beat down by the first emigration."

The scenery along the Lander Road overwhelmed travelers like Brown. "To climb the heights and explore the deep chasms and caverns of a real regular *bona fide* mountain has all along been one of my most ardent wishes. Here then was all I wanted," he rhapsodized. "Yonder to the north West rose Fremont's Peak above the clouds, while nearer were mountains though not so high yet so high that their tops were never bare of snow. Here were thick groves of

Pines upon the mountain sides, the deep silence of whose dark shades were broken by no sounds except that of twigs breaking under our feet."[35]

Lander spent much time and energy trying to establish good relations with the surrounding Indian nations. Bowles said the largest gathering took place on the Fourth of July at the "Big Hole" on Big Sandy and lasted for three days. Lander's expedition, a large crowd of emigrants, and some eight hundred Shoshones under Washakie camped on the sagebrush plain. A gift exchange and general celebration took place on the eve of Independence Day. At nightfall, Washakie appeared in a U.S. Army uniform that Lander had given him, and "the gaudy costumes of the rest as they danced to the sound of the 'tum-tum,' a sort of tambourine, all together was a magnificent sight to us," wrote Albert Bierstadt. "At dark we sent up a few sky-rockets, which terrified the Indians so that some of them ran away. They evidently thought we were a great people to send fire up so high."[36]

The Shoshones accompanied Lander to Green River and some of them stayed there, helping emigrants ford the river and locate lost cattle. Lander judged Washakie's people to be "the truest and most reliable friends of the Whites in the mountains." On the Salt River, however, Lander met about three hundred Bannocks under Mopeah, who the previous winter had stolen horses from the army near Fort Bridger. To prevent attacks on emigrants using the new trail, he held back some gifts until the stolen animals were returned. After the distribution of the presents, another thirty Bannocks under Tashepah arrived. That evening two young warriors took pot shots at Lander and Walter Briscoe as they sat next to a campfire. Lander captured the assailants; Mopeah offered appropriate excuses, but Lander took several Bannocks as hostages when he left the meeting to head to the Raft River.[37]

By the next summer the road described in the 1858 guide had changed dramatically. Working quickly, Lander's men initially ran the Pacific Wagon Road along the bottom of Lander Creek, where little or no trace of it survives today. "The season has been an unusual one; the mountain streams swollen by constant rains, and Green river higher than ever known before in the memory of the oldest mountaineers," Lander wrote in 1859. "These rains compelled the necessity of moving the new road from where originally built along the river bottoms, which became impassable, to the high ground in their vicinity."

[35] Brown, *Journal*, July 26, 27, 1859, 38, 40.
[36] Houstons, "Lander Expedition," 50.
[37] Leland, *Frederick West Lander*, 129–30.

The reports indicate this required considerable grading, and Lander employed more than 150 emigrants. He again busily collected signatures, and nine thousand emigrants petitioned the government to build a bridge across the Green River. (Lander feared local ferry owners would quickly torch the bridge and thought the thirty thousand dollars that it would cost could be more effectively spent bridging smaller creeks.) The emigrants gave testimonials describing the new road's many advantages. "It may now be regarded as an excellent highway, and passable under any event or contingency arising from such causes," Lander wrote proudly. "This road will undoubtedly become the great thoroughfare of stock-drovers and ox-team emigrants to California and Oregon."

"A road starting from this point leads to California avoiding Salt Lake City, said to be 100 miles nearer, it is called Lander's Cut-off," John McTurk Gibson observed in 1859 after learning "that Pike's Peak was the d—st humbug ever got up in any country." Gibson "might probably" have taken the road had conditions not compelled him to go to Salt Lake. "The roads fork here, one goes by Fort Hall and is called the Landers Route, the other goes by Salt Lake," his companion John W. Powell wrote at Gilberts Station. "The Fort Hall Road is said to be the best for feed and water." "We took Landerses cut off represented to be a saving of about 100 miles," wrote Iowan Nancy C. Glenn after reaching Oregon in 1862, "and a good road which we found to be so except where the high water had washed and spoiled the road." The new road won greater praise from California newspapers and from a Rocky Mountain veteran. "There is more grass on it than any route I know," wrote Tim Goodale. He had seen about thirteen thousand emigrants take it that year. "They all bragged on it, and it saved a great deal of stock."[38]

After weeks of cooking over sagebrush, Harriet A. Loughary, who later worked for woman's suffrage in Oregon with Abigail Scott Duniway, was delighted to find "an abundance of wood for our camp fire once more. It is no small disappointment when we were deprived of these when all gathered around our cheerfull bonfire after the days work was done, to rehearse the adventures of the day, mended the numerous rents, washed the childrens faces, dress and tie up the many wounds and bruises and oiled the alkalied faces, hands and toes, while bread, bacon and beans were cooking for the next days travel."[39]

The testimonials of emigrants and mountaineers were useful, but nothing

---

[38] Lander, *Maps and Reports*, 3–4, 11; Gibson, Journal, and Powell, Diary, July 2, 1859; Glenn, "Letter," Oct. 8, 1862, 8:20.

[39] Loughary, "Travels," June 29, 1864, 8:143.

beat the word of a celebrated journalist. "Col. Lander, at the head of a U.S. exploring and pioneer party, has just marked and nearly opened a new road," Horace Greeley of the *New York Tribune* reported that summer from South Pass. Lander's road made "a Northern cut-off, and strikes the old Oregon Trail some fourteen miles south of Fort Hall, saving sixty miles on the journey to Oregon." The new route, Greeley observed, afforded emigrants "cheering hope of a mitigation of the sufferings and hardships of the long journey." He found a great majority of those bound for California and everyone heading for Oregon "turning off on the new route, and I pray that they may find on it food for their weary, famished cattle, and a safe journey to their chosen homes." Greeley missed meeting Lander, "to my regret; but I am sure he is doing a good work, for which thousands will have reason to bless him."[40]

BUILT AT THE EXPENSE OF THE GOVT.: THE LANDER CUTOFF

The later history of the Lander Road is problematic. Overland emigration surged during the Civil War, but it is hard to gauge how heavily westbound emigrants used the new government road. Most travelers apparently preferred to stick with the old trail—and the chance to see something resembling "civilization" at Salt Lake proved irresistible for many travelers. Ironically, the substantial water resources created the cutoff's greatest advantage over the older "desert" routes, but the seasonal flooding that accompanied them made the road difficult to maintain. The records of those who used the trail show that it required continual work to keep the road passable.

Emigrants provide our best picture of life on Lander's road, but many of them were traveling so fast that their accounts often provide few details. They occasionally noted the quality of the road and commented on the landscape. "The scenery through which we have been passing today has been most grand. This A.M., the mountains loomed up into the clouds," overlander Harriet Sanders wrote in 1863 on her way to Idaho Territory. "The clouds on the side of the mountains with the peaks occasionally above them, presented a most beautiful sight. Camped at noon by the Little Sandy, a beautiful stream the water of which flows toward the Pacific." As the trail wound through the aspen groves on the Little Prospect Mountains, Harriet and her companions "all got out and walked at least three miles, had the finest walk and the greatest scenery we

---

[40] Greeley, *An Overland Journey*, 190–91.

have had since leaving home."⁴¹ "We have fine roads, except now and then a steep and rocky descent," Kate Dunlap wrote in 1864. "The last one we passed down was covered with a dense growth of aspen trees, the first grove we have passed through since we left home. It brought to my mind the scenes of home."⁴²

Lucetta Shuey kept her journal sporadically, so it is often difficult to precisely determine her location, but on the first of July her family got an early start and "traveled over good road on the ascent six miles. Crossed a small stream"—perhaps Garnet Creek—"and on over mountainous road through a very pretty grove of quakenasp & pine on the summit of the Rocky Mountains." The road descended "a long hill," perhaps the steep pitch to Lander Creek and then to "a stream of pacific water." Her train formed a corral, "unyoked the cattle, & Ate dinner. There being a number of Indian lodges near us, we had visitors in abundance of the Snake Tribe." The road made a "descent over hilly but rather smooth road" for five miles to the Big Sandy, "a very pretty stream which is twenty feet wide & two feet deep. Very nice stony bottom." Not far from the crossing Shuey came to the grave of a nineteen-year-old man who died two days earlier—"The first fresh grave we had seen." Her train soon went a mile off the road "& camped on the bluff a short distance from the stream in a dry place. Very sandy, no grass." They corralled their wagons in the middle of "nothing but sage, no timber near."⁴³

Emigrant Martha Missouri Bishop Moore crossed the cutoff during a cold spell at the end of July 1860 and took her time. She found "a nice mess of strawberries" on the morning she left Strawberry Creek. Her train nooned at Gilberts Station and took "the Lander route" to Pine Creek, which she called Willow Creek. "Plenty of wood, water & grass some of the prettiest flowers I ever saw," she wrote. The next day the party crossed the Sweetwater for the last time and "camped on a little creek," Lander Creek, "with plenty of wood, water & grass." The next morning, Moore left one of the best surviving descriptions of crossing the Continental Divide on the new road. Her party climbed up the stream "until noon when it suddenly disappeared, passed a slight ascent over a rocky ridge and we were through the South Pass. Crossed Sandy whose foaming & dashing torrent was rushing to join its mad waters with those of the Pacific," she wrote. "Camped on a little branch fine grass and good water." The bad weather continued as August began with a "damp

---

⁴¹ Sanders, "Omaha to Bannack," 15.
⁴² Dunlap, *The Montana Gold Rush Diary*, 81.
⁴³ Shuey, Journal, July 1, 1860, LDS Archives.

& chill" morning and showers that lasted all day. "Come over mountains to Big Sandy where we nooned." She found another nice mess of strawberries before fording the Big Sandy and "starting over a barren desolate country."[44]

The Civil War transformed life on the Lander Cutoff. From St. Joseph to the banks of the Sacramento and the Columbia, Indian relations changed dramatically, as violence surged along the road, especially in Shoshone and Bannock country. Congress created the U.S. Emigrant Escort Service to protect wagon trains.

Captains Henry Maynadier and Medorem Crawford commanded the first party the army shepherded over the "the road built at the expense of the Govt. by Mr. Lannder" starting on July 29, 1861. "Passed over a rough road and camped on the Sweetwater near a canyon," Captain Crawford wrote. The next morning the train climbed over the ridge that separated the Sweetwater and Lander Creek on a "good road and through a wild & desolate country." That night the escort camped on Big Sandy. Two miles from his camp, Crawford noted, there were two springs on the top of a quartz ridge only a few feet apart, "the water from one running to the Sweetwater, Platte, Missouri, Mississippi & Gulph while the other makes its way into the Big Sandy, Green River, Colorado, & Gulph of California." He was not effusive in his praise of the rest of Lander's road: he considered the cutoff and its river crossings "generally bad" and "very bad." The trout fishing, however, was excellent.

Crawford escorted emigrants over the Lander Road for two more years. Shoshones ran off forty-eight of the mules belonging to Capt. Hamer Hayes's Sixth Ohio Volunteer Cavalry company guarding Gilberts Station in 1862. The escort manned the outpost while Hayes and Crawford led the troops in pursuit. They "found most of their stock, but saw no Indians." Meanwhile, 80 wagons and 250 emigrants with 600 head of livestock joined the escort, but another large contingent "struck off to Salt Lake and California." Crawford left the station on August 7 "and took the Lander road" with 98 wagons, 428 souls, and 847 head of livestock under his protection. Thirteen miles of rough road brought the train to Garnet Creek, and the next day they crossed the "hilly road to the Sweet Water," ascended Lander Creek to "the summit of the Rocky mountains in the afternoon, and camped on Little Sandy creek at 5 P.M.," making twenty-two miles.[45]

---

[44] Moore, "The Trip to California," 7:282–83.
[45] Crawford, "Journal of the Expedition," 4–5, 19–26; LeRoy Crawford, Journal III, Aug. 3–8, 1862, 78–82.

Over the next three weeks, Captain Crawford noted how much damage the Lander Trail had suffered during the winter. "I found this road very much injured by the water since last year," he wrote. "Bridges had been carried away, banks of streams so washed out as to render crossing dangerous and frequently impossible; and in many instances emigrants who had preceded us had dug roads along the hill sides to avoid the streams through the cañons." The cutoff was a great improvement over the old trail, of course—it was shorter and better supplied with grass and water—"but unless some repairs are made the road will have to be abandoned." Crawford detailed a squad to go ahead of the train each day to "dig down banks, build bridges, and remove rocks and logs, in order to render the road at all passable." Even with these temporary improvements, "it often required all my company to assist my own and the emigrants' wagons over bad places."

A hard crossing and grim evidence of the dramatic increase in Indian depredations during the Civil War awaited the train at the New Fork—"a grave, from the inscription on which we learned that Patrick Moran, of Missouri, was killed by Indians on the 18th of July, and two men wounded." They saw a second grave near Labarge Creek, but they found a mass grave and evidence of a brutal crime not far from Fort Hall—"the graves of five persons, said to have been killed by Indians on the 9th of August," Crawford reported. "Some of them had been shot with buckshot, which, with other circumstances, leads me to believe that white men had a hand in this massacre."

Further evidence of white criminality awaited the escort on the Portneuf River, "where General Lander constructed a fine bridge, which we last year found in good order, but has since been destroyed and a ferry established by the same parties who owned the ferry on Snake river." Just as Lander had predicted, the men exploiting the trail would stop at nothing when their financial interests were threatened. Crawford refused to use the ferry: he "did not entertain the most favorable opinion" of the ferrymen.[46] The captain was not alone: Nancy C. Glenn believed the body her party found buried in a shallow grave "had been killed by white men as the ferrymen at Ft Hall could tell all about him and how much money he had." The suspects said his name was Camel from Denver and he had five thousand dollars.[47]

When William Smedley camped at the Last Crossing of the Sweetwater

---

[46] Crawford, "Journal of the Expedition," 10–12.
[47] Glenn, "A Letter," Oct. 8, 1862, 8:21.

in July 1862, he heard about the "new road—'Lander's Cut Off'—said to be shorter by eighty miles, with plenty of grass and water, in place of the desert traversed by the old road." The telegraph operator warned "that the road was perilous on account of hostile Indians and impassable from the unusually high water, without building boats and bridges. As we were not prepared for such business we felt doomed to the desert." Indians had stolen some of the livestock belonging to the soldiers "quartered nearby for the protection of emigrants. What protectors!" The arrival of a train from Denver equipped with the tools and ropes needed to cross deep streams persuaded Smedley's train to take the Lander trail. "Here we leave the California road, which, by the way, being a stage road, is kept, for the most part, in excellent repair, and here ended our easy times and comfortable travel and commenced a tour, the hardships and sufferings of which I shall never forget," he wrote. "There being but little travel on the road, grass was abundant," as were hungry mosquitoes.

A day's travel brought the train to the Little Sandy, "an icy cold and rapid stream, where we met with a slight disaster." The stream was so cold that rather than explore it as they usually did, the party "ventured in blindly." Smedley was driving an ox wagon and, fearing a treacherous looking whirlpool, he managed to avoid Charybdis but ran into Scylla. "The deep and swift current carried our cattle with it several feet below the landing, a narrow channel cut out of the bank," creating a three-feet-high wall. "As our cattle attempted to climb out one of them was found tangled in the chain, which detained our wagon so long in deep water that its contents were generally wet, but few seriously damaged." His wagon lost a few crackers and the time it took to dry out its contents.

Smedley enjoyed the abundant mountain trout but found the antelope elusive. He disliked the aggressive Indians and bloodthirsty mosquitoes, flies, and buffalo gnats that claimed the cutoff as their own. He called the "Snakes" he encountered "a tribe notorious for hostilities and a terror to everything west of the Rocky Mountains," a far cry from the reputation the Shoshones had enjoyed only a few years earlier. When his party returned to the old emigrant road after nineteen days "on the long-to-be-remembered 'Lander's Cut-Off,'" Smedley said he had "experienced more hardships, more exposure, more danger and more misery than ever in my life before." Now that it was over, he "rather looked back upon it with satisfaction and pride, as well as with gratitude, for our safe deliverance."[48]

---

[48] Smedley, *Across the Plains in '62*, 6–8 23–33.

Despite Medorem Crawford's concern that a lack of maintenance might make the Lander Road impassible, the army successfully conducted emigrants over the trail in 1863 and 1864. Crawford's brother Le Roy was captain of the Oregon Volunteers in March 1864 and took command of the expedition when Medorem became Oregon's internal-revenue collector. Each year the escort left the frontier late in the season, picking up stragglers as the government train headed west. After reaching the Big Hole in August 1864, W. J. and Julia Campbell reported lying over at Grass Spring "waiting for escort to come." It came in the evening.[49] The escort's wartime journals and overland diarists all describe the rapidly deteriorating relations between emigrants and Indians throughout the Civil War in detail, but there was not an escort for Oregon emigrants in 1865.

Much of the credit for keeping the cutoff passable goes to the emigrants themselves. "The road this afternoon has been very hilly and rocky," Jane Gould wrote as her family set out on Lander's Road in 1862. "The ford over the creek in the hills was washed away. A train that went before us built a bridge so we crossed on." The relatively heavy traffic might have eased the impact of too much water. An anonymous diarist who accompanied the 1864 escort reported spending three days (including a day's layover to let Mrs. Drew deliver twin boys) traversing Lander Creek and finding "good camps all the way in a wet season."[50]

These Dern Pilgrims: F. W. Lander's Legacy

At his cabin at Gilberts Station, Charles H. Miller kept a record of the weather and a count of the "outfits" of men, women, and children, plus horses, mules, oxen, and wagons "going to Salt Lake, and consisting of freight trains" during October and November 1858. Given the season, the totals were remarkable: 59 trains passed Miller's lonely outpost in October and another 36 in November, with 847 travelers in October and 528 in November. Clearly, overland travel had changed dramatically since it began almost twenty years earlier. Now emigrants, freighters, stagecoaches, and mail couriers visited South Pass virtually the year round.[51]

---

[49] Campbells, Memoranda, Aug. 25, 1864.
[50] Gould, *Oregon and California Trail Diary*, July 17, 1862; Anonymous [Ironside?], Journal, Aug. 24, 1864, Beinecke Library.
[51] Campbell, *Pacific Wagon Roads*, 57.

Thirteen thousand emigrants used the Lander Road during the summer of 1859.[52] Col. Reuben F. Maury of the First Oregon Cavalry estimated that thirteen hundred wagons and eight thousand persons made up the 1862 overland migration to Oregon and Washington.[53] Most of them and several thousand California-bound travelers probably used the Lander Road. Rushes to gold discoveries in Idaho and Montana generated more traffic. It is difficult to calculate how many people went west on the trails during their third decade, but a reasonable estimate would be that ten thousand Americans used the route every year between 1859 and 1865. Wagons used the trail until at least 1912, and the total number of people who crossed the Lander Cutoff probably topped one hundred thousand.[54]

With F. W. Lander's departure from Ross Fork on August 1, 1859, his work in the Rocky Mountains came to an end. After surveying of the last section of the Pacific Wagon Road to Honey Lake, in September Lander addressed the Pacific Railroad Convention at San Francisco "on the subject of the construction of a railroad across the American continent." It was a topic, Lander said, that had cost him "so much money, so much time, so much energy, and so much faith." He returned to the West in 1860, but he never visited South Pass again. During his last year as superintendent, Lander helped settle the Pyramid Lake War with the Northern Paiutes and at Sacramento reported "the completion of the Overland Wagon Road" on September 27, 1860. In October he married Jean Margaret Davenport, a popular actress. The following February, Lander completed his final estimates and resigned as superintendent of the Pacific Wagon Road.[55]

The relentless engineer "had traversed the West seven times in seven years, establishing himself as one of the most experienced and recognized frontiersmen in the country." Lander declined Abraham Lincoln's offer to serve as governor of Nevada Territory, but he agreed to carry the president's confidential messages to Sam Houston in a bid to keep Texas in the Union. With the coming of the war, Lander was commissioned a brigadier general and fought brilliantly at Rich Mountain, Philippi, and Bloomery Furnace. After

---

[52] Lander, *Maps and Reports*, 9.

[53] Crawford, "Report," Part 1, 2:36. Captain Crawford inflated Maury's numbers. Migration to Oregon and Washington came "to 1,000 wagons with 5,000 people." Whites "were the instigators and allies of the Indians" in most of that year's depredations. Scott, *War of the Rebellion*, Series 1, Vol. 50, 167–68.

[54] Wight, *The Oregon Trail*, 1:79. A marker at the mouth of Coal Creek says that when a wagon tipped over here in about 1890, "a small girl was downed and was buried in the vicinity." Ibid., 2:50.

[55] Lander to Thompson, Sept. 27, 1860, RG 48, National Archives.

campaigning successfully against Thomas J. "Stonewall" Jackson, Lander was shot at Edward's Ferry in October 1861 and died of the wound on March 2, 1862.[56]

The president, his cabinet, and the Supreme Court all attended the fallen warrior's funeral, but his memory subsequently disappeared in the ocean of blood that was shed over the next three years. This remarkable American is little remembered today, and no highway traces the Lander Cutoff. Yet this does not diminish his service or his accomplishments. "The 'Old Man' cares as much about these dern pilgrims gitting a lame steer to water as ever an old 'Hudson Bayer' did for a black ox skin," said mountaineer Ned Williamson, by way of compliment and complaint.

The twenty-first century has been hard on the heroes of the Old West, but beyond his hard treatment of his horses, there is much to admire about F. W. Lander's integrity, competence, and boundless energy. Overlooked aspects of Lander's legacy are the "worthy relics" created by his corps of artists. "Often on the prairies, where the setting sun shone upon the cheerful campfires of a train of emigrants, the morrow showed no trace to mark their resting-place save, perhaps, the gravestone of some wayworn woman buried in the night," Lander said in an address to the Washington Art Association in 1859. Many nations leave nothing behind to tell of their existence, except their art, he observed. But Frederick W. Lander "left more than a few rock cairns and a road in the West; he left a visual monument to his passage," two perceptive art historians have argued. "With its bounty of images, the trip emerges as one of the most visually (and best chronologically) documented expeditions of the West prior to the government surveys of the 1870s."[57]

F. W. Lander's best monument is his trail, which still "spans the plateau south of the Wind River Range, winds its way to the heights of a three-way continental divide, fords swift mountain streams, passes through mountain meadows and tight canyons, and finally rolls out onto the Snake River Plain," historian Peter T. Harstad wrote forty years ago. "In the well-worn ruts of this nineteenth-century wagon road can be seen a mingling of practicality and romanticism—qualities deeply imbedded in the westward movement as well as in the character of F. W. Lander."[58]

---

[56] Ecelbarger, *Frederick W. Lander*, 54. Lander received a heroic funeral.
[57] Houstons, "Lander Expedition," 57, 70.
[58] Harstad, "The Lander Trail," 14–15.

GRAVESITE OVERLOOKING BURNT RANCH
This may be the spot where James Clyman helped bury Joseph Barnett on August 27, 1844. Below is the Ninth Crossing of the Sweetwater at today's Burnt Ranch. The Oregon Buttes loom on the horizon. At what had been the overland stage stop known as Gilberts Station or Upper Sweetwater Station at the Last Crossing, the U.S. Army built an outpost in June 1862 known as Camp Highland and South Pass Station. *Courtesy Kay Threlkeld, 2005.*

CHAPTER 9

The U.S. Mail and the War for South Pass
1860—1869

THE LAST YEARS OF LARGE-SCALE TRAVEL OVER SOUTH PASS saw the establishment of stagecoach routes and stations, the development of mail service that culminated in the glory days of the Pony Express in 1860 and 1861, and the arrival of electronic communications technology with the construction of the transcontinental telegraph through the pass. Most dramatically, these years witnessed increasing levels of violence, beginning with the Utah War in 1857, as well as the increasingly bitter and bloody Indian wars that make up a forgotten chapter of Civil War history. These conflicts reduced wagon travel over the pass but, with wonderful irony, the close of the trails era coincided with a gold rush to South Pass beginning in 1867.

After two decades of increasing use, South Pass was showing considerable wear and tear. A series of droughts beginning in 1854 transformed the nature of wagon travel. "From Pacific Creek the road is not bad, but at this season the emigrant parties are sorely tried by drought, and when water is found it is often fetid or brackish," Richard Burton wrote in 1860. If there was not too little water, there was too much. Torrential rains in the winter of 1862 washed away much of the overland trail. "The road between this city and the South Pass has been so much damaged that it is with much difficulty the overland mail stages have passed over it since the waters receded," the *Deseret News* reported from Salt Lake. South Pass was always, as William Wagner observed in 1852, "a hard road to travel."[1]

---
[1] Burton, *City of the Saints*, 167; "The Late Rains," *Deseret News*, Jan. 22, 1862, 240/3; Wagner, Journal, June 16, 1852.

The role of South Pass in national communications had deep roots. Private couriers began carrying mail over the pass as early as July 1836, when Henry Spalding dispatched a letter to his mission board, or at least by 1842, when Indian agent Elijah White sent a letter to New York from Fort Hall. A folded lettersheet addressed to John F. Snyder of Belleville, Illinois, and "postmarked" in longhand "South Pass/August 1845" survives.[2]

Not long after establishing the first settlement in the Rocky Mountains, Mormon leaders sent a seven-man mail party from Great Salt Lake City in early March 1848. These hapless couriers experienced their share of troubles crossing South Pass at the end of the month. Their historian, Robert S. Bliss, left the first record of carrying the mail over the pass in winter. "Came 30 miles over the Pass or divide & camped on to Sweet Water," he wrote on March 24. "Last night had some snow & to day frequent snow squalls & verry cold [—] colder than we have seen this winter. This afternoon the snow difficult to pass & injurous to our Animals feet on account of the crust." The weather continued "verry cold & disagreeable," so frigid that on the twenty-sixth they simply stayed in camp. It snowed for the next four days, but the party pushed on, picking up two former soldiers, perhaps deserters from California, at the foot of Rocky Ridge who had left Salt Lake in mid-January and were "in a deplorable condition."[3]

Mormon Battalion veteran Abner Blackburn, who had joined the mail party to rejoin his family in Missouri, recalled these soldiers had come from California the previous fall and "were nearly starved [and] had killed their horse and eat him and were trapping white wolves to eat." The party sought shelter in a small cave and "thought we had cheated the storm, but the hot fire heated the rocks and thawed out the snakes and we left the cave." The party's tent collapsed under the weight of a blizzard and the men had "to make our beds on the snow" as they forged ahead, reaching "Hells Gate" on March 31.[4]

Later mail parties that tried to cross South Pass in winter shared similar hard experiences. Mail agent W. H. Arnall set out for Great Salt Lake City on December 1, 1850, and survived "one of the most perilous trips ever accomplished by a human being." Arnall and two companions "lay near the Pacific Spring for seven weeks where it snowed upon him for seventeen

---

[2] Spalding, "A Letter from the Rocky Mountains," July 11, 1836, 127; Allen, *Ten Years in Oregon*, 155; Jarret, "The First South Pass City," 1,139.
[3] Bliss, "Journal," March 23–31, 1848, 397–99.
[4] Blackburn, *Frontiersman*, 126–27.

successive days and nights." Four of the party's mules froze to death, but the messengers managed to keep three others alive. "For long distances, he and the two men with him were compelled to open roads through the snow five feet deep." When the mail carriers returned to Council Bluffs on June 20, they were "generally supposed to have perished in the mountains during winter."[5]

James Madison Estill's "Express Mail Line for the California Emigration" arrived at Pacific Springs in mid-June 1850 and set up shop. Estill was a classic frontier operator: he had owned mills, a ferry, and a pork-packing house near Weston, Missouri. He contracted to run the "United States farm" at Fort Leavenworth in 1842 and supply the army with twelve thousand bushels of corn and eight thousand of oats. Estill's wide-ranging enterprises ultimately failed and, as a local history put it, he "went to California, to renew his schemes," including this private mail service. Estill's express left St. Joseph on May 15, 1850, with three spring carriages and twenty-four fine horses carrying westbound mail submitted by eighteen agents between St. Louis and the point of departure.[6]

On the morning of June 20, James W. Denver, one of Estill's associates, reached Pacific Springs, which Denver said were "little more than an extensive *swamp*, but there are some fine strong springs in it." He set up camp and a temporary post office, apparently a short distance down Pacific Creek, and began accepting mail. Four days later, Margaret Frink found "the American flag was flying, to mark the private post-office or express office established by Gen. James Estelle, for the accommodation of emigrants wishing to send letters to friends at home."

Anyone lacking the ingredients for a proper frolic could purchase them at Estill's impromptu trading post, which "Had Brandy & Cigars for sale— Brandy $1.50 per pint & cigars 10 cts each," reported John Nevin King on his way to California. Iowa overlander Isaac R. Starr denounced the operation as "one of the old sank manufactures where misery is sold at two-bits a dose. This doggery is connected with the express mail line from California to the U.S.A. They tax 50 cents per letter." Letters could get deluxe treatment for an "express charge" of $1.00, and Mrs. Frink said the firm's messengers "delivered the letters to the postmaster at St. Joseph, and in due time they reached their destination."[7]

---

[5] "Salt Lake Mail," *Frontier Guardian*, June 27, 1851, 2.
[6] Barry, *The Beginning of the West*, 461, 937–39; Paxton, *Annals of Platte County*, 91.
[7] Denver, "The Denver Diary," June 20, 1850, 50; King, Overland Journey, July 1, 1850; Starr, Diary, July 10, 1850, typescript; Frink, "Adventures," June 24, 1850, 2:105–106.

COLD & DISAGREEABLE: THE U.S. MAIL AT SOUTH PASS

Samuel H. Woodson won the first federal postal contract to provide monthly mail service over South Pass to Great Salt Lake City for $19,500 per annum on July 1, 1850. He inaugurated his severely under-funded operation the next August. Woodson contracted with Mormon mail carriers Ephraim Hanks and Feramorz Little, Brigham Young's nephew, to handle the service between Fort Laramie and Salt Lake. They had a tough time making the job pay. Bad weather trapped Little and an Indian assistant with the November mail in 1852. "They were lost for several days about South Pass, and struggled through the snow for almost a month." The two men eventually abandoned their horses, cached the bulk mail, and dragged some of the letters over the mountains. The route proved unprofitable, and Woodson abandoned the business early in 1854.

William M. F. Magraw won a four-year federal contract in March 1854 to provide monthly round-trip mail service between Independence, Missouri, and Utah Territory, but the annual payment was cut by fifty-one hundred dollars. Magraw grumbled that the mail subsidy was inadequate for the task, while Utah's Mormon authorities complained even more loudly about the quality of Magraw's service. He eventually would dump the contract and use his impressive government connections to be appointed head of the Pacific Wagon Road Survey.[8]

Stagecoach service in the West began sporadically. The *Missouri Republican* announced early in 1852 that Blodgett & Co. would establish "a system of express trains from St. Joseph to the Pacific for carrying passengers and letters" and planned to dispatch four trains every season. Nancy and Henry Bradley sent a letter via "Blodgetts Express" from the Platte River in early June, but the proposed passenger line never materialized. That changed dramatically when John M. and Isaac Hockaday advertised a monthly passenger-coach service to Salt Lake in 1854 in association with Magraw. They began laying the groundwork for what become the first effective stage service on the Oregon-California Trail.[9]

Brigham Young hoped to use the federal mail contract he won late in 1856 using Hiram S. Kimball, a merchant who acted as his agent, to build a major

---

[8] Root and Connelley, *Overland Stage to California*, 1; Hafen, *The Overland Mail*, 59–60; MacKinnon, "The Buchanan Spoils System," 132–33.

[9] MacKinnon, "The Buchanan Spoils System," 132–33; *Missouri Republican*, May 10, 1852, in Watkins, "Notes," 239; and Bradley and Bradley, A Daily Journal, June 3, 1852. "This Blodget is of Milwaukie," the Bradleys wrote.

overland freighting company. The venture began as a private business initially proposed in January 1856 to compete directly with the government mail service. Later that month, the Utah Territorial Assembly incorporated the Deseret Express and Road Company. The first of two mass meetings in Salt Lake revealed the proposed corporation's expansive vision of "establishing a daily express and passenger communication between the western States and California, or, more extendedly, between Europe and China."

Both Mormon and non-Mormon leaders in Utah supported the proposal. "Unless the powers at Washington are more alive to the rapid strides of internal progression, they may soon bid farewell to their transportation of the mails," the LDS Church's newspaper warned. With a famine stalking Utah, at least a few citizens were skeptical. After a rousing meeting promoting the plan, "many large speeches were made to 'Buncum' but everyone seems to be in favor of such," observed Mormon diarist and lawman Hosea Stout.[10]

The express was organized as a joint stock company in early February. Brigham Young announced its plans to engage "in the transportation of letters and papers, and, so soon as may be of passengers and freight." A large and enthusiastic audience gathered in the Old Tabernacle to subscribe for a thousand miles' worth of shares—Governor Young offered "to take stock and furnish 300 miles of the route" on his own hook. The assembly "unanimously voted to sustain the chartered company in carrying a daily express from the Missouri river to California, and in extending the line as fast and as far as circumstances may permit." To start operations, Young assigned veteran South Pass trader Bill Hickman to carry the mail from Independence to Fort Laramie and Porter Rockwell to take it from Laramie to Salt Lake. "Forts will be established along the line at distances of twenty-five miles—seventy in number, I believe," British observer John G. Chambers wrote from Salt Lake. "Whether this scheme will fail in consequence of the scarcity of provisions remains to be seen."[11]

By April 1857 the road company had been transformed into the Brigham Young Express and Carrying Company, also known as the B.Y.X. or simply the Y.X. Company. Young sent expeditions to establish square-mile settlements and supply stations at critical points on the overland trail, such as one

---

[10] "Mass Meeting," *Deseret News*, Jan. 30, 1856, 4/4–5/1; Stout, *On the Mormon Frontier*, Jan. 26, 1856, 2:590.

[11] "Express Line" and "Mass Meeting," *Deseret News*, Feb. 6, 1856, 5/3–4; *Western Standard*, May 17, 1856.

hundred miles west of Omaha on Beaver Creek and in Wyoming at Deer Creek, near today's Glenrock; at Horseshoe Creek, now two miles from Glendo; at La Bonte Creek, ten miles south of Douglas; and at Devils Gate, Rocky Ridge, and near Fort Bridger.

"The Y.X. Co. is in a flourishing condition, we are sending out from 40 to 65 animals every mail, which we wish to increasingly continue until we get the road stocked with 1800 horses & mules," Young wrote on the Fourth of July. He sent "Elders A. O. Smoot & N. V. Jones with 80 men, to locate permanent stations in the Black Hills, which we design as resting places to those of our emigration who have not means to come through, or who may be too late as was the case last fall. Of course we shall plentifully supply them with provisions &c."[12]

Stephen A. Markham, a Latter-day Saint and veteran frontiersman who had come west with Brigham Young's Pioneer Camp in 1847, established a Y.X. Company station at the Last Crossing of the Sweetwater. By early July, Mormon surveyor Thomas D. Brown found the post in full operation, trading teams and providing services to "a heavy emigration going West, very many families" and their numerous livestock. Traveling east to inspect stations along the route, Brown left the Little Sandy at 10:30 A.M. "and struck hands with Col. Markham before Sundown, that is as soon as he could get time from Counting the money they had made at Blacksmith, they had over $163. Sixty three of which they made that day."

The outpost, known as Markham's Fort or Markham's Station, was built on the Seminoe Cutoff about a quarter-mile south of the Ninth Crossing on the west bank of Meadow Creek. Markham planned to abandon the operation, Bill Hickman informed Brigham Young. With the U.S. Army's march to Utah Territory, Mormon forces torched the outpost. "Passed a station or trading house of the Mormons which was still smouldering in ruins," wrote Capt. John W. Phelps. "They themselves set fire to it the night before last." Probably built using green logs, some of the station's buildings apparently survived, but this was the first time the spot later known as Burnt Ranch went up in flames.[13]

The government terminated Brigham Young's mail contract shortly after it ordered troops to Utah. Like Burnt Ranch, all the buildings of the Y.X.

---

[12] Kimball, *Mormon Pioneer National Historic Trail*, 69–70; Young to Cannon, July 4, 1857, LDS Archives.
[13] Brown to Young, July 8, 1857, LDS Archives; Haines, *Historic Sites Along the Oregon Trail*, 235; Phelps, "Diary," Sept. 25, 1857, 138; Guenther, "The Burnt Ranch Saga," 9–10.

THE U.S. MAIL AND THE WAR FOR SOUTH PASS   233

Express went up in smoke. "Nearly $200,000 was expended during the winter of 1856–57 to establish way stations, purchase teams and wagons, hire help, and to buy equipment and other supplies," historian Leonard Arrington wrote. "The resources of the Church were almost exhausted in this venture."[14] Brigham Young would not be the last entrepreneur to lose a fortune trying to dominate western trade and transportation.

By 1858, with much of the U.S. Army stationed in Utah, an effective mail service became imperative. Once again, sectional politics prevailed over national interest when the Buchanan administration diverted most funding for overland mail contracts to the longer—2,635 miles by stagecoach—Butterfield Overland Mail route through the Southwest. John M. Hockaday, Magraw's former partner, bid for the Utah mail contract in June 1857 but lost to Stephen B. Miles of Delaware, who took on the difficult task for only $32,000 per annum. Miles failed, and Hockaday and his associates won the St. Joseph–Salt Lake mail contract in May 1858 to provide weekly service until November 1860. The contract paid $190,000 per year to run a four-horse coach to Salt Lake in twenty-two days. Hockaday's service connected to George Chorpenning's Salt Lake–San Francisco route, so by July 1858 "a weekly through overland mail and passenger service was in operation from the Missouri River to California on a thirty-eight day schedule."[15]

"I left St. Joseph, Missouri, on the afternoon of the 1st of May, with the first train started under the Overland Mail contract," former *New York Times* editor James W. Simonton reported that summer. Simonton traveled with Hockaday on the initial run, which did not go well. "Excessive bad roads, consequent upon unusually heavy spring rains, and the high water in the Platte delayed us about five days beyond the contract time of twenty-two days," he wrote. The army hailed even this late arrival with "glad surprise," having "almost come to the conclusion that news from home was never to reach them in much less than about twice that period of time."

Hockaday and his associates were busily "locating stations, one of which they propose to establish in every fifty miles, with relays of mules," Simonton reported. He was confident the mail would go through regularly in eighteen days. On the Fourth of July, Simonton reported that week's mail had arrived from St. Joseph in only eighteen days, a pace that Hockaday's mail coaches

---

[14] Arrington, "Mormon Finance and the Utah War," 220.
[15] Gray, "The Salt Lake Hockaday Mail," 14–15; Mortensen, "A Pioneer Paper," 81.

managed to maintain regularly, at least in reasonable weather. James Bromley made the return trip in a record-setting seventeen days.[16]

Hockaday created the first dependable mail service between Utah and Missouri, eventually establishing thirty-six stations, each of which was entitled to preempt 320 acres of public land. "These mail trains of Hockaday & Co. run on railroad principles," wrote frontier editor Kirk Anderson, praising how they put "passengers as well as mail through in quick time." His "mail train" left St. Joseph on August 14. "Our cavalcade consists of a wagon for carrying the mails and baggage and a fine new ambulance for the accommodation of passengers," he reported. The service intended not only to deliver the mail but to "furnish the people of the plains with merchandise."

To handle this freighting operation, Hockaday partnered with David H. Burr, the former Utah territorial surveyor general, and dispatched four major outfitting parties that summer. The last train alone consisted of 105 wagons, 225 men, 200 mules, 1,000 cattle, 50 horses, and 465,000 pounds of freight: altogether, Hockaday, Burr, & Co. sent 182 wagons west during the summer of 1858. The contractors divided the line into four divisions, with the last one starting at Gilberts Station. "The enterprise he has undertaken is a gigantic one," the *Atchison Champion* commented in August, "but will be a great promoter of civilization and settlement in the vast territory west of here." As winter approached, the mail company anticipated "making all trips within scheduled time," wrote passenger Albert G. Browne. "On the western division, the services of the most experienced mountaineers have been engaged to conduct the mail across the mountains in the winter."[17]

Hockaday could hardly have chosen a worse year to launch his enterprise than 1858. The storms that fall "in the neighborhood of the South Pass and the Sweetwater are pronounced by old mountaineers the most terrible ever experienced in that vicinity," Kirk Anderson reported from Salt Lake. It began storming "almost incessantly" on November 20, and the old veterans swore the blizzard that roared through South Pass during the first three days of December was "the severest known in these parts for the last ten years." It struck just as the east- and westbound mails were due. Gilberts Station, the most remote and isolated outpost on the entire line, was justly "considered

---

[16] "Letter from the Army of Utah" and "Mail Arrangements," *San Francisco Evening Bulletin*, July 21, 1858, 3/2, and July 23, 1858, 1/3; Gray, "The Salt Lake Hockaday Mail," 17.

[17] Gray, "The Salt Lake Hockaday Mail," 18–19; Anderson, "Trip to Utah," 3–4.

by all travelers to be the coldest place on the road from the 'States.' " One of the men trapped at the station said the whiteout was "the worst storm in the memory of old-timers."[18]

The westbound mail under conductor W. J. Brooks, who intended to establish a station on the Sweetwater, arrived at Devils Gate on schedule. He found "the snow was about three feet deep, and now there is no bottom," making it "impossible to put a station on the sixth crossing." Brooks and an assistant named Bevins pressed on, taking shelter at Rocky Ridge, only eight miles short of Gilberts Station, where eight of their nine mules froze to death. After dark on December 4, the badly frostbitten conductors got their single passenger, Carson Valley Indian agent R. B. Jarvis, to shelter at the station. An hour later, nine Salt Lake mail carriers and their passengers, including division agent William Ashton, stumbled into the post after five days struggling to get over South Pass from the station at Big Sandy, only about forty miles away. Both parties had abandoned the mail. Henry Gilbert, Charles H. Miller, and the other hands turned the station into a hospital and set out with a wagon to retrieve the mail. Miller and William Clark somehow managed to deliver the mail at Salt Lake on December 14.[19]

The mail carriers paid dearly for their dedication. "Mr. Ashton has frozen one hand and one foot," reported eastbound passenger John M. Guthrie. "I think he will be bound to loose his hand." Every man who had accompanied him from Salt Lake was frostbitten. "Both the mail boys froze very badly; Mr. Routh, both hands and feet, will probably lose one hand. Little Alex. Montrey, the general favorite with every one on this end of the route, is dreadfully frozen; his whole face, which is quite fleshy, is frozen to the bone; his hands and feet slightly," wrote one of the men, perhaps Charles Miller. "The passengers say he will not get over it."[20]

In December Ashton informed section agent Peter K. Dotson "that his hands are badly frozen and that he would start for Fort Bridger in a few days to have some of his fingers amputated." For four straight days before December 13, "the thermometer stood at 28 degrees below Zero," Ashton reported.[21]

As his men risked their lives and lost limbs trying to deliver the mail under impossible conditions, Hockaday attempted to stage what historian John S.

---

[18]"Cold Weather and the Mails," *The Valley Tan*, Dec. 17, 1858, 2/4.
[19]Ibid., 2/4–5; Gray, "The Salt Lake Hockaday Mail," 2–3.
[20]"Cold Weather and the Mails," *The Valley Tan*, Dec. 17, 1858, 2/4–5.
[21]"Frosty—Very," *The Valley Tan*, Dec. 24, 1858, 2/4.

Gray called "a grandstand play" to show once and for all the advantages the direct road over South Pass had as a mail route over the roundabout and generously subsidized Butterfield line. The plan was to deliver the president's annual message in record time, but the president himself, a notorious Southern sympathizer, sabotaged the scheme when he refused to provide Hockaday's agents with a copy of the text he had expressed to Butterfield's men. Hockaday and Company, the San Francisco *Bulletin* observed, "are heavy sufferers by some piece of jugglery." Historian LeRoy Hafen concluded the Salt Lake mail would have won the overland race, a conclusion strongly supported in the contemporary sources. "If the Government will give him [Hockaday] an equal chance with some others, you will find he can accomplish as wonderful feats as any of Uncle Sam's pets, whether civil or military," wrote the *Bulletin*.[22]

Such justice was not to be. Hockaday began the spring with aggressive plans to provide service to the newly opened gold fields in today's Colorado. The failure of Congress to fund postal operations in March 1858, the death of the postmaster general, and a baffling reversal of the administration's transcontinental mail policy followed, effectively running Hockaday out of business. By the end of May, William H. Russell and John H. Jones, owners of the Leavenworth & Pike's Peak Express, had bought the company. "The winter has been a long, cold and bitter one," observed *The Valley Tan* that spring, reporting that the arrival of two westbound mail deliveries had brought the route up to schedule. "The company certainly have had obstacles of great magnitude to contend against and overcome, and they done all that men could do."[23] There was nothing now for the ruined contractor to do but petition the government for violating its contracts and attempt to recoup some of his losses.

Responding to one of his petitions in 1860, a congressional committee reported that a "discouraged and disheartened" Hockaday had "retired to Salt Lake City, where he now remains in a state of mental and physical debility, which disqualifies him from bestowing any attention whatever to his business." Capt. Albert Tracy, one of the first passengers on a Central Overland California & Pike's Peak Express (C.O.C.&P.P.) eastbound stage that used the stations its predecessor had created, painted an even sadder picture of Hockaday's demise.

---

[22] Gray, "The Salt Lake Hockaday Mail," 3; Hafen, *The Overland Mail*, 114, 125–26.
[23] Gray, "The Salt Lake Hockaday Mail," 5–9; "Mail Obstructions, Snow, &c.," *The Valley Tan*, April 26, 1859, 2/2.

"Bull Trains" Crossing the Plains
Oxen power pulled the thousands of freight wagons that crossed South Pass. They were organized into what contemporary observers called "bull trains," even though no sane teamster ever tried to yoke a bull team to a wagon. From William A. Bell, New Tracks in North America (1869).

Tracy met him at Gilberts Station in "a condition of chronic tremens" in April 1860. Tracy defused a confrontation between Hockaday, "hatless, coatless, and with his hair abroad in a wild, insane manner, above his crimson face," and a stagecoach driver he accused of stealing a mule. After backing down, Hockaday "took more whiskey, from what appeared a favorite blue keg, of the capacity of about two gallons, and was soon asleep." In July 1860 the Bulletin reported that "Hockaday's mental faculties have been seriously affected."[24]

Pony Express Stations at South Pass

William H. Russell picked up the pieces of both John Hockaday and George Chorpenning's shattered transcontinental transportation empires and put them back together as an enterprise that won him fame as "the Napoleon

[24] MacKinnon, "Buchanan Spoils System," 146–47.

of the West." Russell and his partners, Alexander Majors and William B. Waddell, had made a paper fortune transporting army supplies for the Utah Expedition, but the government still owed them most of the money. With its eye on winning the overland mail contract that had already proved fatal to so many entrepreneurs, Russell, Majors & Waddell combined the Leavenworth & Pike's Peak Express with the Hockaday and Chorpenning lines and established the Central Overland California & Pike's Peak Express (C.O.C.&P.P.), the Pony Express.

The new express company promised swift delivery of the U.S. mail from the end of the telegraph line at St. Joseph, Missouri, to San Francisco. Russell, the scheme's mastermind, served as president and financier, while Majors managed day-to-day operations. Majors organized the route into five divisions and in sixty-seven days cobbled together a system of stations purchased from Hockaday, new installations, and a few hopes. Service began on April 3, 1860, and advertised it would carry the mail "from the Missouri to California in eight days."[25]

Majors established "home stations" at intervals of seventy-five to one hundred miles and smaller "relay stations" every ten to fifteen miles. Riders were expected to cover seventy-five miles or more in about ten hours. The operation expanded from 86 stations on the first run to 147 stations by mid-1861.[26] James Bromley, a veteran of Hockaday's express and the Lander Expedition, managed the section from Horseshoe Station on the North Platte to the Weber River, which included South Pass.[27]

Sources identify eight Pony Express stations between Ice Slough and Big Sandy: Warm Springs, Rocky Ridge/St. Marys, Strawberry Creek, Rock Creek, Gilberts Station (Upper Sweetwater/South Pass Station), Pacific Springs, Dry Sandy, and Little Sandy. The U.S. postmaster's schedule of March 12, 1861, however, listed only seven stations, which it called Warm Springs at mile 962; Rocky Ridge at mile 950; Rock Creek at mile 938; Upper Sweetwater at mile 926; Pacific Springs at mile 914; Dry Sandy at mile 902; and Little Sandy at mile 887. Benjamin Franklin Lowe, later one of the first settlers of Lander, Wyoming, and Battese Lorain arrived at the

---

[25] "The Pony Express Starts To day," *St. Joseph Daily Gazette*, April 3, 1860, 1/1. Delivery actually took about ten days during the service's first months of operation.

[26] Historian Joe Nardone provided these numbers from a July 1861 list of stations in his possession. The St. Joseph Museum identified 153 stations in its "Pony Express Stations (1860–1861)."

[27] Settle and Settle, *Saddles and Spurs*, 39.

Upper Sweetwater Station in May 1860 and apparently managed it for the newly organized express company.[28]

The accommodations at "Foot of Ridge Station" below Rocky Ridge on Muskrat Creek failed to impress one famous visitor who was stranded there waiting for a driver in 1860. "The station rather added to than took from our discomfort: it was a terrible unclean hole; milk was not procurable within thirty-five miles, . . . there was no sugar, and the cooking was atrocious," complained English adventurer Richard F. Burton. "We were not sorry when the night came, but then the floor was knobby, the musquetoes seemed rather to enjoy the cold, and the banks [bunks?] swarmed with 'chinches.' " Burton was happier at Pacific Springs, where he spent the next night in a shanty "perhaps a trifle more uncomfortable than the average." Save for the scenery, the hut was "a right melancholy abode," Burton said, but he had "seldom seen a view more beautiful." The "Pony's" couriers impressed Burton much more favorably. "The riders are mostly youths, mounted upon active and lithe Indian nags. They ride 100 miles at a time—about eight per hour—with four changes of horses, and return to their stations the next day," he wrote after seeing them at work in August 1860. "The letters are carried in leathern bags, which are thrown about carelessly enough when the saddle is changed, and the average postage is \$5 = £1 per sheet."

Almost no authentic information survives about who managed the stations near South Pass or whatever adventures the young riders might have had. Fortunately, not far west of the Big Sandy, reliable documentarian Burton's stagecoach met a Pony Express rider. Unlike the stereotype of the hell-bent-for-leather horseman who stopped for nothing, the courier reined in to exchange news with the passengers, something Burton said neither party had. "As he pricked onward over the plain, the driver informed us, with a portentous rolling of the head, that Ichabod was an a'mighty fine 'shyoot,' " Burton concluded.[29]

"I tell you it was no picnic," recalled J. G. Kelley, a rider along the Carson River. "No amount of money could tempt me to repeat my experience of those days." Little is known about the actual running of the Pony Express around South Pass, but William F. Cody told "of several events that took

---

[28] Godfrey, *Pony Express National Historic Trail*, 151–54; U.S. Postmaster Schedule, March 12, 1861, "Overland Mail Company," in Nardone, *Report on Pony Express Route*; Guenther, "The Burnt Ranch Saga," 13.

[29] Burton, *City of the Saints*, Aug. 19, 20, 1860, 29, 161, 163, 166, 169.

place when he was a rider on the lonely Sweetwater area" in the 1898 collection of tall tales he wrote with former army officer Henry Inman as his collaborator. "Buffalo Bill" credited "Pony Bob" Haslam with riding 380 miles with practically no rest, but Cody also claimed he personally rode 322 miles, which he said was the longest ever made by any rider. Generations of gullible historians have accepted Cody's stories without question—former Utah governor Charles R. Mabey even included it in his epic poem celebrating the Pony Express—but as historian John S. Gray has shown, Cody never rode for the C.O.C.&P.P.[30]

Russell, Majors & Waddell had been surviving on loans made against its government contracts for handling most of the Utah Expedition's freighting operations since 1858. The government failed to pay its enormous debts to the company, so the operation was essentially bankrupt when it launched the Pony Express. (This helps explain why many riders said C.O.C.&P.P. stood for "Clean Out of Cash & Poor Pay.") A man who combined the qualities of both a visionary and con artist, Russell counted on winning the overland mail contract to revive the company's fortunes, but Congress adjourned in June 1860 without acting. Russell tried to save his business through an "abstraction of bonds from the Interior Department" that led to a scandal and his arrest. He eventually beat the charges, but these troubles spelled the end of the trail for Russell, Majors & Waddell.

As the Union disintegrated in 1861, Congress finally appropriated money to support the overland mail after the secession of Texas closed the southern routes. But the contract went to the Overland Mail Company, which hired the C.O.C.&P.P. to handle the service east of Salt Lake.[31] With the completion of the transcontinental telegraph in October 1861, the Pony Express officially ceased operations. The *Sacramento Daily Bee* bid "Farewell Pony," saluting the "staunch, wilderness-overcoming, swift-footed messenger" who had "dragged in your train the lightening itself."

The Pony Express made its last ride on November 20, 1861, having carried more than thirty-three thousand pieces of mail. Alexander Majors claimed his firm lost at least a hundred thousand dollars, but historian Raymond W. Settle estimated the actual loss was half a million dollars. The Pony Express,

---

[30] Mabey, "The Pony Express," 7–8; Gray, "Fact versus Fiction in the Kansas Boyhood of Buffalo Bill."
[31] Settle and Settle, *Saddles and Spurs*, 168–71, 178; Ridge, "Reflections on the Pony Express," 7–9; Jackson, "A New Look at Wells Fargo, Stagecoaches and the Pony Express," 303–304, 313.

historian Martin Ridge concluded, was "as risky a venture as any taken on the frontier." Like most such risks, it did not pay off.[32]

The Butterfield Overland Mail contracted to manage the express operations east of Salt Lake in April 1861. The company launched the first daily overland stage and mail service from St. Joseph, Missouri (and later Atchison, Kansas) to Placerville in July 1861. On July 8, its first stage passed diarist Ira H. Butterfield of Michigan on the North Platte River. "We now met the mail-coach coming directly from St. Joseph," eastbound Jewish passenger Israel Joseph Benjamin reported five days later near Antelope Valley, about fifty miles west of today's Utah-Nevada border. "It had left the city on July first and was the first to leave. We were all mutually happy and exchanged news. Since the overland mail now ran daily, from the east as well as from the west, we now met a mail-coach every day which on a journey through the deserts gave us, it may be easily understood, great pleasure." He counted forty-two stations on the 622-mile road from Carson City to Great Salt Lake City and ninety-two stations between Salt Lake and St. Joseph. Benjamin made an insightful comment: "Is it not remarkable that a journey which would take a caravan no less than four to five months can be made by mail-coach in eighteen days?"[33]

Ben Holladay, another transportation mogul who would die broke, began operating the stage line over the Oregon-California Trail. When he took over the assets of Russell, Majors & Waddell in March 1862, Holladay already had plans that would begin the transformation of the South Pass from the nation's major overland transportation corridor into a backcountry byway.[34]

THE PAPER CITY OF SOUTH PASS

Confused travelers sometimes used the same names to identify different South Pass landmarks. It did not help when ambitious promoters established a "paper city" west of the Eighth Crossing of the Sweetwater and a mile beyond Rocky Ridge Station in 1861 that they dubbed "South Pass City." John W. Powell and the mail couriers who wintered there in 1858 had already applied the name to the buildings around Gilberts Station, which helped lead subsequent

---

[32] Settle, "Pony Express," 109, 121, 123; Ridge, "Reflections," 13.
[33] Hafen, *The Overland Mail*, 217–18; Root and Connelley, *Overland Stage*, 40; Butterfield, "Michigan to California," July 8, 1861; Benjamin, *Three Years in America*, July 13, 1861, 2:218, 222, 267.
[34] Hafen, *The Overland Mail*, 227.

RHOBA SULLIVAN
This remarkable woman may have wintered at
South Pass City and given birth to a daughter.
From Morton, Illustrated History of Nebraska
(1905).

writers to assume the real-estate speculation located some fifteen miles to the east was actually at the Ninth Crossing. It was not.

Richard Burton heard "South-Pass City" was founded near Gilberts Station after his visit in August 1860, "one of the many mushroom growths which the presence of gold in the Rocky Mountains has caused to spring up." Mormon overlander Bartlett Tripp stopped for dinner at "S. Pass City" in July 1861 and described it as "a Ranche with it's [sic] accompanying outbuildings of logs as usual." The short-lived establishment's most famous visitor "hove in sight of South Pass City" on the overland mail coach on a sweltering day in August 1861. Young Sam Clemens met the town's "hotel-keeper, the postmaster, the blacksmith, the mayor, the constable, the city marshal and the principal citizen and property holder, all came out and greeted us cheerily, and we gave him good day," he later wrote as Mark Twain. "He gave us a little Indian news, and a little Rocky Mountain news, and we gave him some Plains information in return. He then retired to his lonely grandeur and we climbed on up among the bristling peaks and the ragged clouds." The city "consisted of four log cabins, one of which was unfinished, and the gentleman with all those offices and titles was the chiefest of the ten citizens of the place. Think of hotel-keeper, postmaster, blacksmith, mayor, constable, city marshal and principal citizen all condensed into one person and crammed into one skin." The official was "a perfect Allen's revolver of dignities," commented a passenger who thought he held as many offices as a pepperbox revolver held bullets.[35]

This talented promoter was Potter Charles Sullivan, former speaker of Nebraska's second territorial assembly in 1855 and 1856. Sullivan apparently arrived on the Sweetwater in 1858, and he and his brother Ephraim may have worked for Henry Gilbert. His wife Rhoba Ann seems to have been with him in 1861, for she gave birth to Rhoba May Sullivan in Dakota Territory that year. On May 11, 1862, handcart rescuer and Mormon militia officer Robert Burton arrived at "what is called South Pass City" after a series of Indian raids in late April. "Mr. Sullivan is the proprietor. The city consists of two houses and one stable." By late summer, the Sullivans had decamped for Oregon. James G. Leonard, who served as the first postmaster of South Pass City from March 1861 to September 1862, may have been Sullivan's partner.[36]

When Ruth Warner Turner passed by on her way to California in July 1861, the town had "three or four houses in it, and a post-office near by." Capt. Medorem Crawford laid over for a day "as this is the last Post Office on the road," at least for those who planned to use the Lander Cutoff. The city fathers used rumors to promote their future Metropolis: "The famous paper city of South Pass contains 4 houses, is said to be near gold & silver mines," noted Crawford.[37]

As John W. Hunt's *Wisconsin Gazetteer* observed in 1853, a "paper city" was a real-estate venture "laid out and platted several years in advance of the progress of civilization." Assuming Sullivan and Leonard were partners, they may have envisioned getting in on the ground floor of a gold-rush boomtown, and such characters were not above using rumors to promote a profit. The boosters deployed all the standard promotional tools, including an expansive map of their proposed development. "It was claimed that gold had been discovered near here, and before reaching here we had seen maps of South Pass City showing [the] town regularly laid out and Fremont's Peak represented as within the city limits," Ira H. Butterfield reported on his way west in 1861 as the "super-cargo" for herd of sheep and cattle. "There was no city but two stone shanties, and Fremont's Peak was fifty miles away, and no gold in sight

---

[35] Burton, *City of the Saints*, Aug. 20, 1860, 161; Tripp, Journal, July 29, 1861; Twain, *Roughing It*, 98–99.
[36] Morton, *Illustrated History of Nebraska*, 261–63; Fisher, *Utah and the Civil War*, 121; Jarret, "The First South Pass City," 1,139.
[37] Turner, "A Letter Home," July 8, 1861, 11; Crawford, Diary, July 26, 27, 1861, 19–20.

at least." The scheme apparently met with some success, for during the winter of 1861–62, fifty-two men reportedly wintered over at South Pass City, dreaming of the wealth they would acquire come spring. One story indicates the Shoshones drove them off before they could realize their golden visions.[38]

These descriptions help identify the settlement's location. Crawford said it was five miles from "the canyon of the Sweetwater & where the roads leave the valley, [to] pass over Rocky ridge." In July 1861, Ira H. Butterfield "drove in the morning seven miles to the seventh and eighth crossings of the Sweetwater. Road very hilly. In the afternoon drove four miles to South Pass City. Postoffice here and mail stage station one mile below."[39] Based on these reports, the paper city sprawled out a mile beyond the Rocky Ridge/St. Marys stage station at the mouth of the gap where the Oregon Trail turned up the canyon that led to Rocky Ridge.

Medorem Crawford found the site "deserted, not a soul in the city," when he passed by early in August 1862. A month later, Mormon overlander Jens Weibye described seeing "a station consisting of three houses" where the LDS Church had left seven hundred sacks of flour in the care of "a brother" and his wife. "At this place, there was a store a post-office, and pigs and chickens were seen around the houses," Weibye wrote. While climbing up the draw leading to Rocky Ridge the next morning, Weibye passed "the ruins of three houses built of sandstone," which may have been the abandoned remnants of South Pass City.[40] A year later, Samuel G. Crawford of the Emigrant Escort Service could find "nary house" when he camped "on the paper city of South Pass" in July. A few years later, more skillful boosters would devise a scheme that did create a gold rush, and a longer-lasting South Pass City would be reborn on the head of Willow Creek some twenty miles to the west of the vanished paper city.

The Talking Wire:
The Telegraph Crosses South Pass, 1861

The Pony Express was founded with the full awareness that it would be a short-lived enterprise and would end with the completion of a telegraph

---

[38] Butterfield, "Michigan to California," July 18, 1861, 407; Guenther, "The Burnt Ranch Saga," 11.
[39] Crawford, Diary, 19–20; Butterfield, "Michigan to California," July 18, 1861, 407.
[40] Crawford, "Journal," July 27, 1863, 4; Weibye, Journal, Sept. 4, 5, 1862.

line to San Francisco. Congress had actually passed a Pacific telegraph bill in 1855 granting a 200-foot right of way in perpetuity to the contractors. "The enterprise will be prosecuted with vigor to an early completion," the press reported, but since the project had no funding, nothing came of the act. In 1859 California's legislature appropriated six thousand dollars to help fund a line connecting the state with the East and agreed to pay four thousand dollars to subsidize a backup line that would insure uninterrupted service. "Where shall we build it? Of course on the main line of travel—on the line by which we expect to have most intercourse with the Mississippi valley. That line is by Carson Valley, Salt Lake City, the South Pass, and St. Joseph," editorialized the *Alta Californian*. "By that route nine-tenths of the overland immigrants now in California have come, and it is that route by which the great majority of future immigrants will come."[41]

Congress passed and President Buchanan signed the Pacific Telegraph Act in June 1860. The bill authorized an annual loan of forty thousand dollars for ten years, a maximum fee of three dollars for a single dispatch of ten words, and the use of a quarter-section of public land for every fifteen miles of line to subsidize the building of a telegraph line from west of the state of Missouri to San Francisco, with a branch line to Oregon. The contractors could select any route they pleased.[42]

Hiram Sibley, the president of the Western Union Telegraph Company who had long campaigned for the transcontinental line, submitted the only bid. He sent his partner, Jeptha H. Wade, to California to set up the project's western operations. In April 1860 Salt Lakers learned "all the California telegraph companies had merged in one" and the Pacific Telegraph Company's agents "had perfected arrangements for the early completion of the line of telegraph from California to this city."[43] Wade organized the California State Telegraph Company from the local companies and created a subsidiary, the Overland Telegraph Company, to connect the Carson Valley to Salt Lake City.

Just as politics delayed the construction of a transcontinental railroad, so the question of which route the overland telegraph would take became a political controversy that lasted more than a decade after it was technically

---

[41]"The Pacific Telegraph," *Deseret News*, May 2, 1855, 4/3; Lamar, *New Encyclopedia of the American West*, 1,098; "Overland Mail Routes," *The Valley Tan*, Jan. 4, 1859, 3/3–4.

[42]"Act to Facilitate Communication between the Atlantic and Pacific States," U.S. Statutes, June 16, 1860.

[43]"Telegraph to the Pacific," *Deseret News*, April 10, 1861, 8/3.

Wagons Nearing Mesa

Frontier photographer and artist William Henry Jackson based this drawing on his experiences in 1866 as an overland teamster (and occasional pronghorn antelope hunter). His sketch shows the Oregon Buttes looming in the distance as wagons follow the transcontinental telegraph line to South Pass. *Courtesy Scotts Bluff National Monument and the National Park Service.*

possible. The principals considered running the line up the Arkansas River or over the old Butterfield Mail route through the Southwest, and the burgeoning new metropolis at Denver might have won the prize had it delivered its promised twenty thousand dollars in stock subscriptions. Instead, the builders chose the logical direct route up the Platte River and over South Pass to take advantage of the existing stage and mail stations.

The companies, all controlled by Western Union, secured extremely talented men to run the project, with Edward Creighton managing construction of the Pacific Telegraph to Salt Lake and James Gamble the Overland Telegraph. Creighton spent the summer of 1860 surveying routes west from Omaha before selecting the road over South Pass, while the western managers decided to follow the overland stage and Pony Express trail across the central Great Basin.

After almost a year, the project finally got underway. The Nebraska territorial legislature incorporated the Pacific Telegraph Company in June 1861 to enforce the terms of the eastern leg of the contract. (The ubiquitous B. F. Ficklin was one of the incorporators). James Gamble set out with twenty-six wagons from Sacramento on May 27, 1861, to start running the Overland Telegraph Company line from the existing line at Carson City to Salt Lake. On June 20, 1861, J. M. Hubbard raised the "first pole of the Telegraph line" at Fort Churchill on Carson River, while James Street started building the Overland Telegraph west from Great Salt Lake City in July.

On the Fourth of July, Edward Creighton began stringing wire for the Pacific Telegraph line west from Omaha. Preparations may have started even earlier, for on May 21, Ira H. Butterfield could see a telegraph line, "or at least one being constructed," on the south side of the Platte. A week after Creighton's official start, W. H. Stebbins, director of construction for the four hundred miles of wire going east from Salt Lake over South Pass, raised the first Pacific Telegraph pole on Salt Lake's East Temple Street, today's Main Street.[44]

Considerable skepticism greeted the project, which the Pacific Telegraph Act directed was to be completed by July 31, 1862. It was a wild scheme, since it would be "next to impossible to get your poles and materials distributed on the plains, and as fast as you build the line the Indians will cut it down," Abraham Lincoln told Hiram Sibley. James Gamble solved this problem by

---

[44]"The Western Telegraph," *Deseret News*, July 3, 1861, 141/4; Butterfield, "Michigan to California," May 21, 1861, 397; Root and Hickman, "The Pony Express and Pacific Telegraph," 67.

hiring Indians to take care of the operation's livestock. "I never had any reason to regret the confidence I placed in them," he recalled.[45]

Even as the nation was mobilizing for war, Edward Creighton purchased five hundred oxen and mules, provisions, and one hundred wagons. He recruited four hundred men at Omaha and armed them with rifles and Navy revolvers. Far to the west, Gamble kept in close communication with Creighton's eastern division, with the two men "advising each other at frequent intervals of the progress of the work." They made a bet about who would reach Salt Lake first. Both superintendents "thoroughly organized and systematized" the work: "The line was first measured and staked off; the hole-diggers followed; then came the pole-setters, and next the wire party," Gamble wrote. The contract required no fewer than twenty-five durable poles per mile, and the line "was strung up at the rate of from three to eight miles a day," he recalled.[46]

The Central Overland California stage line announced telegraph stations between Fort Kearny and Salt Lake would include Cottonwood Springs, Overland City (Julesburg), Fort Laramie, Horse Shoe, Pacific Springs, and Fort Bridger, but James Gamble recalled that stations were established forty to fifty miles apart. By the time the Civil War began, the nearest station to South Pass was at the Last Crossing, and was known as Gilberts Station, Upper Sweetwater Station, and often as South Pass Station.[47]

The superintendents built the line with astonishing speed: at the end of July, Gamble's crew was already 125 miles east of Carson Valley. By August, Creighton was ninety-five miles west of Fort Kearny. At Scotts Bluff on July 24, eastbound sojourner Israel Joseph Benjamin reported the line "was already completed, and here they lay much material to carry it forward." A month later, "Telegraph completed to Deer Creek this evening," wrote Charles Scott while marching east with the last remnants of the Utah Expedition. Meanwhile, in the Great Basin, Gamble's crew built sixteen miles of line in one day, an effort spurred on by the need to get to water.

Work crews "were busy completing the telegraph line to the East," Benjamin commented at Salt Lake City on July 15. "There were various gaps but in many places the line was completed for stretches of fifty to eighty miles." The project almost failed to reach Salt Lake when Hubbard's crew ran out of poles

---

[45] Root and Hickman, "The Pony Express and Pacific Telegraph," 66; Gamble, "Wiring a Continent," 558.
[46] Gamble, "Wiring a Continent," 558; Thompson, *Wiring a Continent*, 363.
[47] Root and Hickman. "The Pony Express and Pacific Telegraph," 69; Gamble, "Wiring a Continent," 561.

in early October, but Gamble located suitable timber near Egan Canyon in today's Nevada and directed his reluctant men to become loggers. Despite being buried by an overnight snowstorm, the men cut twenty wagonloads of poles.[48]

This delay gave Creighton the edge he needed to win the race to Salt Lake. On October 18, Brigham Young had the honor of sending the first eastbound message from Great Salt Lake City. "Utah has not seceded but is firm for the Constitution and laws of our once happy country," the Mormon prophet assured the Western Union's Jeptha H. Wade, "and is warmly interested in such useful enterprises as the one so far completed." Acting Governor Frank Fuller used the second wire to congratulate President Lincoln "upon the completion of an enterprise which spans a continent, unites two oceans, and connects with nerve of iron the remote extremities of the body politic, with the great Governmental heart."[49]

The "last link in the great transcontinental chain was finally forged" on October 24, 1861, when both lines were connected at Salt Lake. In a little more than four months, the hard-driving superintendents and their hard-driven men had wired a continent, crossing prairies, deserts, and mountains. As the first messages indicated, the bond of galvanized iron wire they forged helped unite a nation. Chief Justice Stephen J. Field of the California Supreme Court (the older brother of Cyrus Field, the man who managed laying the first transatlantic telegraph cable) sent the first transcontinental message to congratulate Abraham Lincoln "on the completion of this great work" and to assure the president of California's "determination to stand by the government."

The transcontinental connection "will be the means of strengthening the attachment which binds both the East and the West to the Union," Field said. Horace W. Carpentier, president of the Overland Telegraph Company, telegraphed Lincoln from San Francisco, celebrating the critical need for such a link: "I announce to you that the telegraph to California has this day been completed." Carpentier proclaimed. "May it be a bond of perpetuity between the states of the Atlantic and those of the Pacific."[50]

The transcontinental line proved immensely profitable. Despite the authorizing legislation's limiting the charge for ten words to three dollars, the line

---

[48] Root and Hickman, "The Pony Express and Pacific Telegraph," 67; Benjamin, *Three Years in America*, 2:222, 262; Scott, "Diary," Aug. 24, 1861, 398; Gamble, "Wiring a Continent," 558.
[49] "The Completion of the Telegraph," *Deseret News*, Oct. 23, 1861, 5/3.
[50] Thompson, *Wiring a Continent*, 368.

began transmitting messages at a dollar a word before the rate settled down to a little more than eighty-seven cents to send a message from New York to San Francisco. For Sibley, Wade, Creighton, Gamble, and a small inner circle of Western Union men, the transcontinental telegraph was "a glorious triumph, both financially and strategically." The line between Salt Lake and Brownsville, Nebraska, over South Pass had cost only $147,000, even with two Western Union directors adding enormous "financing" charges. This investment quickly represented six million dollars in Western Union stock. After suitable "watering," the company's shareholders transformed that amount into many millions more.[51]

Whatever financial shenanigans accompanied the building of the transcontinental telegraph, the link between east and west proved its value during the Civil War—and on the trail. The poles, wires, and the string of stations reminded overland travelers that civilization was continuing its relentless march to the West. Evidence of the line long survived in the high, dry climate of the Rockies. "The first transcontinental telegraph line paralleled the south side of the old trail through the Pass," trail expert Paul Henderson wrote after visiting South Pass in 1955. "One often finds the stubs of the old cedar and pine poles, and tie wires. Occasionally one of the early wood shell insulators are found."[52]

Life was not easy for the men who tended the talking wire. "In the vicinity of South Pass the operators are sometimes 'snowed in' for months at a time. All communication with the outer world, save by telegraph, is completely cut off," journalist J. Ross Browne reported. "A more isolated life than these poor fellows lead can scarcely be conceived. Around them as far as the eye can reach the mountains and plains are covered with snow. All traces of human life are obliterated. The station-houses are covered up, high over the roofs, and it is only by cutting a way out and keeping it clear that the occupants save themselves from being buried alive."[53] The isolation led most operators to welcome passing emigrants, and they sometimes proved useful for more than conversation. When overlander Jennie Eakin Hanna's family's camped on Little Sandy Creek in 1866, the telegraph operator "had father draw a tooth for him."[54]

---

[51] Ibid., 370.
[52] "Dickie Springs Quadrangle," in Paul Henderson, "A Tour along the Old Oregon Trail," copy in author's possession.
[53] Browne, *Resources of the Pacific Slope*, 437.
[54] Eakin, Diary, June 29, 1866, typescript, 4–5.

An Indian War Is Inevitable

"It is really surprising to see what a vast Train of human beings are pushing forward Male Indians [toward] the Three great points of attraction 'viz' Salt Lake, California, & Oregon," William Wagner wrote as he watched the cavalcade of humanity marching up the Platte River to South Pass in 1852. "The young, the old, the great & small, of both sexes & colors—from the infant a few days old, to the gray haired veteran of three score years & Ten, are alike braving the dangers, encountering the hardships, enduring the privations of a long, tedious, & perilous Journey through, an uncultivated, uncivilized & unfriendly country."

Like most of his countrymen, Wagner felt he and his companions were fulfilling a national destiny. Unlike many other Americans, Wagner realized that someone would pay dearly for the triumph of the bold pioneers: "But westward ho! The Star of empire makes its way, & the time is not far distant when the Broad & uncultivated prairies & plains, that are now the Hunting grounds of the rude Savage, will be converted into beautiful Farms & Homes for the Pale faces—'Where then will be the Red mans Home?'"[55] At South Pass, the answer to Wagner's question was much the same as it was throughout the United States.

Male Indians spent virtually all their time hunting and making war with neighboring tribes, James Clyman observed in 1824. The tradition endured. Medorem Crawford told of meeting as many as one hundred raiders in the Sweetwater Valley in 1842. At Ice Springs (also known as Ice Slough), Crawford found "a war party of Sues & Shians who had been to fight the Snakes." The South Pass section of Charles Preuss's seven-part "Topographical Map of the Road from Missouri to Oregon" proclaimed in bold type, "War-Ground of the Snake and Sioux Indians."[56]

Oregon pioneer J. M. Harrison used the phrase: "The Sweetwater is the warground of the Snake, Crow, Blackfoot, and Sioux Indians," he recalled; "there many sanguinary conflicts have taken place between them." South Pass and its approaches were contested ground, where young warriors from many Indian nations came to test their mettle. He remembered "some of the young braves" belonging to a war party of about five hundred Arapahos—no doubt

---

[55] Wagner, Journal, May 23, 1852, 78.
[56] Clyman, *James Clyman, Frontiersman*, 20; Crawford, "Journal," July 23, 1842, 13; Spence and Jackson, *The Expeditions of John Charles Frémont*, Map Portfolio, Map 4, Section 4.

an enormous exaggeration—attempted to rob six wagons on their way to South Pass, "reaching over from their ponies and cutting through the wagon cover [and] pulling out whatever they could lay their hands on." Harrison claimed the train's leader rushed up and struck the young men on their backs with the flat of a sword and soon persuaded them to desist, while the whites thought "it best not to shoot unless there was not an other alternative."[57]

Despite occasional conflicts such as the one Harrison reported, good relations between Indians and the whites passing through the homelands characterized the first decades of overland emigration. The Shoshone were the dominant tribe at South Pass well into the 1860s. Washakie repeatedly pledged his bond with the Americans: in his role as Indian agent, F. W. Lander spoke highly of "Washikee, who is also known by the term of 'the White man's friend.'" Any steps the government could take "to augment the power of Washikee, who is perfectly safe in his attachment to the Americans and northern mountaineers, would also prove beneficial," Lander wrote.[58] But Washakie was unable to fulfill his pledges to his people when whites broke their own promises after the Utah War, empowering younger, angrier Shoshone leaders.

Until and even after 1861, most violence near South Pass involved Indians fighting Indians. When Jean Rio Baker heard Cheyenne warriors had killed two Shoshones on their way to the 1851 peace conference at Fort Laramie, she wrote, "the Shoshones had in return slaughtered 27 out of 30 Cheyenes" bound for "the Great Counsel of the Tribes." The situation deteriorated over the next ten years: "nearly every tribe of Indians in this country are at war with one another," Lt. Caspar Collins wrote in 1862. Unfortunately, conflict between emigrants and Indians also escalated steadily. Bvt. 2nd Lt. John L. Grattan's disastrous attempt to "crack it to the Sioux" near Laramie in 1854 resulted in the obliteration of his command. In response, a year later Gen. William Harney's troops massacred a Brulé village on Blue Water Creek near Ash Hollow.[59]

On the road to South Pass after the Utah War, violence begat violence as travelers witnessed a steady increase in bloodshed along the entire Platte River system. West of the Three Crossings of the Sweetwater in 1860, Richard Burton met "an Italian driven from the low country by a band of Sioux, who had slain his Shoshonee wife, and at one time had thought of adding his scalp

---

[57] Harrison, Recollections of 1846 [1875], 10–11.
[58] Lander to Greenwood, Feb. 18, 1860, in Morgan, *Shoshonean Peoples*, 254.
[59] Baker, "By Windjammer and Prairie Schooner," 270; Spring, *Caspar Collins*, 120; Utley, *Frontiersmen in Blue*, 114–15.

THE U.S. MAIL AND THE WAR FOR SOUTH PASS   253

to his squaw's." When he stopped at the at what he called the Foot of Ridge Station "a war party of Sioux rode in, en route to provide themselves with a few Shoshonee scalps," Burton reported.[60]

With the onset of the Civil War and the withdrawal of virtually all the troops on the frontier, violence broke out all along the trail, beginning with a surge in intertribal warfare. The Shoshones and Sioux had a battle near Strawberry Creek, Capt. Medorem Crawford reported on July 24, 1861.[61] This may have been the clash four days earlier on Willow Creek between two hundred Lakota and a hundred Shoshone warriors under Washakie, who personally killed the first of the attackers. His oldest son, Nan-nag-gai, arrived in camp after the attack began. Washakie rebuked him: "I, an old man, have killed this Sioux our enemy, while you, like a squaw, come into camp after the fight is over."

"I will make for myself a name as great as is yours, or die in the attempt," the indignant son replied as he turned to charge the Lakota. "He killed and scalped several of the enemy, but was finally slain, and his body was scalped and hacked into pieces in sight of his father, who had followed after him," wrote historian Grace Hebard. "All day long Washakie with his men fought the Sioux to avenge the death of his cherished boy, and with the coming of twilight the enemy was forced to retreat, with the loss of a number of their braves." According to legend, Washakie's grief turned his hair white overnight. Some believe the Lakota war leader Crazy Horse led the assault.[62]

Such incidents undermined Washakie's power, which was already under siege. In April 1861, Washakie was in trouble, Indian agent William "Billy" Rogers told William H. Russell of the Pony Express: "his tribe have deserted him, or as they say they have thrown him away, he has always ruled them and could hold them in complete subjigation until now," Rogers warned. "He told me last summer that his Indians have lost confidence in him that he had made them promises of goods on the word of the Superintendent." No goods had arrived, and now "the Snakes say they do not intend to let the Mail or Emigrants pass through their Country if they do not get some presents this spring." Rogers considered the Shoshones the best Indians in the Rocky Mountains: they "pride themselves that they have never spilled the blood of a white man."

---

[60] Burton, *City of the Saints*, Aug. 19, 1860, 158–59, 175.
[61] Crawford, Diary, July 27, 1861, 19.
[62] Hebard, *Washakie*, 98, 101; Guenther, "Burnt Ranch Saga," 14, 31n51. Hebard dated Nan-nag-gai's death to fall 1866.

Pony Express agent James Bromley, who had just returned from South Pass, told Rogers "that if something is not done soon, there will be trouble in the Snake Country, which is in his division. There are not enough U.S. Troops in Utah to whip this tribe, they are the best fighters and the bravest in the Territory and better prepared for fighting" than the handful of soldiers still left in Utah. Rogers asked Russell to appeal to the commissioner of Indian affairs to send him eight or ten thousand dollars to get Washakie reinstated. Farther west, the agent warned, the Goshutes were "becoming daily more and more hostile towards the Whites who keep the Stations. I have had reliable information if something is not done soon that they intend wiping out the Stations and Stock."[63]

Nothing happened in response to Rogers's plea. Except for a sergeant's guard at Fort Bridger, the last U.S. troops left Utah Territory by December 1861 to join the war for the Union. Former sutler William Carter organized a force of mountaineers and Shoshones loyal to Washakie to fill the void until Company I of the Third California Volunteers arrived to garrison the fort a year later.

Early in the spring of 1862, the violence that Rogers had predicted along the mail and telegraph lines exploded as Shoshones, Bannocks, and white renegades began attacking mail stations from the North Platte to Green River, notably at Split Rock. The marauders burned coaches, ran off livestock, and killed stage drivers.[64]

Overland Mail Company agent Louis McLane demanded that the army station troops on the mail route permanently "for the protection of the mails and treasure." At Brigham Young's suggestion, acting governor Frank Fuller enlisted a mounted company of Utah militia "for the purpose of protecting the Overland Mail Route" for thirty days. (Young also wanted an escort for several Mormon officials on their way to Washington.) Under Utah War veteran Col. Robert T. Burton, they marched from Salt Lake on April 26, 1862, after the wettest winter anyone in the Rocky Mountains could remember.

The volunteers saw bags of mail scattered along the trail and more stacked in abandoned stations, notably at Ice Springs, where they found "twenty-six sacks, a great portion of which had been cut open and scattered over the prairie." Every station between Green River and the North Platte was deserted,

---

[63] Rogers to Russell, April 18, 1861, in Morgan, *Shoshonean Peoples*, 263–64.
[64] Gowans and Campbell, *Fort Bridger*, 118–20; Long, *The Saints and the Union*, 82.

Burton informed Fuller in May, and "all stock having been stolen or removed and other property abandoned to the mercy of Indians or white men." The fact that the mail bags had been pilfered and all the cash and checks taken proved to Burton "conclusively that some renegade whites were connected with the Indians in the robbery."[65]

To fill the void created by the army's withdrawal, on April 28, 1862, President Lincoln called on Brigham Young "to raise, arm, and equip a company of cavalry for service of ninety days to protect the overland mail and telegraph against Indian attack" along the overland trail between Independence Rock and the Green River. In two days, the company, consisting of a captain, two lieutenants, six sergeants, eight corporals, and seventy-two privates, was ready for service. The commander was Lot Smith, best remembered for burning U.S. Army supply wagons in 1857. The Mormon volunteers rode out of Salt Lake on May 1. At the mouth of Emigration Canyon, Brigham Young bade them farewell, encouraging the soldiers to "conduct themselves as gentlemen, remembering their allegiance and loyalty to the government" while not forgetting their religion.[66]

After contending with the swollen spring runoff fed by the winter's storms, Smith's men reached the deserted mail station at Pacific Springs on May 18. "The traveling is awful, snow deep, waters high," wrote ferry proprietor Lewis Robison. "There is no bottom to the mud." The soldiers took the Seminoe Cut-off to Warm Springs and three days later reached Independence Rock, where they met Burton's company. On the way east, Pvt. Joseph A. Fisher recalled, "we passed many mail stations—one every ten miles. All we encountered along the way, lay in heaps of blackened ashes." Fisher, a former Pony Express rider, exaggerated the devastation, but the company found derelict stations and sacks of stolen or abandoned mail scattered along the trail. Near Split Rock they discovered the wreckage of a stage attacked and looted by Indians.[67]

Abraham Lincoln had declined a chance to become secretary of Oregon Territory in 1849, but he maintained an avid interest in the West throughout his career.[68] The new president viewed the region and its mineral wealth as vital to the Union cause. It was a keen insight, and during the war California's

---

[65] Scott, *The War of the Rebellion*, Series 1, Vol. 50, 1023; Fisher, *Utah and the Civil War*, 115, 133–34; Daniel H. Wells to Joshua Terry, April 24, 1862, Brigham Young Collection, LDS Archives.
[66] Bigler, *Forgotten Kingdom*, 207; *Deseret News*, April 30, 1862, 348; Long, *Saints and the Union*, 87.
[67] Fisher, *Utah and the Civil War*, 33, 37, 45, 48.
[68] Lincoln to Clayton, Sept. 27, 1849, Lincoln Papers, Library of Congress.

mines contributed $185 million to help finance the war, with Nevada adding another $45 million.[69] Lincoln's Indian policy focused on making treaties that extinguished Indian land claims and made western lands "secure for the advancing settler"—and prospector.

One of Lincoln's forgotten achievements was "to organize the entire West into viable political units, each with a government that was loyal to the Union." This led to the creation of Dakota, Colorado, and Nevada territories in 1861, Idaho in 1862, Arizona in 1863, and Montana in 1864. These territories, Lincoln said in 1864, would soon be prosperous enough to be admitted to the Union as states. "The immense mineral resources of some of those Territories ought to be developed as rapidly as possible," the president wrote. He encouraged Congress to consider adopting extraordinary measures to promote that end. Lincoln recognized the Oregon-California Trail as an essential link between the eastern and western United States: by 1865 the U.S. Army had twenty thousand troops stationed throughout the West and at strategic locations along the overland trail.[70]

Organizing the defense of the trail, however, took time. The army assigned two skeleton companies of the U.S. Fourth Regiment of Cavalry and sent the First Independent Battalion of Ohio Volunteer Cavalry (later renamed the Sixth and then consolidated with the Eleventh Regiment of Ohio Volunteer Cavalry) under Lt. Col. William O. Collins to police the overland road and protect the mail and telegraph.

In the summer of 1862, Gen. James Craig, the federal officer in charge of guarding the wagon road from the Missouri River to Utah Territory, took the stagecoach west to Pacific Springs to size up the problem. Craig had already crossed South Pass as a gold seeker. He told Lot Smith he recalled "the pleasant time he had spent in Salt Lake City in 1849 at the Dinner for the 24th of July," where the Mormons celebrated their arrival in Zion and entertained more than two thousand guests.[71]

Colonel Collins hired no less an expert than Jim Bridger to guide the Ohio Volunteers up the Platte. Shortly after reaching Fort Laramie, Collins led four companies to Independence Rock, where Lot Smith's Nauvoo Legionnaires joined him on June 16 for a march to South Pass. On the way, the troops

---

[69] Josephy, *The Civil War in the American West*, 262.
[70] Lincoln, Annual Message, 1864; Lamar, *The New Encyclopedia of the American West*, 215.
[71] Smith to Young, June 16, 1862, LDS Archives.

began converting Ben Holladay's stage stations into military outposts at Three Crossings, St. Marys, and the Last/Ninth Crossing of the Sweetwater. What had been Gilberts Station was renamed Camp Highland and later South Pass Station. Collins assigned ten to twelve men at each post. The garrisons transformed the old mail and stage stops into properly picketed military outposts with sentinel boxes, fenced corrals, stables, kitchens, telegraph rooms, and parade grounds.

Collins and the Sixth Ohio Volunteers arrived at the Last Crossing on June 29 via the Seminoe Cutoff. They established a permanent camp on the east side of the river, which was still running so high it was impossible to cross. "This is a tolerably pleasant place, but there is no timber within two miles," wrote the colonel's eighteen-year-old son, Caspar Collins. "Game was plenty here in the earlier part of the season, but the emigrants have nearly chased it all off and their oxen have eaten nearly all the grass."[72]

"Col. Collins is decidedly against killing Indians indiscriminately," Lot Smith informed Brigham Young from Pacific Springs, "and will not take any general measures, save on the defensive, until he can ascertain satisfactorily by whom the depredations have been committed, and then not resort to killing until he is satisfied that peaceable measures have failed." Collins ordered Smith to move his headquarters to Fort Bridger and directed him to guard the trail between Green River and Salt Lake.[73]

Meanwhile, Collins and the men at South Pass Station did their best to kill Indians after word arrived on June 29 that raiders had killed two emigrants. Within an hour, the colonel had left camp with over one hundred picked men, only to find that the attackers had vanished. "I never saw so many men so anxious in my life to have a fight with the Indians," wrote Caspar Collins. "But ponies are faster than American horses, and I think they will be disappointed."[74]

The men at Camp Highland "had our first trouble with Indians," Pvt. Amberson Shaw recalled, when raiders ran off a supply train's mules and killed a camp teamster. "They robbed him of all his clothes, and they found him naked and stiff, lying in the sage. He had three bullet holes through him," wrote Lt. Caspar Collins. Capt. Hamer Hayes led the pursuit, during which the raiders stampeded the soldier's mounts, but his men were able to recover

---

[72] Jones, *Guarding the Overland Trails*, 75–79; Spring, *Caspar Collins*, 119.
[73] Long, *The Saints and the Union*, 87.
[74] Spring, *Caspar Collins*, 121–22.

almost all the mules, Hayes reported. "After we returned to our old camp we were ordered to cut timber to build a stockade," Shaw wrote. "Pine saplings were selected and a barricade that would accomodate the entire command was erected with sufficient loopholes to afford the men ample scope to protect all sides. The Indians never attacked our Fort and we were left in peace." The men who replaced Shaw were not so fortunate.[75]

To Rob the Trains and Destroy the Wires

When he returned to Fort Laramie after a tour of the trail, Gen. James Craig was not reassured. All the tribes in the mountains charged the government with bad faith and breaches of promise for failing to send the agreed-upon agents, food, and annuities. "They have come in by hundreds from the Upper Missouri, attacked and robbed emigrant trains and mail stations, and in one instance last week—they robbed a mail station within two hours after a detachment of Colonel Collins's troops had passed," Craig reported in July. He had no doubt that renegade white men encouraged and participated in the attacks.

Craig had only about 360 men to patrol the four hundred miles between Laramie and Bridger. "I need not say that this force cannot protect a line of such length unless the Indians are willing to behave well. I think I am doing all that can be done with so small a force mounted as they are and without any grain forage." Craig had recently learned that his impossible task had just got harder: "the Postmaster-General has ordered the Overland Mail Company to abandon the North Platte and Sweet Water portion of the route and remove their stages and stock to a route south of this running through Bridger Pass."

Postmaster General Montgomery Blair was only technically a general, but his decision had enormous military implications. Instead of shortening the overland road it had to guard, the directive essentially doubled the army's problem. "My instructions require me to protect the overland mail along the telegraph line, and the emigration not being mentioned, I have up to this time directed my attention to the safety of all these," Craig explained. He had ordered two detachments of twenty-five and thirty men to escort the stages on the road over Bridger Pass, but he had decided to keep most of his troops on the South Pass road "to protect the telegraph line and the emigration, at

---

[75] Shaw, "Capt. A. G. Shaw to Tell History," 1917; Spring, *Caspar Collins*, 126; and Jones, *Guarding the Overland Trails*, 88.

least until the emigration, which consists principally of family trains, has passed through my district. I do this," he wrote, "because the Indians evince a disposition to rob the trains and destroy the wires. Indeed I am satisfied that unless the Government is ready to abandon this route both for mails and emigrants an Indian war is inevitable."

If he abandoned the South Pass route, Craig feared the tribes would suppose they had frightened the soldiers away and seize the opportunity to "destroy the telegraph line and probably rob and murder such small parties as are not able to defend themselves." He had encouraged his officers "to urge upon the emigrants the necessity of forming strong companies and exercising vigilance." He explained he had sent Lot Smith's Utah troops to Fort Bridger, which left him with three hundred men in the Sixth Ohio and two skeleton companies of the Fourth Cavalry Regiment, consisting of only about sixty men mounted upon horses purchased seven years ago, to protect the long road to South Pass. To make matters worse, in August Brigham Young declined a request to extend the Mormon volunteers' tour.[76]

Craig dutifully set about transferring the mail stations to the Bridger Pass trail and opened Fort Halleck south of Laramie to defend the new line. In the meantime, he kept garrisons on the Sweetwater to protect the telegraph line—which Indians perceptively called "the talking wire." By 1864 Utah's first daily newspaper reported "a very large part of the emigration, which usually travels along the South Pass and telegraph route, has this year come by the stage road and routes to the southward."[77] Many sojourners continued to use the old trail over South Pass, but most freighting operations adopted the stagecoach and the mail route to the south. The postmaster's decision to move the U.S. Mail to a more direct route began the transformation of South Pass from the key to a continent into a remote backwater.

Violence continued to flare at South Pass Station, usually in the form of Indian raiding. A desperate telegraph message to Sweetwater Station reported "several hundred" Indians attacked on November 24, 1862, killing Private Joseph Good with an arrow. A subsequent investigation indicated the attacking army had in fact been a Shoshone raiding party of perhaps eight warriors that had almost managed to pry the pickets of the corral apart and make off

---

[76] Craig to Blunt, July 11, 1862, in Scott, *War of the Rebellion*, Series 1, Vol. 13, 468–69; Bigler, *Forgotten Kingdom*, 208.

[77] "Indian Troubles of the Eastward," *Union Vedette*, July 26, 1864, 2/2.

with the post's mounts. The soldiers had failed to mount a guard, and only the station's dogs raised the alarm.[78]

Two massacres far from South Pass had a devastating impact on Indian relations across the Far West. In May 1862 the commander of the Department of the Pacific ordered the Third Regiment of California Infantry under Col. P. E. Connor to march to Salt Lake and protect the western sections of the overland mail line. Supplemented by companies of the Second California Cavalry, in August the command marched across the overland stage line through central Nevada. On the way, Connor dispatched Maj. Edward McGarry with orders to "shoot every male Indian in the region of the late murders" on the Humboldt River, where raiders had reportedly slain emigrants near Gravelly Ford. McGarry killed some two dozen Indians, reflecting the iron hand Connor adopted for subsequent campaigns.

At dawn on January 29, 1863, the California Volunteers attacked Shoshone leader Bear Hunter's winter camp on Bear River to avenge the band's alleged murders of emigrants and miners. The desperate fight that followed degenerated into a massacre of women and children. At its end, Connor reported his men had killed 224 Shoshones, but contemporary reports put the number much higher. How many Shoshones died is impossible to determine, but Bear River saw the largest slaughter of Indians in the history of the American West.[79]

Connor warned the leaders of the three hundred Shoshones he met with on the Snake River in May 1863 "that the troops he left at Camp Connor would exterminate any of them who molested travelers or settlers." This brutal policy and the atrocity at Bear River helped persuade about seven hundred Shoshones to attend negotiations at Fort Bridger in July 1863, where they insisted they were tired of fighting soldiers on the Oregon Trail. Washakie and other leaders signed a treaty granting the government the right to build roads, establish military and agricultural settlements, and to operate telegraph and stage lines—and eventually a railroad—on Shoshone lands. In exchange, the treaty promised twenty thousand dollars in annuities for twenty years, paid in goods, of course. Congress reduced the annuity to ten thousand dollars per anum.[80]

Connor's victory and subsequent negotiations with the Bannocks and Shoshone at least restored peace along the trail west, but when the First Colorado

---

[78] Pvt. Bazil Glaize was the casualty. Jones, *Guarding the Overland Trails*, 94n32.
[79] Bigler, *Forgotten Kingdom*, 224–26. Brigham D. Madsen's *The Shoshoni Frontier and the Bear River Massacre* is the definitive account.
[80] Josephy, *The Civil War in the American West*, 260; Hebard, *Washakie*, 109–10.

SOUTH PASS STATION, IDAHO TERRITORY, 1863
Bugler Charles Frederick Moellmann's sketch shows the overland telegraph line when South Pass was briefly part of Idaho Territory. The figure in the lower center indicates the fishing was good at the Last Crossing of the Sweetwater.
Courtesy Grace Raymond Hebard Papers, American Heritage Center, University of Wyoming.

TREATY OF FORT BRIDGER, JULY 2, 1862
Among the prominent Eastern Shoshone leaders who signed this document were Washakee, Wanapitz, Pantoshiga, Ninabitze, Narkawk, (and on its last page) Taboonshea, Weerango, Tootsahp, Weeahyukee, and Bazile, who historian Grace Hebard believed was the son of Sacajawea. *Courtesy National Archives.*

Cavalry attacked a band of Southern Cheyenne warriors at Fremont's Orchard on the South Platte in April, the skirmish ignited the Indian War of 1864. "I find Indians at war with us through the entire District of Nebraska from South Pass to the Blue, a distance of 800 miles and more, and have laid waste to the country, driven off the stock, and murdered men, women, and children in large numbers," Gen. Samuel Sturgis reported in August 1864 after assuming command of the district. He was convinced white men had led every Indian raid, but his solution was still to "exterminate the leading tribes engaged in this terrible slaughter."[81]

A report from Big Sandy, "this side of South Pass, states that the Indians appeared in the neighborhood but left again, going Eastward, on Sunday evening," Salt Lake's *Union Vedette* wrote. They were said to be Lakotas, Arapahos, and Cheyennes seeking revenge for past wrongs. "Everything possible will be done by the military to protect the telegraph and emigrant roads, and rid them of Indians," the paper pledged. In reality, the situation quickly got worse: "The Indians were getting bad west of Laramie, destroying trains, killing pilgrims and carrying off women," recalled Capt. Eugene Ware. "Far down in the east they were making violent incursions upon the road between Cottonwood Springs and Fort Kearney." A similar "condition of war" prevailed from Fort Laramie to South Pass.[82]

Lakota and Cheyenne raids along the Platte River road shut down mail service in August 1864. "Overland route closed until road is better protected," Lewis Byram Hull wrote at Fort Laramie. By fall Denver was cut off from the East, but Hull reported the handful of soldiers at the Platte's upper crossing had found something better to do than fight Indians. "Capt. Koehne, Sergt. Patton, and one of the Co. A men came down yesterday. They report new silver and gold leads discovered near Deer creek and South Pass," he wrote in August. "Gold and silver have been discovered at South Pass and almost every soldier who was stationed there the past summer has a claim," Pvt. Hervey Johnson wrote home. "They intend coming out next spring to work their claims. The Diggings are principly quartz and are said to be rich." One of his unit's officers even planned to bring out a quartz crusher in the spring. "Emigration will soon be directed thither and times will be as lively as they were in Bannac and Virginia cities on the discovery of gold at those places," Johnson predicted.[83]

---

[81] Jones, *Guarding the Overland Trails*, 168.
[82] "Indian Troubles," *Union Vedette*, July 26, 1864, 2/2; Ware, *The Indian War of 1864*, 216.
[83] Hull, "Soldiering on the High Plains," Aug. 19, 20, 1864; Johnson, *Tending the Talking Wire*, Oct. 9, 1864, 177.

"Among the brilliant feats of arms in Indian warfare" that followed, the assault of the Colorado and New Mexico volunteers on a peaceful Cheyenne and Arapahoe village (which was flying both white and American flags) still stands "in history with few rivals, and none to exceed it in final results," as a Denver newspaper proclaimed. At Sand Creek at dawn on November 29, 1864, Col. John M. Chivington, a Methodist minister known as the "Fighting Parson," attacked Black Kettle's band and systematically executed a wholesale massacre of some 150 Natives. A congressional committee concluded Chivington "surprised and murdered, in cold blood, the unsuspecting men, women, and children on Sand creek, who had every reason to believe they were under the protection of the United States authorities, and then returned to Denver and boasted of the brave deed he and the men under his command had performed." Such harsh actions were immensely popular in the American West. On the road to Denver three years after Sand Creek, journalist Alexander McClure heard citizens demand "Give us Chivington or Connor!"[84]

The practical peacemaking results of such policies were, at best, mixed. Connor's devastation of the Northern Shoshones strengthened Washakie and those who supported his peace policy. East of South Pass, Chivington's bloodbath ignited a "general Indian war" in 1865. "The Sioux, Arrapahoes and Cheyennes, seem to have broken out all along the line of the telegraph and are committing depredations along the South Pass road, from the eastward of Laramie west as far as the Rocky Mountains," an army newspaper reported. "A very large part of the emigration, which usually travels along the South Pass and telegraph route, has this year come by the stage road and routes to the southward." The *Union Vedette* hoped the Indians would let the overland road alone, but it was not to be. Chivington's cowardly massacre intensified the crisis. "I found that the Indians after the Chivington affair had combined and moved north; had struck the Platte Valley and held the overland route from Julesburg to Junction Station; had captured trains, demolished ranches, murdered men, women, and children; [and] destroyed fifty miles of telegraph lines," a general reported.[85]

It fell to Companies E and G of the Eleventh Ohio Volunteers to guard the telegraph line between Deer Creek and South Pass from its six outposts.

---

[84] "Battle of Sand Creek," *Rocky Mountain News*, Dec. 17, 1864; Thrapp, *Encyclopedia of Frontier Biography*, 1:265; McClure, *Three Thousand Miles*, 66.

[85] "Indian Troubles," *Union Vedette*, July 26, 1864, 2/2; Scott, *War of the Rebellion*, Series 1, Vol. 48, 331.

THE U.S. MAIL AND THE WAR FOR SOUTH PASS   265

On his way to Montana, John S. Collins described "an abandoned log house on the side of the mountain, where a few soldiers wintered in 1863." The hut might have been associated with South Pass Station but more probably was a miner's shack. The garrison's worst enemy proved to be cold: at Laramie the mercury froze in the fort's thermometers each night between January 3 and 5, indicating a temperature of fifty or sixty below zero. Sanitary whiskey placed in a tin cup froze solid in twenty minutes.[86]

Two of Caspar Collins's men froze at South Pass in early spring 1865, "though not very seriously," he wrote. "I have just returned from that abominable section of country. Dr. Rich and I went up together. We were two days getting twenty-five miles, and then had to leave our horses on account of the snow and walk in." The doctor profited from his trip: a frostbitten miner paid him one hundred dollars in gold dust to cut off his toes. Collins complained he was shut up "in one of the most desolate regions on the American continent. I think this is the natural penitentiary of the United States."

In addition to South Pass, the young lieutenant had four posts under his jurisdiction, each about forty miles apart. "I have to go up in that part of the country to make inspections once a month, and have the privilege of going as often extra as I may desire," he informed his aunt. "That permission I make little use of, however," he admitted. The weather at his headquarters at Sweetwater Bridge near Independence Rock was "not much colder than in Ohio, but is a great deal dryer and windier; but at the posts above, it excels anything" in an arctic explorer's journal.[87]

General Connor took command of military operations in the Rocky Mountains in 1865. He planned to make "one of the most thorough campaigns against the Indians during the summer and fall ever made in the West," the *Omaha Daily Nebraskan* reported, "and will force them to fight or surrender, and is only fearful they may adopt the latter policy."[88] On May 5, Connor ordered that two non-commissioned officers, twelve infantrymen, and four cavalry troopers would garrison each of the army's telegraph posts.

The order was not implemented soon enough to protect all the stations: five hundred Indians attacked Three Crossings and tore down the telegraph line, he reported. Connor concluded the large force of Indians coming from

---

[86] Collins, *Across the Plains*, May 13, 1864; Jones, *Guarding the Overland Trails*, 189, 100.
[87] Spring, *Caspar Collins*, 169–73.
[88] "Gen. Connor and the Indians," *Union Vedette*, May 29, 1865, 2/2.

the north threatened "the line all the way to Salt Lake." Grenville Dodge, commander of the Department of the Missouri, complained that if he was compelled "to throw in more troops on the South Pass line it will take some three regiments more."[89]

For most Americans, the Civil War had ended in April at Appomattox, but at 10 A.M. on May 27, 1865, "Indians in considerable force" appeared at St. Marys Station "and cut and carried away some of the line, [and] pulled down and burned the poles." An hour later they attacked the post and burned it to the ground. "St. Mary's being a depot of telegraph supplies the Indians were very anxious for plunder," but the fire detonated its store of hundreds of metal cartridges: "the indians thought it wasn't medicine to stay around and left," Hervey Johnson reported. The operator and four soldiers climbed out a back window and "took refuge in the cellar, pulling the main line with them, which remained unbroken west and telegraphed they were surrounded with no chance for escape until rescued by troops." The men escaped to South Pass Station "saving nothing but their arms and the clothes they had on."

Capt. Joseph H. Mathewson immediately marched east from Fort Bridger with a company of cavalry. Such events threatened "trouble to the immigration and bodes no good to the savages themselves. For there is little disposition anywhere to permit their longer interruption at their own good pleasure of the great trans continental thoroughfare," Salt Lake's *Union Vedette* warned. After a courier reported the raid to the post at Platte Bridge, Col. Preston Plumb dispatched sixty men from the Eleventh Kansas Volunteers "to go up the road as far as Rock Ridge, with instructions to repair the telegraph line and take the necessary measures for the immediate rebuilding of the station." They found Mathewson's Nevada Volunteers already rebuilding the post.[90]

With the Civil War over, morale and discipline among the troops stationed along the Sweetwater collapsed. Desertions had long been endemic in their units, and 1864 saw the arrival of the Third U.S. Volunteers, former Confederate prisoners of war known as "galvanized Yanks." All they wanted was "to get out of prison, were tired of the war, didn't want to go back into the service, did not want any more of the Southern Confederacy, did not want to be exchanged, and were willing to go into the United States service for

---

[89] Guenther, "The Burnt Ranch Saga," 17; and Dodge to Pope, May 22, 1865; Scott, *War of the Rebellion*, Series 1, Vol. 48, Part 2, 544.

[90] "Gen. Connor and the Indians," 2/2; "On the War-Path," 2:1, both *Union Vedette*, May 29, 1865; Johnson, *Tending the Talking Wire*, 252; Scott, *War of the Rebellion*, Series 1, Vol. 48, Part 2, 724.

the purpose of fighting the Indians," Eugene Ware recalled.[91] These men had even less attachment to the service than those who had enlisted. Some of the reformed rebels were integrated into the Eleventh Ohio and found themselves stationed at South Pass.

Lt. Col. Milo George, Capt. Mathewson, and Lt. Stephen P. Jocelyn left Fort Bridger with an escort of twenty men on the last day of June to repair the telegraph line at least as far as South Pass. They also intended to investigate whether the troops stationed there "had refused to go out and repair the line in consequence of the fears with which the hostile Indians had inspired them," Jocelyn reported "It was deemed a matter of the last importance that the line should be placed in working order at as early a day as possible." After repairing the line between Bridger and Hams Fork, what the officers found was not inspiring. At Little Sandy the telegraph was out of order and the operator more interested "in an old deck of cards than in repairing his apparatus, [so] we were forced to wait for news until we reached Sweetwater station."

The soldiers crossed South Pass in a severe storm. "At Sweetwater we found everything to be in this direction precisely as we had heard, line down and [the] troops afraid to go out and fix it up." George determined to press on and repair the line.[92]

The next day the officers met several large emigrant trains, generally bound for Montana and Oregon. The new station at St. Marys, "a substantial stone structure built by troops from Fort Bridger," stood half a mile below the ruins of the old station. George's command found thirty-five men from the Eleventh Kansas who had been sent from Platte Bridge to repair the line at Independence Rock. "These troops are called 'jayhawkers' by the soldiers," wrote Jocelyn, "and, so far as we can judge, are not misnamed. There is absolutely no idea of discipline among them, and obedience seems to depend entirely on individual inclination." The Jayhawkers had failed to repair eight hundred yards of line, a job Mathewson and ten men completed in an hour and ten minutes. "There is a great want of *something* among the troops with whom we came in contact on the Sweetwater," Jocelyn mourned.[93]

The young lieutenant concluded his report with an analysis of what was wrong the detachment of "galvanized rebs" and the Eleventh Ohio at South

---
[91] Ware, *The Indian War of 1864*, 401.
[92] J., "Editorial Correspondence," *Union Vedette*, July 17, 1865, 2/1–2.
[93] "Down the Sweetwater," *Union Vedette*, July 18, 1865, 2/2.

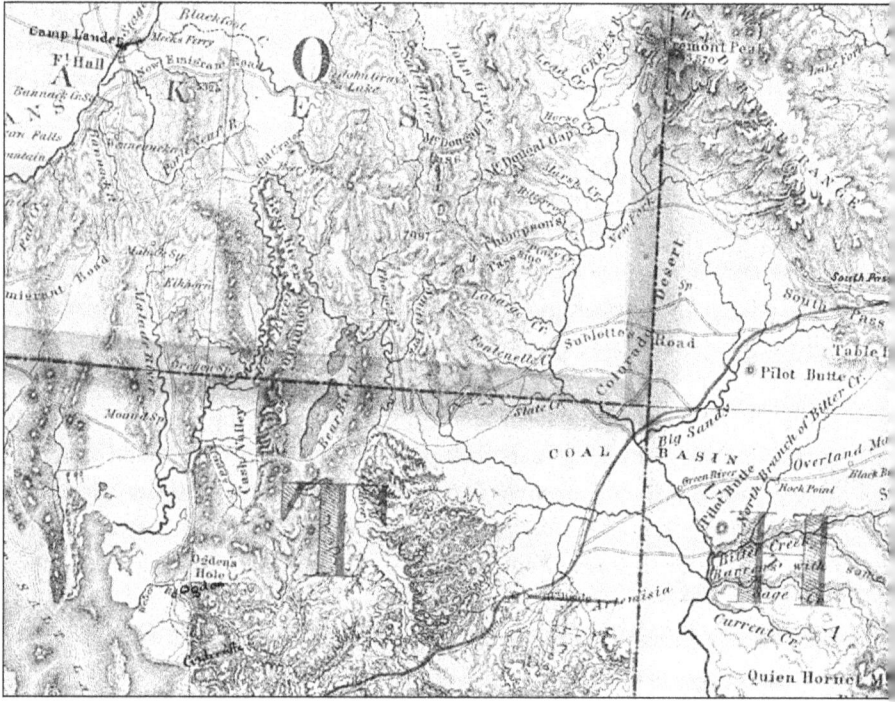

Pass. Similar garrisons manned the stations at St. Marys and Sweetwater Bridge, while about forty men were posted at Three Crossings. Four cavalrymen were not enough to secure or repair the line, "even if they were properly mounted, which they are not," Jocelyn argued.

The soldiers who had chosen to serve on the plains to escape the prisoner-of-war camp at Rock Island, Illinois—notoriously called the "Bull Pen"—were unmistakably poor whites. Few of them could write their names, but they were intelligent and obedient and made better soldiers than the Jayhawkers. The force deployed to defend the telegraph line on the Sweetwater should be sufficient, Jocelyn concluded, but the hapless troopers frankly admitted "that the Indians could whip them man for man in almost any kind of fight." The men "seemed wanting in no quality of good soldiers, except the essential one of discipline." Their officers' conduct was "simply disgraceful" and needed to be investigated, since the safety of the line depended on them.

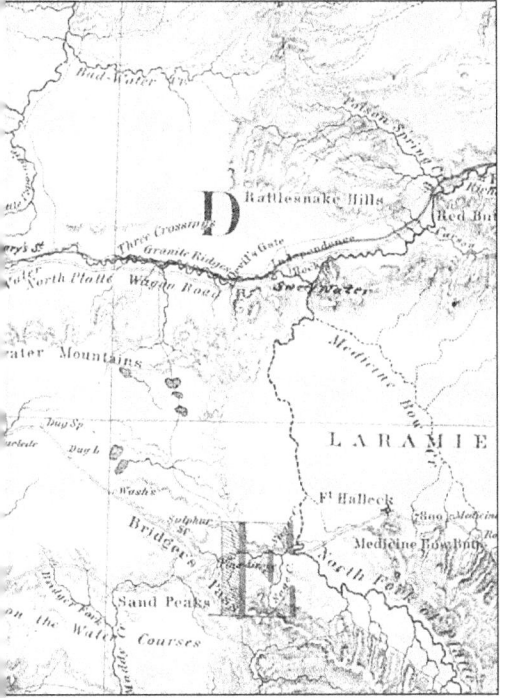

ROADS THROUGH
GREATER SOUTH PASS
Map of the Territory of the
United States from the Mississippi
River to the Pacific Ocean, 1867.
Edward Freyhold redrew G. K.
Warren's original 1857 map from the
Pacific Railroad Survey to show the
latest territorial boundaries,
the classic "North Platte Wagon Road"
up the Sweetwater River, and the
"Overland Mail Route" across greater
South Pass. *Original engraving by
Julius Bien, New York. Courtesy of
the David Rumsey Map Collection,
Cartography Associates.*

The lieutenant ended on a particularly grim note: even though the telegraph had been completed less than four years earlier, in many places the poles were unsound, "being quite rotten in and near the ground. Unless the entire line has a thorough overhauling before winter no amount of care can keep it up during that season, as the heavy winds will certainly prostrate long stretches of it at times, when inclement weather will render repairs nearly impracticable or at best difficult."[94]

THE ROAD TO THE WILD AND ROMANTIC

All over America, the young soldiers who marched to fight in the Civil War did so with dreams of glory that died in the mud of Virginia or the dust of Wyoming. "We were all young fellows," one of the Ohio Volunteers recalled.

---
[94]"Beyond the Mountains," *Union Vedette*, July 23, 1865, 2/1–2.

"The West was new to us and we were anxious to get on the road to the wild and romantic regions about which so many stories had been told." The war beyond the Mississippi was very much a sideshow, but for the seventy-six Buckeyes who were killed in action or died of wounds or disease patrolling the overland trail with the Eleventh Ohio, the conflict mattered very much.[95]

On June 23, 1865, Stand Watie, the last Confederate general still fighting, surrendered at Doaksville, Indian Territory. For most citizens of the United States, it was the end of a long national nightmare, but for thousands of Lakota, Cheyenne, and Arapaho families the event meant nothing. More than a month later, on July 26, 1865, warriors attacked Platte Bridge Station and a supply train a few miles away. They rubbed out twenty-six soldiers, including Lt. Caspar Collins. That summer, a massive campaign by the allied Indians systematically burned the stage stations along the Overland Trail, while General Connor's campaign on Powder River disintegrated into a wild-goose chase. After the bloodiest year in the history of the Oregon Trail, the army withdrew the garrisons at Three Crossings, Sweetwater, St. Marys, and South Pass in September. That winter raiders burned down South Pass Station.[96]

Twenty months after the U.S. Army truly needed a line along the Overland Trail that would shorten the miles of trail it had to protect, it finally happened. The Western Union Telegraph Company announced in November 1866 it had opened a "line to California via Denver, Bridgers Pass, and where the overland stage route is now traveled." It had been "constructed in a superior manner" to the hastily built and now rotting line over South Pass. The company maintained the old wires, probably to provide service to Fort Laramie, but it was one more sign that the glory days of South Pass were over. Other troubles, however, worsened. As a Salt Lake newspaper announced in June 1867, "The telegraph line between Fort Caspar and South Pass, a distance of 175 miles, is now, and has been for two weeks, in the hands of the Indians."[97]

The Civil War was over, but a long and brutal Indian war had just begun.

---
[95] Josephy, *The Civil War in the American West*, 250.
[96] Guenther, "The Burnt Ranch Saga," 18.
[97] "Midnight Dispatches," *Union Vedette*, Nov. 23, 1866, 2/3; "By Pacific Telegraph," *Union Vedette*, June 28, 1867, 2/2.

CHAPTER 10

"Gold, Slathers of It"
The Rush to South Pass
1867

Rumors that gold could be found around South Pass—and rumors about rumors—began early in its written history. "Ever since 1849, when the first overland emigration to California set in, rumors have from time to time reached the ear of the mining public of a remarkable rich mineral belt lying somewhere in the Wind River range of mountains, to the east of what is known as the South Pass, on the old emigrant overland route," a frontier newspaper reported in early 1868. Trappers and Indians brought gold and gold-bearing quartz into the settlements, saying they had picked it up in the Sweetwater country. Occasionally some brave soul offered "to hunt up the locality of the new Eldorado, but in almost every instance they were driven out by the Indians." Some of the goldseekers, the paper said, came in but never came out, having had their hair raised by the Shoshones "and induced by them to take up a quiet residence there."

A Georgian working for the American Fur Company, who had come to the country for his health, had discovered gold near South Pass in 1842, the *Sweetwater Mines* reported in 1869, but Indians killed him before he could leave the country.[1] This has all the hallmarks of a legend, but as early as 1845, Capt. Philip St. George Cooke had praised the beautiful Sweetwater, "which flows over golden (mica) sands," identifying the source of at least some of the tales.[2]

Deposits of fool's gold intrigued at least three Forty-niners. "There was a large quantity of yellow mica in the sands of the streams, and in all of its

---
[1] "The Sweetwater Country," in Chisolm, *South Pass, 1868*, 39, 216.
[2] Cooke to Dear Sir, Sept. 9, 1845, *Niles' National Register*, Oct. 25, 1845.

affluants, and some of our men could hardly relinquish the idea of its being gold," Alonzo Delano wrote in 1849. "But, alas! the application of nitric acid dispelled their pleasant dreams." William B. Lorton found the banks of the Sweetwater "covered with shining particles, supposed to be gold; the sand is full, but the particles are light and difficult to wash."[3]

Some of Forty-niner James Godfrey's companions left the wagon road at the foot of South Pass and followed the Sweetwater "up a ways and found, as they imagined, large quantities of the glittering ore and brought up a large quantity of it. We all looked at it with greedy eyes and hoped for awhile that we had arrived at our journeys end," he wrote. They examined the mineral closely, talked about it for much of the day, and gave it the nitric acid test before concluding it could not be gold, which "set our minds to rest. What it was, I know not, but it certainly resembled it (gold) very much. It was in fine scales and found in black sand on the bank of the river and would have been very rich had it been gold." The mysterious mineral dancing in the bed of the Sweetwater made "a beautifull appearance, flashing in the Sunlight,"[4] Carmi P. Garlick observed a year later. He might have seen not fool's gold but the real thing, for at least some of these placer deposits probably did contain the precious nuggets and dust.

The most detailed report of early mining projects near South Pass appeared in 1855. Joseph Hollman, U.S. attorney for Utah Territory, arrived in Missouri carrying army dispatches from Great Salt Lake City. Hollman had seen thirty or forty men "exploring for gold, where it is supposed it will be found in pretty large quantities." Led by C. L. Craig of St. Joseph, the workers were Mormons from Salt Lake who "were industriously engaged at damming and turning the bed of the Sweetwater" not far from Devils Gate. The men had supposedly found large quantities of silver, and one man was said to have found forty dollars' worth of gold in a single day. "There is no doubt in my mind but rich deposits of gold will be found in the Sweetwater country," Hollman's story concluded.[5]

By the mid-1850s the gold in the Wind River Range was no secret. On his way to Utah with an army supply train in 1858, Richard Ackley "did some hunting for gold by washing with one of our pans, and found very good indication. There have been large quantities found nearer the head." The range had more than its beauty to recommend it, Richard F. Burton observed. At a stage stop

---

[3] Delano, *Life on the Plains*, June 27, 1849, 109; Lorton, Diary, July 23 [24], 1849.
[4] Godfrey, "Overland Diary," June 20, 1849; Garlick, A Trip Overland, June 24, 1850, 26.
[5] "From Utah and the Plains," *St. Louis Luminary*, Aug. 4, 1855, 147; "Interesting From the Plains," *New York Daily Times*, July 31, 1855.

in the Black Hills in 1860, he saw "a quill full of large gold-grains from a new digging" in the Wind Rivers. "Probably all the primitive masses of the Rocky Mountains will be found to contain the precious metal," he commented.[6]

The promoters of the first South Pass City failed to ignite a gold rush in 1862, but two years later the officers and men of the Eleventh Ohio Volunteers were convinced there was enough gold on the upper Sweetwater to make them rich. Harriet A. Loughary, at the scene of the action, was less impressed. Near a noon stopover at "Soap Suds," probably today's Lewiston Lakes near the top of Rocky Ridge, was "a mining camp, men prospecting for gold." The party met a miner named J. D. Jones, "once a neighbor in Iowa, who asked us to stop and look over the gold mines." The train's captain agreed: "Soon all with spades, dishpans, buckets, butcher knives, and wash pans started for the gold, but after some hours of useless toil returned without sight of gold," Loughary concluded.[7]

Many of the California Volunteers who came to Utah were experienced miners, and by the end of the Civil War the Far West was overrun with prospectors. Fort Bridger commandant Maj. Noyes Baldwin and Capt. John F. Skelton grubstaked John A. James and D. C. Moreland to spend six months surveying the mineral prospects of South Pass. Along with miners they found operating in the area, the men organized the region's first mining district, the Lincoln, on November 11, 1864, on a tributary of Beaver Creek and elected James secretary. The prospectors often had "to shovel about ten feet of snow drift off before we could reach the ground, but what little we have done, satisfies us that there is near by a good lead of gold bearing rock," James reported next March. "The gold that we get is entirely unwashed, being of rough irregular shape bearing the appearance of having just tumbled out of decomposed rock in the immediate vicinity."

The prospectors found all types of the element, ranging from very fine-quality flour gold to coarse gold. "In fact Major, it is the finest quality of gold I ever saw," one veteran said, except for the ore he had mined in British Columbia, "and that coined $21 per oz." The men hoped to run water to the prospects soon, and James cagily requested Baldwin's support. "We should like to share with you still in the search, and [the] profits of a part of the hiden treasures of the mountains, which we are determined to persevere in the pursuit of until we find it, knowing that there are plenty of good fortunes in these mountains." Before Indians drove them out, Moreland, James, and

---

[6] Ackley, "Across the Plains," Aug. 14, 1858, 204; Burton, *City of the Saints*, Aug. 10, 1860, 165.
[7] Loughary, "Travels," June 27, 1864, 8:142.

their associates apparently began mining on Willow Creek, where South Pass City eventually rose, "leaving behind them evidences of their work in the shape of some cabins and small prospect holes."[8]

Rich Gold Discovery! The Rush

One of the great ironies of America's age of golden rushes is that during the journeys that hundreds of thousands of Americans made across the California Trail, they passed over the place that became the scene of the era's last gold rush—South Pass. On June 27, 1867, mountain man Lewis Robison, the grizzled Mormon veteran who ten years earlier had set the torch to Fort Bridger as the U.S. Army approached, rode into Great Salt Lake City with two other men. They entered the East Temple Street offices of Bohm & Mollitor, assayers. The men carried forty ounces of gold dust reportedly crushed from quartz rock in two days. The assayers refined the ore into a gold bar valued at $740.06, with a fineness of 934½. "The only account the discoverers have as yet given is that the mines are about 200 miles from here and are rich," the *Union Vedette* reported.

The strike had to be somewhere near Green River, men who knew Robison guessed, since he had lived there for years and now owned the main ferry across that dangerous stream. "That there are good gold mines in Utah is beyond a doubt, but they are concealed by those who know where they are, and prospecting is very much discouraged," the newspaper said. It advised interested parties "to remain where they are until something more definite about the place where those mines are situated can be learned. Let there be no rush until something more definite will be ascertained." With the gold bar on display at the National Bank, such reasonable advice proved as effective as admonishing a prairie fire not to burn too quickly through tinder-dry grass.[9]

Within a week, the road to Green River was crowded with citizens from Salt Lake, including many Mormons, whose leaders had long discouraged such speculations. The *Union Vedette*, the territory's most vocal booster of mining, continued trying to calm the excitement. "We have no doubt that Lewis Robinson [sic] and his party have found rich mines," it advised, "but it is just as well to wait a few days or a few weeks until the matter is confirmed as to go wild in the start!" Since they were located closer to the mines than

---

[8] Chisolm, *South Pass, 1868*, 39, 216–17, 220–21.
[9] "Rich Gold Discovery!" *Union Vedette*, July 1, 1867, 2/2.

anyone, local citizens should sit tight and wait until reports sorted themselves out. "It will be just as safe to keep cool!"[10]

It was hopeless. "THE NEW GOLD MINES" had "set the people wild in this locality," the *Vedette* reported five days later. Even William Hooper, the Mormon territorial delegate to Congress, had gone to the diggings. The paper added fuel to the fire when it said the mines could be found at the head of the Sweetwater River. Robison and his associates distributed sixty-dollar "presents" to influential parties and disposed of an additional forty ounces of quartz and placer gold. "All of which," surmised the *Vedette*, "goes to prove the existence of very rich gold mines not far from this city."[11]

Robison and his colleagues actually proved that they knew how to start a gold rush. The key, of course, was their use of newspapers to promote public excitement. Influential eastern newspapers, notably the *Times* and *Tribune* of Chicago, picked up the initial announcements in the *Vedette*, and the Salt Lake journal kept up a steady drumbeat of reports: such stories undoubtedly sold newspapers. "At last, we are enabled to give our distant readers what we consider reliable news of the character, extent and richness of the new gold discoveries on the heads of Strawberry and Willow Creek near the South Pass," the *Vedette* promised at the end of July. Derived from the reports of trustworthy, experienced men who would not get excited about a two-bit prospect and could "tell the difference between a piece of quartz rock and a burnt brick," the existence of numerous gold-bearing quartz ledges on the north side of the Sweetwater was now "a demonstrated fact." The claims of Robison, Joshua Terry, "and that company" had proved exceedingly rich. A single ordinary hand mortar could pound out $25 to $40 a day from "selected rock," and "even as high as $100." News that Indians had killed three men named Scholl, Lawrence, and Taylor nearby did little to allay the subsequent excitement.[12]

What Robison and Terry discovered in June 1867 was the Carisso ledge, which soon became the renowned Carissa Mine. John H. Gerrish reportedly selected thirteen pounds of the poorest quartz ore from three different places on the ledge to insure a fair test, but Bohm & Mollitor still assayed the ore at $75.24 worth of gold and $1.56 in silver to the ton. By late July several other prospects looked as good if not better, notably the Morning Star, Melrose, Copperopolis, and Last Chance.

[10] "In Quest of the Gold Mines," *Union Vedette*, July 6, 1867, 2/3.
[11] "The New Gold Mines," *Union Vedette*, July 11, 1867, 3/1.
[12] "Gold Mines on the Tributaries of the Sweetwater," *Union Vedette*, July 31, 1867, 2/1.

Gold hunter George Roberts fled when the Indians killed one Captain Lawrence and Tony Scholl, but he joined twenty-seven "well armed, determined men" at Robison's ferry and turned back to South Pass. The militant miners built a stockade and corral and quickly "resumed their prospecting for 18 or 20 miles around. They found plenty of rich gold quartz ledges." Roberts was convinced it was the most extensive quartz camp in the world. On August 4, Lakota warriors tried to stampede the miners' stock. Before the sun went down, Roberts claimed, all that was mortal of sixteen young Sioux braves lay "lifeless, dead! dead! dead!"[13] Several hundred peaceful Shoshones visited the settlement that fall, but the Lakota do not seem to have returned.

Half a mile below the Carissa Mine, prospectors began building a third and more enduring South Pass City. By early November, the settlement boasted fifty houses and several stamping mills. At year's end, the Dakota territorial legislature made the boomtown the seat of Sweetwater County.[14]

Maj. Patrick A. Gallagher of the California Volunteers left Salt Lake in late August with "a strong party of prospectors" bound for the "extensively rich mining camp."[15] East of the new metropolis, prospector Frank McGovern discovered a lode in September that became famous as the Miners Delight. McGovern quickly sold his claim to Gallagher and his associates, who built a second settlement at the site. (McGovern went on to become the mining camp's first justice of the peace.) By October such discoveries were drawing crowds at Salt Lake to gawk at the front window of J. Bauman & Co.'s Drug Store, which displayed "an enormous piece of gold quartz weighing some fifty odd pounds, and literally 'lousy' with gold." The specimen came from the Miners Delight ledge, the Union Vedette reported. There was gold at South Pass, the newspaper trumpeted, "slathers of it."[16]

Robison and his partners sold out not long after the rush began and settled down to rake in cash at their revitalized Green River ferry. Prospectors left a slightly more enduring legacy in the towns they established at South Pass City, Atlantic City, and Miners Delight, soon renamed Hamilton. Over the next two years, mines with colorful names such as the Young American, the King Solomon, the Mary Ellen, the Caribou, and the Buckeye sprang into operation. They discovered some fifteen hundred lodes, "some valuable,

---

[13] "Assay of Rock," Union Vedette, Aug. 2, 1867, 3/1; "Important News," Union Vedette, Aug. 22, 1867, 2/1.
[14] Chisolm, South Pass, 1868, 6, 40.
[15] "Still Going to the Sweetwater Mines," Union Vedette, Aug. 18, 1867, 3/1.
[16] "Gold, Slathers of It," Union Vedette, Oct. 17, 1867, 3/1.

many worthless." Boosters said as many as ten thousand citizens moved to the boomtowns, claims that historian Lola M. Homsher observed seemed to have no basis in fact. The transient population gathered at the pass was as ephemeral as a morning frost on a hot summer day.

In April 1868 the *Sweetwater Mines* reported the virtual demise of South Pass City, whose population had decamped to rumored strikes in the Big Horn Mountains, while the Union Pacific's demand for laborers lured away more strong backs. By July, the paper reported there were 1,030 men in the area, and a U.S. marshal's census in 1869 gave the total population of the mining area as 1,517. The official U.S. Census of 1870 lowered this number to 1,166. "By 1872 it was reported that the population of the three South Pass mining towns probably numbered less than one hundred each."[17]

After its short but meteoric burst of glory, mining at South Pass proved extraordinarily enduring. The brief impact of mineral development is still visible along the emigrant road west of Radium Springs. A man named Lewis reportedly discovered the Bullion Lode on Strawberry Creek in 1876 and "took out a small fortune" from a drift he ran under the creek. A boomtown named Lewiston flourished briefly as a home to families such as the Nickersons and Gustins, while a mill stood half a mile away on the creek. The Bullion Mine is said to have yielded some twenty-one thousand ounces of gold during its heyday, and evidence of mining activity abounds along the old trail. According to legend, the abandoned outbuildings and ranch house at Gillespie Ranch near Radium Springs provided a place for sexual services for Lewiston's miners.

Emile Granier launched an unsuccessful hydraulic mining operation at Rock Creek in 1879, but the E. T. Fisher Company made money dredging the creek during the 1930s.[18] (Today the LDS Church runs a campsite for handcart re-enactors built on the Fisher operation's tailings.) By the 1890s the mines at South Pass had played out, but mining operations continued in the area until the late 1970s, and amateur prospectors still search for elusive gold nuggets to this day. The collapsing ruins of Lewiston are now on private property, and cows frequent two disintegrating, roofless log wrecks, said to be the old Gustin store and a livery stable.[19]

---

[17] Chisolm, *South Pass, 1868*, 217–18.
[18] Chisolm, *South Pass, 1868*, 218–19.
[19] Much of this information is available at Jean Mathisen's "Lewiston" and G. B. Dobson's "Wyoming Tales and Trails" websites, www.ghosttowns.com/states/wy/lewiston.html and www.wyomingtalesandtrails.com [Sept. 6, 2013].

The Last Covered Wagons: South Pass after 1869

Judge S. W. Dexter of Ann Arbor, Michigan, proposed "Something New" in his newspaper in February 1832—"*to unite New York and the Oregon by a rail way*"—so that the United States could use that distant country's fur and agriculture resources to trade with India. Dexter's suggested route would cross "the Rocky Mountains, not by that difficult and northern route which Lewis and Clark first essayed, but that more moderate and pleasant one called the '*southern pass.*'"[20]

Other visionaries, notably Hartwell Carver and George Wilkes, carried the proposal forward, while Asa Whitney, who had made a fortune in the China trade, sent a memorial to Congress in 1845 presenting the transcontinental line as a road to national enlightenment that could sell land to potential settlers and pay for itself. "There would be no difficulty in the way of constructing a rail road from the Atlantic to the Pacific ocean," missionary Samuel Parker observed as he crossed South Pass on his way to Oregon in August 1835, "and probably the time may not be very far distant, when trips will be made across the continent, as they have been made to the Niagara Falls, to see nature's wonders."[21]

During the Civil War, America's main east-west corridor shifted south from the Oregon Trail to the drier but shorter Overland Trail. During 1868 the transcontinental railroad headed directly west from the Laramie Plains to cross the deserts and passes of central Wyoming to new railroad towns at Green River and Evanston, the same route Interstate 80 followed a century later. Grenville M. Dodge, chief engineer of the Union Pacific Railroad, considered that South Pass was "the southern end of the Wind River Mountains and all the country there gives down into a level valley until the Medicine Bow Range is reached, some one hundred and fifty miles southeast. It forms a natural depression through the continent, and it is through this depression that the Union Pacific Railroad was built," he wrote. "This depression is a basin smaller than Salt Lake, but has no water in it. It is known as the Red Desert, and extends about one hundred miles east and west, and sixty or seventy miles north and south. The east and west rims of this basin make two divides of the continent."[22]

The completion of the transcontinental railroad in 1869 diminished wagon travel to the West, but there were still tens of thousands of Americans with a

---

[20] Dexter, "Something New," *The Emigrant*, Feb. 8, 1832, 2/3–4. Larry Mullaly transcription.
[21] Parker, *Journal of an Exploring Tour*, 60.
[22] Dodge, *Biographical Sketch of James Bridger*, 160–61.

hankering to follow the sun in hopes of finding a better life. How many people carried on the generations-old tradition of heading west in a wagon is hard to estimate, but anecdotal evidence indicates overland emigration remained sizeable for the next three decades—for there were tens of thousands of Americans too poor to pay for a railroad ticket to chase their dreams beyond the Continental Divide.

The stories of these latter emigrants have much in common with those who went west before the railroad, but they have surprising differences. On a spring day in 1881, forty-seven people gathered in Mercer County, Missouri, to begin their "long and eventful journey westward to the much-talked of Oregon Territory," emigrant Emily Towell recalled. "There was much excitement that day. Every imagination was fired with dreams and visions of new homes and fortunes to be made in the fertile West." Three weeks later, the Towells camped among the many wagons gathered on the outskirts of Kearney, Nebraska, near the iron road. "The cars on the railroad were speeding past every few minutes. The passengers had a great deal of fun waving to the occupants of the wagons on the road," Emily wrote. "They motioned with their hands, pointing westward to show how much faster they could travel than we. The wagons were just plodding snails in comparison with the speeding cars."

The railroad diverted most wagon traffic away from South Pass, and the majority of overland emigrants followed the tracks of the Union Pacific across the deserts of southern Wyoming. But during the 1880s a surprising number of families left the Union Pacific line at Rawlins and headed north to the old trail, where "the women-folk washed clothing at the Sweet Water river. This is a very swift stream." Emily Towell found the constant wind aggravating, but Rock Creek, with its "lovely thick carpet of green grass, near a huge bank of snow, provided a lovely camp site." When the family crossed South Pass on July 8, 1881, "Soft fleecy clouds hung in the sky and the wind seemed a little more tolerant. The children explored everything within their reach. They found delicious wild strawberries and brought them back to camp. A great part of the day was spent driving on the sumit of the mountains. The roads were in good condition. The night was spent three miles south of Pacific Springs." The Towells camped on the Little Sandy the next day with "a band of cattle from Idaho, about seventeen hundred head."[23]

---
[23] Towell, "Missouri to Idaho," 10:198, 203–204, 211–12.

Four years later, the Springer family left Rawlins on July 14, 1885, "through a lot of this red dirt. The road was as red as brick," overlander Viola Springer wrote. Stage stations and stores lined the road to South Pass. She saw considerable wagon traffic heading east and west, including gypsies from Oregon and Shoshones from the "Weishakee tribe" driving a large flock of sheep. She met prospectors at Lewiston, which sported two houses, while Rock Creek was the site of a quartz mill. Game was plentiful: she saw deer one morning, "a lot of sage hens," and droves of antelope—"I seen as many as a hundred all together," Miss Springer reported one day, and her father said he saw some two hundred near Oregon Slough. Springer described "an old house and stable which used to be an old Stage Station" at Pacific Springs, where the marsh was flourishing.

When the Springer train left Rawlins, "there was 27 freight teams went past. They was Indians freighting." Springer was witnessing yet another South Pass phenomenon: Indian teamsters in trains consisting of up to one hundred wagons. The creation of the Arapaho-Shoshone Reservation obliged the federal government to transport an annual shipment of goods from the railroad to Fort Washakie. The Fort Bridger Treaty of 1868 created the 2,774,400-acre Wind River Indian Reservation for the Eastern Band of the Shoshone Nation: the Brunot Land Cession of 1874 took away the southern third of the Shoshone's land and opened it to white settlement. The government began transferring their old rivals, the Arapahos, from their temporary confinement in northwest Nebraska and northeast Wyoming to the Shoshone reservation in 1878.

Freighting operations were underway by next summer. In December the last wagon trains found themselves snowbound at Pacific Springs, where the Indian teamsters had to store tons of supplies until spring. The trains operated until the railroad reached Lander in 1906. Amelia Hall recalled that before they set out, the teamsters stopped at Lander to buy all the available woman's hats in town—"the bigger and more wildly plumed the better."[24]

What was now remembered as the Old Oregon Trail saw considerable use by freighters and cattlemen in the last decades of the nineteenth century. "Most herds followed the Oregon Trail," John K. Rollinson recalled in his *Wyoming Cattle Trails*, but he drove livestock over the Lander Cutoff in 1883. A year earlier, Tom Sun "trailed 3,000 cattle over the Lander Road" from Oregon to his ranch at Devils Gate.[25]

---

[24] Guenther, "The Burnt Ranch Saga," 22, 31n85.
[25] Boyack, "Oregon Trail Trek No. 8," 85.

WAGON TRAIN, 1882
Overland wagon travel did not end with the driving of the Golden Spike at Promontory, Utah, in 1869. Railroads did not provide service to the Northwest for decades, and their fares were beyond the means of most families that wanted to move west. *Courtesy Utah State Historical Society.*

Joseph M. Huston of Daniel, Wyoming, worked as hunter for an Oregon Trail wagon train in 1891. He lost the chance of bidding "the sweet pleasure of a fond farewell" to a charming young lady when her family left the rest of the train to follow the Lander Road, but he remembered "that when he reached Green River at the mouth of Slate Creek there were 500 wagons camped there."

According to a 1958 account of a Wyoming trail trek, Fred Graham and his bride were working at a ranger station in Snyder Basin on the Lander Cutoff in 1912 when "they talked with Oregon-bound emigrants and saw the last of the covered wagons on the old Trail."[26]

---

[26] Carley, "Oregon Trail Trek No. 6," 50–51.

Stand on South Pass now, and you will find it as still and peaceful as if no clamor of empire had ever surged through it. Antelope will drift close to see what you are up to; no smokes stain the dark blue sky; the riotous rendezvous of the fur hunters, held for a dozen years after 1825, have left neither mark nor echo, not even a tepee ring. The wheels that between 1836 and 1869 rocked and creaked and squealed up the Sweetwater and down past the westward-falling trickle of Pacific Creek have left ruts that are still visible in places among the sage and bunchgrass if you look hard, but modern travel does not go this way. Both Highway 30 and the railroad cross the divide at Creston. All that crosses South Pass now is Wyoming 28, a secondary road. And here is a lesson, not only in history, but in the fallibility of prophecy based on false premises.

WALLACE STEGNER
MARKING THE SPARROW'S FALL

Afterword
The Legacy of South Pass

WITH THE DRIVING OF THE GOLDEN SPIKE IN MAY 1869, the glory days of South Pass as the most important crossing of the Rocky Mountains came to an end. Late in the summer of 1870, at the end of the overland era, the Hayden Survey and its photographer, William H. Jackson, camped a dozen miles from South Pass. Nearby on Willow Creek, the mobile village of Washakie's Shoshone band stood on a site their ancestors had used for many centuries. After three decades of intensive hunting and grazing by overland wagon trains and the cattle herds they drove west, the old trail was deeply etched into the hard earth. Now that few wagons used the road to South Pass, the range was once again healthy enough to support bison.

After the linking of the rails, the historic road up the Sweetwater would never again be a major transportation corridor. Prior to World War I, the federal government considered building a national military highway over the old trail, but while the region's geography was ideal for oxen and wagons, it was not a natural route for steam and gasoline engines.[1] Even today the state highways surrounding South Pass avoid the historic wagon road.

Over the last century, South Pass has seen booms in sheep and cattle ranching, oil and gas exploration and extraction, uranium mining and processing, and even steel ore production—in 1962 the opening of U.S. Steel's Atlantic City iron mine and mill finally brought a railroad across South Pass. Apparently inevitable busts followed all these booms. A few determined optimists still hammer at outcroppings of the South Pass greenstone belt and prospect the dry washes along its broad plain, but even the well-funded Fremont Gold

[1] Hebard, "First White Women in Wyoming," 29.

Corporation exploration project less than three miles from South Pass in 2006 failed to locate viable deposits at Dickie Springs. "Although my grandfather and father both mined gold in the South Pass–Atlantic City areas, the gold rush is over for this country," Wyoming native Joe Greig observed. "It's time to mine the historical and inspirational gold this area holds."[2]

Only ranching has endured as a way to make a living in the high country and harsh climate of South Pass. Raising cattle began surprisingly early in the shadow of the Wind River Range—the great western ranching tradition can trace some of its earliest origins to the range around South Pass. There was, after all, "plenty of good water, [an] abundance of grass, and wood enough to satisfy any reasonable man," William Glaze and nearly three hundred other emigrants observed when they sang the praises of Frederick Lander's new Pacific wagon road in 1859.

The next year Lander himself described the famous mountain man, army scout, and trailblazer Tim Goodale, as "a mountaineer who resided at the South Pass." As Richard F. Burton rode the stage west, he complained that the passengers were constantly "hurried on to some distant wretched ranch." (He defined "Rancho" in Mexico as "a rude thatched hut where herdsmen pass the night" and "rancharia" as a sheep-walk or cattle-run. In California it was "a large farm with grounds often measured by leagues," but it also applied "to any dirty hovel in the Mississippian Valley.") On the Sweetwater Burton visited "another ranch belonging to a Portuguese named Luis Silva, married to an Englishwoman who had deserted the Salt Lake Saints." He "staid a piece" and was unimpressed, but a "stout, active, middle-aged matron" at the station at the Three Crossings impressed him mightily. She was "an Englishwoman, a Miss Moore—Miss is still used for Mrs. by Western men and negroes—celebrated for cleanliness, tidiness, civility, and housewifery in general." Miss Moore deserved "all the praises that had so liberally been bestowed upon her," and her "little ranch was neatly swept and garnished, papered and ornamented." He praised the well-built ranch at Willow Creek where two Canadian traders had "apparently settled for life," although it appears their main business was not raising livestock but selling whiskey. Burton said it did not poison him, but "that is about all that I can say for it."[3]

---
[2] U.S. Dept. of the Interior, BLM, *Environmental Assessment for Dickie Springs Placer Gold Exploration*, 1–8, 22–23; and personal communications with Rock Springs District BLM officers.
[3] Lander, *Maps and Reports*, 3, 10; Burton, *City of the Saints*, 5, 154, 161.

Other journal keepers described the early ranches around South Pass. Harriet Sanders met "a mountaineer on the track of stray cow" near Strawberry Creek in 1863 who said he was six miles from his ranch. Viola Springer camped on Little Sandy "not far from a sheep ranch" in July 1885.[4] Many if not most of these early operations served as trading, stage, or mail stations. Some of them, such as Burnt Ranch at the Ninth Crossing and the Halter and Flick Ranch at Pacific Springs, are legendary.

Ranching at South Pass experienced a golden age at the beginning of the twentieth century. Homesteaders opened dozens of land claims along its streams and creeks. The climate often made them difficult to "prove up," but small homesteads created virtually all the private land holdings that exist in the area. "My grandparents had filed a claim on the ranch at Pacific Springs when mother was a little girl," recalled William Earl "Bill" Carr, who was born at South Pass City in 1895 to William Carr and Ella Thomas Potter. "My Great-grandmother Thomas is buried there on the ranch in an unmarked grave." Carr described the history of this important ranch in his memoirs. His grandfather, William Joseph Carr, "sold the place to George Flick and Bill Halter who used to operate a road house for freighters hauling from Point of Rocks to South Pass and Atlantic City [with a] store, a bar, and blacksmith shop. They later sold out to John Hay."

The Hay family of cattlemen and bankers still owns this historic spot. Carr recalled working at the nearby Sweetwater Ranch belonging to his uncle, John Sherlock, and a man named Smith next door at the Baldy Williams Ranch. The Halter and Flick ranch at Pacific Springs included a post office and, legend has it, a cathouse for freighters on the Point of Rocks Road that connected South Pass with the Union Pacific line at Point of Rocks, twenty-five miles east of Rock Springs, Wyoming.[5]

Commemorating South Pass

"South Pass was perhaps the most important landmark along the emigrant trails," the National Park Service concluded.[6] Today, two small, simple stone

---
[4] Sanders, "Omaha to Bannack," 14; Springer, "From Princeton," July 23, 1885, 11:103.
[5] Reta Carr, "Stories from the Past," in *Tales of the Seeds-Ke-Dee*, 173–86; Carr Family Record, Family History Library.
[6] National Park Service, *California and Pony Express National Historic Trails*, 256.

monuments mark the summit of South Pass. Overland veteran Ezra Meeker first crossed South Pass in 1852, and erected the first marker on June 24, 1906, as part of what the seventy-five-year-old pioneer and promoter called his "Ox-Team Monument Expedition." The Meeker marker is one of he many placed at landmarks between The Dalles and Independence. Like the others, it reads, "Old Oregon Trail 1843–57." (Meeker never seems to have explained why he used those dates to mark the "Old" Oregon Trail, but perhaps he chose the "Great Migration" of 1843 as the beginning and the exploration of the Lander Cutoff as the concluding date.) "Recovering the Lost Trail has a deeper meaning than merely gratifying a whim or satisfying a feeling of curiosity," Meeker said in 1915.[7] It is still true.

"I was working there when Ezra Meeker, who was setting markers on the Oregon Trail, came by that way to have his oxen shod," Bill Carr remembered. "There were no oxen shoes in the shop so Mr. Halter made them. After he had made them, he told me I could nail them on since my back bent much easier than his. That was my only experience in shoeing oxen." Meeker spent four days at South Pass, and "searched for a suitable stone for a monument to be placed on the summit of the range, and after almost despairing of finding one, had come upon exactly what was wanted," Carr recalled. It required four men to drag it down the mountains and load the stone onto Halter's wagon. It was "a monument hewed by the hand of Nature," Meeker wrote, and the men estimated it weighed half a ton.[8]

Herman G. Nickerson of the Wyoming Oregon Trail Commission raised the second monument at the summit of South Pass in June 1916. This black monolith commemorates Narcissa Prentiss Whitman and Eliza Hart Spalding as the "FIRST WHITE WOMEN TO CROSS THIS PASS July.4.1836." Whitman and Spalding were traveling with a fur-trade caravan bound for the rendezvous near today's Pinedale, so they did not cross South Pass on what later became the emigrant road: they crossed some twenty-three miles to the northwest. When Nickerson erected his monument, he righted Meeker's toppled 1906 marker and set both in concrete.[9]

Early in the twentieth century, technology began to alter the topography of South Pass. Civil engineer John Linn told Meeker the survey line of a canal

---

[7] Meeker, *Ox-team Days*, 192–93; and Meeker, *Story of the Lost Trail*, 7.
[8] Meeker, *Story of the Lost Trail*, 7; Carr, "Stories," 179–81.
[9] Noble, "Marking Wyoming's Oregon Trail," 20–21; Duffin, "Whitman-Spalding Marker"; Guenther, Hammer, and Chaney, "The Women Who Carried the Star of Empire," 137–38, has a map of the route.

ran within a hundred feet of Meeker's monument. A few years later, John W. Hay, the patriarch of the Wyoming ranching family, began digging the canal, hoping to transport irrigation water from the Sweetwater River at his Old Sweetwater Ranch across the Continental Divide to Pacific Springs. The Pacific Springs and Dickie Springs 7.5-minute quadrangles actually indicate that the ditch did reach the Sweetwater, but the project never persuaded water to run uphill. The abandoned canal is still visible.

After the iron mines near Atlantic City closed in 1983, a company bought salvage rights to the abandoned railroad line. It removed the rails and ties but went bankrupt before it had removed the roadbed. Ironically, there appears to be enough material in the roadbed to fill the canal and restore the immediate vicinity of South Pass to something resembling its original topography. "In spite of an abandoned railroad grade, a diversion ditch, and the physical evidence of an AT&T buried cable," the California/Pony Express National Historic Trails *Comprehensive Management Plan* observed, the site "has an exceptional historic character and should be protected from any additional visual intrusions."

During the farming depression of the 1920s, a few large holdings and grazing associations consolidated most of the smaller ranches around South Pass. Today relatively few families and corporations control most of the area's private land. Beyond fence lines, two-track roads, and the occasional ranch house, corral, and windmill, these widely scattered ranches have had little impact on the landscape. The ranchers who manage these operations and use the Bureau of Land Management's range allotments around South Pass have proven to be excellent stewards of the land.

Preservation and Protection

Congress took its first step toward commemorating and protecting significant historical sites with the American Antiquities Act of 1906, which gave the president the right to designate "historic landmarks, historic and prehistoric structures, and other objects of historic or scientific interest" as national monuments. The Historic Sites Act of 1935 "declared that it is a national policy to preserve for public use historic sites, buildings, and objects of national significance for the inspiration and benefit of the people of the United States." The act directed the secretary of the interior to conduct "a survey of historic and archaeologic[al] sites, buildings, and objects for the purpose of determining which possess exceptional value as commemorating or illustrating the history of the United States" and authorized the government to acquire historic properties.

World War II interrupted the Department of the Interior's National Survey of Historic Sites and Buildings. The government had assembled extensive reports and by 1959 had "a classified list of sites and buildings of exceptional value" that was not made public. "Much invaluable material has languished in Government files, unused," National Parks Service director Conrad L. Wirth complained to Secretary of the Interior Frederick Andrew Seaton. "Consequently, the full effective value of the survey for State agencies, regional historical organizations, and semi-public preservation groups and for the Nation as a whole was not realized." Wirth proposed creating a "category of *Registered National Historic Landmarks*" and granting the secretary the right to issue a certificate to the owner of any survey site found to possess exceptional value "upon application and agreement to certain simple conditions." The only cost to the federal government, Wirth pointed out, "would be that of issuing and administering the certificate system." It would "provide an official and impartial basis for averting encroachments and other indiscriminate threats to preservation."

The Eisenhower Administration announced the historic landmark program on October 9, 1960. That December, South Pass was among the first sites Secretary Seaton proposed as a national historic landmark.[10] After passage of the National Historic Preservation Act in 1966, South Pass was one of the first sites listed on the National Register of Historic Places.

Even with such actions, threats to the integrity of South Pass and its landscape increased rather than diminished over time. To deliver natural gas to southern California, in May 1989 the Altamont Gas Transmission Company proposed building a thirty-inch pipeline capable of moving 719 million cubic feet of gas per day over a 620-mile route from Wild Horse, Montana, across South Pass, and on to Muddy Creek in southwest Wyoming. Rather than use established energy corridors, Altamont claimed that developing a new route over South Pass would save forty miles and forty million dollars. Despite an intense controversy, the BLM approved the South Pass route in July 1994. Due to the proposed pipeline, in 1995 the National Trust for Historic Places included the South Pass Historic Landscape on its list of America's eleven most endangered places, noting the "need to document the South Pass Historic

---

[10] Mackintosh, "The Historic Sites Survey," 46–47, 135–38.

Landscape and nominate the entire 100,000 acre area to the National Register of Historic Places."[11]

A dramatic drop in natural gas prices led Altamont to delay the project, and ultimately the BLM rejected it. Since that time, "To protect the visual and historical integrity of the historic trails," the BLM's Rock Springs and Lander Field Offices have worked to create a management plan for the resources they administer for the American public. To protect the Oregon, Mormon Pioneer, and California National Historic Trails corridor, in 1997 the agency designated 53,780 acres of BLM-administered public lands as the South Pass Historic Landscape and an area of critical environmental concern (ACEC).[12] Public comment for the *Proposed Resource Management Plan and Final Environmental Impact Statement for the Lander Field Office Planning Area* closed in February 2013, but the agency has yet to issue a Record of Decision about the plan and its alternative approaches to protecting South Pass.

SOUTH PASS NATIONAL HISTORICAL PARK: A 1969 VISION

In June 1969 the chief historian of the National Park Service returned from a field trip to the Rocky Mountains with a remarkable vision. In a memo to the service's assistant director in charge of planning, Robert M. Utley proposed creating a South Pass National Historical Park extending from Independence Rock to Pacific Springs—a distance of more than one hundred miles. It is worth quoting in detail:

> South Pass City is but one of a truly outstanding array of historic resources concentrated in the Sweetwater–South Pass area. Districts, sites, and buildings have survived with good to excellent integrity to represent the themes of "Overland Migrations," "The Mining Frontier," "The Cattleman's Empire," and of Western expansion. . . .
>
> Located south of the Wind River Range, in sight of which the emigrants had traveled for many days, South Pass was both deceiving and disappointing. Although its elevation exceeds 7,500 feet, it did not conform to the emigrant's picture of a Rocky Mountain pass. Some crossed it without knowing it. Elizabeth

---

[11] Bama, "Founder Fights His Last Fight," *High Country News*, Aug. 21, 1995; "America's 11 Most Endangered Historic Places" at http://en.wikipedia.org/wiki/America%27s_Most_Endangered_Places#1995_Places.

[12] Bureau of Land Management, *Green River Resource Management Plan*.

WAGONS, RIDERS, AND THE OREGON BUTTES
Lander photographer Andy Blair captured this wagon train on the way to South Pass in 2006 with the Oregon Buttes on the horizon.

Wood thought the road on the summit to be as level as the streets of Peoria. William Newby expressed disappointment: "If you dident now it was the mountian," he wrote in 1843, "you wouldent now it from aney outher plane."

Some twenty miles wide, South Pass is flanked on the north by the Wind River Mountains, on the south by high, barren hills. The continental divide cuts southeast across the pass, occupying the crests of rolling, sage-covered hills. The Sweetwater River, rising in the Wind River Mountains, flows south immediately east of the divide, then, just south of the bridge by which Highway 28 crosses it, turns abruptly east toward the Platte. The land is used almost exclusively for grazing, and the historic setting therefore remains virtually unaltered—although a railroad has recently been built through the pass to serve mining operations to the north.

Extensive evidence of the Oregon Trail may still be seen [and] markers abound. The state has fenced a generous stretch of trail ruts five miles west of the divide. BLM and the state have erected a highway turnout featuring an impressive interpretive display and . . . the National Historic Landmark plaque. Pacific Springs, a major emigrant campsite and the first water source after leaving the Sweetwater, lies just west of the summit. Actually a bog several acres in area, it remains essentially as it was in Oregon Trail days. South Pass lands are held both privately and by BLM.

I am convinced that there is an unrivaled opportunity in the South Pass–Sweetwater area to preserve and interpret a complex of sites of superlative historical significance and public interest associated with the Western Movement. As the BLM presentation indicates, locally there is an awareness in both public and private sectors of the need for preservation and a desire to get started. The area is attracting mounting numbers of visitors whose unregulated use of resources threatens serious damage as time goes on.

A South Pass National Historical Park might . . . include a generous segment of Oregon Trail ruts and Pacific Springs and provide a site for administrative and interpretive development. A cooperative agreement with the State would cover Independence Rock. Another would bring the Tom Sun Ranch into the park. Others might be concluded with the owners, public and private, of Devils Gate and other significant sites along the Sweetwater, together with the best evidences of trail ruts, to link the Independence Rock unit on the east with the South Pass unit to the west.[13]

Robert M. Utley, a remarkable public servant, became one of the most highly regarded historians of the American West. Sad to say, nothing came of his vision. Most of what he described is still intact, and Bob Utley's call to action remains as timely today as it was almost fifty years ago.

South Pass Today

Between 1840 and 1870 some five hundred thousand Americans crossed South Pass on the Oregon, California, and Mormon Pioneer National Historic Trails.[14] When the movement began in 1840, only three trading posts—Fort Laramie, Fort Hall, and Fort Boise—represented "civilization" between the Missouri and the Columbia River. When it ended, there were cities at Denver, Salt Lake, Boise, Carson City—and even South Pass. Over a little more than a generation, South Pass played an essential role in the transformation of America.

---

[13] Robert M. Utley, Memorandum on Sweetwater–South Pass Historic Sites, Wyo., June 23, 1969, of the National Trails System Office files, Salt Lake City.

[14] Mattes, *Platte River Road Narratives*, 5.

When J. Ross Browne published his survey of the American West's mineral resources in 1869, he called South Pass "that great gateway of American immigration to the Pacific States and Territories." Browne described the place as "a point to which travellers in future ages will probably make pilgrimages, as the Mahometans now do to Mecca. It is the heart of the North American continent, from which flow the great arteries of commerce."[15] He was partly wrong, for the paths of commerce that connect America's coasts have bypassed the great gateway, but Browne was still a prophet. Tens of thousands of American pilgrims still follow the rough wagon traces to South Pass to touch the past and tread the trails their ancestors followed to find new lives and homes in the Far West.

"The country remains as it was in '52. There the trail can be seen for miles and miles ahead, worn bare and deep, with but one narrow track where there used to be a dozen, with the beaten path that vegetation has not yet recovered from the scourge of passing hoofs and tires of wagons years ago," Ezra Meeker wrote after his visit to South Pass in 1906. The livestock hooves and the passage of time had leveled the graves of the pioneers, he wrote, and the smell of carrion around each campground was gone. "But where were the camp fires? Where was the herd of gaunt cattle? Where the sound of the din of bells? The hallooing for lost children? Or the little groups off on the hillside to bury the dead?" he asked. "All were gone."[16] Only ashes now remain of the pioneers' campfires, but to the northwest 3,737 Eastern Shoshones and 8,177 Northern Arapahos called the 2,268,000 acres of the Wind River Reservation home in 2011. The two nations share almost 3,474 square miles of America's seventh-largest Indian reservation, with most Shoshones living in the west around Fort Washakie, while the Arapahos gather to the east around Ethete and Arapahoe.

Today the wide prairie at the foot of the Wind River Range appears much as it did to historic travelers. The place transforms the very face of nature. At South Pass everything "seemed to have undergone a change," J. Quinn Thornton observed in 1846. "The temperature, the atmosphere, and the heavens, seemed to have changed" until the sublime and grand scenery "appeared to gleam up awfully through wild depths of azure."[17]

---

[15] Browne, *Resources of the Pacific Slope*, 437, 2:183.
[16] Meeker, *Ox-team Days*, 195–96.
[17] Thornton, *Oregon and California*, 137–38.

The rugged landscape still eloquently evokes openness and freedom, rich with the grandeur and desolation that so impressed early pioneers. The "profound silence and terrible stillness and solitude" of the pass Richard Burton experienced in 1860 endures, broken only when the high, cold wind blows relentlessly through the break in the mountains. Summer days still grow blazing hot after freezing nights, and winter snows still bury the countryside. Visitors find a wide variety of the spectacular wildflowers early emigrants described—wild roses, lupines, larkspurs, daisies, pinks, white shooting stars, honeysuckles, irises, buttercups, sunflowers, and butterfly milkweed— blooming close to banks of snow, "lingering relics of winter, thus attesting the aptitude of Nature to respond to her environment whatever its character," as Forty-niner David Leeper recalled.[18]

South Pass is a history-haunted place. Each year, several thousand Americans leave the pavement of Wyoming State Highway 28 to follow three miles of gravel road to the trace of the Oregon, California, Mormon, and Pony Express National Historic Trails. Here an aging BLM sign describes South Pass. Visitors cross another third of a mile of rougher road to the Continental Divide. Between the first of May and the end of October 2006, 2,773 SUVs, trucks, and cars hauling an estimated 7,487 visitors rattled across the cattle guard at the entrance to the buck-and-pole fence surrounding the forty acres the BLM has set aside for South Pass. A few hundred yards to the west, Ezra Meeker's granite-and-quartz boulder and Captain Nickerson's black slate slab are the only indication that this spot marks the division of the waters.

Ironically, the view from the summit is one of the least impressive and most cluttered on the twenty-mile-wide prairie dividing the Winds and Pacific Butte. Looking east, the old wagon road winds its sinuous way over the rolling plain that forms South Pass. Looking west, a badlands bluff stands on the far side of Highway 28. Its brilliant red Wasatch formation rocks shut off the view. A PacifiCorp high-power transmission line runs across the landscape. The abandoned trough of the Hay ditch seems to be waiting to be backfilled with the gravel and taconite pellets—bounced out of ore cars decades ago—from the remnants of the railroad bed. Few visitors notice these intrusions, which are disappearing beneath the sagebrush and blowing away in the eternal wind.

The South Pass trail corridor's highly significant historical sites include Independence Rock, Devils Gate, Martins Cove, Split Rock, Ice Slough, Sixth

---

[18] Leeper, *The Argonauts of 'Forty-nine*, 39.

Crossing, Rocky Ridge, and Burnt Ranch, the BLM reported in November 2011. The landscape at South Pass has remained relatively unchanged for 150 years, the National Park Service concluded, and retains its "excellent historical integrity across almost all of the Lander Field Office—the most intact in the State of Wyoming and among the most pristine in the nation." These federal agencies rightly believe this "fragile, sensitive, rare, irreplaceable, exemplary, unique, and vulnerable to adverse change" spot is a national treasure. The importance of the South Pass landscape is its similarity to "that which was witnessed by the original travelers across the trail corridor. This landscape is mentioned in countless journals of pioneers who were amazed at the landscape's vast wide open prairies."[19]

The American past has an almost magical ability to disappear. Since 1624, when the inhabitants agreed to let the Dutch establish New Amsterdam, a fur-trading post on their hilly island of Manhattan, the City of New York has been created and destroyed a hundred times. A sprawling metropolis now surrounds the Alamo. The cabins where the Donner party spent a miserable winter are now not much more than a stone's throw from Interstate 80—and one of them may well lie buried under the pavement of the agricultural inspection station blocking the interstate highway. Malls and suburbs now cover much of the hallowed ground brave men consecrated with their life's blood during the Civil War. But beneath the looming majesty of Pacific Butte, South Pass endures.

Americans still make pilgrimages to South Pass, for it is a place whose wide-open landscape breathes history. "I can stand on South Pass and close my eyes, and hear the hoof beats of the Pony Express riders, the cracking of ox-team drivers' whips, the creak of wagon wheels, the voices of women and children," wrote Wyoming native Tom Bell, whose great-great-grandmother crossed South Pass in the 1850s. "South Pass is one of the few places where you can stand in 2006 and 1846 at the same time," archaeologist Terry Del Bene observed. "That's pretty special. We're running out of places like that."[20] For many, South Pass represents a national treasure. We can either squander what makes it precious, or protect and defend the qualities that make it unique and a worthy legacy to bequeath to future generations.

---

[19] U.S. Dept. of the Interior, Lander BLM Field Office, *Resource Management Plan Revision: Areas of Critical Environmental Concern Report*, 43–45.

[20] Bama, "Founder Fights His Last Fight"; Vita, "Trail of Fears: Will the Federal Government Allow Gold Mining along Wyoming's Oregon Trail?"

Selected Bibliography

THIS BIBLIOGRAPHY IS DIVIDED INTO PRIMARY SOURCES, Secondary Sources, and Government Documents. It lists only the sources cited in this study, which represent only a fraction of the material about South Pass. Digital versions are available for many if not most of these sources. Many of the LDS Archives sources can be found at the Church of Jesus Christ of Latter-day Saints' Church History Library and Archives website, notably at the Mormon Pioneer Overland Travel, 1847–68, site at http://lds.org/churchhistory/library/pioneercompanysearch/.

ABBREVIATED ARCHIVAL REFERENCES

Beinecke Library: Yale Collection of Western Americana, Beinecke Rare Book and Manuscript Library, Yale Univ.
BYU Library: Special Collections, Harold B. Lee Library, Brigham Young Univ.
Huntington Library: Henry E. Huntington Library, San Marino, Calif.
Journal History: Journal History of The Church of Jesus Christ of Latter-day Saints.
LDS Archives: Church History Library and Archives, The Church of Jesus Christ of Latter-day Saints, Salt Lake City, Utah.
Marriott Library: Special Collections, J. Willard Marriott Library, Univ. of Utah.
Mattes Library: Merrill J. Mattes Research Library, National Frontier Trails Center, Independence, Mo.
Oregon Hist. Soc: Oregon Historical Society Research Library, Portland, Ore.

PRIMARY SOURCES

Abbey, James. *California: A Trip across the Plains, in the Spring of 1850.* New Albany, Ind.: Kent & Norman, and J. R. Nunemacher, 1850.

SELECTED BIBLIOGRAPHY

Ackley, Richard Thomas. "Across the Plains in 1858." Ed. by Dale L. Morgan. *Utah Hist. Qrtly.* (July, October 1941): 190–228.

Ahmanson, John. *Vor Tids Muhamed* [1856]. Omaha: Press of the Danish Pioneer, 1876. Republished as *Secret History: A Translation of Vor Tids Muhamed.* Trans. by Gleason L. Archer. Chicago: Moody Press, 1984.

Aitken, William Knox. "Adventures of a Mormon," July 11, 1857. *London Advertiser,* August 9, 1857.

Ajax, William. Journal 1862. MSS 1488. Special Collections, BYU Library.

Allen, O. *Guide Book to the Gold Fields of Kansas and Nebraska and Great Salt Lake City, 1858–9.* Washington, D.C.: R. A. Walters, 1859.

Alley, George, to Geo. H. Alley, August 24, 1848, Pacific Springs. Copy of holograph in possession of Gail Robinson, Green River, Wyo. Will Bagley transcription.

Anderson, Kirk. "Trip to Utah, 1858." *Missouri Hist. Soc. Bulletin* (October 1961): 3–15.

Anderson, William Marshall. *The Rocky Mountain Journals of William Marshall Anderson: The West in 1834.* Ed. by Dale L. Morgan and Eleanor Towles Harris. Lincoln: Univ. of Nebraska Press, 1987.

Anonymous [Dr. R. B. Ironside?]. Journals of the United States Emigrant Escort Service, 1861–1864. Journal V, Saddle Creek to Boise City, 1864. WA MSS 116. Beinecke Library.

Arthur, David. "Across the Plains in 1843." *Sunday Oregonian,* 1889.

Baker, Jean Rio Griffiths. Diary, 1851. "By Windjammer and Prairie Schooner." In Holmes, *Covered Wagon Women,* 3:203–81.

Ball, John. *Autobiography of John Ball: Compiled by His Daughters Kate Ball Powers, Flora Ball Hopkins, Lucy Ball.* Grand Rapids, Mich.: The Dean-Hicks Co., 1925.

Beckwourth, James Pierson. *The Life and Adventures of James P. Beckwourth, mountaineer, scout, and pioneer, and chief of the Crow Nation of Indians. Written from his own dictation, by T. D. Bonner.* New York: Harper & Brothers, 1856.

Beesley, Sarah Hancock. Reminiscences. In Handcart Stories, 28–34. LDS Archives.

Benjamin, Israel Joseph. *Three Years in America, 1859–1862.* 2 vols. Philadelphia: Jewish Publication Soc. of America, 1956.

Bidwell, John. *A Journey to California.* In Nunis, *The Bidwell-Bartleson Party,* 26–70.

———. "The First Emigrant Train to California." *Century Magazine* (November 1890): 106–30.

Blackburn, Abner. *Frontiersman: Abner Blackburn's Narrative.* Ed. by Will Bagley. Salt Lake City: Univ. of Utah Press, 1992.

Blank, Parthenia McMillan [and Cecilia Emily McMillen Adams]. "Twin Sisters on the Oregon Trail." In Holmes, *Covered Wagon Women,* 5:253–312.

Bleak, James Godson. Journal, 1856. LDS Archives.

Blevins, Alexander. "An Interesting Interview with An Aged Couple." Reminiscence of 1843 Emigration. *The Valley Review,* March 29, 1879.

SELECTED BIBLIOGRAPHY 297

Bliss, Robert S. "Journal [1848]." Ed. By Everett L. Cooley. *Utah Hist. Qrtly.* (October 1959): 381–404.
Bowles, John. "California—The Trip over the Plains," September 9, 1859. *The Republican* (Lawrence, Kansas), October 20, 1859. Manuscript. Mattes Library.
———. *The Stormy Petrel: An Historical Romance.* New York: A. Lovell & Co., 1892.
Bradley, Nancy Jane and Henry. A Daily Journal, 1852. WA MSS 45. Beinecke Library. Richard L. Rieck transcription.
Brown, Delia Thompson. Diary Kept, 1860–1869. Typescript. Print /NC 79/1/1. Nevada Hist. Soc. Jesse G. Petersen transcription.
Brown, J. Robert. *Journal of a Trip across the Plains of the U.S. from Missouri to California in the Year 1856.* Columbus, Ohio: By the Author, 1860.
Brown, James Berry. *Journal of a Journey across the Plains in 1859.* Ed. by George A. Stewart. San Francisco: The Book Club of California, 1970.
Brown, James S. *Life of a Pioneer, Being the Autobiography of James S. Brown.* Salt Lake City: Geo. Q. Cannon & Sons, 1900.
Browne, Albert G. "The Utah Expedition: Its Causes and Consequences," *Atlantic Monthly* (March, April, May 1859): 361–584.
Browne, J. Ross. *Resources of the Pacific Slope: A Statistical and Descriptive Summary.* New York: D. Appleton, 1869.
Bryant, Edwin. *What I Saw in California: Being the Journal of a Tour by the Emigrant Route and South Pass of the Rocky Mountains, across the Continent of North America, the Great Basin, and through California.* New York: D. Appleton & Co., 1848. Kristin Johnson transcription.
Buffum, Joseph Curtis. The Diary, 1849. Typescript. Bancroft Library.
Bullock, Thomas. 1848 Journal, MS 1385:5. LDS Archives.
———. A Mormon Trail Journal of Thomas Bullock, May–June 1858. Typescript. Vault MSS 772. BYU Library.
———. *The Pioneer Camp of the Saints: The 1846 and 1847 Mormon Trail Journals of Thomas Bullock.* Ed. by Will Bagley. Spokane, Wash.: The Arthur H. Clark Co., 1997.
Burnett, Peter H. *Recollections and Opinions of an Old Pioneer.* New York: D. Appleton & Co., 1880.
Burrell, Mary. "Council Bluffs to California, 1854." In Holmes, *Covered Wagon Women*, 6:255–61.
Burton, Richard F. *The City of the Saints and across the Rocky Mountains to California.* London: Longman, Green, Longman, and Roberts, 1861.
Butterfield, Ira H. "Michigan to California in 1861." *Michigan History Magazine* (July 1927): 392–423.
Camp, Herman. Letter, July 8, 1849. In *The Gold Rush: Letters from the Wolverine Rangers, 1849–1851.* Ed. by John Cumming. Mount Pleasant, Mich.: Cumming Press, 1974, 48–55.

Campbell, Robert. "Interesting News from the Plains." *Frontier Guardian*, July 24, 1850, 1–2.

Campbell, W. J. and Julia. Memoranda of Travel from Iowa to Oregon, 1864. April Dauenhauer transcription. Copy in author's possession.

Carnes, David. Journal of a Trip, 1849. MSS 83/66 c. Bancroft Library. Richard L. Rieck transcription.

Carson, Christopher. *Kit Carson's Own Story of His Life, as Dictated to Col. and Mrs. D. C. Peters about 1856–57, and Never Before Published.* Ed. by Blanche C. Grant. Taos, N.Mex.: Kit Carson Memorial Foundation, 1955.

Carter, William A. "Diary Describes Life on the Trail in 1857." *Annals of Wyoming* (April 1939): 75–113.

Chisolm, James. *South Pass, 1868: James Chisholm's Journal of the Wyoming Gold Rush.* Ed. by Lola M. Homsher. Lincoln: Univ. of Nebraska Press, 1975.

Christy, Thomas. *Thomas Christy's Road Across the Plains, 1850.* Ed. by Robert H. Becker. Denver: Old West Publishing Co., 1969.

Clark, John Hawkins. "Overland to the Gold Fields of California in 1852." Ed. by Louise Barry. *Kansas Hist. Qrtly.* (August 1942): 227–96.

Clayton, William. *An Intimate Chronicle: The Journals of William Clayton.* Ed. by George D. Smith. Salt Lake City: Signature Books, 1991.

Clyman, James. *James Clyman, Frontiersman.* Ed. by Charles L. Camp. Portland: The Champoeg Press, 1960.

Collins, John S. *Across the Plains in '64.* Omaha: National Printing Co., 1911.

Cone, Gordon C. Journal of Travels from Waukesha, Wisconsin, to California, by the "south pass" in the summer of 1849. Vault MSS 661. Special Collections, BYU Library.

Conyers, E. W. "Diary of Enoch W. Conyers, A Pioneer of 1852." *Transactions of the Oregon Pioneer Association* (1905), 423–512. Kay Threlkeld transcription.

Cooke, Lucy Rutledge. "Letters on the Way to California." In Holmes, *Covered Wagon Women,* 4:209–95.

Crawford, Medorem. "Journal of Medorem Crawford: An account of his trip across the plains with the Oregon Pioneers of 1842." Ed. by F. G. Young. *Sources of the History of Oregon* (1897).

———. "Journal of the Expedition Organized for the Protection of Emigrants to Oregon, &c." Sen. Exec. Doc. 17 (37:3), 1863. Serial 1149.

———. Journals of the United States Emigrant Escort Service, 1861–1864. Journal 1: Diary Omaha to Portland, 1861. WA MSS 116. Beinecke Library.

Crawford, Samuel Gillespie. Journals of the United States Emigrant Escort Service, 1861–1864. Journal 4, Loup Fork to Grande Ronde Valley, 1863. WA MSS 116. Beinecke Library.

Decker, Peter. *The Diaries of Peter Decker: Overland to California in 1849 and Life in the Mines, 1850–1851.* Ed. by Helen S. Griffen. Georgetown, Calif.: The Talisman Press, 1966.

Delano, Alonzo. *Life on the Plains and among the Diggings.* New York: Miller, Orton & Co., 1857.
Denver, James W. "The Denver Diary: Overland to California in 1850." Ed. by Richard E. Meyer. *Arizona and the West* (Spring 1975): 35–62.
De Smet, Pierre-Jean. *Life, Letters and Travels.* 4 vols. Ed. by Hiram Martin Chittenden and Alfred Talbot Richardson. New York: F. P. Harper, 1905.
Dinwiddie, David. "Overland from Indiana to Oregon." Ed. by Margaret Booth. *Sources of Northwestern History No. 2*, 1928, 3–14.
Dodge, Grenville M. *Biographical Sketch of James Bridger*, 1905. Annals of Wyoming 33, no. 2 (October 1961): 160–61.
Downes, Clara E. Journal Across the Plains, 1860. MSS 84/161 c. Bancroft Library. Excerpted in Melody M. Miyamoto, "'A Novel Sight': The 1860 Overland Adventure of Clara E. Downes." *Overland Journal* (Fall 2002): 86–97.
Dorius, Carl C. N. Journal. In Earl N. Dorius and Ruth C. Rasmussen, *The Dorius Heritage.* Salt Lake City: E. N. Dorius, 86–88.
Duncan, Elizabeth. "This Far Off Land: The Overland Diary, June–October, 1867, and California Diary, January–March, 1868, of Elizabeth 'Bettie' Duncan." Ed. by Katie H. Armitage. *Overland Journal* 17, no. 3 (Fall 1999): 12–25.
Dunlap, Kate. *The Montana Gold Rush Diary* [1864]. Ed by S. Lyman Tyler. Denver: Old West Publishing Co., 1969.
Eakin, Jane [Jennie Eakin Hanna]. Diary, 1866. Typescript, A30. Special Collections, Univ. of Oregon Library.
Erickson, Kersten. Recollections of Coming to Zion in 1857. Benson Biographical File, 1–3. LDS Archives.
Farmer, James, Journal, 1853. Collection of Mormon Diaries, Library of Congress, reel 11, item 3, 2:2–42. See also Journal, Apr. 1851–Nov. 1856, fd. 1. LDS Archives.
Farnham, Thomas Jefferson. *Travels in the Great Western Prairies.* Poughkeepsie, N.Y.: Killy & Lossing, Printers, 1841.
Ferris, Warren Angus. *Life in the Rocky Mountains.* Ed. by LeRoy Hafen and Paul C. Phillips. Rev. ed., Denver: Fred A. Rosenstock, the Old West Publishing Co., 1983.
Fishburn, Robert Leeming, "Autobiography." In Daughters of Utah Pioneers, *Chronicles of Courage*, 2:204–208.
Ford, Nineveh. Recollections: The Pioneer Road Makers, 1843. MSS P-A 32. Bancroft Library.
Frink, Margaret A. "Adventures of a Party of Gold Seekers." In Holmes, *Covered Wagon Women*, 2:55–167.
Frizzell, Lodisa. *Across the Plains to California in 1852.* Ed. by Victor Hugo Paltsits. New York: New York Public Library, 1915.
Garlick, Dr. Carmi P. A Trip Overland to California, 1850. WA MSS S-2343 G184. Beinecke Library.

300   SELECTED BIBLIOGRAPHY

Garrison, A. H. "Reminiscences of Abraham Henry Garrison—Over the Oregon Trail in 1846." Ed. by James M. Tompkins. *Overland Journal* 11, no. 2 (Summer 1993), 10–31.

Gibson, John McTurk. Journal of Western Travel [1859]. Saunders County Hist. Soc. Museum, Wahoo, Neb.

Glenn, Nancy C. "A Letter from La Grande Ronde, 1862." In Holmes, *Covered Wagon Women*, 8:19–26.

Godfrey, James. "The Overland Diary of James Godfrey [1849]." Ed. by Peter van der Pas. *Nevada County Hist. Soc. Bulletin* (April–July 1990), 10–23; (July–October 1992), 18–27. Kay Threlkeld transcription.

Gould, Jane Augusta Holbrook. *The Oregon and California Trail Diary*. Ed. by Bert Webber. Medford, Ore: Webb Research Group, 1997.

Gove, Jesse A. *The Utah Expedition, 1857–1858: Letters of Capt. Jesse A. Gove, 10th Inf., U.S.A.* Ed. by Otis G. Hammond. Concord: New Hampshire Hist. Soc., 1928.

Gray, William H. *A History of Oregon, 1792–1849*. Portland: Harris & Holman, 1870.

Greeley, Horace. *An Overland Journey, from New York to San Francisco in the Summer of 1859*. New York: C. M. Saxton, Barker & Co., San Francisco: H. H. Bancroft & Co., 1860.

Green, Caleb. Journal Containing A Visit to the Great Salt Lake or Observations during a five month's Residence in Utah (1856, 1857). A0612, Caleb Green Collection, 1862. See also Caleb Grant [sic], Report, December 12, 1856, in "Church Emigration Book." LDS Archives.

Gunnison, John W. *The Mormons, or, Latter-day Saints, in the Valley of the Great Salt Lake*. Philadelphia: Lippincott, Grambo & Co., 1852. Second edition, 1860.

Hancock, Samuel. *The Narrative, 1845–1860*. New York: R. M. McBride, 1927.

Harmon, Appleton Milo. Autobiography and Diary, 1850–1853. Vault MSS 75. BYU Library.

Harrison, J. M. Recollections of 1846, 1875. Oregon Hist. Soc. Kay Threlkeld transcription.

Hart, William Henry. Diaries, 1852. MSS 1411. BYU Library.

Hastings, Lansford W. *The Emigrants' Guid*. Cincinnati: George Conclin, 1845.

Haven, Jesse, Journal, 1856. Vols. 4–5. LDS Archives.

Hobbs, Henry. Journal. May 1859 to July 1860. LDS Archives.

Hoffman, William. Journal of William Hoffman, April 13, 1853, to August 1, 1853. Typescript. Idaho State Hist. Soc. Selections published as "An Accurate Observer." Ed. by Arthur S. Taylor and William McKinney. *Idaho Yesterdays* (Summer 1964): 20–25.

Houston, A. H. Letter to Dear Father, October 16, 1849. "From California." *Indiana American* (Brookville), January 4, 1850.

Hull, Lewis Byram. "Soldiering on the High Plains: The Diary of Lewis Byram Hull, 1864–1866." Ed. by Myra E. Hull. *Kansas Hist. Qrtly.* 1 (February 1938): 3–53.

Jaques, John [J. J.]. "Some Reminiscences." *Salt Lake Daily Herald*, December 1, 8, 15, 22, 29, 1878, January 12, 19, 1879.

Jensen, James. Reminiscence. Journal History, September 13, 1857.

SELECTED BIBLIOGRAPHY 301

Johnson, Hervey. *Tending the Talking Wire: A Buck Soldier's View of Indian Country, 1863–1866.* Ed. by William E. Unrau. Salt Lake City: Univ. of Utah Press, 1979.
Johnson, John Peter Rasmus. A Journal Kept While Travelling across the Plains, 1864. Vault MSS 21. BYU Library.
Jones, Daniel W. *Forty Years Among the Indians: A True and Thrilling Narrative of the Author's Experiences among the Natives.* Salt Lake City: Juvenile Instructor Office, 1890.
Kelly, William. *An Excursion to California over the Prairie, Rocky Mountains, and Great Sierra Nevada.* 2 vols. London: Chapman and Hall, 1851.
Kenderdine, Thaddeus S. *A California Tramp and Later Footprints; or, Life on the Plains and in the Golden State Thirty Years Ago.* Newton, Penn.: Globe Printing House, 1888.
King, John Nevin. Overland Journey to California. WA MSS S-723 K5825. Beinecke Library. Richard L. Rieck transcription.
Kingsford, Elizabeth Horrocks Jackson. *Leaves from the Life of Elizabeth Horrocks Jackson Kingsford.* Ogden, Utah: Privately printed, 1908, 2–6.
Langworthy, Franklin. *Scenery of the Plains, Mountains and Mines: A Diary.* Ogdensburg, N.Y.: J. C. Sprague, Book-Seller, 1855. Republished with an introduction by Paul C. Philips. Princeton: Princeton Univ. Press, 1932.
Lapish, Hannah. Recollections. In Handcart Stories, 37–40. LDS Archives.
Larkin, Elijah. Diary, 1863. MSS 175. BYU Library.
Lee, Jason. "Diary of Rev. Jason Lee [1834]." Ed. by F. G. Young. *Qrtly. of the Oregon Hist. Soc.* (June 1916): 116–266.
Lee, John D. *A Mormon Chronicle: The Diaries of John D. Lee 1848–1876.* 2 vols. Ed. by Robert Glass Cleland and Juanita Brooks. San Marino: The Huntington Library, 1955.
Leeper, David Rohrer. *The Argonauts of 'Forty-nine: Some Recollections of the Plains and the Diggings.* South Bend, Ore.: J.B. Stoll & Co., Printers, 1894.
Lieuallen, William. The Journal, 1864. Copy in author's possession.
Lippincott, Benjamin S. Letters, 1847–1851. MSS 95/15 c. Bancroft Library.
Looney, Jesse, to John C. Bond. October 27, 1843, Waiilatpu, Oregon Territorial Manuscripts, Mss 2263, Typescript, Folder 30, T-177. Oregon Hist. Soc.
Lorton, William B. Diary, September 1848–January 1850. Original diaries and Dale L. Morgan typescript, C-F 190. Bancroft Library.
Loughary, Harriet A. "Travels and Incidents, 1864." In Holmes, *Covered Wagon Women*, 8:115–62.
Lovejoy, Asa. "Lovejoy's Pioneer Narrative, 1842–48." Ed. by Henry E. Reed. *Oregon Hist. Qrtly.* (September 1930): 236–60.
Lowe, Percival G. *Five Years a Dragoon ('49 to '54) and Other Adventures on the Great Plains.* Kansas City, Mo.: The F. Hudson Publishing Co., 1906. Second ed., Norman: University of Oklahoma Press, 1965.
Mackintosh, Daniel. "Correspondence." *The Mormon*, July 4, 1857, 3.
Manlove, Jonathan. An Overland Trip to the California Gold Fields. Typescript. Manuscript SMCII Box 17, Folder 13. California State Library, Sacramento.

Margetts, Phillip. Letter to Elizabeth Margetts, June 14, 1857, near St. Joseph, Missouri. Michelle Margetts transcription.
Mason, J. D. "Letter from California." *Fort Wayne Times*, December 12, 1850, 1/1–3. Kristin Johnson transcription.
May, Richard Martin. *The Schreek of Wagons: 1848 Diary of Richard M. May.* Ed. by Devere Helfrich and Trudy Ackerman. Hopkinton, Mass.: Rigel Publications, 1993.
McAllister, John Daniel Thompson. Journal, 1862. LDS Archives.
McClure, Alexander Kelly. *Three Thousand Miles through the Rocky Mountains* [1867]. Philadelphia: J. B. Lippincott & Co., 1869.
Meeker, Ezra. *Ox-team Days on the Oregon Trail.* Ed. by Howard R. Driggs. Yonkers-on-Hudson: World Book Co., 1922.
———. *Story of the Lost Trail to Oregon.* Seattle: By the author, 1915.
Moore, Martha Missouri Bishop. "The Trip to California, 1860." In Holmes, *Covered Wagon Women*, 7:280–83.
Munger, Asahel. "Diary of Asahel Munger." *Qrtly. of the Oregon Hist. Soc.* 8, no. 4 (December 1907): 388–405.
Murrell, George McKinley. To Dear Father, September 17, 1849. Huntington Library.
Newton, Jotham. Trip to California—Overland, May 9 to September 14, 1853, and draft letter, October 6, 1853. Jotham Newton Papers. MSS C-F 75. Bancroft Library. Richard L. Rieck transcription.
Newell, Robert. "Memorandum of Travels in the Teritory of Missourie." In Hafen, *The Mountain Men and the Fur Trade of the Far West*, 8:253–74.
Palmer, Harriet Scott. *Crossing Over the Great Plains by Ox-Wagons.* Pamphlet. Oregon Hist. Soc.
Parke, Charles Ross, M.D. *Dreams to Dust: A Diary of the California Gold Rush, 1849–1850.* Ed. by James E. Davis. Lincoln: Univ. of Nebraska Press, 1989, 45–46.
Parker, Samuel. *Journal of an Exploring Tour beyond the Rocky Mountains.* Minneapolis: Ross & Haines, 1967.
Parkman, Francis, Jr. *The California and Oregon Trail: Being Sketches of Prairie and Rocky Mountain Life.* New York: George P. Putnam, 1849.
Phelps, John W. "Diary." In Hafen and Hafen, *The Utah Expedition, 1857–1858*, 89–138.
Platt, P. L., and N. Slater. *The Travelers' Guide across the Plains, upon the Overland Route to California Showing Distances from Point to Point, accurately measured by Roadometer.* Chicago: The Daily Journal Office, 1852. Second edition, ed. by Dale L. Morgan. San Francisco: John Howell Books, 1963.
Pratt, Orson. *The Orson Pratt Journals.* Ed. by Elden J. Watson. Salt Lake City: E. J. Watson, 1975, 375–457.
Pritchard, James A. *The Overland Diary of James A. Pritchard, from Kentucky to California in 1849.* Ed. by Dale L. Morgan. Denver: Old West Publishing Co., 1959.
Reynolds, William P. Letter to John Reynolds, December 27, 1848. HM 4157. Huntington Library.

SELECTED BIBLIOGRAPHY 303

Richardson, Caroline L. 1852 Journal and Commonplace Book. MSS C-F 102. Bancroft Library. Richard L. Rieck transcription.
Root, Frank A., and William E. Connelley. *The Overland Stage to California: Personal Reminiscences and Authentic History of the Great Overland Stage Line and Pony Express.* Topeka, Kans.: By the Authors, 1901.
Ross, Alexander. *Adventures of the First Settlers on the Oregon or Columbia River, 1810–1813.* London: Smith, Elder and Co., 1849. Republished in Thwaites, ed., *Early Western Travels,* vol. 7, 1904.
Russell, Osborne. *Journal of a Trapper.* Ed. by Aubrey L Haines. Portland: Oregon Hist. Soc., 1955.
Sanders, Harriet. "Omaha to Bannack [in 1863]." In W. F. Sanders II and Robert W. Taylor. *Biscuits and Badmen: The Sanders Story.* Butte, Mont.: Editorial Rev. Press, 1983, 4–20.
Savage, Levi. Excerpts from Levi Savage's Journal, 1856. Typescript. LDS Archives.
Scharmann, Hermann B. *Overland Journey to California.* Trans. and ed. by Margaret Hoff Zimmermann and Erich W. Zimmermann, 1918, from *New Yorker Staats-Zeitung,* 1852.
Scott, Abigail Jane Duniway. "Journal of a Trip to Oregon." In Holmes, *Covered Wagon Women,* 5:21–138.
Scott, Charles A. "Diary of the Utah Expedition, 1857–1861." Ed. by Robert E. Stowers and John M. Ellis. *Utah Hist. Qrtly.* (April and October 1960): 155–76, 389–402.
Shaw, Amberson Gary. "Capt. A. G. Shaw to Tell History [1862, 1865]." *Valentine Democrat* (Nebraska), January 17 to August 1917.
Shaw, David Augustus. *Eldorado; or, California As Seen by a Pioneer.* Los Angeles: B. R. Baumgardt & Co., 1900.
Shepard, Cyrus. Diary, 1834–1835. Ed. by Gerry Gilman. Vancouver, Wash.: Clark County Genealogical Soc., 1986.
Shuey, Lucetta. Journal, Adams County, Illinois, to Calaveras County, California, 1860. LDS Archives. Michael N. Landon transcription.
Simpson, George. *Part of Dispatch from George Simpson, Esqr., Governor of Ruperts Land, 1829.* Ed. by E. E. Rich. Toronto, Canada: Champlain Soc., for the Hudson's Bay Record Soc., 1947.
Smedley, William. *Across the Plains in '62.* Ed. by E. R. Warner. Denver, 1916.
Smith, Edward. "A Journal of Scenes and Incidents on a Journey from Missouri to California in 1848." Typescript, California DAR, Genealogical Records Committee Report: Series 2, Volume 4, Miscellaneous Records of Several States and Counties. Copy at CS 68 C 34 v. 4. California State Library. Sarcamento.
Smith, Elias, Journal, 1851. LDS Archives.
Smith, George A. "Captain A. O. Smoot's Company," *Deseret News,* June 11, 1856, 106.
Smith, Samuel R. "From California: Letter from a California Emigrant." (Wellsboro, Penn.) *Tioga Eagle,* November 11, 1849, 4/1–3. Richard L. Rieck transcription.
Spalding, Eliza Hart. "Diary of Mrs. H. H. Spalding." In Drury, *First White Women Over the Rockies,* 1:183–98.

SELECTED BIBLIOGRAPHY

Spalding, Henry H. "A Letter from the Rocky Mountains." *Oregon Hist. Qrtly.* 51 (1950): 127–33.
Spooner, Elijah Allen. Letters and Diary, 1849–1850. Vault MSS 662. BYU Library.
Springer, Viola. "From Princeton, Missouri, to Harney Valley, Oregon, 1885." In Holmes, *Covered Wagon Women*, 11:73–142.
Stansbury, Howard. *Exploration and Survey of the Valley of the Great Salt Lake*. Philadelphia: Lippincott, Grambo & Co., 1852.
Stanton, Charles T., to Sidney Stanton, "South Pass," July 19, 1846. In Morgan, *Overland in 1846*, 615–20.
Starr, Isaac R. Diary, 1850. MSS 2473, Oregon Hist. Soc. Kay Threlkeld transcription.
Stevenson, Edward. Letter to the Editor, August 17, 1855. *Deseret News*, September 5, 1855, 208.
Stickney, Ann Jarvis. "Autobiography." In Kate B. Carter, ed. *Our Pioneer Heritage*. 20 vols. (Salt Lake City: Daughters of Utah Pioneers, 1958–77), 9:439.
Stone, Minerva. Letter to Dear Parents, Sweet Water River, September 11, 1850. LDS Archives.
Stout, Hosea. *On the Mormon Frontier: The Diary of Hosea Stout*. 2 vols. Ed. by Juanita Brooks. Salt Lake City: Univ. of Utah Press, 1964.
Stuart, Robert. *The Discovery of the Oregon Trail: Robert Stuart's Narratives of His Overland Trip Eastward from Astoria in 1812–13*. Ed. by Philip Ashton Rollins. New York: Eberstadt & Sons, 1935.
———. *On the Oregon Trail: Robert Stuart's Journey of Discovery*. Ed. by Kenneth A. Spaulding. Norman: Univ. of Oklahoma Press, 1953.
Stucki, John S. *Family History Journal of John S. Stucki: A Handcart Pioneer of 1860, from Switzerland to Utah in 1860*. Salt Lake City: Pyramid Press, 1932.
Taylor, Calvin. "Overland to California in 1850: The Journal of Calvin Taylor." Ed. by Burton J. Williams. *Utah Hist. Qrtly.* 38, no. 4 (Fall 1970): 312–49.
Terry, Chloe. Diary of Chloe Terry (Doyle), 1852. Typescript, Accession Number 3234, Manuscripts, Special Collections, Allen Library, Univ. of Washington. Kay Threlkeld transcription.
Thomas, Preston. John Brown Emigrating Company Journal, July–Sept. 1851. Special Collections, Marriott Library, Univ. of Utah.
Thornton, Jessy Quinn. *Oregon and California in 1848*. 2 vols. New York: Harper & Bros., 1849.
Towell, Emily. "Missouri to Idaho, 1881." In Holmes, *Covered Wagon Women*, 10:197–219.
Townsend, John Kirk. *Across the Rockies to the Columbia*. Intro. by Donald Jackson. Lincoln: Univ. of Nebraska Press/Bison Books, 1978.
Tracy, Albert. "Journal of Captain Albert Tracy." Ed. by J. Cecil Alter and Robert J. Dwyer. *Utah Hist. Qrtly.* (1943): 1–119.
Tripp, Bartlett. Journal, July 24 to August 1861. LDS Archives.
Truman, Ben C. "Across the Plains in Winter." *New York Times*, February 11, 1867, 2.

Turner, Ruth Warner. "A Letter Home—1861." *The Humboldt Historian* (Fall 1981): 2–28.
Twain, Mark. *Roughing It.* Hartford: American Publishing Co., 1872.
Wagner, William. Journal of an Ox Team Driver, 1852. Typescript. Oregon-California Trails Association Manuscripts. Mattes Library. Richard L. Rieck transcription.
Walker, Joel Pickens. *A Pioneer of Pioneers; Narrative of Adventures thro' Alabama, Florida, New Mexico, Oregon, California, &c.* Los Angeles: Glen Dawson, 1953.
Ware, Eugene. *The Indian War of 1864.* Topeka, Kans.: Crane & Co., 1911.
Watson, William J. *Journal of an Overland Journey to Oregon Made in the Year 1849.* Fairfield, Wash.: Ye Galleon Press, 1985.
Weibye, Jens C. A. Journal, 1862. September 23, 1862, 2–28. Journal History. LDS Archives.
Whipple, E. P. "The Mormons in California." *Gettysburg Star and Banner.* February 16, 1849. Ardis Parshall transcription.
Whitman, Marcus. "Journal Kept by Dr. Marcus Whitman of His Tour of Exploration with Rev. Samuel Parker in 1835 Beyond the Rocky Mountains." Ed. by F. G. Young. *Oregon Hist. Qrtly.* (September 1927): 239–57.
Whitman, Narcissa. *The Letters of Narcissa Whitman, 1836–1847.* Ed. by Glen Adams. Fairfield, Wash.: Ye Galleon Press, 1986.
Whitworth, George Frederick. Diary, 1853. Whitworth College Archives. Janet Hauck transcription.
Wilkins, James F. *An Artist on the Overland Trail.* Ed. by John Francis McDermott. San Marino, Calif.: The Huntington Library, 1968.
Williams, Joseph. *Narrative of a Tour from the State of Indiana to the Oregon Territory in the Years 1841–2.* Cincinnati: J. B. Wilson for the author, 1843.
Williams, P. L. "Personal Recollections of Wash-A-Kie, Chief of the Shoshones." *Utah Hist. Qrtly.* (October 1928): 101–107.
Wiman, Henry E., to Dear Parents, October 25, 1849. Robert H. Miller Papers. Missouri Hist. Soc.
Wislizenus, Frederick Adolph. *A Journey to the Rocky Mountains in the year 1839, by F. A. Wislizenus, M. D. Trans. from the German, with a sketch of the author's life, by Frederick A. Wislizenus, esq.* St. Louis: Missouri Hist. Soc., 1912.
Wood, Joseph Warren. Diary, 1849. HM 318. Huntington Library. Richard L. Rieck transcription. Selections published as "The Diary of Joe Wood, '49er: Young Lawyer Becomes Victim of Gold Fever," *Peoria Star*, October 1954.
Woodruff, Wilford. Journal. Journals and Papers. LDS Archives.
Woodward, William, Clerk. James G. Willie Emigrating Company Journal, 1856, 16–53. LDS Archives.
———, to Joseph F. Smith, 1907. Utah State Hist. Soc.
Woolley, Frank. Autobiography. LDS Archives.
Wyeth, John B. *Oregon; or, A Short History of a Long Journey.* Cambridge: Printed for J. B. Wyeth, 1833.
Wyeth, Nathaniel Jarvis. *The Journals of Captain Nathaniel J. Wyeth's Expeditions to the Oregon Country, 1831–1836.* Ed. by Don Johnson. Fairfield, Wash.: Ye Galleon Press, 1997.

Young, Ann Eliza Webb. *Wife No. 19, or the Story of a Life in Bondage.* Hartford, Conn.: Dustin, Gilman & Co., 1875.

SECONDARY SOURCES

Aird, Polly. "Bound for Zion: The Ten- and Thirteen-Pound Emigrating Companies, 1853–54." *Utah Hist. Qrtly.* (Fall 2002): 300–25.
Allen, John Logan. "Division of the Waters: Changing Concepts of the Continental Divide, 1804–44." *Journal of Hist. Geography* (1978): 357–70.
———. "The Invention of the American West: Fur Trade Exploration, 1821–1839." In John Logan Allen. *A Continent Comprehended.* Vol. 3 of *North American Exploration.* Lincoln: Univ. of Nebraska Press, 1997.
Anonymous. *Minutes of the Apostles of The Church of Jesus Christ of Latter-day Saints, 1835–1893.* 5 vols. Salt Lake City: Privately published, 2010.
Arrington, Leonard J. *Great Basin Kingdom: An Economic History of the Latter-day Saints, 1830–1900.* Cambridge: Harvard Univ. Press, 1958.
———. "Mormon Finance and the Utah War." *Utah Hist. Qrtly.* 20, no. 3 (July 1952): 219–38.
Bama, Lynne. "HCN's Founder Fights His Last Fight, Yet Again." *High Country News,* August 21, 1995.
Bancroft, Hubert Howe. *History of Utah, 1540–1886.* San Francisco: The History Company, 1889.
Barry, Louise. *The Beginning of the West: Annals of the Kansas Gateway to the American West, 1540–1854.* Foreword by Dale L. Morgan. Topeka: Kansas State Hist. Soc., 1972.
Bashore, Melvin L. "Avoiding Rocky Ridge: Mormons on the Seminoe Cutoff." *Annals of Wyoming* 79, no. 2 (Spring 2007): 2–11.
Bigler, David L. *Forgotten Kingdom: The Mormon Theocracy in the American West, 1847–1896.* Spokane, Wash.: The Arthur H. Clark Co., 1998.
Bigler, David L., and Will Bagley. *The Mormon Rebellion: America's First Civil War, 1857–1858.* Norman: University of Oklahoma Press, 2012.
Bishop, L. C. *Historical Emigrant Road Series.* Cheyenne: Wyoming State Archives and Hist. Dept., 1959.
Boyack, Hazel Nobel. "Oregon Trail Trek No. 8: Lander Road." *Annals of Wyoming* (April 1959): 77–93.
Branch, E. Douglas. "Frederick West Lander, Road-Builder." *Mississippi Valley Hist. Rev.* (Sept. 1929): 172–87.
Brown, Randy. "The Grave of Ephraim Brown." *Overland Journal* (1989): 25–27.
Bryant, Thomas J. "Seminoe vs. Seminole." *Annals of Wyoming* 6, no. 1–2 (July–October 1929): 237–38. From the *Rawlins Journal,* reprinted in the *Cheyenne Daily Leader,* March 22, 1882.

SELECTED BIBLIOGRAPHY

Carley, Maurine. "Oregon Trail Trek No. 6: [East of South Pass]." *Annals of Wyoming* (April 1958): 36–52.

———. "Oregon Trail Trek No. 7: [West of South Pass]." *Annals of Wyoming* (October 1958): 193–213.

Carr, Reta. "Stories from the Past," 173–86. In Sublette County Artists' Guild, *Tales of the Seeds-Ke-Dee*. Denver: Big Mountain Press, 1963.

Carr Family Record. AFN: MN77-CL, Family History Library. FamilySearch website, familysearch.org.

Carter, Lyndia McDowell. "The Mormon Handcart Companies." *Overland Journal* (Spring 1995): 2–18.

Chaffin, Tom. *Pathfinder: John Charles Frémont and the Course of American Empire*. New York: Hill & Wang, 2002.

Chittenden, Hiram Martin. *The American Fur Trade in the Far West*. 2 vols. Foreword by James P. Ronda. Lincoln: Univ. of Nebraska Press, 1986.

Christy, Howard A. "Weather, Disaster, and Responsibility: An Essay on the Willie and Martin Handcart Story." *BYU Studies* (1997–98): 6–74.

Clark, Malcolm, Jr. *Eden Seekers: The Settlement of Oregon, 1818–1862*. Boston: Houghton Mifflin & Company, 1981.

Dale, Harrison Clifford. *The Ashley-Smith Explorations and the Discovery of a Central Route to the Pacific, 1822–1829, with the original journals*. Second edition, Glendale, Calif.: The Arthur H. Clark Co., 1941.

Dary, David. *The Oregon Trail: An American Saga*. New York: Alfred A. Knopf, 2004.

Daughters of Utah Pioneers Lesson Committee. *Chronicles of Courage*. 8 vols. Salt Lake City: Daughters of Utah Pioneers, 1990–97.

DeVoto, Bernard. *Across the Wide Missouri*. New York: Houghton Mifflin & Co., 1947.

———. *The Year of Decision, 1846*. New York: Houghton Mifflin & Co., 1943.

Drury, Clifford M. *First White Women Over the Rockies: Diaries, Letters and Biographical Sketches of the Six Women of the Oregon Mission Who Made the Overland Journey in 1836 and 1838*. 3 vols. Vol. 1: Narcissa Prentiss Whitman, Eliza Hart Spaulding, Mary Augusta Dix Gray, and Sarah White Smith, Vol. 2: Mary Richardson Walker and Myra Fairbanks Eells; Vol. 3: Diary of Sarah White Smith, Letters of Asa B. Smith and other documents relating to the 1838 Reenforcement to the Oregon Mission. Glendale, Calif.: The Arthur H. Clark Co., 1963, 1966.

———. *Marcus and Narcissa Whitman and the Opening of Old Oregon*. 2 vols. Glendale, Calif.: The Arthur H. Clark Co., 1973.

Duffin, Dorothy B. "The Whitman-Spalding Marker at South Pass." *Overland Journal* (Spring 2000): 4–5.

Eaton, Herbert. *The Overland Trail to California in 1852*. New York: Capricorn Books, 1974.

Ecelbarger, Gary. *Frederick W. Lander: The Great Natural American Soldier*. Baton Rouge: Louisiana State Univ. Press, 2000.

Eells, Myron. *Marcus Whitman, Pathfinder and Patriot.* Seattle: The Alice Harriman Co., 1909.

Eldredge, John. *The Utah War: A Guide to the Historic Sites, South Pass to Salt Lake City.* Salt Lake City: Trailbuff.com Press, 2007.

———. "Who Was Roy? Discovering whose name was chiseled in 1814 on a rock in southwest Wyoming provides the earliest evidence for American traders west of South Pass." *Rocky Mountain Fur Trade Journal* 6 (2012): 21–29.

Fisher, Margaret M. *Utah and the Civil War: Being the Story of the Part Played by the People of Utah in that Great Conflict, with Special Reference to the Lot Smith Expedition, and the Robert T. Burton.* Salt Lake City: Deseret Book Co., 1929.

Fletcher, Patricia, Jack Fletcher, and Lee Whitely. *Cherokee Trail Diaries. Volume I—1849: A New Route to the California Gold Fields. Volume II—1850: Another New Route to the California Gold Fields.* Caldwell, Idaho: The Caxton Printers, Ltd., 1999.

Fletcher, Patricia, and Jack Fletcher. *Cherokee Trail Diaries. Volume III—1851–1900: Emigrants, Goldseekers, Cattle Drives, and Outlaws.* Sequim, Wash.: The Fletcher Family Trust, 2001.

Franzwa, Gregory M. *The Oregon Trail Revisited.* Tucson: The Patrice Press, 1997.

———. "The Reconstruction of Seminoe's Fort." *folio* (August 2003).

Furniss, Norman F. *The Mormon Conflict, 1850–1859.* New Haven: Yale Univ. Press, 1960.

Gamble, James. "Wiring a Continent." *The Californian* 3 (May 1881): 556–63.

Goetzmann, William H. *Exploration and Empire: The Explorer and the Scientist in the Winning of the West.* Austin: Texas Hist. Association, 1993.

Gowans, Fred R. *Rocky Mountain Rendezvous: A History of the Fur Trade Rendezvous, 1825–1840.* Layton, Utah: Peregrine Smith Books, 1985.

———, and Eugene E. Campbell. *Fort Bridger: Island in the Wilderness.* Provo: Brigham Young Univ. Press, 1975.

Gray, John S. "Fact versus Fiction in the Kansas Boyhood of Buffalo Bill." *Kansas History* (Spring 1985): 2–20.

———. "The Salt Lake Hockaday Mail." *Annals of Wyoming.* Part 1 (Fall 1984): 12–20; Part 2, (Spring 1985): 2–12.

Guenther, Todd. "The Burnt Ranch Saga: A History of the Last Crossing of the Sweetwater." *Overland Journal* (Winter 1999–2000): 2–32.

———, Erin Hammer, and Fred Chaney. "The Women Who Carried the Star of Empire Westward: Eliza Spalding and Narcissa Whitman." *Overland Journal* (Winter 2002): 130–51.

Hafen, LeRoy R. *Broken Hand: The Life of Thomas Fitzpatrick, Mountain Man, Guide and Indian Agent.* Lincoln: Univ. of Nebraska Press/Bison Books, 1981.

———. *The Mountain Men and the Fur Trade of the Far West.* 10 vols. Glendale, Calif.: The Arthur H. Clark Co., 1965–72.

———. *The Overland Mail, 1849–1869: Promoter of Railroads, Precursor of Settlement.* Cleveland, Ohio: The Arthur H. Clark Co., 1926.

———, and Ann W. Hafen. *The Utah Expedition, 1857–1858: A Documentary Account of the United States Military Movement under Colonel Albert Sidney Johnston, and The Resistance by Brigham Young and the Mormon Nauvoo Legion*. Glendale, Calif.: The Arthur H. Clark Co., 1958.

Haines, Aubrey L. *Historic Sites along the Oregon Trail*. Tucson: The Patrice Press, 1994.

Hanson, James A. "The Myth of the Silk Hat and the End of the Rendezvous." *Museum Fur Trade Qrtly.* (Spring 2000): 2–11.

Harstad, Peter T. "The Lander Trail." *Idaho Yesterdays* (Fall 1968): 14–28.

Hebard, Grace Raymond. "The First White Women in Wyoming." *Washington Hist. Qrtly.* (January 1917): 29–31.

———. *Washakie, Chief of the Shoshones*. Intro. by Richard O. Clemmer. Lincoln: Univ. of Nebraska Press, 1995.

Heilig, Dan, "Director's Message." *Frontline*, Wyoming Outdoor Council Newsletter (Summer 2000).

Holmes, Kenneth L. *Covered Wagon Women: Diaries and Letters from the Western Trails, 1840–1890*. 11 vols. Glendale, Calif., and Spokane, Wash.: The Arthur H. Clark Co., 1983–93.

Holmes, Reuben. "The Five Scalps (Edward Rose)." Ed. by Stella M. Drumm. Missouri Historical Society, *Glimpses of the Past* 5, no. 3 (January–March 1938): 5–54.

Homer, Michael W. *On the Way to Somewhere Else: European Sojourners in the Mormon West, 1834–1930*. Spokane, Wash.: The Arthur H. Clark Co., 2006.

Houston, Alan, and Jourdan Houston. "The 1859 Lander Expedition Revisited: 'Worthy Relics' Tell New Tales of a Wind River Wagon Road." *Montana* (Summer 1999): 50–71.

Hulbert, Archer Butler, and Dorothy Printup Hulbert, eds. *Marcus Whitman, Crusader*. 3 vols. Colorado Springs and Denver: Colorado College and the Denver Public Library, 1936, 1938, 1941.

Irving, Washington. *The Rocky Mountains: or Scenes, Incidents, and Adventures in the Far West; digested from the Journal of Capt. B. L. E. Bonneville*. Reprinted as *The Adventures of Captain Bonneville, U.S.A.* Ed. by Edgeley W. Todd. Norman: Univ. of Oklahoma Press, 1961.

Jackson, W. Turrentine. "A New Look at Wells Fargo, Stagecoaches, and the Pony Express." *California Hist. Soc. Qrtly.* (December 1966): 291–324.

———. *Wagon Roads West: A Study of Federal Road Surveys and Construction in the Trans-Mississippi West, 1846–1869*. Berkeley: Univ. of California Press, 1952.

Jarret, David L. "The First South Pass City: An Overland Stage Stop." *American Philatelist* (November 1976): 1138–40.

Jones, Robert Huhn. *Guarding the Overland Trails: The Eleventh Ohio Cavalry in the Civil War*. Spokane, Wash.: The Arthur H. Clark Co., 2005.

Josephy, Alvin M. *The Civil War in the American West*. New York: Alfred A. Knopf, 1991.

Lamar, Howard R. *The New Encyclopedia of the American West*. New Haven: Yale Univ. Press, 1998.

Lavender, David. *Westward Vision: The Story of the Oregon Trail.* New York: McGraw Hill Book Co., 1963.
Leland, Joy. *Frederick West Lander, A Biographical Sketch, 1822–1862.* Reno: Desert Research Institute, 1993.
Long, E. B. *The Saints and the Union: Utah Territory during the Civil War.* Urbana and Chicago: Univ. of Illinois Press, 1981.
Lindstrom, Matthew J. *Encyclopedia of the U.S. Government and the Environment: History, Policy, and Politics.* 2 vols. in 1. Santa Barbara, Calif: ABC CLIO, 2011.
Mabey, Charles R. "The Pony Express." *Utah Hist. Qrtly.* (January 1954): 1–14.
MacKinnon, William P. *At Sword's Point: A Documentary History of the Utah War to 1858.* Norman: The Arthur H. Clark Co., 2008.
———. "The Buchanan Spoils System and the Utah Expedition: Careers of W. M. F. Magraw and John M. Hockaday." *Utah Hist. Qrtly.* (Spring 1963): 127–50.
Madsen, Brigham D. *Exploring the Great Salt Lake: The Stansbury Expedition of 1849–50.* Salt Lake City: Univ. of Utah Press, 1989.
———. *The Shoshoni Frontier and the Bear River Massacre.* Salt Lake City: Univ. of Utah Press, 1985.
Marshall, William I. *Acquisition of Oregon and the Long Suppressed Evidence about Marcus Whitman.* Seattle: Lowman & Hanford Co., 1911.
Mattes, Merrill J. *Platte River Road Narratives: A Descriptive Bibliography of Travel over the Great Central Overland Route to Oregon, California, Utah, Colorado, Montana, and Other Western States and Territories, 1812–1866.* Urbana: Univ. of Illinois Press, 1988.
Matteson, Edith, and Jean Matteson, "Mormon Influence on Scandinavian Settlement in Nebraska." In Henning Bender, Birgit Flemming Larsen, and Karen Veien, eds., *On Distant Shores: Proceedings of the Marcus Lee Hansen Immigration Conference.* Aalborg: Danes Worldwide Archives and Danish Soc. for Emigration History, 1993.
McCartney, Laton. *Across the Great Divide: Robert Stuart and the Discovery of the Oregon Trail.* New York: Free Press, 2003.
Meldahl, Keith H. *Hard Road West: History and Geology along the Gold Rush Trail.* Chicago: Univ. of Chicago Press, 2007.
———. "Wyoming's Rivers and the Overland Trails." *Overland Journal* (Winter 2005–2006): 158–69.
Morgan, Dale L. *Jedediah Smith and the Opening of the West.* Indianapolis: Bobbs-Merrill Co., 1953.
———. *Overland in 1846: Diaries and Letters of the California-Oregon Trail.* 2 vols. Georgetown, Calif.: The Talisman Press, 1963.
———. *Shoshonean Peoples and the Overland Trail: Frontiers of the Utah Superintendency of Indian Affairs, 1849–1869.* Ed. by Richard L. Saunders, with an ethnohistorical essay by Gregory E. Smoak. Logan: Utah State Univ. Press, 2007.
———. *The State of Deseret.* Logan: Utah State University Press, 1987.
———. *The West of William Ashley: The international struggle for the fur trade of the Missouri,*

the Rocky Mountains, and the Columbia, with explorations beyond the Continental Divide, recorded in the diaries and letters of William H. Ashley and his contemporaries, 1822–1838. Denver: The Old West Publishing Co., 1964.

Mortensen, A. R. "A Pioneer Paper Mirrors the Breakup of Isolation in the Great Basin." *Utah Hist. Qrtly.* (January 1952): 77–92.

Morton, J. Sterling. *Illustrated History of Nebraska*. Lincoln: Jacob North & Co., 1905.

Nardone, Joe. *Report on Pony Express Route, Sacramento to Placerville*. Laguna Hills, Calif.: Pony Express Trail Association, 2003.

Newman, Peter C. *Caesars of the Wilderness: The Story of the Hudson's Bay Company*. New York: Viking Penguin, 1987.

Noble, Bruce J., Jr. "Marking Wyoming's Oregon Trail." *Overland Journal* (Summer 1986): 19–31.

Nunis, Doyce B., Jr. *The Bidwell-Bartleson Party: 1841 California Emigrant Adventure: Documents and Memoirs of the Overland Pioneers*. Santa Cruz, Calif.: Western Tanager Press, 1991.

Paxton, W. M. *Annals of Platte County, Missouri*. Kansas City, Mo.: Hudson-Kimberly, 1897.

Poll, Richard, Thomas Alexander, Eugene Campbell, and David E. Miller. *Utah's History*. Logan: Utah State Univ. Press, 1989.

Prucha, Francis Paul. *Documents of United States Indian Policy*. Lincoln: Univ. of Nebraska Press, 2000.

Rea, Tom. *Devil's Gate: Owning the Land, Owning the Story*. Norman: Univ. of Oklahoma Press, 2006.

Ridge, Martin. "Reflections on the Pony Express: The Significance of a National Icon." *Montana The Magazine of Western History* (Autumn 1996): 2–13.

Roberts, Brigham H. *A Comprehensive History of The Church of Jesus Christ of Latter-day Saints*. 6 vols. Salt Lake City: Deseret News Press, 1930.

Ronda, James P. *Astoria and Empire*. Lincoln: Univ. of Nebraska Press, 1990.

Root, George A., and Russell K. Hickman. "The Pony Express and Pacific Telegraph." *Kansas Hist. Qrtly.* (February 1946): 36–92.

Settle, Mary Lund, and Raymond W. Settle. *Saddles and Spurs. The Pony Express Saga*. New York: Bonanza Books, 1950. Reprint, Lincoln: Univ. of Nebraska Press, 1972.

Settle, Raymond W. "The Pony Express, Heroic Effort, Tragic End." *Utah Hist. Qrtly.* (April 1959): 103–28.

Spence, Mary Lee, and Donald Jackson, eds. *The Expeditions of John Charles Frémont*. 4 vols. Chicago: Univ. of Illinois Press, 1970.

Spring, Agnes Wright. *Caspar Collins: The Life and Exploits of an Indian Fighter of the Sixties*. New York: AMS Press, 1967.

Stamm, Henry E., IV. *People of the Wind River: The Eastern Shoshones, 1825–1900*. Norman: Univ. of Oklahoma Press, 1999.

Stegner, Wallace. *The Gathering of Zion: The Story of the Mormon Trail*. New York: McGraw Hill, 1964.

Stenhouse, T. B. H. *The Rocky Mountain Saints: A Full and Complete History of the Mormons.* New York: D. Appleton and Co., 1873.

Thompson, Robert Luther. *Wiring a Continent: The History of The Telegraph Industry in the United States, 1832–1866.* Princeton: Princeton Univ. Press, 1947.

Thrapp, Dan L. *Encyclopedia of Frontier Biography.* 4 vols. Glendale, Calif., and Spokane, Wash.: The Arthur H. Clark Co., 1988, 1994.

Thwaites, Reuben Gold, ed. *Early Western Travels, 1748–1846: A series of annotated reprints of some of the best and rarest contemporary volumes of travel, descriptive of the aborigines and social and economic conditions in the middle and far west, during the period of early American settlement.* 32 vols. Cleveland, Ohio: The Arthur H. Clark Company, 1904–1907.

Tobie, Harvey E. *No Man Like Joe: The Life and Times of Joseph L. Meek.* Portland, Ore.: Binfords & Mort, 1949.

Unruh, John D., Jr. *The Plains Across: The Overland Emigrants and the Trans-Mississippi West, 1840–1860.* Urbana: Univ. of Illinois Press, 1979.

Utley, Robert M. *Frontiersmen in Blue: The United States Army and the Indian, 1848–1865.* New York: The Macmillan Co., 1967.

———. *A Life Wild and Perilous: Mountain Men and the Paths to the Pacific.* New York: Henry Holt and Co., 1997.

Victor, Frances Fuller. *The River of the West: The Adventures of Joe Meek.* 2 vols. Classics of the Fur Trade Series. Ed. by Win Blevins. Missoula, Mont.: Mountain Press Publishing Co., 1984.

Vita, Tricia. "Trail of Fears: Will the Federal Government Allow Gold Mining along Wyoming's Oregon Trail?" *Preservation Online,* May 5, 2006.

Volpe, Vernon L. "The Origins of the Fremont Expeditions: John J. Abert and the Scientific Exploration of the Trans-Mississippi West." *Historian* (Winter 2000): 245–63.

Vrooman, Nicholas. "The Métis Red River Cart." *Journal of the West* (Spring 2003): 8–20.

Watkins, Albert. "Notes of the Early History of the Nebraska Country" *Publications of the Nebraska State Hist. Soc.* (1922): 1–379.

White, David A. *News of the Plains and the Rockies, 1803–1865.* 8 vols. Spokane, Wash.: The Arthur H. Clark Co., 1996–2001.

Whiteley, Lee. *The Cherokee Trail: Bent's Fort to Fort Bridger.* Denver: The Denver Posse of Westerners, 1999.

Wight, Jermy Benton. *The Oregon Trail, Book One: Frederick W. Lander and the Lander Trail.* Bedford, Wyo.: Star Valley Lama, 1993.

Wishart, David J. *The Fur Trade of the American West, 1807–1840: A Geographical Synthesis.* Lincoln: Univ. of Nebraska, 1992.

———, ed. *Encyclopedia of the Great Plains: A Project of the Center for Great Plains Studies.* Lincoln: University of Nebraska Press, 2004.

SELECTED BIBLIOGRAPHY 313

GOVERNMENT DOCUMENTS

Bryan, Lt. Francis T. "Road from Ft. Riley to Bridger's Pass in 1856." Sen. Doc. 35:1, Vol. 3 1857–58, Serial 920.

Campbell, Arthur H. *Report upon the Pacific Wagon Roads, Constructed under the direction of the Hon. Jacob Thompson, Secretary of the Interior, in 1857–'58–'59*. H. Exec. Doc. 108 (35:2), 1859, Serial 1008. See also Sen. Exec. Doc. 36 (35:2).

Commissioner of Indian Affairs. *Annual Report*, 1851. Sen. Exec. Doc. 1, pt. 3 (32-1). Serial 613-3.

———. *Annual Report*, 1852. Sen. Exec. Doc. 1, pt. 1, (32-2). Serial 658.

———. *Annual Report*, 1854. Sen. Exec Doc. 1, pt. 1 (33-2). Serial 746-1.

Donaldson, Thomas. *The Public Domain: Its History, with Statistics*. Washington, D.C.: U.S. Govt. Print. Off., 1881.

Godfrey, Anthony. *Historic Resource Study: Pony Express National Historic Trail*. Washington, D.C.: United States Department of the Interior/National Park Service, 1994.

Jackson, Andrew. "Message from the President of the United States, in answer to a resolution of the Senate relative to the British Establishments on the Columbia, and the state of the fur trade, etc." Sen. Exec. Doc. 39 (21:2), Serial 203.

Kimball, Stanley B. *Historic Resource Study: Mormon Pioneer National Historic Trail*. Washington, D.C.: United States Department of the Interior/National Park Service, 1991.

Lander, Frederick W. *Additional Estimate for Fort Kearney, South Pass, and Honey Lake Wagon Road: Letter from the Acting Secretary of the Interior Transmitting a Communication from Colonel Lander in regard to the Fort Kearney, South Pass and Honey Lake Wagon Road*. Washington, D.C.: Govt. Print. Off., 1861. Serial 1100-63.

———. *Report and Map of the Fort Kearney, South Pass, and Honey Lake Wagon Road*. Sen. Exec. Doc. 36, 35:2, 1859. Serial 984.

———. *Report of the Reconnaissance of a Railroad Route from Puget Sound via the South Pass to the Mississippi River by Fred. W. Lander*. H. Exec. Doc. 129 (33:1). Serial 738.

———, and U.S. Dept. of the Interior. *Maps and Reports of the Fort Kearney, South Pass, and Honey Lake Wagon Road: Letter from the acting Secretary of the Interior transmitting reports and maps* [by F. W. Lander] *of the Fort Kearney, South Pass, and Honey Lake wagon road*. H. Exec. Doc. 64 (36:2), 1861. Serial 1100.

Mackintosh, Barry. "The Historic Sites Survey and National Historic Landmarks Program: A History." Washington, D.C.: History Division, National Park Service, 1985.

National Archives. Records of the Fort Kearney, South Pass, and Honey Lake Road. RG 48, Microcopy 95.

National Park Service. *Comprehensive Management and Use Plan for the California and Pony Express National Historic Trails, Management and Use Plan Update for the Oregon and Mormon Pioneer National Historic Trails/Final Environmental Impact Statement*. Denver: Resource Planning Group, National Park Service, 1999.

Scott, Lt. Col. Robert N. *The War of the Rebellion: A Compilation of the Official Records of the Union and Confederate Armies.* "Operations in Missouri, Arkansas, Kansas, the Indian Territory, and the Department of the Northwest." Series 1, Vol. 13. Washington, D.C.: Govt. Print. Off., 1885.

———. *The War of the Rebellion: A Compilation of the Official Records of the Union and the Confederate Armies.* Series 1, Vol. 48, Part 2. "Operations in Louisiana and the Trans-Mississippi States and Territories. January 1–June 30, 1865." Washington, D.C.: Govt. Print. Off., 1896.

U.S. Dept. of the Interior, Bureau of Land Management. *Environmental Assessment for Dickie Springs Placer Gold Exploration.* Rock Springs, Wyo.: BLM Field Office, June 2005. WY/040/EA04-262. Searching for this title on the Internet will produce a cached PDF copy of this document.

———. *Final Environmental Impact Statement for the Jack Morrow Hills [and] Coordinated Activity Plan/Proposed Green River Resource Management Plan Amendment for Public Lands Administered by the Bureau of Land Management Rock Springs Field Office.* 2 vols. Rock Springs, Wyo.: BLM Field Office, June 2004. Searching for this title on the Internet will produce a cached PDF copy of this document.

———. *Proposed Resource Management Plan and Final Environmental Impact Statement for the Lander Field Office Planning Area.* 2 vols. Lander, Wyo.: BLM Field Office, February 2013. Digital copy at http://www.blm.gov/wy/st/en/programs/Planning/rmps/lander.html [May 20, 2013].

———. *Resource Management Plan Revision: Areas of Critical Environmental Concern Report.* Lander, Wyo.: BLM Field Office, November 2011. Digital copy at http://www.blm.gov/pgdata/etc/medialib/blm/wy/programs/planning/rmps/lander.Par.74315.File.dat/ACEC.pdf [May 20, 2013].

U.S. War Department. *Reports of Explorations and Surveys, to ascertain the most practicable and economical route for a railroad from the Mississippi River to the Pacific Ocean. Made under the direction of the Secretary of War, in 1853–56.* Washington, D.C.: A. O. P. Nicholson, Printer, 1855–61.

Index

References to illustrations appear in italic type.

Abbey, James, 139, *157*
Abert, John J., 120
Ackley, Richard, 117, 272
Adams, John Quincy, 54
Adams, Thomas, 206, 209
Ahmanson, John A., 194
Aird, Polly, 167
Ais, John, 97
Aitken, William Knox, 33, 178
Ajax, William, 160–61
Alexander, Edmund, 185–88
Allen, John Logan, 24, 27, 86, 196
Alley, George, 131
American Fur Company, 36, 67, 75, 79, 84–86, 97, 105, 144, 271
Anderson, Kirk, 234–35
Anderson, Nils, 177
Anderson, William Marshall, 60, 88, 91, 103, 144
Angus, John O., 170
Antelope Hills, 26, 30, 46
Antelope Meadow, 211
Antelope Springs, 146
Archambault, Auguste, 145–46
Arnall, W. H., 228–29

Arthur, David, 127–28
Ashley, William, 29, 52–55, 57, 61, 64–66, 68–77, 87, 196
Ashton, William, 235
Astor, John Jacob, 35–37, 51
Atlantic City, Wyo., 276, 283–85, 287

Babbitt, Almon W., 146
Bailey, Elizabeth, 52
Baker, Jean Rio Griffiths, 142, 252
Barnett, Joseph, 159, 226
Bartletson, John, 199
Bear River, 40–41, 75, *181*, 260
Beckwourth, James, 68, 73–74, 196
Beesley, Sarah Hancock, 192–95
Bell, Tom, 294
Benjamin, Israel Joseph, 241, 248
Benson, Kersten Erickson, 192
Benton, Thomas Hart, 51, 119–21
Bertrand, Louis, 190
Bidwell, John, 113, 115–16, 118–19, 133–34
Bierstadt, Albert, 213, *215*, *216*
Bigler, David L., 176–77, 195
Big Sandy River, 41, 43, 81, 88, 90, 99,

INDEX

Big Sandy River *(continued)*, 130, 135, 154, 159, 186, 203, 205, 208, 210–12, 214, 216, 219–20, 235, 238–39, 263
Black, Arthur, 57
Blackburn, Abner, 228
Black Hills (Wyo.), 30, 54, 92, 95, 159, 196, 198, 232, 273
Blacks Fork, 61, 116, 149, 164, 189, 198, 199
Bonneville, Benjamin L. E., 79, 80–85, 95
Bowles, John, 135, 214, 216
Bradley, Henry and Nancy, 152, 230
Branch, Alexander K., 57–58, 62, 63
Bridger, Jim, 79, 93, 109, 115, 163–64, 196–98, 256
Bridger Pass, 70, 149, 198–99, 203, 258, 270
Bromley, James E., 206, 234, 238, 254
Brown, Delia Thompson, 159
Brown, James Berry, 214–16
Brown, Thomas D., 232
Browne, Albert G., 234
Browne, J. Ross, 250, 292
Bryan, Francis T., 199
Bryant, Edwin, 127, 133–34
Buchanan, James, 190, 233, 245
Buffum, Joseph Curtis, 152, 155
Bullock, Thomas, 196
Burnett, Peter, 116, 159
Burnt Ranch, 17, 114, *226*, 232, 239, 285, 294
Burr, David H., 86, 234
Burrell, Mary, 144
Burton, Richard F., 26, 29, 124, 149, 157, 227, 239, 242–43, 252–53, 272–73, 284, 293
Burton, Robert, 149, 254–55
Butterfield, Ira H., 241, 243–44, 247
Butterfield Overland Mail, 233, 236, 241, 247

California Trail, 21, 104, 138, 150, 212, 274
Camp, Elmon S., 160
Campbell, Robert (fur trader), 41, 73–74
Campbell, Robert (Mormon), 34, 170
Campbell, W. J. and Julia, 223
Carnes, David, 139, 154
Carr, William Earl "Bill," 285–86
Carson, Christopher "Kit," 112, 121, 146
Carter, Lyndia, 150, 193–94, 196
Carter, William A., 148, 149, 188, 254
Carver, Jonathan, 28
Central Overland California & Pike's Peak Express. *See* Pony Express
Champlain, Jean Baptiste, 39
Cherokee Trail, 70, 149, 196–99
Chorpenning, George, 233, 237, 238
Chouteau, Pierre, 104, 109
Christy, Thomas, 139
Clark, John Hawkins, 141, 152, 157, 160
Clark, William (explorer/Indian agent), 26–28, 65, 89
Clark, William (mailman), 235
Clarke, Emeline, 107
Clayton, William, 128–29
Clemens, Sam, 158, 242
Clyman, James, 29, 50, 53–63, 62, 65, 68, 70, 159, 196, *226*, 251
Cody, William F., 43, 239–40
Collins, Caspar, 252, 257, 265, 270
Collins, John S., 265
Collins, William O., 256–58
Cone, Gordon, 156
Connor, P. E., 260, 264–65, 270
Conyer, Enoch, 143, 145
Cooke, Lucy Rutledge, 139
Cooke, P. St. George, 149, 188–89, 271
Continental Divide, 2, 23–25, 27, 30,

INDEX

36, 75, 78, 81, 90, 99, 103, 105, 115, 119, 133, 139–40, 151, 153, 160, 211, 219, 225, 279, 287, 280, 293
Craig, Isabel, 103
Craig, James, 256, 258–59
Crane, Addison Moses, 141
Crawford, Medorem, 122, 220–21, 224, 243–44, 251, 253
Crawford, Samuel G., 244
Creighton, Edward, 247–50
Crooks, Ramsay, 35, 37, 42, 45, 51–55

Dansie, Charlotte Rudland, 160–62; family of, 161–62
Dawson, Nicholas, 118
Day, John, 37
Decker, Peter, 130, 151
Deer Creek, Wyo., 192, 232, 248, 263–64
Delano, Alonzo, 126, 272
Del Bene, Terry, 17, 294
De Smet, Pierre-Jean, 115, 117–19
Devils Gate, 47, 48, 117, 143–45, 149, 151, 185, 173, 190–92, 207, 232, 235, 272, 291, 293
Dexter, S. W., 278
Dodge, Grenville M., 203, 266, 278
Dodge, Henry, 94–95
Dorion, Marie and Pierre, 36
Dotson, Peter K., 235
Dorius, Carl, 192
Downes, Clara, 165
Drips, Andrew, 76, 109
Dry Sandy Creek, 44–45, 70, 134, 238
Duncan, Elizabeth, 159
Dunlap, Kate, 158, 205, 219

Eddie, Thomas, 57
Eells, Myra Fairbanks, 89, 104–106
Eisenhower, Dwight D., 22, 162, 288
Ermatinger, Francis, 105–106

Estill, James Madison, 152, 229
Evans, Israel, 193
Evans, Lewis, 197–98

Farmer, James, 144
Farnham, Thomas Jefferson, 113–14
Ferguson, James, 189
Ferris, Warren, 59, 67, 82
Ficklin, B. F., 189–90, 206, 247
Fishburn, Robert, 193
Fisher, Joseph A., 255
Fitzpatrick, Thomas ("Broken-Hand," "White Hair"), 29, 53–57, 60–65, 68, 70, 79, 84–85, 90, 92, 98, 109, 118, 121, 163
Flick, George, 285
Floyd, Dr. John, 51–52, 65
Fontenelle, Lucien, 64, 76, 81, 89, 92–93
Ford, Nineveh, 115–17, 133
Fort Kearney, South Pass, and Honey Lake Wagon Road (Pacific Wagon Road), 200, 202–204, 207, 213–16, 224, 230, 284
Forts: Astoria, 35–39; Atkinson, 63–65; Boise, 100, 101, 292; Bridger, 30, 34–35, 145, 178–81, 187–90, 196–99, 208, 216, 232, 325, 248, 254, 266–67, 274, 280; Caspar, 270; Churchill, 247; Hall, 71, 88, 100–101, 105, 110, 113, 187, 207, 209, 212, 217–18, 221, 228, 291; Halleck, 259; Kearny, 146, 248; Laramie, 84, 92, 98, 105, 109, 116, 139, 145, 149, 163–65, 193, 266–67, 274, 280, 197, 199, 248, 252, 256, 291; Leavenworth, 97, 184, 229; Limhi, 190, 209; Nonsense (Bonneville), 81–82, 99, 105; Pueblo, 197; Seminoe, 144, 149, 151; St. Vrain, 197; Thompson, 206–208;

Forts *(continued)*: Vancouver, 71, 82, 85, 92, 107, 110; Walla Walla, 93, 102, 106; Washakie, 280, 292
Fraeb, Henry, 79, 109
Frapp, Isaac ("Shoshonee Aleck"), 209
Frémont, John C., 26, 29, 63, 112, 115, 117, 119–24, *120*, *144*, *145*
Fremont Butte, 43
Fremont Gold Corp., 284
Fremont Peak, 135, 214, 215, 243
Fremont Orchard, 263
Frink, Margaret, 152, 229
Frizzell, Lodisa, 143
Frost, Frances Seth, 213

Gabriel, Peter, 209
Gadd, Samuel, 177
Gallagher, Patrick A., 276
Gamble, James, 247–50
Gibson, John McTurk, 217
Gilbert, Henry S., 210, 243
Gilberts Station, 210–12, 214, 217, 219–20, 223, *226*, 234–35, 237–38, 241–42, 248, 257
Glenn, Nancy C., 217, 221
Good, Joseph, 259
Goodale, Tim, 203, 209, 214, 217, 284
Goodyear, Miles, 97, 101, 130
Gould, Jane, 205, 208, 223
Gove, Jesse, 186–87, 190, 206
Graham, Fred, 281
Granier, Emile, 277
Grant, George D., 168
Grant, Richard, 71
Gray, Mary Augusta Dix, 89, 104
Gray, William H., 92, 95–97, 104
Great Basin, 21–22, 39, 67, 85, 100, 114–15, 128, 138, 167, 184, 204, 247–48
Great Divide Basin, 46–47, 70, 196, 198, 203

Greeley, Horace, 218
Green, Caleb, 180
Green River (Spanish River), 21, 43–46, 54, 57, 60–61, 73, 81, 109, 119, 141–42, 165, 186–87, 194, 196, 198, 203, 209, 212, 216–17, 254–55, 257, 274, 276, 281; Seeds-ke-dee, 26, 57, 70
Green River Basin/Valley, 31, 33, 35, 42, 60, 64, 117, 207
Green River desert, 204
Greig, Joe, 284
Gulf of Mexico, 15, 27, 152
Gunnison, John W., 30, 146, 165–66

Hall, Amelia, 280
Halter, Bill, 285–86
Ham, Zacharias, 68
Hams Fork, 74, 85, 91, 149, 187–88, 267
Hancock, Samuel, 116
Handcart scheme, 169–84, 190–96
Hanks, Ephraim, 147, 181–82, 230
Hanks Cutoff, 148
Hanna, Jennie Eakin, 250
Harmon, Ansil P., 160, 162
Harmon, Appleton Milo, 34
Harris, Moses ("Black"), 73, 75, 104, 109, 130, 196
Harrison, J. M., 251–52
Hart, James H., 179
Hart, William H., 143
Haslam, Robert ("Pony Bob"), 240
Haven, Jesse, 182
Hay, John W., 285, 287; and ditch across South Pass, 293
Hayes, Hamer, 220, 257–58
Hellyer, Robert, 17
Henderson, Paul, 24, 250
Henry, Andrew, 39, 53–54, 60, 64–65
Hickman, William Adams ("Bill"), 231–32

Hitchings, Henry, 213
Hoback, John, 40
Hoback River, 36, 42
Hobbs, Henry, 193–94
Hockaday, Isaac, 230
Hockaday, John M., 210, 230, 233–38
Hoffman, Lt. Col. William, 149
Hoffman, William, 158
Holladay, Ben, 241
Hollman, Joseph, 272
Hudson's Bay Company, 57, 82–83, 85–88, 92, 100, 105, 110, 124, 127
Hull, Lewis Byram, 263
Humboldt, Alexander von, 28, 86
Humboldt River, 213–14, 260
Hunt, Wilson Price, 35–40, 55
Huston, Joseph M., 281

Ice cream, 154
Ice Spring, 139, 154, 181, 251, 254
Ice Slough, 238, 293
Ide, William, 127
Independence Rock, 21, 59, 146, 149, 255–56, 265, 267, 289, 293
Indians: 26, 31, 33, 37, 52, 64, 71–72, 88, 99–101, 103, 114, 121, 126, 163, 165, 199, 150–51, 163–65, 187, 192, 251, 204–205, 220–23, 251–60, 263–68, 280, 292; Absarokas (Crows), 26, 33, 40–43, 45, 54–57, 70, 76, 80, 115–17; Arapahos, 39–40, 150, 280, 292; Arikaras, 36, 53–54; Bannocks, 33, 41n24, 72, 165, 190, 207, 209, 216, 220, 254, 260; Blackfeet, 33–34, 42, 53, 81, 91, 93; Cheyennes, 33, 55–56, 104, 121, 144, 146, 149, 163–64, 252, 263–64, 270; Gros Ventres, 72, 76, 81; Lakotas (Sioux), 104, 33, 54, 121, 144, 150, 165, 251–53, 263–64, 270, 276; Nez Perce, 27, 33, 73, 89, 93, 97–100, 103; Pawnees, 63, 68, 144; Salish (Flatheads), 72, 89, 93, 189; Shoshones (Snakes), 26, 33–35, 39, 43, 48, 62, 70, 72, 76, 91, 101, 106, 121, 135, 149–50, 163–66, 187, 190, 206–207, 209, 214, 216, 220, 222, 244, 251–54, 259–60, 262, 271, 276, 280, 283, 292; Utes, 26, 33, 72, 76, 165, 168
Irving, Washington, 54–56, 79, 81–82

Jack Morrow Hills, 20, 24, 70
Jackson, David, 75, 78
Jackson, William H., 283
Jaques, John, 175, 181–82, 195
Jarvis, R. B., 235
Jefferson, Thomas, 28, 51
Jensen, James, 192
Jensen Meadow, 99, 211
Jocelyn, Stephen P., 267–68
Johnson, Hervey, 263, 266
Johnston, Albert Sidney, 149, 185, 188–90, 199
Jones, Benjamin, 37, 41, 45
Jones, Dan W., 148–49
Jones, Samuel, 177

Kearny, Stephen W., 128
Keemle, Charles, 55, 78
Kelley, Hall Jackson, 83, 111
Kelley, J. G., 239
Kenderdine, Thaddeus, 142
Kimball, Heber C., 185
Kimball, Hiram, 230
Kimball, William H., 168, 175n34, 178
King, John Nevin, 229

Lajeunesse, Basil Cimineau, 144
Lajeunesse, Charles ("Seminoe"), 144–45, 148–51
Lajeunesse, Lucy ("Mi-Coo-Sah"), 149

320 INDEX

Lander, Frederick William, 135, 201–18, 221, 252; legacy of, 224–25
Lander, Wyo., 57, 201, 206, 238, 280
Lander Creek, 99, 103n35, 211, 216, 219–20, 223
Lander Cutoff/Trail/Road, 23, 42, 44, 81, 90, 99, 201, 215; later history, 218–25, 280–81
Langworthy, Franklin, 138, 156–57
Lapish, Hannah, 194
Latter-day Saints. *See* Mormons
Lavatti, Thomas, 209
LeClerc, Francois, 37, 42, 45
Lee, Jason, 84, 88–92, 105
Lee, John D., 140
Leeper, David, 293
Leonard, James G., 243
Lewiston, Wyo., 277, 280
Lewiston Lakes, 273
Lincoln, Abraham, 54, 247, 249, 255–56
Lipe, Oliver Wack, 198
Lippincott, Benjamin S., 125–26
Little, Feramorz, 230
Little Sandy River/Creek, 17, 21, 23, 60, 81, 99, 103, 106, 114, 119, 130, 134, 157, 179, 211, 218–20, 222, 232, 238, 250, 267, 279, 285
Lodgepole Creek, 30, 197–99
Lorton, William B., 139, 140, 154, 159, 272
Loughary, Harriet A., 217, 273

MacKenzie, Donald, 32
Mackintosh, Daniel, 191
Madsen, Ole, 177
Magraw, William M. F., 191, 203, 205–208, 212, 230
Major, William Warner, 168
Majors, Alexander, 238, 240

Manlove, Jonathan, 155
Marcy, Randolph B., 189–90, 199
Margetts, Philip, 191–92
Markham, Stephen A., 232
Martin, Edward, handcart company, 148, 176, 181–82
Martin, Michael ("Bad-Hand"), 209
Martins Ravine/Cove, 176, 181, 293. *See also* Devils Gate
Mason, J. D., 155
Mathewson, Joseph H., 266–67
May, Richard Martin, 152
McAllister, John D. T., 160–61
McClellan, Robert, 37, 45
McGovern, Frank, 276
McKay, Thomas, 92, 100
McLaughlin, John, 92, 105, 110
Meek, Joe, 84, 98–100, *108*, 109
Meek, Virginia, 103
Meeker, Ezra, 286, 292; monument, 24, 287, 293
Mexico, 15, 25, 27, 81, 114, 119, 124, 128, 136, 138, 284; U.S. war with, 21, 11, 128
Miller, Alfred Jacob, 109
Miller, Charles H., 209, 223, 235
Miller, Joseph, 40, 45
Missions and missionaries, 21, 31, 66, 68, 87–110, 113, 117–18, 124, 128, 146–48, 168, 171–73, 177, 191, 208, 228, 278
Mitchell, D. D., 163–64
Moffet, John R., 203
Montrey, Alex, 235
Moore, Martha Missouri Bishop, 219–20
Moreland, D. C., 273
Morgan, Dale L., 51, 54n7, 57, 61, 63, 66, 70, 139
Mormons, 34, 114, 128–31, 140, 142,

146, 149, 164–65, 167–96, 206–207, 209, 213, 228, 230–33, 242–44, 249, 254–56, 259, 272, 274; Kingdom of God, 114, 165, 167–68, 189
Mormon Trail, 15, 17, 21, 23, 32, 29, 72, 99, 128–31, 141, 147–48, 150, 289, 291, 293
Morris, Esther Hobart, 103
Mortinsen, Bodil, 177
Mountains/Ranges: Bear River, 30, 100, 205; Blue, 39, 92, 100–101, 109, 111; Granite, 25, 47; Medicine Bow, 24, 30, 69, 198, 278; Uinta, 27, 30, 35, 70; Wind River, 20–21, 24, 26–27, 30, 35–36, 57, 70, 72, 98, 106, 112, 133, 156–58, 205, 207, 225, 271–73, 278, 284, 289–90; Wyoming, 31
Muddy Gap, Wyo., 48, 117, 144, 196
Munger, Sarah Elizabeth ("Eliza"), 107
Murrell, George McKinley, 129
Myers, Caroline, 160–61

National Historic Landmark, 2, 22, 288, 290
National Historic Trails, 15, 17, 23, 99, 285, 287, 289, 291, 293
National Park Service (NPS), 16–17, 22, 285, 289, 294
National Register of Historic Places, 16, 288–89
Newby, William, 290
Newell, Francis Ermatinger, 103
Newell, Kittie M., 103
Newell, Robert ("Doc"), 103, 109–10
New Mexico, 67, 189–90, 199, 264
Newton, Jotham, 142
Nickerson, Herman G., 277, 286
Nicollet, Joseph N., 119–20
Nilson, Ella and Jens, 177

North West Company, 72, 82
Nutt, Robert, 57

O'Fallon, Benjamin, 64
Olsen, Anne, 177
Oregon Buttes, 20, 24, 27, 30, 112, 133, 136, 155, *226*, *246*, 290
Oregon-California Trail, 33, 44, 90, 197–98, 202, 205, 207–209, 230, 241, 256. *See also* California Trail
Oregon Trail, 21, 29, 31, 41, 46, 48, 107–108, 116, 119, 121, 124–28, 139, 144, 196, 203–204, 218, 244, 260, 270, 278, 280–81, 286, 290–91

Pacific Butte, 20, 24, 26, *32*, 132–33, *136*, 155–56, 293–94
Pacific Creek, 24, 45n33, 70, 122, 141–42, 155, 159–60, 227, 229, 282
Pacific Fur Company, 28, 35, 39, 72
Pacific Springs, 23–24, 26, 31, 91, 99, 114, 119, 130, 132, 139, 152–53, 155, 158–62, 182, 186, 204, 229, 238–39, 248, 255–57, 279–80, 285, 287, 289–91
Palmer, Harriet Scott, 159
Pambrun, Pierre Chrysologue, 102
Parke, Charles Ross, 153–54
Parker, Samuel, 92–94, 104, 278
Parkman, Francis, 84, 87, 126 27
Pembrun [Pambrun?], Thomas, 209
Phelps, John W., 203. 232
Pike, Zebulon, 28, 86
Pike's Peak, 213, 215, 217
Pilcher, Joshua, 76–77
Pine Creek, 43, 208, 211, 219
Pinedale, Wyo., 43, 99, 286
Platte River, 25–26, 28, 40, 58, 62–65, 67–68, 71, 73, 76–78, 80, 97–98, 113–14, 116, 121, 123,

Platte River *(continued)*: 129, 138, 164–65, 176, 199, 215, 230, 233, 247, 251–52, 256, 290; North Fork, 30, 48, 69, 75, 80, 88, 145, 173, 179, 196, 198, 238, 241, 254, 258, 266–67, 270; South Fork, 30, 68–69, 94, 197, 263
Pony Express, 21, 31, 227, 240–41, 244; riders, 165, 239, 255, 294; stations, 237–38; trail, 17, 23, 44, 99, 247, 287
Poor, Richard L., 211
Popo Agie River, 26, 57–58, 105, 116, 206
Potts, Daniel T., 53, 74
Powell, John W., 217, 241
Pratt, Orson, 129–30, 148
Provost, Etienne, 60, 71, 144
Pyeatt, John Rankin, 197

Rawlins, Wyo., 70, 196, 198, 279–80
Red Desert (Wyo.), 198, 278
Reed, James F., 137
Reed, John, 36–37
Religion, 87, 128–29, 255
Rendezvous, 44, 71–76, 78, 81–82, 84–86, 88–89, 91, 93, 95, 97–102, 104–105, 109–10, 115, 204, 282, 286
Reynolds, William, 137–38
Rezner, Jacob, 40
Richards, Franklin D., 147–48, 168, 171, 173, 175–76, 183
Richards, Samuel, 168
Richardson, Caroline, 159
Robb, John S. "Solitaire," 54n7, 55–56, 63, 66
Roberts, George, 276
Robison, Lewis, 255, 274–76
Rock Creek, 20, 46, 131, 146, 160, 177, 238, 277, 279–80
Rockwell, Orrin Porter, 148, 186, 231

Rocky Mountain Fur Company, 53, 79, 85, 89, 91, 145
Rocky Ridge, 58, 122, 140, 146–47, 156, 177–78, 195, 208, 219, 228, 232, 238–39, 241, 244, 266, 273, 294
Rogers, Cornelius, 86, 104
Rogers, William "Billy," 253–54
Rose, Edward ("Chee-ho-cart"), 54–57
Rowley, George, 193–94
Russell, Majors & Waddell, 238, 240–41. *See also* Pony Express
Russell, Osborne, 34, 87, 99
Russell, William H., 236–38, 240, 253–54

Sanders, Harriet, 218, 285
Savage, Levi, 177
Scharmann, Hermann B., 139
Scholl, Tony, 275–76
Scott, Charles, 248
Scott, Hiram, 73, 76
Seaton, Frederick Andrew, 288
Seminoe Cutoff, 146–49, 232, 255, 257
Seville, William, 199
Shaw, Amberson, 257–58
Shaw, David, 153, 158
Shepard, Cyrus, 89–91
Shuey, Lucetta, 219
Sibley, Hiram, 245, 247, 250
Simonton, James W., 233
Simpson, George, 82–83, 87–88
Simpson, Lewis, 186
Smedley, William, 221–22
Smith, Abigail Raymond and Asa B., 107
Smith, Edward, 145
Smith, Elias, 142
Smith, George A., 148, 168
Smith, Jedediah S., 29, 53–57, 60–68, 70–76, 78–79, 86, 88
Smith, Joseph, 128, 167–68, 184

INDEX 323

Smith, Lot, 186, 255–57, 259
Smith, Samuel R., 131
Smith, Sarah Gilbert White, 89, 104–106
Smoot, Abraham O., 179–80, 232
Snow, Erastus, 169, 179
South Pass, 5, 15–16; altitude of, 24, 27, 112, 122–23, 130, 289; burials and graves at, 17, 39, 130, 141, 158–62, 178, 219, 225, 226, 285, 292; geology and geography of, 23–25, 27–29; gold rush to, 271–78; importance of, 22–23, 25, 29–31, 64–66, 76–78, 110 113–14, 123–24, 131, 138, 165; landscape and scenery at, 15–17, 20–21, 31, 98, 101, 105, 124, 131–35, 155–58, 199, 205, 213–16, 218–19, 282, 287–89, 292–94; location and discovery of, 2, 21, 45–52, 123–24; Pacific Telegraph at, 244–50, 258–61, 270; and Pony Express, 237–41, 253–54; ranching at, 284–85; trails through, 91, 114–19, 139–43, 196–204, 207–10, 278–81; wagons cross, 78–81
South Pass City, Wyo., 2, 20, 34–35, 103, 276–77, 285, 289; 1861 "paper city," 241–44, 273
Spalding, Eliza Hart, 89, 94–100, 102–104, 106, 108–109, 286
Spalding, Henry Harmon, 95, 97, 100, 102–103, 109, 228
Spooner, Elijah Allen, 152
Springer, Viola, 280, 285
Stansbury, Howard, 146, 198
Stansbury Expedition, 98
Stanton, Charles T., 134
Starr, Isaac R., 229
Stevenson, Edward, 146–47
Stewart, Sir William Drummond, 92, 97, 104, 109, 145

Stickney, Ann Jarvis, 193–94
Stone, S., 57, 62–64
Stout, Hosea, 231
Stratton, Joseph, 147
Strawberry Creek, 153–54, 157, 208, 219, 238, 253, 275, 277, 285
Stuart, Granville, 26
Stuart, Robert, 28–29, 35–48, 37, 51–52, 87, 115
Stucki, John S., 194
Sublette, Milton, 79, 85–86, 90, 97
Sublette, William L., 54, 57–58, 60, 67, 75–76, 78–79, 81, 84, 86, 116, 144
Sublette Cutoff, 141, 215, 235
Sullivan, Ephraim, 243
Sullivan, Potter Charles, 242–43
Sullivan, Rhoba Ann, 242, 243
Sullivan, Rhoba May, 243
Sun, Tom, 280
Sun Ranch, 150, 291
Sweetwater Canyon, 59, 244
Sweetwater Hills, 25, 158
Sweetwater River, 46, 48, 57–60, 62–63, 70, 72–72, 76, 81, 90–91, 112, 117, 121–22, 129, 133, 141, 144, 146–48, 158, 161, 179, 184. 196, 204, 211, 219–20, 235, 240, 243, 259, 267, 271–73, 275, 282–85, 287, 289–91; Bridge/First Crossing, 265, 268; Three Crossings, 17, 122, 159, 252, 257, 265, 268, 270, 284; Fifth Crossing, 146; Eighth (Sweetwater Station), 58, 241, 244; Ninth/last crossing/South Pass Station/Camp Highland, 18, 20, 23, 114, 140, 146, 153, 159, 192, 207–208, 210, 221, 226, 232, 234, 238–39, 248, 257–58, 261
Sweetwater Valley, 24–25, 29, 121, 170, 198, 251. See also Burnt Ranch; Gilberts Station; Sweetwater Bridge

Taylor, Calvin, 132, 156
Taylor, John, 130, 172–73, 179, 183–84, 196
Telegraph, 21, 222, 227, 238, 240, 244–50, 254–60, 261, 263–70
Temoni, Samuel, 97
Terry, Chloe, 143
Terry, Joshua, 275
Terry, Stephen, 57
Thing, Joseph, 91, 204–205
Thomas, Preston, 142
Thompson, Jacob, 203, 207
Thorn, Jonathan, 35–36
Thornton, J. Quinn, 29, 134, 292
Towell, Emily, 279
Townsend, John, 89–91, 102
Tracy, Albert, 210, 236–37
Tripp, Bartlett, 149, 242
Trout, 42, 81, 125–26, 204, 220, 222
Turner, Ruth Warner, 243
Twain, Mark, 158, 242–43

U.S. Army, 63–64, 72, 77, 79, 149, 165, 184, 189, 192, 206–207, 216, 223, 226–33, 254–60, 263–72, 274; Army of Utah, 188, 199, 234n16; Corps of Engineers, 199; Corps of Topographical Engineers, 119–21. *See also* Utah Expedition
U.S. Mail, 192, 203–204, 210, 230–38, 242, 244, 237, 254–60, 263, 285. *See also* Pony Express
Utah Expedition, 149, 184–90, 199, 207, 238, 240, 248
Utley, Robert M., 22, 67n1, 71, 289–91

Vallé, André, 37, 45
Vasquez, Louis, 53, 73, 196–97

Waddell, William B., 238, 240–41
Wade, Jeptha H., 245, 249–50

Wagner, William, 227, 251
Wagner, William H., 200, 207, 213
Walker, Joel Pickens and Mary Young, family, 110
Walker, Joseph R., 80, 82, 110
Walker, Mary Richardson and Elkanah, 89, 104–107
Ward, Barney, 147
Ware, Eugene, 263, 267
Washakie, 34, 163–65, 166, 187, 209, 216, 252–54, 260, 264, 280, 283; Fort, 292; Mount, 26
Watson, William, 154–55
Webb, Chauncey, 191
Weber, John H., 53, 60, 64, 70–71
Weibye, Jens, 244
White, David A., 28, 46
White, Elijah, 121, 228
Whitman, Narcissa Prentiss and Marcus, 20, 89, 92–104, 106–109, 286
Whitworth, George F., 147
Wildflowers, 132, 155, 159, 205, 219, 293
Wildlife: antelope, 34, 42, 43, 69, 209, 211, 280, 282; beaver, 42, 50, 53–54, 56, 60–63, 71–72, 82–83, 85–87, 109–10; bighorn sheep, 46, 50, 58–59; buffalo (bison), 33–34, 42–43, 44–46, 56–58, 60, 68–69, 72, 80, 88, 90–91, 100, 106, 118–19, 125, 144, 164, 181, 283; wolves, 127, 142, 159, 178, 228
Williams, Ezekiel, 39
Williams, Joseph, 116, 119
Williams, P. L., 34–35
Williamson, Ned, 209, 225
Willie, James G., handcart company of, 176–78, 181–83
Willow Creek, 20, 43, 131, 158, 177, 219, 244, 253, 274–75, 283–84

Wilson, John, 34, 197
Wiman, Henry, 153
Wind River Arapaho-Shoshone
  Reservation, 280, 292
Wislizenus, Frederick, 85, 116
Women, 35, 43, 89, 94–109, 111, 114,
  118, 121, 125–26, 128, 138, 143, 153,
  160–61, 164, 177, 180, 184, 191, 195,
  223, 260, 263–64, 279, 286, 294
Wood, Elizabeth, 289–90
Wood, Joseph Warren, 155–56
Woodruff, Wilford, 147, 174
Woodson, Samuel H., 230
Woodward, William, 169, 177, 181
Wyeth, John B., 84

Wyeth, Nathaniel, *83*, 84–86, 88–91,
  124, 205

Yates, Edmund L., 214
Young, Brigham, 20, 128–31, 147–48,
  164–65, 167–68, 206, 209, 230; and
  Civil War, 249, 254–55, 257, 259;
  and handcarts 174, 176, 179–84,
  191–93, 195; and Utah War, 184–90
Young, Brigham, Express & Carrying
  Co., 149, 192, 231–33
Young, Martha, 110

Zachary, Alexander, Jr., 126

www.ingramcontent.com/pod-product-compliance
Lightning Source LLC
Chambersburg PA
CBHW020829160426
43192CB00007B/584